# Contemporary Readings in
# **Globalization**

# Contemporary Readings in
# Globalization

Editor
## Scott R.Sernau
*Indiana University South Bend*

Contemporary
**CRS**
Readings Series

PINE FORGE PRESS
An Imprint of Sage Publications, Inc.
Los Angeles • London • New Delhi • Singapore

*For information:*

Pine Forge Press
A Sage Publications Company
2455 Teller Road
Thousand Oaks, California 91320
E-mail: order@sagepub.com

Sage Publications Ltd.
1 Oliver's Yard
55 City Road
London EC1Y 1SP
United Kingdom

Sage Publications India Pvt. Ltd.
B-42, Panchsheel Enclave
Post Box 4109
New Delhi 110–017  India

Sage Publications Asia-Pacific Pte. Ltd.
33 Pekin Street #02–01
East Square
Singapore 048763

Printed in the United States of America.

*Library of Congress Cataloging-in-Publication Data*

Contemporary readings in globalization / edited by Scott R. Sernau.
    p. cm.
Includes bibliographical references and index.
ISBN 978-1-4129-4471-7 (pbk.: alk. paper)
1. Globalization. 2. Globalization—Social aspects. 3. Poverty. I. Sernau, Scott.
JZ1318.C6574 2008
303.48'2—dc22                                    2007029748

This book is printed on acid-free paper.

07   08   09   10   11      10  9  8  7  6  5  4  3  2  1

| | |
|---|---|
| *Acquisitions Editor:* | Benjamin Penner |
| *Editorial Assistant:* | Nancy Scrofano |
| *Production Editor:* | Sarah K. Quesenberry |
| *Copy Editor:* | Renee Willers |
| *Proofreader:* | Susan Schon |
| *Typesetter:* | C&M Digitals (P) Ltd. |
| *Indexer:* | Nara Wood |
| *Marketing Manager:* | Jennifer Reed |
| *Cover Designer:* | Michelle Kenny |

# CONTENTS

Topics Guide     vii

Advisory Board     x

About the Editor     xi

Preface     xiii

PART I: A CHANGING WORLD     1

1. Awakening Giants, Feet of Clay: A Comparative Assessment
   of the Rise of China and India     3
   *Pranab Bardhan*

2. The Wal-Mart You Don't Know     15
   *Charles Fishman*

3. The "Radical" Thesis on Globalization and the Case of Venezuela's Hugo Chavez     19
   *Steve Ellner*

4. A Coffee Connoisseur on a Mission: Buy High and Sell High     23
   *Michaele Weissman*

5. The Great Turning: From Empire to Earth Community     27
   *David Korten*

PART II: INEQUALITY AND POVERTY     31

6. Always With Us: Jeffrey Sachs's Plan to Eradicate World Poverty     33
   *John Cassidy*

7. Born Into Bondage     37
   *Paul Raffaele*

8. Pulling Rickshaws in the City of Dhaka: A Way Out of Poverty?     43
   *Sharifa Begum and Binayak Sen*

9. The Good Samaritans: Melinda Gates, Bono, and Bill Gates     55
   *Nancy Gibbs*

10. Violencia Femicida: Violence Against Women and Mexico's Structural Crisis     59
    *Mercedes Olivera*

11. How One Company Brought Hope to the Poor     65
    *Marco Visscher*

PART III: EDUCATION     69

12. The Right to Education in a Globalized World     71
    *Ronald Lindahl*

13. Breaking Down Notions of Us and Them:
    Answering Globalization With Global Learning     83
    *Angelo Carfagna*

14. A Would-Be Pilot, Hitting Turbulence on the Ground                                87
    *Michael Wines*

PART IV: CONFLICT                                                                      91

15. France: The Riots and the Republic                                                 93
    *Graham Murray*

16. Torture: The Struggle Over a Peremptory Norm in a Counter-Terrorist Era           105
    *Rosemary Foot*

17. Peace and Democracy for Haiti: A UN Mission Impossible?                           119
    *Sebastian von Einsiedel and David M. Malone*

18. Globalization and the Study of International Security                             127
    *Victor D. Cha*

19. The Biggest Failure: A New Approach to Help the World's Internally Displaced People   133
    *Ray Wilkinson*

PART V: HEALTH                                                                        141

20. Outsourcing Your Heart                                                            143
    *Unmesh Kher*

21. Rumor, Fear and Fatigue Hinder Final Push to End Polio                            147
    *Celia W. Dugger and Donald G. McNeil, Jr.*

22. AIDS and Health-Policy Responses in European Welfare States                       151
    *Monika Steffen*

23. U.S. Plan to Lure Nurses May Hurt Poor Nations                                    159
    *Celia W. Dugger*

PART VI: ENERGY                                                                       161

24. Exploitation of Energy Resources in Africa                                        163
    *Julia Maxted*

25. While Washington Slept                                                            169
    *Mark Hertsgaard*

26. Some Convenient Truths                                                            177
    *Gregg Easterbrook*

PART VII: ENVIRONMENT                                                                 181

27. A Financial Framework for Reducing Slums:
    Lessons From Experience in Latin America                                          183
    *Bruce Ferguson and Jesus Navarrete*

28. Tropic of Answer: Charles Munn, a Pioneer of South American Ecotourism,
    Answers Readers' Questions                                                        197
    *Charles Munn*

29. Strangers in the Forest                                                           201
    *Lawrence Osborne*

30. In American Waters                                                                209
    *Scott R. Sernau*

**Internet Resources**                                                               **211**

**Index**                                                                            **215**

# TOPICS GUIDE

AFRICA

6. Always With Us: Jeffrey Sachs's Plan to Eradicate World Poverty
7. Born Into Bondage
9. The Good Samaritans: Melinda Gates, Bono, and Bill Gates
14. A Would-Be Pilot, Hitting Turbulence on the Ground
24. Exploitation of Energy Resources in Africa

AGRICULTURE

4. A Coffee Connoisseur on a Mission: Buy High and Sell High
6. Always With Us: Jeffrey Sachs's Plan to Eradicate World Poverty
7. Born Into Bondage

ASIA

1. Awakening Giants, Feet of Clay: A Comparative Assessment of the Rise of China and India
8. Pulling Rickshaws in the City of Dhaka: A Way Out of Poverty?
11. How One Company Brought Hope to the Poor
20. Outsourcing Your Heart
21. Rumor, Fear and Fatigue Hinder Final Push to End Polio
23. U.S. Plan to Lure Nurses May Hurt Poor Nations
29. Strangers in the Forest

BUSINESS

2. The Wal-Mart You Don't Know
4. A Coffee Connoisseur on a Mission: Buy High and Sell High
9. The Good Samaritans: Melinda Gates, Bono, and Bill Gates
11. How One Company Brought Hope to the Poor

CROSS-CULTURAL UNDERSTANDING

5. The Great Turning: From Empire to Earth Community
13. Breaking Down Notions of Us and Them: Answering Globalization With Global Learning
15. France: The Riots and the Republic
28. Tropic of Answer: Charles Munn, a Pioneer of South American Ecotourism, Answers Readers' Questions
29. Strangers in the Forest
30. In American Waters

EUROPE

    15. France: The Riots and the Republic
    22. AIDS and Health-Policy Responses in European Welfare States
    25. While Washington Slept

GENDER

    5. The Great Turning: From Empire to Earth Community
    10. Violencia Femicida: Violence Against Women and Mexico's Structural Crisis
    11. How One Company Brought Hope to the Poor
    23. U.S. Plan to Lure Nurses May Hurt Poor Nations

LATIN AMERICA AND CARIBBEAN

    3. The "Radical" Thesis on Globalization and the Case of Venezuela's Hugo Chavez
    10. Violencia Femicida: Violence Against Women and Mexico's Structural Crisis
    17. Peace and Democracy for Haiti: A UN Mission Impossible?

LAW AND HUMAN RIGHTS

    10. Violencia Femicida: Violence Against Women and Mexico's Structural Crisis
    12. The Right to Education in a Globalized World
    15. France: The Riots and the Republic
    16. Torture: The Struggle Over a Peremptory Norm in a Counter-Terrorist Era
    17. Peace and Democracy for Haiti: A UN Mission Impossible?
    19. The Biggest Failure: A New Approach to Help the World's Internally Displaced People

NATURAL RESOURCES

    3. The "Radical" Thesis on Globalization and the Case of Venezuela's Hugo Chavez
    5. The Great Turning: From Empire to Earth Community
    24. Exploitation of Energy Resources in Africa
    25. While Washington Slept
    26. Some Convenient Truths

NORTH AMERICA

    2. The Wal-Mart You Don't Know
    13. Breaking Down Notions of Us and Them: Answering Globalization With Global Learning
    20. Outsourcing Your Heart
    23. U.S. Plan to Lure Nurses May Hurt Poor Nations
    25. While Washington Slept
    30. In American Waters

PHILANTHROPY AND AID

    6. Always With Us: Jeffrey Sachs's Plan to Eradicate World Poverty
    9. The Good Samaritans: Melinda Gates, Bono, and Bill Gates

## RURAL POVERTY

  6. Always With Us: Jeffrey Sachs's Plan to Eradicate World Poverty
  7. Born Into Bondage
11. How One Company Brought Hope to the Poor


## TERRORISM

16. Torture: The Struggle Over a Peremptory Norm in a Counter-Terrorist Era
18. Globalization and the Study of International Security


## TRADE

  1. Awakening Giants, Feet of Clay: A Comparative Assessment of the Rise of China and India
  2. The Wal-Mart You Don't Know
  3. The "Radical" Thesis on Globalization and the Case of Venezuela's Hugo Chavez
  4. A Coffee Connoisseur on a Mission: Buy High and Sell High
  6. Always With Us: Jeffrey Sachs's Plan to Eradicate World Poverty


## TRAVEL AND TOURISM

20. Outsourcing Your Heart
28. Tropic of Answer: Charles Munn, a Pioneer of South American Ecotourism, Answers Readers' Questions
29. Strangers in the Forest
30. In American Waters


## URBAN POVERTY

  8. Pulling Rickshaws in the City of Dhaka: A Way Out of Poverty?
14. A Would-Be Pilot, Hitting Turbulence on the Ground
15. France: The Riots and the Republic
27. A Financial Framework for Reducing Slums: Lessons From Experience in Latin America


## VALUES

  5. The Great Turning: From Empire to Earth Community
  9. The Good Samaritans: Melinda Gates, Bono, and Bill Gates
13. Breaking Down Notions of Us and Them: Answering Globalization With Global Learning
30. In American Waters

# ADVISORY BOARD

# ABOUT THE EDITOR

**Scott R. Sernau** (PhD, Cornell University) is Professor of Sociology and Director of International Programs at Indiana University, South Bend, where he regularly teaches courses on global issues, international inequalities, family, urban society, and race and ethnic relations. He has taught courses in Mexico and Costa Rica, as well as while circling the globe with Semester at Sea. He has won numerous campus and statewide teaching awards, including the Sylvia Bowman Award for distinguished teaching, and serves on the IU Faculty Colloquium on Excellence in Teaching. He is the author of several books, including *Global Problems: The Search for Equity, Peace, and Sustainability; Worlds Apart: Social Inequalities in a Global Economy;* and *Bound: Living in the Globalized World.*

# PREFACE

Those who ignore the changing world around them have always done so at their peril. The outside world comes to their door soon enough. Sometimes, it comes as a threat: disease, invasion, domination. Other times, the world arrives with a friendlier face: an unexpected new neighbor, a distant job assignment.

Some of my students are intensely interested in what is going on in the world and others believe they have more pressing needs. They are worried about their education. They are worried about their health. They are worried if they will find a job when they graduate and what sort it will be. What I hope they will come to see is that these personal issues are increasingly a part of an interconnected world of global issues. In their education, their accomplishments are not just being compared to the accomplishments of their classmates, but their knowledge and skills are also being compared to those of students in technology-savvy India and China, Brazil, and even Estonia. Even their classmates may have roots in distant parts of the world. Whether or not they will get through the semester without coming down with a miserable case of the flu may depend on who their roommate is, but also on who gets on an airplane in Hong Kong or Bangkok. And, of course, what sorts of jobs will be available to them is going to depend a great deal on the global economy. The former jobs of many of my students' parents no longer exist in our community. Many of the growing jobs in the business world, and even in medicine and education, involve complex international connections and the ability to collaborate around the globe.

Our changing world looms larger in their lives than ever before in other ways as well. Will our ROTC students be deployed to Iraq or Afghanistan, serve missions in Africa, or provide emergency assistance following a hurricane in the United States? Will this year's graduates enter a new era of international cooperation, or will their lives, families and careers be continually interrupted by war, terror, and outbreaks of conflict? And will their adult lives be filled with amazing new useful technology undreamed of just a few years ago, or by the continued struggle to live on a planet wracked by resource depletion, degraded environments, and the uncertain effects of climate change?

In some measure, we are deciding the answers to some of these questions right now. I have brought together a wide range of ideas and examples, along with both warnings and signs of hope from very diverse sources, ranging from the popular press to the alternative press to scholarly journals. The common thread in the articles is that each provides a new vantage point for better understanding the forces that are reshaping our world and our future.

# PART I

# A CHANGING WORLD

Globalization is a recently popularized term that refers to the growing interconnectedness of our world. Globalization is fueled by economic forces, such as the search for inexpensive labor and for ever-growing markets. At the same time, it has broad political, social, and cultural implications that extend beyond outsourcing and trade. This section examines facets of the process of globalization that are changing the way we live in the world.

The latter half of the 20th century was molded by the Cold War struggle between the United States and the Soviet Union. The world's largest economies at the end of the last century were the United States, Japan, and Germany. Soon, the world's largest economies may be those of the United States, China, and India. The dramatic economic growth of the world's two most populous countries, China and India, stands to reshape the global system. Will they also become major political and cultural forces in the world? The first article looks at the dramatic rise of China and India and considers both their strengths and underlying weaknesses.

But in the 21st century many of the world's most powerful players are not countries but corporations. One of the world's largest, fastest growing and most aggressive in marketing is Wal-Mart. Wal-Mart has become a familiar part of the commercial landscape around the world. Article 2 contends, however, that there are sides to this corporate phenomenon that we may not know. The argument that multinational corporations are destructive to the world's social fabric is a key contention of the antiglobalization movement. In Latin America, Venezuela's president, Hugo Chavez, has built a political career out of decrying the destructive elements of American-led globalization. Article 3 explores this criticism, which seems to resonate with many of Latin America's poor.

While "radicals" denounce globalization, reformers contend that it can be made to better serve the world's economic, social and environmental needs. Article 4 considers the world's second most traded commodity after oil, well known to everyone from businesspeople to college students. Can the trend toward gourmet and specialty coffee be a force for more socially and environmentally sensitive trade? Article 5 contends that the entire world is in need of a new way of doing business. Examining new thinking in business, social movements, politics, and spirituality, David Korten contends we are poised on a momentous shift from the demands of global empires to a new way of thinking that he calls "earth community."

1. Awakening Giants, Feet of Clay: A Comparative Assessment of the Rise of China and India.
   Pranab Bardhan. *Journal of South Asian Development.* Vol. 1, No. 1. 2006.

2. The Wal-Mart You Don't Know.
   Charles Fishman. *Fast Company.* December 2003.

3. The "Radical" Thesis on Globalization and the Case of Venezuela's Hugo Chavez.
   Steve Ellner. *Latin American Perspectives.* Vol. 29, No. 6. 2002.

4. A Coffee Connoisseur on a Mission: Buy High and Sell High.
   Michaele Weissman. *The New York Times.* June 22, 2006.

5. The Great Turning: From Empire to Earth Community.
   David Korten. *Yes! Magazine.* Summer 2006.

# CHAPTER 1

## Awakening Giants, Feet of Clay

### A Comparative Assessment of the Rise of China and India

Pranab Bardhan

China and India are the economic superstars of the last quarter century, with China in particular showing remarkable annual economic growth. At the same time, both struggle with entrenched structural problems that could hobble their continued growth. This article compares the two economies and the development indicators of each. Then it looks at deeper social and historical issues as well as ongoing political problems that continue to limit each country.

## Introduction

The media, particularly the financial press, are all agog over the rise of China and India in the international economy. After a long period of relative stagnation, these two largest countries of the world, containing nearly two-fifths of the world's population, have had their incomes growing at remarkably high rates over the last two decades or so. India was slightly ahead of China in 1870 as well as early 1970 in terms of the level of per capita income at 1990 international prices—see Maddison (2005)—but since then China has surged well ahead of India. India's per capita income growth rate in the last two decades has been nearly 4 percent, while China's has been at least double that rate, and even discounting for some overstatement in the Chinese official rates of growth, the rate of growth in China has been significantly faster. Journalists have referred to the economic reforms and integration of these large economies into the world economy in all kinds of colorful metaphors: giants shaking off their "socialist slumber," "caged tigers" unshackled, and so on. Newspaper columnists and media pundits have sent breathless reports from Beijing and Bangalore about the imminent and inexorable competition from these two new whiz kids

in our complacent neighborhood in a "flattened," globalized, playing field. Others have warned about the momentous implications of "3 billion new capitalists," largely from China and India, redefining the next phase of globalization (see, for example, Friedman 2005; Prestowitz 2005).

While there is much to admire in the changes in these two large economies (which the West has to learn to live with) and to appreciate their great potential in the rest of this century, it is important not to exaggerate their undoubted achievements. There are many pitfalls and roadblocks that they have to overcome in the near future before they can become significant players in the international economic scene on a sustained basis. At this point the hype about the Indian economy seems quite premature, and the risks on the horizon for the Chinese polity (and hence for economic stability) highly underestimated. In this article, after a comparative study of the two economies in terms of broad development indicators, we will explore some deeper social and historical issues that underlie their differential ability to resolve collective action problems in long-run investment and to manage political conflicts, which go beyond the usual simple aggregative comparisons of an authoritarian and a democratic political regime.

## Poverty and Underemployment

Both China and India are still desperately poor countries. Of the total of 2.3 billion people in these two countries (counted among the "3 billion new capitalists"), it is sobering to note that nearly 1.5 billion live on less than $2 a day (at 1993 purchasing power parity) according to World Bank calculations (see Table 1.1). The absolute number of such poor people in the two countries together in 2001 was about the same as in 1981 (with the large decline in China since then mostly neutralized by the significant rise in India). Of course, the lifting of hundreds of millions of people above poverty in China has been historic. Through repeated assertions in the international financial press, it has become generally accepted that this has been accomplished by globalization. Yet from Table 1.1 one cannot ignore the fact that a substantial part of the decline of poverty in China since 1980 already happened by the mid-1980s (maybe largely as a result of the spurt in agricultural growth following decollectivization and land reform), *before* the big strides in foreign trade and investment in the 1990s (Chen and Ravallion 2004b). The assertions about Indian poverty reduction primarily through trade liberalization in the 1990s are even shakier. The Green Revolution in agriculture from the mid-1960s to the mid-1980s helped many farmers and agricultural laborers climb out of poverty. But in the 1990s, the decade of major trade liberalization, the rate of decline in poverty by some aggregative estimates has slowed down.[1] One careful disaggregated study (Topalova, forthcoming) across districts in India suggests that trade liberalization did not affect urban poverty significantly, but agricultural tariff reduction may have (differentially across districts) slowed down the decline in rural poverty. Such results mainly indicate the difficulty of displaced workers in adjusting to new activities and sectors on account of various constraints (for example, in getting credit or information or infrastructural facilities, and labor market rigidities). In any case, India is as yet a minor player in world trade, contributing less than 1 percent of world exports (China's share is about 6 percent).

What about the hordes of software engineers, call center operators and back room programmers of India supposedly hollowing out white-collar jobs in rich countries? They must be transforming the economy of India, right? While this is no doubt a major event for the Indian economy that makes the Indian elite proud, one should not lose one's sense of proportion. The total number of workers in all forms of information technology (most broadly defined) jobs and business process outsourcing

**Table 1.1**      People Below the Poverty Line (Million)

|                                        | 1981  | 1987  | 2001  |
| -------------------------------------- | ----- | ----- | ----- |
| *Poverty line of $1.08 a day (1993 PPP)* |       |       |       |
| China                                  | 633.7 | 308.4 | 211.6 |
| India                                  | 382.4 | 369.8 | 358.6 |
| *Poverty line of $2.15 a day (1993 PPP)* |       |       |       |
| China                                  | 875.8 | 730.8 | 593.6 |
| India                                  | 630.0 | 697.1 | 826.0 |

*Source:* Chen and Ravallion (2004a).

*Note:* PPP = purchasing power parity.

to India comes to less than a million workers, which is about one quarter of 1 percent of the Indian labor force. And even if the number of such workers were to double or triple in the next 10 years, this will remain only a blip on the screen if you are thinking of affecting the conditions of Indian workers in general. For all its Nobel Prizes and brilliant scholars and professionals, one should not overlook the fact that India is the largest single-country contributor to the pool of illiterate people in the world, and nearly two-thirds of India's children drop out of school before the eighth grade. (As for quality of education, one dismal indicator noted by Pratham, a large education NGO, is that even in the fifth grade some 35 percent of the children cannot read or write.) To lift these people out of poverty and dead-end menial jobs and make them part of the billions of "new capitalists" (even if that is what they wanted to be) will remain a Herculean task over many decades to come.

Only 7 percent of the 18 to 23 age group enroll in higher education institutions in India (compared to more than 15 percent in China). As a matter of fact, India's educational inequality is one of the worst in the world. According to World Bank (2006b) estimates, inequality in adult schooling years in the general population[2] in India is not just much higher than it is in China and other neighboring countries (like Sri Lanka, Thailand, Vietnam and Indonesia), but it is significantly higher than in most Latin American countries and even in some African countries (like Kenya, Tanzania and Ghana). Of course, even a microscopic minority of the highly educated in a large country is sizeable in absolute numbers and can make a splash in the world markets—for example, it has been reported for some time that there are more IT workers in Bangalore now than in Silicon Valley in California. But the sustainability of this for India as a whole is in some doubt, particularly when the majority of higher education institutions in the country are currently dysfunctional (with the student's university performance as signal of quality increasingly replaced by that in competitive examinations outside), strapped for government funds[3] (and yet ways of mobilizing private resources for public institutions remain largely blocked), over-regulated and politicized, and low in research productivity (measured, for example, by top journal citation index) in science and technology. Already talent shortage is reported to have hit India's capital goods industry, and even for the information-related sector it is felt in some quarters that the reservoir of India's technical and managerial skills may prove rather shallow in the near future.[4]

Apart from information-related services (including interactive design software), India is now doing well in international competition in pharmaceuticals and biotech products, and also lately in some auto parts,[5] vehicles, and some varieties of steel and equipment. But most of these activities are either highly skill-intensive or capital-intensive. For various reasons India has not yet succeeded in the kind of labor-intensive manufacturing jobs that have transformed the economies of China and now Vietnam. Which of these reasons are more important than others is not yet resolved at the analytical level. But most people agree on the problem of inadequate long-term finance for small firms or of infrastructural deficiencies in India (which we will discuss shortly). Many economists and businessmen also point to the debilitating effects of two long-standing policies in India: one relates to the reservation of a large number of products for small-scale industries (more than 600 such products are reserved for this sector even now), and the other to rigid labor laws, neither policies afflicting China[6] or Vietnam. The former policy of reservation is supposed to have prevented the utilization of economies of scale and rationalization of production in efficient large factories that can compete in world markets (particularly in terms of quality standardization and timely delivery), apart from acting as a built-in disincentive for a successful small firm to expand its operations. The labor laws (particularly Chapter V-B of the Industrial Disputes Act) make it very difficult to sack workers in large firms even when they are inefficient (or when the market in some line of production declines) or to employ short-term contract labor. This discourages new hires by employers, induces capital-intensity in production, and inhibits entry and exit of firms. The adverse effect of these two policies are particularly visible, critics point out, in the textile and garment sector, where Chinese success in recent years has far outstripped that of India (a country with a long history of textiles). Even after the de-reservation of the garment

sector in India from 2001 onwards and the lifting of the MFA quotas in the US and Europe, India's market share in the world has not substantially improved, while China has already established a dominant share.

Others have pointed out that the impact of these two policies are somewhat exaggerated. On account of various (overt and covert) exemptions, large companies have not always been kept outside the products under small-scale reservation. In textiles there are clear economies of scale in spinning, but not so much in weaving, printing and garments. Indian spinning mills, both on cotton and manmade fiber, have acquired international scales. That production scale did not matter in weaving and garments is evident from Japanese and Taiwanese experience where textiles firms were small, but were supported by large trading houses that secured economies of scale in marketing. Chinese textile firms used to be state-owned and large, and there is an alternative hypothesis of the large size of those Chinese firms: China's huge state-owned textile factories may have partly reflected inadequate development of market-based inter-firm relationships that is evident in industrial clusters like Tiruppur in Tamil Nadu. But now many of the textile firms under joint venture and foreign ownership are relatively small.

On labor laws it has been found by Dutta Roy (2004), in one of the very few statistical studies at the industry level in India, that over the period 1960–1961 to 1994–1995 the impact of job security regulations was statistically insignificant in 15 of the 16 industries studied: the rigidities in the adjustment of labor were about the same even before the introduction of stringent job security clauses in the law (the 1976 and 1982 amendments to the Industrial Disputes Act). More recent case studies of labor practices in 10 states and nine industries over 1991–1998 by Deshpande (2004) also suggest that the Indian labor market is not as inflexible as it is made out to be: many firms were able to change employment as they wanted or increase the share of nonpermanent (casual and temporary) workers. Labor laws are implemented at the state level, and it is well known that many state governments look the other way when they are openly violated—Jenkins (2000) has referred to this as "reform by stealth." Clearly, there has to be a package deal on job security; allowing more flexibility in hiring and firing has to be combined with a reasonable scheme of unemployment compensation or adjustment assistance, from an earmarked fund to which employers as well as employees should contribute. No Indian politician has yet gathered the courage or imagination to come up with such a deal.

In any case it is evident that without a massive expansion of low-skill labor-intensive manufacturing jobs labor-surplus countries like India cannot lift the conditions of its poor workers in the near future. Manufacturing contributes less than a fifth of India's GDP, whereas in China it is more like half. For all its high rate of growth of income, job growth rates in India have not kept up, and, on evidence from National Sample Survey data, may have even declined from about 2.5 percent in 1983–1993 to about 1 percent in the period 1993–2000 (much below the rate of growth of the labor force). Since on an average India's labor force is younger than China's, it is often said that India has a demographic window of opportunity in the next two or three decades before the burden of supporting the aged hits the economy hard, as it will hit China sooner (the median age of the population is about 24 years in India, 33 years in China). But this assumes India can provide good jobs to this surge of young people in the labor force. So far in the last couple of decades the job expansion rates have been, as we have seen, rather bleak. Even in China, which is now being described as the manufacturing workshop of the world (though as yet, in 2004, China's share in the worldwide manufacturing value added is less than 9 percent, compared to Japan's 21 percent and the US' 24 percent), less than one-fifth of its labor force is employed in manufacturing, mining and construction combined (Banister 2005)—(China actually lost tens of millions of manufacturing jobs since the mid-1990s).[7] Nearly half of the labor force is still in agriculture in China (about 60 percent in India). As per acre productivity growth has stagnated in agriculture in both countries, how and where the hundreds of millions of peasants will be absorbed is a worrisome question in the foreseeable future for both countries. (The problem is likely to be more acute for India as by the midcentury India is expected to have 220 million more workers than China).

## Infrastructure

As indicated earlier, a major difference between China and India in terms of preconditions for job creation and general economic growth is in the area of building and maintenance of infrastructure. Let us now elaborate on this. We shall discuss four kinds of infrastructure: (a) physical (like roads, transportation, communication, power, ports, irrigation, etc.); (b) social (particularly health and education); (c) regulatory (in contract enforcement, starting a business, etc.); and (d) financial (particularly the banking sector).

It is now generally agreed that investment in Chinese physical infrastructure in the last two decades has been simply phenomenal compared to India's, the results of which are now obvious for business. The cost of power for manufacturing is reported to be about 35 percent higher in India than in China. A recent study by the accounting firm KPMG has estimated that a company can expect about 17 significant power shutdowns a month in India, whereas in China the corresponding number is about five. The number of days in turnaround time for ships in Mumbai port is several times that in Shanghai. The number of days it takes for Indian textile exports to go from factory gate to a New York retail outlet is about twice that for China and other East Asian countries. The number of telephone (fixed plus mobile) subscribers per 1,000 in China is about six times that in India, and the number of Internet users per 1,000 in China is nearly four times that in India. Glitzy airport terminals and transportation, industrial parks and multilane highways[8] that dazzle many a visitor to coastal China are nowhere to be found in India. There have been some noticeable improvements in India in roads, civil aviation, ports and telecommunication in recent years. But in electricity, railway and irrigation water populist politics continues to make it very difficult to charge or enforce appropriate user prices, and this has inhibited both private and public investment in new projects. Firms are resorting to private supply of electricity through generators at a high cost; commercial freight rates on the railways, which bear the burden of cross-subsidizing passenger fares, are much higher than in China; heavily subsidized irrigation water is leading to groundwater depletion through over-extraction and to wasteful production of inappropriate crops (like rice in Punjab or sugarcane in Maharashtra). In any case a fiscal deficit of about 10 percent of GDP makes it hard for the Indian government to invest adequately in public infrastructure. The Chinese fiscal deficit is much lower (about 2 percent) and their tax–GDP ratio (at about 20 percent)[9] much higher, which along with larger household and corporate savings and foreign investment has made possible the massive investment in infrastructure.

In social infrastructure, particularly in education and health, China has been far ahead of India for several decades now. Adult literacy rate is 91 percent (87 percent for women) in China compared to India's 61 percent (48 percent for women). The student–teacher ratio in secondary schools is about 18 in China to India's 34. Infant mortality rate is 30 per 1,000 to India's 65. Of India's under-5 children, as many as 47 percent are underweight compared to China's 10 percent. The percentage of population with access to improved sanitation facilities is 44 in China, to India's 30. Ninety-seven percent of births in China are attended by skilled health personnel; in India it is 43 percent. Doctors per 1,000 people, low as it is in both countries, is more than three times as many in China. According to WHO estimates for 1998, the burden of infectious and parasitic diseases (measured in terms of DALY's—disability-adjusted life years—per capita) is seven times as high in India compared to China. But China's health advantage is diminishing, particularly in rural areas and remote provinces, on account of the decline in public health services and increased dependence on private financing of health, which the poor can ill afford.[10] The number of doctors per 1,000 people in China may have even declined somewhat between 1990 and 2002. Some experts have noted that the erosion of public health coverage, coupled with the stringent family planning policy, have resulted in some deterioration in the female child mortality situation in China in the last two decades (in the 0 to 6 age group China now has 119 boys per 100 girls, the corresponding number in India is 108). In both countries the overwhelming majority of people does not have health insurance and turn to poorly regulated private health care providers and quacks. In both countries the HIV/AIDS pandemic is spreading fast and has the potential of a catastrophe (by one conservative estimate the expected number of HIV-infected people in India will be about 20 million in 2010 and about 10 million in China). Another health-related issue is environmental pollution. Reflecting its much higher rate of growth, the per capita carbon dioxide emission in China is more than twice that of India. China has 7 of the world's 10 most polluted cities. (It has been recently reported that 400,000 people die prematurely every year in China from diseases linked to air pollution.) Energy use even per unit of GDP is somewhat higher in China.

Both China and India have the crushing legacy of a heavy-handed and corrupt regulatory bureaucracy. But there are significant differences between the two countries in regulatory delays and entry barriers now. According to the World Bank report on *Doing Business in 2006* (2006a) to start a business requires in India 71 days and a cost amounting to 62 percent of the annual per capita income in the country, whereas in China it is 48 days and about 14 percent of per capita income. Registering property requires 67 days and costs about 9 percent of property value in India, whereas in China it is 32 days and 3 percent. Complying with licensing and permit requirements for ongoing operations requires 363 days and 126 percent of per capita income in China; 270 days and 679 percent in India. Time required for exporting a standardized shipment of goods is 20 days in China and 36 days in India. In enforcing debt contracts it requires 425 days and costs about 43 percent of debt value in India, whereas in China it is 241 days and 26 percent of debt value. On closing an insolvent business it takes about 10 years in India; in China 2.4 years. As we have discussed before, in hiring and firing of employees in large factories Chinese labor markets are more flexible than India's. Tens of millions of employees have been laid off from Chinese state-owned enterprises with a rapidity (20 million reportedly laid off just in 4 years between 1995 and 1999) that is simply breathtaking and politically unthinkable in the Indian context.[11]

China's financial stock in relation to its GDP is much higher than India's, largely reflecting the former's much higher savings rate, and accordingly cost of capital is significantly lower than in India. But it is mainly in the efficiency of operation of financial infrastructure that India's condition is significantly better than China's. Even though in both countries the state dominates the financial sector and regularly parks its politically inspired debts there, banks in China are burdened with "bad" loans to a much larger extent than in India.[12] Chinese banks are much more beholden to decisions at the political party level, but (with the exception of some small and innovative new banks) the bureaucracy in the Indian banks is often much too "lazy" and risk-averse (particularly with respect to small borrowers) in its lending policies. In both countries corporate bond markets are anaemic and equity markets are not very important as a source of finance. While insider trading and financial scandals have been rampant in both countries, the Indian stock market is now much healthier, better managed and much less mired in government intervention than its Chinese counterpart, and this has had some differential impact in corporate governance in the two countries. The Indian corporate sector provides more opportunities for domestic private entrepreneurial ventures, and in recent years has nurtured private companies that play a more dynamic role in the global innovation chain. (In any case the public sector still accounts for about 38 percent of GDP in China, while in India it is about 24 percent.) The much larger foreign investment in China than in India may be partly due to the weaker domestic capital market in the former, apart from the differences in physical, social and regulatory infrastructure mentioned earlier.

It is often claimed that China falls into the East Asian growth pattern of recent history where a high savings rate enables large amounts of investment to be shoveled into the growth engine, without much of technical progress to show for it.

First of all, such a characterization of East Asian growth is somewhat misleading for two reasons: (a) when imports of new capital goods embody new technology, it is difficult to disentangle the effects of capital accumulation from those of technical progress; and (b) this is nothing special about East Asia, as almost all countries, including the United States through much of the 19th century (Eichengreen 2002) show a similar pattern in the early stages of industrialization. For China in particular, the analysis of decomposition of economic growth shows (Jun 2003; Wang and Yao 2003; Wu 2003) that between 14 and 25 percent (depending on methods of estimation) of total output growth between 1978 and 2000 is attributable to technical progress. Scattered micro-level evidence seems to suggest a more wasteful use of capital, fuel and other production inputs in China than in India. *Business Week* (2005) reports an analysis of financial data from Standard and Poor's CompuStat for 340 publicly quoted companies from 1999 to 2003, which shows that Indian companies mostly outperformed their Chinese counterparts on returns to invested capital.[13] At the aggregative level the efficiency with which investment has been used is often (crudely) measured by the incremental capital–output ratio (the ratio of investment to increase in GDP). The current measure for China is about 4 (while that for India is about 3). Thus measured, while investment efficiency is somewhat higher in India, the Chinese level is not out of line with most developing countries. In fact there is some evidence that for much of the period of 1978–2000 there has been an upward trend in this efficiency in China, largely reflecting the pre-eminence of rural industrialization there.

One factor that is reported to have influenced the remarkable pace of Chinese rural industrialization in this period largely under nonstate (and until recently, also nonprivate) auspices is the extensive decentralization that was part of the reform in governance. Fiscal decentralization allowed local governments to retain a large part of the profits made in the village and township enterprises (TVE's), which provided incentives for their further development, and competition for mobile resources among local-government-controlled enterprises induced efficiency (Qian and Roland 1998). Both China (since the early 1980s) and India (since the early 1990s) went for serious decentralization, but their nature was quite different. In India this took the form of regular elections at the local level, but there has been as yet very little devolution of real authority and revenue-raising powers to local governments (Chaudhuri, forthcoming; Government of India 2001). The role of elected officials at the village or district level in most parts of the country is largely to select beneficiaries of projects (like employment or credit programs) funded from above. In many states the resources meant for the poor have been diverted to nontarget groups through collusion between the local powerful people and the bureaucrats. In China, Party functionaries at the local level (non-Party leaders occasionally chosen in village elections were less effective if their agenda differed from that of Party functionaries) had some real authority and some local revenue shares, which motivated them to play a leading role in local business development particularly in the coastal areas. Unlike in the case of Chinese TVE's (up to the end of the 1990s), in India local business development has not usually been in the agenda of local governments.[14]

## Institutional and Political Issues

The large autonomy and incentives offered to local governments in China sometimes also induced them to engage in regional protectionism, raising barriers to inter-regional trade. This has meant that while China was getting integrated into the international economy, the domestic market was often territorially segmented, and there is some evidence that internal trade barriers may have even increased in the 1990s (Poncet 2004). India also has many restrictions and taxes on internal trade, and, in spite of 55 years of federalism, is far from approaching an internal common market. In both countries market reforms have been associated with increased regional inequality, with the gulf between the backward regions (western provinces in China and the central heartland in India) and the advanced regions increasing, regular doses of redistributive transfers by the central government notwithstanding.

It has been widely noted that in the economic reform process the Chinese leadership has often been able to take bold decisions and implement them relatively quickly and decisively, whereas in India reform has been halting and hesitant, often marked by two steps forward and one step backward. This is usually attributed to the inevitably slow processes of democracy in India. No doubt there is something to this. For example, given the feverish construction boom in China, highways and dams are built over hitherto inhabited or environmentally sensitive land in a relatively short period of time, whereas in India the decisions will be usually engulfed in massive agitations and intricate political negotiations, the outcome of which is usually uncertain and often long-delayed. The exigencies of political mobilization and electoral cycles often dictate a rather short political time horizon of decisions in India, and short-run populist compromises with vocal interest groups and buyouts of political support with expensive patronage prevail over long-run policy commitments. The limited ability of the Indian political system to bear the short-run costs of beneficial long-run reforms and a continuing erosion of the institutional mechanisms that enable credible commitments to coherent long-term development policies (including investing in the improvement of India's creaking infrastructure) indicate the extreme difficulties of resolving collective action problems that the contending interest groups face in the matter of much of economic reform in India, even though most of these groups have the potential of benefiting from the reform in the long run.

That the superior Chinese ability to resolve collective action problems and take (and stick to) hard decisions in contrast to India is not a matter simply of authoritarianism versus democracy. I believe authoritarianism is neither necessary nor sufficient for credible commitment to long-run policy. That it is not sufficient is obvious from the cases, say, of many African dictators presiding over weak states and vacillating decisions. That it is not necessary is clear from examples of the post-war history of Scandinavian or Japanese democracies where many coordinated macroeconomic adjustment decisions rising above short-run political pressures have been taken (although in the macroeconomic crisis of the last decade or so the famed Japanese ability to coordinate on hard decisions is looking a bit frayed). I think deeper issues than the formal pattern of the political regime are involved here, and some of these deeper factors may simultaneously influence the nature of collective action in economic management and the pattern of political regime in a country.

The literature on collective action in economics and political science suggests[15] that social heterogeneity and economic inequality tend to have a negative effect on coordination and cooperation in matters of collective action. This has a bearing on the India–China comparison both at the micro and aggregative levels (just as the better coordinating ability of the Scandinavians and the Japanese may be linked to their remarkable social homogeneity and economic equality). In terms of ethnicity, language or religion Chinese society is much less heterogeneous than the Indian (some of the social homogeneity is, of course, the artificial outcome of the centuries-old domination of the Han Chinese and their forcible ironing out of ethnic and linguistic differences).[16] Since the revolution the Chinese economy, both rural and urban, has been characterized by far less inequality in assets (land,

financial assets and human capital) and income. Even in the last quarter century, when inequality has been increasing sharply in China (there is, however, some evidence of a turnaround in the rise in income inequality in both rural and urban areas since 1995, but the rural–urban disparity keeps mounting; Khan 2004),[17] by all accounts the levels of asset inequality even now are significantly below those in India. This relative social and economic homogeneity over several decades has facilitated taking coordinated action in long-term policies in China, and made it easier to enlist the support of a broad range of social groups for necessary short-run sacrifices. In particular, the disruptions and hardships of restructuring in the domestic economy, as the cold wind of international competition blew over enterprises and activities nurtured by decades of Party control, were rendered somewhat tolerable by the fact that China has had some kind of a minimum rural safety net, made possible to a large extent by an egalitarian distribution of land cultivation rights that followed the decollectivization of 1978 (the size of land cultivated by a household was assigned in terms of the demographic size of the household).[18] In most parts of India, for the poor there is no similar rural safety net. Table 1.2 shows that Indian wealth distribution was much more unequal than that in China. In addition, the more severe educational inequality in India, which we have noted before, makes the absorption of shocks in the industrial labor market more difficult (to the extent that education and training provide some means of flexibility in retraining and redeployment). So the resistance to the competitive process that market reform entails is that much stiffer in India.

But China is far behind India in the ability to politically manage conflicts. I was in Beijing the day of the Tiananmen killings and had visited the Square two days before. The scale of (unarmed) demonstration I saw there was something that Indian authorities routinely face every day in several parts of the country. Large societies always generate many kinds of conflict, and an extremely heterogeneous society like India with a great deal of economic disparities and social inequalities is always in some kind of turmoil somewhere. Yet it is remarkable how over the last half century or so the Indian political system has been able to douse the fires and contain many of the conflicts,[19] starting with the language riots in the 1950s, to the armed rebellions of militant peasants or regional separatists, to the sporadic outbreaks of inter-caste and inter-community violence that continue to this day. Defying many dire predictions of the Indian state breaking up, the system has by and large managed conflicts in some ways even better than

**Table 1.2**  Gini Coefficients of Inequality in Wealth Distribution

|              | Rural | Urban |
| ------------ | ----- | ----- |
| China (1995) | 0.33  | 0.52  |
| China (2002) | 0.39  | 0.47  |
| India (1991) | 0.62  | 0.68  |
| India (2002) | 0.63  | 0.66  |

*Source:* For China, Li et al. (2005); for India, author's estimate from National Sample Survey data.

a far less heterogeneous and less poor Europe has fared over, say, the last 200 years.

The standard comment is, of course, that democracy acts as a safety valve for smoldering tensions, and this is no doubt true. But again I think there are some deeper forces involved. The same heterogeneity of socioeconomic groups that has hindered collective action in the matter of economic management of long-term policies and investment in India may have also strengthened the demand for democratic rules in inter-group negotiations and bargaining, thereby contributing to the continued survival of democratic processes against all odds.[20] Thus, without minimizing the importance of a certain tradition of tolerance and pluralism in the Indian political culture and legal system, and a degree of continuing commitment on the part of India's political and military officials, one can suggest that the general persistence of democracy and the form it has taken has also something to do with the political exigencies of bargaining within a divided ruling class, and the constant need to absorb dissent and co-opt potential rebel leaders and newly emergent groups.

For many centuries Chinese high culture, language and political and historiographical tradition have not given much scope to pluralism and diversity, and a centralizing and authoritarian Communist Party has carried on with this tradition. Jenner (1992) in his provocative book analyzing the link between the "history of tyranny" and the "tyranny of history" in China, describes one of the most basic tenets of Chinese civilization as "that uniformity is inherently desirable, that conflict is bad, that there should be only one empire, one culture, one script . . . one tradition," and that "what is local and different is treated (by the high culture) as deviant." Nurtured in this tradition, there is a certain preoccupation with order and stability in China (not just in the Party) and a quickness to brand dissenting movements and local autonomy efforts as seditious, and it is in this context that one sees some dark clouds on the horizon for China's future. Not merely has the fast pace of economic growth created

many inequalities and job disruptions and dislocations, coastal China is moving far ahead of the inland provinces, as we have noted before. Those left behind are bound to get restive, particularly as fiscal decentralization has meant that the lagging regions have to live with large cuts in community services. These tensions of fiscal federalism are increasing in India too. The better-performing state governments are now openly protesting large redistributive transfers to laggard states ordained by the Finance Commission. In the Indian democratic system, however, some of these laggard populous states (like UP or Bihar) send a very large number of members to the Parliament, and the (shaky) coalition governments at the center can ill afford to alienate them. But in China the hard budget constraint bites and the laggard regions were quite often left to fend for themselves.[21] This led local officials to impose arbitrary levies on farmers; on top of this, official corruption and increasingly frequent seizures of land for more profitable urban or industrial use (it is reported that at least 40 million farmers have lost their land to the demands of modernization and development) have inflamed many in the countryside. All this, in addition to the increased incidence of industrial dumping that poisons streams and farmland, and, of course, the large numbers of workers laid off from failing state enterprises in the rust-belt provinces (where they sometimes see the rampant asset-stripping by managers), has explosive potential for the future. (From police records it already appears that the number of recorded incidents of social unrest multiplied more than seven-fold in the 10 years since 1994, though most of these incidents are as yet largely localized.)

Of course, the leadership is trying campaigns and exhortations to paper over the cracks, with nationalism fast replacing socialism as the necessary social glue, apart from some genuine attempts at improvements in benefits for laid-off workers, fiscal transfers to backward regions, pollution abatement, and reduction in the disequalizing effects of subsidies and taxes.[22] The Party is also slowly (and intermittently) relaxing some of its rigid controls. Some people (wistfully) suggest that in many ways mainland China in recent decades may be in effect following in the footsteps of Taiwan. Taiwan also had a highly disciplined authoritarian (organized on similar quasi-Leninist lines) ruling party—the Kuomintang—presiding over a capitalist transformation, with party committees playing an important role in economic management of enterprises. Taiwan also had a very large state-owned sector, and instead of drastic large-scale privatization of this sector, they allowed the non-state sector (often in small industries) to grow and gradually eclipse the importance of the state sector. As the economy gathered momentum in high growth the prospering middle classes started demanding political and civic rights and gradually won them, until Taiwan became a full-scale democracy in recent years. Things are, however, unlikely to be as smooth in this transition process in mainland China, and the authorities' preoccupation with maintaining order and stability, and the Party's monopoly of power may make them overreact to difficult situations, sometimes with disastrous consequences. Some others predict that even if China manages a soft landing into some form of quasi-democracy, it will be of the corrupt oligarchic kind under a predominant party like the one that prevailed in Mexico under the Partido Revolucionario Institucional (PRI) for many decades.

## Conclusion

Both China and India have made remarkable economic progress in the last quarter century, but both have severe structural and institutional problems that will hobble them for many years to come, and accounts of their blowing away jobs and incomes from the rest of the world are often patently exaggerated. Such exaggeration, in an echo chamber of the "giant sucking sound," only helps the protectionist lobbies in the other countries, and it is music to the ears of the preening ultra-nationalists in China and India. Between the two countries, Chinese economic performance has been on balance much better than that of India, although India's domestic private enterprise in industry and services has been arguably more robust and autonomous. In this article I have tried to probe underneath the contrasting performances of these two vast countries and offer some broad speculative hypotheses. Economic reform and commitment to long-run policies require hard collective decisions (and follow-up collective actions), and I have tried to trace the relative difficulty for India to take these decisions and actions in its more heterogeneous society and conflict-ridden polity. But Indian heterogeneity and pluralism have also provided the basis for a better ability to politically manage conflicts, which I am not sure China's overarching homogenizing bureaucratic state has so far acquired, even though this ability is likely to be sorely needed in the future years of increasing conflicts, inevitable in a fast-growing, internationally integrated economy with mounting disparities and tensions. I have suggested that this requires looking at deeper social and historical forces than simply referring to an aggregative comparison of an authoritarian and a democratic political regime, which is the standard fare in China–India comparative studies.

## Questions

1. What are the factors driving the growth of China and of India? How do they differ?

2. Given the information in the article, do you believe this growth will continue? Are the challenges greater for India or China? Why?

## Notes

1. For alternative estimates and discussion on this phenomenon in rural India, see Kijima and Lanjouw (2005).

2. The Gini coefficient of inequality in years of schooling was 0.56 for India in 1998–2000; for China in 2000, it was 0.37.

3. In contrast, state financing for higher education more than doubled just in 5 years between 1998 and 2003 in China.

4. According to the McKinsey Global Institute, talent shortage is looming in both China and India. China is producing more engineering graduates than India, but the proportion of them who are, according to them, "suitable" for the professional jobs particularly at the international standard is somewhat higher in India than in China. In 2003 the total number of suitable young engineers (excluding civil and agricultural engineers, but including those with IT and computer science degrees) was 160,000 in China and 130,000 in India.

5. Sutton (2004), in his study of the auto component supply chain in China and India, finds that the performance of car seat and exhaust makers, as well as the performance of the general run of first-tier suppliers to the new car makers in both countries, has reached levels that are at, or close to, international best practice.

6. One major restriction in the Chinese labor market has been that a large part of the floating migrant workers (estimated to be about 120 million in total) did not have housing registration (hukou), a system that has only recently been discontinued; they also face other kinds of discrimination.

7. In India the corresponding fraction of the labor force is about one-seventh.

8. China, that hardly had any superhighways in 1990, has built 30,000 km of it since then (making the system the second longest in the world). In 2004 India spent $2 billion on its road network; China spent $30 billion.

9. Just before the fiscal reform of 1994, the Chinese fiscal revenue as share of GDP was more similar to what India's is now.

10. Even the state enterprises that remain in business have largely shed their social protection functions for their employees (including provision of housing, daycare, hospitals and schools).

11. See the estimate of Banister (2005), after adjusting for statistical anomalies in official data.

12. Since 2002 asset reconstruction companies have disposed of a large fraction of the bad loans in China. The Chinese government has poured large sums of money to back these companies and to spruce up the four major state-owned banks for partial sales of shares to foreign banks. The credit ratings for Chinese banks are sometimes better than for Indian banks simply because of this greater ability and willingness of the Chinese government to provide substantial capital infusions.

13. Some unpublished work by Chang-Tai Hsieh and Peter Klenow using Chinese and Indian manufacturing censuses finds that

even though productivity at the four-digit industry level is low in both countries, China has a longer distance to cover.

14.   There are some exceptions in Kerala. Consider, for instance, the Manjeri municipality in the relatively backward district of Malappuram in north Kerala. In collaboration with some social groups and bankers, municipal authorities succeeded in converting it into a booming hosiery manufacturing center, after developing the necessary skills at the local level and the finance.

15.   For a review of the literature, see Baland and Platteau (2003).

16.   The sinologist and historian Jenner (1992) writes on this issue:

Nowhere has the homogenizing effect been more successful than in creating the impression that the Han Chinese themselves are a single ethnic group, despite the mutual incomprehensibility of many of their mother tongues and the ancient hostility between such Han Chinese nationalities as the Cantonese and the Hakkas. While the occupation of Tibet and East Turkestan has failed to persuade most Tibetans and Uighurs that they are Chinese, so that they can be kept in the empire only by force, historical myth-making has so far been remarkably effective, not just in inventing a single Han Chinese ethnicity, but also—and this is a far bigger triumph—in winning acceptance for it.

17.   The Gini coefficient of income inequality in China in 2002 is estimated there to be about 0.45 (the same as it was in 1995). From the Market Information Survey of Households data of the National Council of Applied Economic Research, Lal et al. (2001) suggest that the Gini coefficient of income inequality in India is about 0.41 in 1997–98. According to Li et al. (2005), the Gini coefficient of wealth inequality in China increased from 0.40 in 1995 to 0.55 in 2002.

18.   Even after some reassignments of landholdings, we can see from Khan (2004) that the Gini coefficient of inequality of per capita landholdings in China in both 1988 and 2002 were about 0.49. For India the data from the 2001 landholdings survey are not yet available, but already in 1991 the Gini coefficient of inequality was about 0.64.

19.   Kashmir and the north-east are, however, two areas where the Indian state has repeatedly failed in accommodation and containment.

20.   For an elaboration of this argument see Bardhan (1984[1998]).

21.   An econometric estimate by Jin et al. (2005) on the basis of a panel dataset from 29 provinces in China suggests that while in the period 1970–1979 the central government extracted about 83 percent of any increase provincial revenue, in the period 1982–1991, with the implementation of the "fiscal contracting system" (*caizheng chengbao zhi*), the percentage fell dramatically to about 25 percent, and to that extent the central government's capacity to transfer from high-revenue to low-revenue provinces declined. Since the 1994 fiscal reform, however, transfers to laggard provinces have increased substantially.

22.   The agricultural taxes and levies are to be eliminated nationwide by 2006.

# References

Baland, J.-M. and J. P. Platteau. 2003. "Economics of Common Property Management Regimes," in K.-G. Maler and J. R. Vincent (eds), *Handbook of Environmental Economics*, pp. 127–90. Amsterdam: Elsevier.

Banister, J. 2005. "Manufacturing Employment in China," *Monthly Labor Review, 128*(7): 11–29.

Bardhan, P. 1984 [1998]. *The Political Economy of Development in India.* New Delhi: Oxford University Press.

*Business Week.* 2005. 22 August.

Chaudhuri, S. Forthcoming. "What Difference Does a Constitutional Amendment Make? The 1994 Panchayat Raj Act and the Attempt to Revitalize Rural Local Government in India," in P. Bardhan and D. Mookherjee (eds), *Decentralization to Local Governments in Developing Countries: A Comparative Perspective*, Cambridge, MA: MIT Press.

Chen, S. and M. Ravallion. 2004a. "How Have the World's Poorest Fared Since the Early 1980's?" *World Bank Research Observer, 19*(2): 141–70.

———.2004b. "China's (Uneven) Progress Against Poverty." Policy Research Working Paper No. 3408, World Bank, Washington, DC.

Deshpande, L. K. 2004. *Liberalization and Labor: Labor Flexibility in Indian Manufacturing.* New Delhi: Institute of Human Development.

Dutta Roy, S. 2004. "Employment Dynamics in Indian Industry: Adjustment Lags and the Impact of Job Security Regulations," *Journal of Development Economics, 73*(1): 233–56.

Eichengreen, B. 2002. "Capitalizing on Globalization," *Asian Development Review, 19*(1): 17–69.

Friedman, T. L. 2005. *The World is Flat: A Brief History of the Twenty-first Century.* New York: Farrar, Straus and Giroux.

Government of India. 2001. *Report of Working Group on Decentralized Planning and Panchayat Raj Institutions.* New Delhi: Ministry of Rural Development.

Jenkins, R. S. 2000. *Democratic Politics and Economic Reform in India.* Cambridge: Cambridge University Press.

Jenner, W. J. F. 1992. *The Tyranny of History: The Roots of China's Crisis.* London: Penguin Press.

Jin, H., Y. Qian and B.R. Weingast. 2005. "Regional Decentralisation and Fiscal Incentives: Federalism, Chinese Style," *Journal of Public Economics, 89*(9–10): 1719–42.

Jun, Z. 2003. "Investment, Investment Efficiency, and Economic Growth in China," *Journal of Asian Economics, 14*(5): 713–34.

Khan, A. R. 2004. "Growth, Inequality and Poverty in China: A Comparative Study of the Experience in the Periods Before and After the Asian Crisis." Issues in Employment and Poverty Discussion Paper No. 15, International Labour Office, Geneva.

Kijima, Y. and P. Lanjouw. 2005. "Agricultural Wages, Non-Farm Employment and Poverty in Rural India." Unpublished, World Bank, Washington, DC.

Lal, D., R. Mohan and I. Natarajan. 2001. "Economic Reforms and Poverty Alleviation: A Tale of Two Surveys," *Economic and Political Weekly, 36*(12): 1017–28.

Li, S., Z. Wei and S. Jing. 2005. "Inequality of Wealth Distribution of Chinese People: An Empirical Analysis of its Cause." FED Working Paper No. 65, China Center of Economic Research, Peking University, Beijing.

Maddison, A. 2005. *Growth and Interaction in the World Economy: Roots of Modernity.* Washington, DC: AEI Press.

Poncet, S. 2004. "A Fragmented China." Tinbergen Institute Working Paper No. 103/2, Erasmus University, Rotterdam.

Prestowitz, C. 2005. *Three Billion New Capitalists: The Great Shift of Wealth and Power to the East.* New York: Basic Books.

Qian, Y. and G. Roland. 1998. "Federalism and the Soft Budget Constraint," *American Economic Review,* 88(5): 1143–62.

Sutton, J. 2004. "The Auto-component Supply Chain in China and India: A Benchmarking Study." Unpublished, London School of Economics, London.

Topalova, P. Forthcoming. "Trade Liberalization, Poverty and Inequality: Evidence for Indian Districts," in A. Harrison (ed.), *Globalization and Poverty.* Chicago: University of Chicago Press.

Wang, Y. and Y. Yao. 2003. "Sources of China's Economic Growth, 1952–1999: Incorporating Human Capital Accumulation," *China Economic Review,* 14(1): 32–52.

Wu, Y. 2003. "Has Productivity Contributed to China's Growth?" *Pacific Economic Review,* 8(1): 15–30.

World Bank. 2006a. *Doing Business in 2006.* Washington, DC: World Bank.

———. 2006b. *World Development Report.* Washington, DC: World Bank and Oxford University Press.

WHO. 1998. *World Health Report.* Geneva: WHO.

*Source:* From Bardhan, Pranab (2006). Awakening Giants, Feet of Clay: A Comparative Assessment of the Rise of China and India. *Journal of South Asian Development.* Vol. 1 No. 1. Reprinted with permission from Sage Publications, Inc.

# CHAPTER 2

## The Wal-Mart You Don't Know

Charles Fishman

Wal-Mart has become one of the United States' most familiar shopping icons. Already the largest retailer in the world, and one of the world's largest corporations, it is starting to dominate and transform markets in Latin America and Asia. It is also extremely controversial. To some it represents opportunity, bargain prices for all, and a consumer-first ethic of service. To others it represents low wages, union-busting, and the decimation of small business by a corporate giant. This article examines the hidden, and maybe darker, side of the global mass marketing phenomenon.

A gallon-sized jar of whole pickles is something to behold. The jar is the size of a small aquarium. The fat green pickles, floating in swampy juice, look reptilian, their shapes exaggerated by the glass. It weighs 12 pounds, too big to carry with one hand. The gallon jar of pickles is a display of abundance and excess; it is entrancing, and also vaguely unsettling. This is the product that Wal-Mart fell in love with: Vlasic's gallon jar of pickles.

Wal-Mart priced it at $2.97—a year's supply of pickles for less than $3! "They were using it as a 'statement' item," says Pat Hunn, who calls himself the "mad scientist" of Vlasic's gallon jar. "Wal-Mart was putting it before consumers, saying, 'This represents what Wal-Mart's about. You can buy a stinkin' gallon of pickles for $2.97. And it's the nation's number-one brand.'"

Therein lies the basic conundrum of doing business with the world's largest retailer. By selling a gallon of kosher dills for less than most grocers sell a quart, Wal-Mart may have provided a service for its customers. But what did it do for Vlasic? The pickle maker had spent decades convincing customers that they should pay a premium for its brand. Now Wal-Mart was practically giving them away. And the fevered buying spree that resulted distorted every aspect of Vlasic's operations, from farm field to factory to financial statement.

Indeed, as Vlasic discovered, the real story of Wal-Mart, the story that never gets told, is the story of the pressure the biggest retailer relentlessly applies to its suppliers in the name of bringing us "every day low prices." It's the story of what that pressure does to the companies Wal-Mart does business with, to U.S. manufacturing, and to the economy as a whole. That story can be found floating in a gallon jar of pickles at Wal-Mart.

Wal-Mart is not just the world's largest retailer. It's the world's largest company—bigger than ExxonMobil, General Motors, and General Electric. The scale can be hard to absorb. Wal-Mart sold $244.5 billion worth of goods last year. It sells in 3 months what number-two retailer Home Depot sells in a year. And in its own category of general merchandise and groceries, Wal-Mart no longer has any real rivals. It does more business than Target, Sears, Kmart, J.C. Penney, Safeway, and Kroger combined. "Clearly," says Edward Fox, head of Southern Methodist University's J.C. Penney Center for Retailing Excellence, "Wal-Mart is more powerful than any retailer has ever been." It is, in fact, so big and so furtively powerful as to have become an entirely different order of corporate being.

Wal-Mart wields its power for just one purpose: to bring the lowest possible prices to its customers. At Wal-Mart, that goal is never reached. The retailer has a clear policy for suppliers: On basic products that don't change, the price Wal-Mart will pay, and will charge shoppers, must drop year after year. But what almost no one outside the world of Wal-Mart and its 21,000 suppliers knows is the high cost of those low prices. Wal-Mart has the power to squeeze profit-killing concessions from vendors. To survive in the face of its pricing demands, makers of everything from bras to bicycles to blue jeans have had to lay off employees and close U.S. plants in favor of outsourcing products from overseas.

Of course, U.S. companies have been moving jobs offshore for decades, long before Wal-Mart was a retailing power. But there is no question that the chain is helping accelerate the loss of American jobs to low-wage countries such as China. Wal-Mart, which in the late 1980s and early 1990s trumpeted its claim to "Buy American," has doubled its imports from China in the past 5 years alone, buying some $12 billion in merchandise in 2002. That's nearly 10% of all Chinese exports to the United States.

One way to think of Wal-Mart is as a vast pipeline that gives non-U.S. companies direct access to the American market. "One of the things that limits or slows the growth of imports is the cost of establishing connections and networks," says Paul Krugman, the Princeton University economist. "Wal-Mart is so big and so centralized that it can all at once hook Chinese and other suppliers into its digital system. So—wham!—you have a large switch to overseas sourcing in a period quicker than under the old rules of retailing."

Steve Dobbins has been bearing the brunt of that switch. He's president and CEO of Carolina Mills, a 75-year-old North Carolina company that supplies thread, yarn, and textile finishing to apparel makers—half of which supply Wal-Mart. Carolina Mills grew steadily until 2000. But in the past 3 years, as its customers have gone either overseas or out of business, it has shrunk from 17 factories to seven and from 2,600 employees to 1,200. Dobbins's customers have begun to face imported clothing sold so cheaply to Wal-Mart that they could not compete even if they paid their workers nothing.

"People ask, 'How can it be bad for things to come into the U.S. cheaply? How can it be bad to have a bargain at Wal-Mart?' Sure, it's held inflation down, and it's great to have bargains," says Dobbins. "But you can't buy anything if you're not employed. We are shopping ourselves out of jobs."

The gallon jar of pickles at Wal-Mart became a devastating success, giving Vlasic strong sales and growth numbers—but slashing its profits by millions of dollars.

There is no question that Wal-Mart's relentless drive to squeeze out costs has benefited consumers. The giant retailer is at least partly responsible for the low rate of U.S. inflation, and a McKinsey & Co. study concluded that about 12% of the economy's productivity gains in the second half of the 1990s could be traced to Wal-Mart alone.

There is also no question that doing business with Wal-Mart can give a supplier a fast, heady jolt of sales and market share. But that fix can come with long-term consequences for the health of a brand and a business. Vlasic, for example, wasn't looking to build its brand on a gallon of whole pickles. Pickle companies make money on "the cut," slicing cucumbers into spears and hamburger chips. "Cucumbers in the jar, you don't make a whole lot of money there," says Steve Young, a former vice president of grocery marketing for pickles at Vlasic, who has since left the company.

At some point in the late 1990s, a Wal-Mart buyer saw Vlasic's gallon jar and started talking to Pat Hunn about it. Hunn, who has also since left Vlasic, was then head of Vlasic's Wal-Mart sales team, based in Dallas. The gallon intrigued the buyer. In sales tests, priced somewhere over $3, "the gallon sold like crazy," says Hunn, "surprising us all." The Wal-Mart buyer had a brainstorm: What would happen to the gallon if they offered it nationwide and got it below $3? Hunn was skeptical, but his job was to look for ways to sell pickles at Wal-Mart. Why not?

And so Vlasic's gallon jar of pickles went into every Wal-Mart, some 3,000 stores, at $2.97, a price so low that Vlasic and Wal-Mart were making only a penny or two on a jar, if that. It was showcased on big pallets near the front of stores. It was an abundance of abundance. "It was selling 80 jars a week, on average, in every store," says Young. Doesn't sound like much, until you do the math: That's 240,000 gallons of pickles, just in gallon jars, just at Wal-Mart, every week. Whole fields of cucumbers were heading out the door.

For Vlasic, the gallon jar of pickles became what might be called a devastating success. "Quickly, it started cannibalizing our non-Wal-Mart business," says Young. "We saw consumers who used to buy the spears and the chips in supermarkets buying the Wal-Mart gallons. They'd eat a quarter of a jar and throw the thing away when they got moldy. A family can't eat them fast enough."

The gallon jar reshaped Vlasic's pickle business: It chewed up the profit margin of the business with Wal-Mart, and of pickles generally. Procurement had to scramble to find enough pickles to fill the gallons, but the volume gave Vlasic strong sales numbers, strong growth numbers, and a powerful place in the world of pickles at Wal-Mart. Which accounted for 30% of Vlasic's business. But the company's profits from pickles had shriveled 25% or more, Young says—millions of dollars.

The gallon was hoisting Vlasic and hurting it at the same time.

Young remembers begging Wal-Mart for relief. "They said, 'No way,'" says Young. "We said we'll increase the price"—even $3.49 would have helped tremendously—"and they said, 'If you do that, all the other products of yours we buy, we'll stop buying.' It was a clear threat." Hunn recalls things a little differently, if just as ominously: "They said, 'We want the $2.97 gallon of pickles. If you don't do it, we'll see if someone else might.' I knew our competitors were saying to Wal-Mart, 'We'll do the $2.97 gallons if you give us your other business.'" Wal-Mart's business was so indispensable to Vlasic, and the gallon so central to the Wal-Mart relationship, that decisions about the future of the gallon were made at the CEO level. . . .

By now, it is accepted wisdom that Wal-Mart makes the companies it does business with more efficient and focused, leaner and faster. Wal-Mart itself is known for continuous improvement in its ability to handle, move, and track merchandise. It expects the same of its suppliers. But the ability to operate at peak efficiency only gets you in the door at Wal-Mart. Then the real demands start. The public image Wal-Mart projects may be as cheery as its yellow smiley-face mascot, but there is nothing genial about the process by which Wal-Mart gets its suppliers to provide tires and contact lenses, guns and underarm deodorant at every day low prices. Wal-Mart is legendary for forcing its suppliers to redesign everything from their packaging to their computer systems. It is also legendary for quite straightforwardly telling them what it will pay for their goods. . . .

It also is not unheard of for Wal-Mart to demand to examine the private financial records of a supplier and to insist that its margins are too high and must be cut. And the smaller the supplier, one academic study shows, the greater the likelihood that it will be forced into damaging concessions. Melissa Berryhill, a Wal-Mart spokeswoman, disagrees: "The fact is Wal-Mart, perhaps like no other retailer, seeks to establish collaborative and mutually beneficial relationships with our suppliers."

For many suppliers, though, the only thing worse than doing business with Wal-Mart may be not doing business with Wal-Mart. Last year, 7.5 cents of every dollar spent in any store in the United States (other than auto-parts stores) went to the retailer. That means a contract with Wal-Mart can be critical even for the largest consumer-goods companies. Dial Corp., for example, does 28% of its business with Wal-Mart. If Dial lost that one account, it would have to double its sales to its next nine customers just to stay even. "Wal-Mart is the essential retailer, in a way no other retailer is," says Gib Carey, a partner at Bain & Co., who is leading a yearlong study of how to do business with Wal-Mart. "Our clients cannot grow without finding a way to be successful with Wal-Mart."

Many companies and their executives frankly admit that supplying Wal-Mart is like getting into the company version of basic training with an implacable Army drill sergeant. The process may be unpleasant. But there can be some positive results.

"Everyone from the forklift driver on up to me, the CEO, knew we had to deliver [to Wal-Mart] on time. Not 10 minutes late. And not 45 minutes early, either," says Robin Prever, who was CEO of Saratoga Beverage Group from 1992 to 2000 and made private-label water sold at Wal-Mart. "The message came through clearly: You have this 30-second delivery window. Either you're there, or you're out. With a customer like that, it changes your organization. For the better. It wakes everybody up. And all our customers benefited. We changed our whole approach to doing business."

But you won't hear evenhanded stories like that from Wal-Mart, or from its current suppliers. Despite being a publicly traded company, Wal-Mart is intensely private. It declined to talk in detail about its relationships with its suppliers for this story. More strikingly, dozens of companies contacted declined to talk about even the basics of their business with Wal-Mart. . . .

"You won't hear anything negative from most people," says Paul Kelly, founder of Silvermine Consulting Group, a company that helps businesses work more effectively with retailers. "It would be committing suicide. If Wal-Mart takes something the wrong way, it's like Saddam Hussein. You just don't want to piss them off." . . .

To a person, all those interviewed credit Wal-Mart with a fundamental integrity in its dealings that's unusual in the world of consumer goods, retailing, and groceries. Wal-Mart does not cheat suppliers, it keeps its word, and it pays its bills briskly. "They are tough people but very honest; they treat you honestly," says Peter Campanella, who ran the business that sold Corning kitchenware products, both at Corning and then at World Kitchen. "It was a joke to do business with most of their competitors. A fiasco."

But Wal-Mart also clearly does not hesitate to use its power, magnifying the Darwinian forces already at work in modern global capitalism.

Caught in the Wal-Mart squeeze, Huffy didn't just relinquish profits to keep its commitment to the retailer. It handed those profits to the competition.

What does the squeeze look like at Wal-Mart? It is usually thoroughly rational, sometimes devastatingly so.

John Mariotti is a veteran of the consumer-products world—he spent 9 years as president of Huffy Bicycle Co., a division of Huffy Corp., and is now chairman of World Kitchen, the company that sells Oxo, Revere, Corning, and Ekco brand housewares. . . .

Mariotti describes one episode from Huffy's relationship with Wal-Mart. It's a tale he tells to illustrate an admiring point he makes about the retailer. "They demand you do what you say you are going to do." But it's also a classic example of the damned-if-you-do, damned-if-you-don't Wal-Mart squeeze. When Mariotti was at Huffy throughout the 1980s, the company sold a range of bikes to Wal-Mart, 20 or so models, in a spread of prices and profitability. It was a leading manufacturer of bikes in the United States, in places like Ponca City, Oklahoma; Celina, Ohio; and Farmington, Missouri.

One year, Huffy had committed to supply Wal-Mart with an entry-level, thin-margin bike—as many as Wal-Mart needed. Sales of the low-end bike took off. "I woke up May 1"—the heart of the bike production cycle for the summer—"and I needed 900,000 bikes," he says. "My factories could only run 450,000." As it happened, that same year, Huffy's fancier, more-profitable bikes were doing well, too, at Wal-Mart and other places. Huffy found itself in a bind.

With other retailers, perhaps, Mariotti might have sat down, renegotiated, tried to talk his way out of the corner. Not with Wal-Mart. "I made the deal up front with them," he says. "I knew how high was up. I was duty-bound to supply my customer." So he did something extraordinary. To free up production in order to make Wal-Mart's cheap bikes, he gave the designs for four of his higher-end, higher-margin products to rival manufacturers. "I conceded business to my competitors, because I just ran out of capacity," he says. Huffy didn't just relinquish profits to keep Wal-Mart happy—it handed those profits to its competition. "Wal-Mart didn't

tell me what to do," Mariotti says. "They didn't have to." "The retailer," he adds, "is tough as nails. But they give you a chance to compete. If you can't compete, that's your problem."

In the years since Mariotti left Huffy, the bike maker's relationship with Wal-Mart has been vital (though Huffy Corp. has lost money in 3 out of the last 5 years). It is the number-three seller of bikes in the United States. And Wal-Mart is the number-one retailer of bikes. But here's one last statistic about bicycles: Roughly 98% are now imported from places such as China, Mexico, and Taiwan. Huffy made its last bike in the United States in 1999. . . .

There is very little academic and statistical study of Wal-Mart's impact on the health of its suppliers and virtually nothing in the last decade, when Wal-Mart's size has increased by a factor of five. This while the retail industry has become much more concentrated. In large part, that's because it's nearly impossible to get meaningful data that would allow researchers to track the influence of Wal-Mart's business on companies over time. You'd need cooperation from the vendor companies or Wal-Mart or both—and neither Wal-Mart nor its suppliers are interested in sharing such intimate detail. . . .

In the end, of course, it is we as shoppers who have the power and who have given that power to Wal-Mart. Part of Wal-Mart's dominance, part of its insight, and part of its arrogance is that it presumes to speak for American shoppers.

If Wal-Mart doesn't like the pricing on something, says Andrew Whitman, who helped service Wal-Mart for years when he worked at General Foods and Kraft, they simply say, "At that price we no longer think it's a good value to our shopper. Therefore, we don't think we should carry it."

## Questions

1. What are the opportunities and the problems created by Wal-Mart's rapid growth?

2. Do the problems created by Wal-Mart outweigh the benefits? Would you support the expansion of Wal-Mart in your community?

*Source:* The Wal-Mart You Don't Know. Charles Fishman. *Fast Company.* December 2003. Reprinted by permission of Mansueto Ventures LLC via Copyright Clearance Center.

# CHAPTER 3

## The "Radical" Thesis on Globalization and the Case of Venezuela's Hugo Chávez

Steve Ellner

Economic globalization has brought great wealth to some, and also brought wide gaps between rich and poor in many places. Venezuela's President, Hugo Chávez, has become a leading figure in the Latin American opposition to economic globalization, especially as it has been promoted by the United States.

The best way to evaluate the accuracy of theories about globalization is to examine concrete developments and trends in the past two decades. This approach is especially revealing in the case of the "radical" thesis on globalization, which posits that transnational capital and structures are inexorably undermining the state and national sovereignty. The "radicals" argue that since globalization promotes uniformity and capital is no longer nationally based, Third World nations will receive equal if not favorable treatment from international investors and equality between nations will eventually prevail. But the facts speak for themselves: globalization has had the opposite effect of widening the gap between rich and poor nations.

A second assertion of the radical thesis has, however, withstood the test of time fairly well. The radicals point out that, given the narrow range of options now available to the state, any government that defies multinational structures and spurns neoliberal policies will eventually back down or else be removed from power. Examples of this dynamic in Latin America abound. In Venezuela, for instance, the veteran politicians Carlos Andrés Pérez and Rafael Caldera, who had staunchly supported state interventionism and attacked neoliberal policies, ended up yielding to pressure and embracing neoliberalism in their second terms in office. Indeed, Pérez claimed that his decision to accept an International Monetary Fund-imposed program was inspired by the example of Peru's Alan García, whose confrontation with multilateral lending agencies had had devastating political and economic consequences.

Venezuela's President Hugo Chávez is the first elected Latin American head of state since Alan García to defy the hegemonic powers of the "new world order." He has been the only president throughout the continent to pursue a truly independent foreign policy and preach far-reaching changes at home. In this sense he may be considered a path-breaker who is defining the limits of change in the age of globalization and putting the radical thesis on globalization to the test. Like García, Chávez has opposed neoliberalism and defied powerful international actors, but unlike the Peruvian president he has clashed with national economic groups as well. García was successful during his first year in office on both political and economic fronts, but then the economy went into a tailspin and he fell into political disgrace. Similarly, Chávez got off to a good start politically and even scored better in the 2000 elections than in his original electoral triumph, but since then his popularity has significantly declined.

Chávez's critics in both political and academic arenas reflect the logic of the radical thesis on globalization. From the outset they called Chávez's policies "obsolete" and prognosticated political disaster. Their line of reasoning, explicit or implicit, is that no president can defy powerful international actors and get away with it (Quirós Corradi, 1999: 291–296; 1998: 187). Nevertheless, with the exception of occasionally harsh remarks by State Department spokesmen, Washington has assumed a relatively passive stance toward Chávez. Some political analysts consider this restraint amazing given the leftist thrust of Chávez's discourse and stands (Gott, 2000: 228). The radicals explain this moderation in terms of globalization logic. According to them, the United States is confident that global imperatives will force Chávez to back down or else face destabilization. They add that, given globalization's preference for uniformity, the United States is more committed to democracy today than in the past and thus would prefer to avoid a Pinochet-type sequence of events as long as Chávez enjoys widespread popularity. In essence it is seen as anticipating two possible scenarios: Chávez either "rectifies" his positions or doggedly adheres to them, in which case the economy contracts and his popularity plummets, leading to his overthrow with or without U.S. collaboration (Romero, 2000).

Members of the far left, among others, write the Chávez phenomenon off as pure rhetoric devoid of leftist content. Underlying their skepticism regarding the goals of the Chávez movement—and everything else short of a full-fledged revolution—is the deterministic notion of the globalization radicals that successfully challenging the "new world order" is virtually impossible. Thus, for instance, the ex-guerrilla-turned-neoliberal Teodoro Petkoff argues that Chávez has reneged on his leftist positions and embraced neoliberalism as Pérez and Caldera were forced to do before him. Petkoff points to specific neoliberal proposals designed by the Caldera administration on issues such as the social security and severance-payment systems that Chávez allegedly is coming around to accept. He concludes that Chávez is "the negation of all revolutionary ideas" and adds that "Marx would have turned over in his grave" (Petkoff, 2001a; 2001b; 2001c). A former comrade-in-arms of Petkoff, the legendary Douglas Bravo, is equally pessimistic about the direction of the Chavista movement. His arguments appear to be a wish list of revolutionary plans that Chávez had pledged to carry out and then reneged on. The list begins with Chávez's refusal to make good on his alleged promise to distribute arms to the people on the day of the abortive 1992 coup attempt in order to activate a mass insurrection. Bravo concludes that Chávez's retreat on a number of issues demonstrates "his acceptance of globalization" (1999: 30–34). The arguments of Petkoff and Bravo coincide with the theory that the only way antiglobalization

governments can stay in power is to abandon their positions and accept the imperatives of the "new world order." The Petkoff-Bravo discussion of Chávez's revised positions, however, tells only part of the story.

Chávez's discourse, which stresses globalization's unequal distribution of wealth, underpins specific policies and actions that are adverse to the "new world order." The "multipolar world" slogan that he frequently employs on his trips abroad is thus more than empty rhetoric or megalomania as his adversaries claim. Although he stops short of being explicit on this point, the multipolar model is intended to counter U.S. hegemony. He does make clear that the "multipolar" world consists of blocs of nations to two of which Venezuela belongs: OPEC and the community of Latin American nations. After his assumption of power in 1998, he was instrumental in persuading OPEC members to comply with production quotas and establish a band system in which prices oscillate between US$22 and US$28 a barrel. The objective of shoring up and stabilizing oil prices overrides all other considerations and has a major impact on the global economy. Nevertheless, some actors misinterpret Venezuela's priorities. Thus, for instance, in order to generate support for the band system, Chávez traveled to all 10 fellow OPEC nations in preparation for the organization's second summit meeting in September 2000.

The U.S. State Department and Chávez's opposition at home criticized his visits to Iraq and Libya, which they portrayed as a manifestation of solidarity with the "Arab cause" if not with international terrorism. Had he omitted these two nations from his tour, however, OPEC unity would have been seriously compromised. Similarly, his insistence that the United States refrain from bombing fellow-OPEC nations in the Middle East after the September 11 attacks was designed to contribute to OPEC cohesion, criticisms by his adversaries notwithstanding. In a congressional address in which he explained his government's position on the September 11 attacks, Chávez emphasized that both OPEC unity and Latin American integration are designed to strengthen national sovereignty. In his speech, he alluded to the radical-globalization writer Francis Fukuyama when he said that "somebody has argued that mankind has reached the 'end of history' and that national sovereignty no longer means anything." His vision of regional integration as an assertion of national sovereignty (Cardozo, 2001) is diametrically opposed to the radical-globalization thesis, which sees these agreements among neighboring countries as a step in the direction of tearing down all national barriers.

Chávez and the military officers who support him are particularly sensitive about the defense of national sovereignty, which they consider to be the armed forces' raison d'être. Many of them are convinced that with the end of the Cold War, Washington would prefer to phase out the Latin American armed forces or convert them into police forces in charge of combating crime (particularly drug trafficking) and keeping public order. Behind these fears is the realization that radical globalization implies the erosion of sovereignty and the concomitant transformation of the military into a superfluous institution. Thus, for instance, Rear Admiral Hernán Gruber Odremán, who conspired against the government along with Chávez in 1992, called globalization "nothing other than a trap leading to a new colonialism" that includes the elimination of the armed forces as the United States did when it invaded Panama in 1989 (Gruber, 1999: 41). Chávez addresses himself to these concerns by linking the defense of national sovereignty to the new role assigned to the armed forces based on its active participation in the political and economic life of the nation. To achieve these objectives, he has granted the military the right to vote, appointed scores of officers to important positions in his administration and his party, and involved the military in community and welfare projects.

Ultimately, it is Chávez's economic policy, more than his foreign policy or reformulation of the role of the armed forces, that will determine whether Venezuela is successful in overcoming the constraints imposed by globalization. Chávez has vocally denounced neoliberalism, but a new economic strategy to replace it has yet to be formulated. This lack of precision does not mean that he has made his peace with powerful economic and political groups as some leftist adversaries (and ex-leftist ones like Petkoff) claim. Many specific actions and policies give the lie to the assertion that Chávez is a neoliberal with leftist trappings. Thus he has refrained from privatizing state companies en masse as his predecessors did and instead has sought to establish terms of sale for the all-important aluminum sector in accordance with national interests. He has also begun to roll back the partial privatization of the petroleum industry by proposing majority state ownership of all joint oil ventures. When all government measures dealing with the economy are taken into account, it is clear that the delineation of a genuine "third way" that avoids state domination of the economy but clearly spurns neoliberal formulas is a major challenge for nationalistic regimes in the age of globalization (Buxton, n.d.).

Apart from oil policy, the most important issue in Venezuela with regard to global capital is the payment of the foreign debt. Chávez inveighs against the injustice of Third World debt and calls for collective negotiation among all debtor and creditor nations, but until now Venezuela has dutifully made its payments. Nevertheless, a member of the government coalition Patria Para Todo (Fatherland for All—PPT) stresses that the nation should be obliged to pay only a reasonable amount of the debt over a reasonable period of time.

Chávez faces powerful enemies who by late 2001 had begun to organize with the aim of ousting him from power by any means possible. The opposition is aided by the errors committed by Chávez and his movement, not the least of which are his rhetorical excesses and the alienation of the middle class. Political analysts will have to objectively identify shortcomings in the Chavista strategy in order to demonstrate that there is nothing inevitable about the final outcome. Such a focus will serve to refute the notion that any deviation from the globalization-imposed model will inexorably lead to great economic hardship and force those in power to choose between recanting and being removed from office.

## Questions

1. Why does President Chávez oppose many forces of globalization?

2. Does Chávez present a reasonable alternative? Can he succeed in preserving national sovereignty and in charting a different path to development?

## References

Bravo, Douglas. 1999. "Chávez es un hombre inteligente, audaz, conversador, carismático . . . ," pp. 5–40 in Alberto Garrido, *Guerrilla y conspiración militar en Venezuela*. Caracas: Fondo Editorial Nacional José Agustín Catalá.

Buxton, Julia. n.d. "Economic policy and the rise of Hugo Chávez," in Steve Ellner and Daniel Hellinger (eds.), *Venezuelan Politics in the Chávez Era: Class, Polarization,* and *Conflict*. Boulder, CO: Lynne Rienner.

Cardozo, Elsa. 2001. "La administración Chávez y su proyecto continental de política exterior." Paper presented at 23d Congress of the Latin American Studies Association, Washington, DC, September 7.

Gott, Richard. 2000. *In the Shadow of the Liberator: Hugo Chávez and the Transformation of Venezuela*. London: Verso.

Petkoff, Teodoro. 2001a. "Hugo el Calderista." *Teodoro en Tierra,* September 30.

Petkoff, Teodoro. 2001b. "Prologue," pp. 11–18 in Américo Martín, *América y Fidel Castro.* 3d edition. Caracas: Editorial Panapo.

Petkoff, Teodoro. 2001c. "Una linea, tal cual, de vida." *Producto:* La *Revista de Negocios en* Venezuela (April). hhtp://www .producto.com.ve/211/notas/medios.html

Quirós Corradi, Alberto. 1998. *¿Un receso para la democracia?* Caracas: El Texto.

Quirós Corradi, Alberto. 1999. *La cultura de lo obsoleto.* Caracas: El Texto.

Romero, Anibal. 2000. "La política de Washington ante Hugo Chávez." *Venezuela Analítica* (February).

*Source:* Ellner, Steve (2002). The "Radical" Thesis on Globalization and the Case of Venezuela's Hugo Chávez. *Latin American Perspectives 29(6).*
Copyright © Sage Publications. Reprinted by permission of Sage Publications, Inc.

# CHAPTER 4

## A Coffee Connoisseur on a Mission

*Buy High and Sell High*

Michaele Weissman

Coffee is big business in the United States and is the second most valuable global commodity after petroleum. The last decade has seen a surge of interest in gourmet coffee, blended coffee drinks, and regional specialty blends. At the same time, across North America and Europe, there is growing interest in the idea of fair trade and of building equitable working relationships with the often poor and rural producers of global commodities. This article follows the trail of a coffee connoisseur as he seeks to build relationships in his search for the finest coffee beans.

GRANADA, Nicaragua—Geoff Watts turned up recently at the ceremony capping Nicaragua's 2006 Cup of Excellence coffee competition in the steamy 500-year-old Convent of San Francisco here. Mr. Watts, 32, is the green coffee buyer for Intelligentsia Coffee, a fast-growing, privately owned retail and wholesale company in Chicago.

Coffee, Mr. Watts says, is his life, and he tries to attend most of the competitions in Latin America each year to find the best beans and build lasting relationships with growers.

"Relationship coffee" is one term Mr. Watts uses to describe how he does business—another is "direct trade."

"I find a coffee I love, build a direct relationship with the grower and then pay at least 25 percent above the Fair Trade price," he said in an interview. He also lavishes time and resources on his growers, inviting groups of them to Chicago to learn about the consumer side of the coffee business. Fair Trade certification, which is monitored by an international nonprofit organization, is intended to guarantee fair wages and labor conditions for farmers in developing countries.

Mr. Watts and the founder and chief executive of Intelligentsia, Doug Zell, do not ascribe to the "buy low, sell high" business model. They buy high and sell high. In the coming years, both say they expect to pay 50 percent, 100 percent, even 200 percent above Fair Trade rates for beans so good that customers will pay $20 and more a pound retail. "On the grower side and the consumer side, we're trying to create a culture of quality," Mr. Watts said.

Mr. Zell underwrites the $150,000 to $200,000 annual cost of Mr. Watts's relationship-building and his seven months of travel each year in coffee-growing countries because he expects these investments to pay off as quality increases and customers learn to appreciate artisanal coffees from around the world.

To speed this development, Intelligentsia has devised a plan that offers farmers financial incentives for improving growing methods and producing superior beans. Mr. Watts was in Nicaragua to introduce this new approach, which mandates direct dealings with farmers and limits the role of the cooperatives that currently market most Nicaraguan coffee.

Some in the specialty coffee business have had their doubts about Intelligentsia's business model and its high-flying ways. "Intelligentsia was known as this stupid and naïve company that overpaid farmers and carried too much debt," said a coffee buyer, Peter Giuliano, a principal of Counter Culture Coffee in Durham, N.C., one of a handful of top-quality roasters that pay a premium for quality. Stumptown, based in Portland, Ore., is another.

Mr. Watts acknowledges that in the past the company had sometimes overemphasized altruism and underemphasized business. Recently, however, the tut-tutting has been silenced as Mr. Zell has turned Intelligentsia into a profit-making venture, with 2005 sales of $9.4 million and a 2006 growth rate of 21 percent, according to company figures.

Coffee matters in Nicaragua, and all the important people were gathered for the Cup of Excellence ceremony: government officials, mill owners, exporters and representatives from the cooperatives that represent the country's 27,000 small coffee growers.

As darkness fell and the speeches dragged on, Mr. Watts, milling about in the relative cool of the church's loggia, greeted a coffee grower, Norman Canales. He is the son of the 2004 Cup of Excellence first-place winner, Daniel Canales, who was the first organic grower to win. Norman and his brothers Milton and Donald also grow organic coffee recognized by Cup of Excellence. Intelligentsia is the sole buyer of the Canales family's coffee.

"My family thanks God for Cup of Excellence," Norman Canales said, giving Mr. Watts an exuberant hug. "Cup of Excellence helped Geoff Watts and Intelligentsia find us. Now we get a high price for our coffee and we consider Geoff to be our guardian angel."

The morning after the Cup of Excellence ceremony, Mr. Watts rose early in preparation for the real business at hand. He was to meet the growers of the Las Brumas coffee cooperative, four hours from Granada in the hills above Matagalpa. In 2003, these farmers walked away with many Cup of Excellence honors. Since then, Mr. Watts has been buying much of their coffee.

As the driver, who had arrived hours late, played pothole hopscotch on the rutted highway, Mr. Watts and his companions—Mr. Giuliano of Counter Culture Coffee and K. C. O'Keefe, an Intelligentsia consultant based in Lima, Peru—talked coffee. Time and again, they returned to the financial differential between ordinary and extraordinary coffee. Farmers growing the best beans earn only pennies more than those whose crop is ordinary, though they work much harder, the men agreed.

While others recognized the problem, Intelligentsia was instituting a policy for changing this. But to do so, it would have to alter the way the cooperative system works, because all coffee growers within the co-op would no longer be paid the same. Like the growers of estate-quality wines, some would be paid a premium for

excellence. Mr. Watts was going to Las Brumas to explain the new pricing structure.

A fiesta, paid for by Intelligentsia, was already under way at Las Brumas—4,400 feet above sea level, with no electricity—when the group arrived. After socializing, 35 coffee growers and their families crowded into an outbuilding to hear Mr. Watts. Speaking in somewhat tortured Spanish, he began his presentation by praising the growers of Las Brumas and offering to underwrite several capital improvements.

With Mr. O'Keefe, the consultant, translating, Mr. Watts then addressed the purpose of the meeting. He told the farmers that from now on he would pay $1.60 a pound for AA coffee that earned a cupping score of 84 to 87 (on a scale of 100); $1.85 a pound for AAA coffees that earned scores of 88–93; and an unheard-of $3 a pound for extraordinary coffee that scored 94 and above. Furthermore, Mr. Watts said, these rates would never decline, they would only increase.

The response was muted, perhaps fearful. Growers in Las Brumas had never before been offered direct payment: in the past, the co-op received payment, and all farmers were paid the same price for their coffee.

The growers wanted to know how much Cecocafen, the huge cooperative that includes the small Las Brumas co-op as a member, would skim off the top.

None, Mr. Watts, answered. "Cecocafen would be paid a separate fee of around 26 cents per pound."

But why should Cecocafen take money, any money from Las Brumas growers? Mr. Watts was asked. Cecocafen, he answered, was paid for performing "essential services," like dry-milling the beans, prefinancing the crop and providing technical assistance.

And then the question that went to the heart of the matter: How could Las Brumas farmers be sure that the judging of their coffees—on which their pay rate would depend—would be fair, impartial and consistent?

Mr. Watts tried to reassure the farmers, telling them that Intelligentsia would build a cupping lab in the village and teach Las Brumas growers to judge their own coffee.

Then the sun began to set and Mr. Watts departed, leaving the mountain cool for the heat and humidity of Managua, where another flight awaited him. Nothing was settled. But Mr. Watts would be back in the fall, and he was relying on the relationship of trust he had established with Las Brumas to persuade farmers to accept his offer for next year's crop.

Mr. Giuliano, who is sometimes a partner with Mr. Watts in buying beans at auction, praised Intelligentsia's direct trade program, calling the promise never to reduce rates "unprecedented." The current Fair Trade price for coffee is $1.26 a pound for nonorganic beans and $1.41 for organic. What many do not understand is that Fair Trade relates to working conditions, not the quality of coffee beans.

In the meantime, on June 22, the top 10 Cup of Excellence coffees will be auctioned online. Buyers from the United States, Europe and Japan are expected to bid on this year's top coffees. The winning growers are traveling to Managua to watch the monitor as bids are placed and the prices for their coffees rise. The rates paid for Cup of Excellence coffees have risen wildly in the last few years. Intelligentsia and other buyers have paid $40 a pound and more for microlots of estate-quality coffees—they incur these costs for their promotional value.

Because chance and the weather play such a role in growing coffee, winners change every year. If they are lucky, this year's auction winners will get a once-in-a-lifetime cash infusion large enough to buy another piece of land or upgrade equipment. And if they are luckier still, their victory may lead to a visit from Mr. Watts of Intelligentsia or someone like him offering not just a sales agreement, but a relationship.

## Questions

1. Why does this coffee buyer intentionally seek out expensive coffee? What is driving his decisions?

2. Do you believe that "relationship coffee" will benefit the coffee growers or just the coffee buyers?

---

# CHAPTER 5

## The Great Turning

*From Empire to Earth Community*

David Korten

The author contends that for 5,000 years the planet has been dominated by a form of social organization and ideology that he terms "empire." He argues that new attitudes are emerging, with people from many different backgrounds and concerns calling for a new social order: earth community.

*By what name will future generations know our time?*

Will they speak in anger and frustration of the time of the Great Unraveling, when profligate consumption exceeded Earth's capacity to sustain and led to an accelerating wave of collapsing environmental systems, violent competition for what remained of the planet's resources, and a dramatic dieback of the human population? Or will they look back in joyful celebration on the time of the Great Turning, when their forebears embraced the higher-order potential of their human nature, turned crisis into opportunity, and learned to live in creative partnership with one another and Earth?

## A Defining Choice

We face a defining choice between two contrasting models for organizing human affairs. Give them the generic names Empire and Earth Community. Absent an understanding of the history and implications of this choice, we may squander valuable time and resources on efforts to preserve or mend cultures and institutions that cannot be fixed and must be replaced.

Empire organizes by domination at all levels, from relations among nations to relations among family members. Empire brings fortune to the few, condemns the majority to misery and servitude, suppresses the creative potential of all, and appropriates much of the wealth of human societies to maintain the institutions of domination.

Earth Community, by contrast, organizes by partnership, unleashes the human potential for creative co-operation, and shares resources and surpluses for the good of all. Supporting evidence for the possibilities of Earth Community comes from the findings of quantum physics, evolutionary biology, developmental psychology, anthropology, archaeology, and religious mysticism. It was the human way before Empire; we must make a choice to re-learn how to live by its principles.

Developments distinctive to our time are telling us that Empire has reached the limits of the exploitation that people and Earth will sustain. A mounting perfect economic storm born of a convergence of peak oil, climate change, and an imbalanced U.S. economy dependent on debts it can never repay is poised to bring a dramatic restructuring of every aspect of modern life. We have the power to choose, however, whether the consequences play out as a terminal crisis or an epic opportunity. The Great Turning is not a prophecy. It is a possibility.

## A Turn From Life

According to cultural historian Riane Eisler, early humans evolved within a cultural and institutional frame of Earth Community. They organized to meet their needs by cooperating with life rather than by dominating it. Then some 5,000 years ago, beginning in Mesopotamia, our ancestors made a tragic turn from Earth Community to Empire. They turned away from a reverence for the generative power of life—represented by female gods or nature spirits—to a reverence for hierarchy and the power of the sword—represented by distant, usually male, gods. The wisdom of the elder and the priestess gave way to the arbitrary rule of the powerful, often ruthless, king.

## Paying the Price

The peoples of the dominant human societies lost their sense of attachment to the living earth, and societies became divided between the rulers and the ruled, exploiters and exploited. The brutal competition for power created a relentless play-or-die, rule-or-be-ruled dynamic of violence and oppression and served to elevate the most ruthless to the highest positions of power. Since the fateful turn, the major portion of the resources available to human societies has been diverted from meeting the needs of life to supporting the military forces, prisons, palaces, temples, and patronage for retainers and propagandists on which the system of domination in turn depends. Great civilizations built by ambitious rulers fell to successive waves of corruption and conquest.

The primary institutional form of Empire has morphed from the city-state to the nation-state to the global corporation, but the underlying pattern of domination remains. It is axiomatic: for a few to be on top, many must be on the bottom. The powerful control and institutionalize the processes by which it will be decided who enjoys the privilege and who pays the price, a choice that commonly results in arbitrarily excluding from power whole groups of persons based on race and gender.

## Troubling Truths

Herein lies a crucial insight. If we look for the source of the social pathologies increasingly evident in our culture, we find they have a common origin in the dominator relations of Empire that have survived largely intact in spite of the democratic reforms of the past two centuries. The sexism, racism, economic injustice, violence, and environmental destruction that have plagued human societies for 5,000 years, and have now brought us to the brink of a potential terminal crisis, all flow from this common source. Freeing ourselves from these pathologies depends on a common solution—replacing the underlying dominator cultures and institutions of Empire with the partnership cultures and institutions of Earth Community. Unfortunately, we cannot look to imperial power holders to lead the way.

## Beyond Denial

History shows that as empires crumble the ruling elites become ever more corrupt and ruthless in their drive to secure their own power—a dynamic now playing out in the United States. . . .

Americans acculturated to the ideals of America find it difficult to comprehend what our rulers are doing, most of which is at odds with notions of egalitarianism, justice, and democracy. Within the frame of historical reality, it is perfectly clear: they are playing out the endgame of Empire, seeking to consolidate power through increasingly authoritarian and anti-democratic policies.

Wise choices necessarily rest on a foundation of truth. The Great Turning depends on awakening to deep truths long denied.

## Global Awakening

It is fortuitous that we humans have achieved the means to make a collective choice as a species to free ourselves from Empire's seemingly inexorable compete-or-die logic at the precise moment we face the imperative to do so. The speed at which institutional and technological advances have created possibilities wholly new to the human experience is stunning.

> *Just over 60 years ago*, we created the United Nations, which, for all its imperfections, made it possible for the first time for representatives of all the world's nations and people to meet in a neutral space to resolve differences through dialogue rather than force of arms.

> *Less than 50 years ago*, our species ventured into space to look back and see ourselves as one people sharing a common destiny on a living space ship.

*In little more than 10 years* our communications technologies have given us the ability, should we choose to use it, to link every human on the planet into a seamless web of nearly costless communication and cooperation.

Already our new technological capability has made possible the interconnection of the millions of people who are learning to work as a dynamic, self-directing social organism that transcends boundaries of race, class, religion, and nationality and functions as a shared conscience of the species. We call this social organism global civil society. On February 15, 2003, it brought more than 10 million people to the streets of the world's cities, towns, and villages to call for peace in the face of the buildup to the U.S. invasion of Iraq. They accomplished this monumental collective action without a central organization, budget, or charismatic leader through social processes never before possible on such a scale. This was but a foretaste of the possibilities for radically new forms of partnership organization now within our reach.

## Break the Silence, End the Isolation, Change the Story

We humans live by stories. The key to making a choice for Earth Community is recognizing that the foundation of Empire's power does not lie in its instruments of physical violence. It lies in Empire's ability to control the stories by which we define ourselves and our possibilities in order to perpetuate the myths on which the legitimacy of the dominator relations of Empire depend. To change the human future, we must change our defining stories.

## Story Power

For 5,000 years, the ruling class has cultivated, rewarded, and amplified the voices of those storytellers whose stories affirm the righteousness of Empire and deny the higher-order potentials of our nature that would allow us to live with one another in peace and cooperation. There have always been those among us who sense the possibilities of Earth Community, but their stories have been marginalized or silenced by Empire's instruments of intimidation. The stories endlessly repeated by the scribes of Empire become the stories most believed. Stories of more hopeful possibilities go unheard or unheeded and those who discern the truth are unable to

identify and support one another in the common cause of truth telling. Fortunately, the new communications technologies are breaking this pattern. As truth-tellers reach a wider audience, the myths of Empire become harder to maintain. . . .

It is not enough, as many in the United States are doing, to debate the details of tax and education policies, budgets, war, and trade agreements in search of a positive political agenda. Nor is it enough to craft slogans with broad mass appeal aimed at winning the next election or policy debate. We must infuse the mainstream culture with stories of Earth Community. As the stories of Empire nurture a culture of domination, the stories of Earth Community nurture a culture of partnership. They affirm the positive potentials of our human nature and show that realizing true prosperity, security, and meaning depends on creating vibrant, caring, interlinked communities that support all persons in realizing their full humanity. Sharing the joyful news of our human possibilities through word and action is perhaps the most important aspect of the Great Work of our time.

Changing the prevailing stories in the United States may be easier to accomplish than we might think. The apparent political divisions notwithstanding, U.S. polling data reveal a startling degree of consensus on key issues. Eighty-three percent of Americans believe that as a society the United States is focused on the wrong priorities. Supermajorities want to see greater priority given to children, family, community, and a healthy environment. Americans also want a world that puts people ahead of profits, spiritual values ahead of financial values, and international cooperation ahead of international domination. These Earth Community values are in fact widely shared by both conservatives and liberals.

Our nation is on the wrong course not because Americans have the wrong values. It is on the wrong course because of remnant imperial institutions that give unaccountable power to a small alliance of right-wing extremists who call themselves conservative and claim to support family and community values, but whose preferred economic and social policies constitute a ruthless war against children, families, communities, and the environment.

The distinctive human capacity for reflection and intentional choice carries a corresponding moral responsibility to care for one another and the planet. Indeed, our deepest desire is to live in loving relationships with one another. The hunger for loving families and communities is a powerful, but latent, unifying force and the potential foundation of a winning political coalition dedicated to creating societies that support every person in actualizing his or her highest potential.

In these turbulent and often frightening times, it is important to remind ourselves that we are privileged to live at the most exciting moment in the whole of the human experience. We have the opportunity to turn away from Empire and to embrace Earth Community as a conscious collective choice. We are the ones we have been waiting for.

## Questions

1.  What are the main characteristics of "empire" and of "earth community" according to Korten?

2.  Are you convinced that world attitudes and organization are changing from "empire" to "earth community"? What evidence do you see for or against this?

*Source:* The Great Turning: From Empire to Earth Community. David Korten. *Yes! Magazine.* Summer 2006. Reprinted by permission of Positive Futures Network.

# PART II

# INEQUALITY AND POVERTY

In our globalized economy, huge gaps remain between rich and poor. A long-standing gap is between rich and poor nations. Some low-income Asian countries have begun to close this gap with dramatic economic growth, from the "four dragons" of Taiwan, Hong Kong, South Korea, and Singapore to the huge economies of China and India. While both China and India still have vast numbers of poor people, especially in rural areas, their growth alone has reduced the numbers of the world's poor. At the same time, many Latin American economies have stagnated and some African economies have actually lost ground, with a wider gap than ever between the world's richest countries and its poorest.

Within many countries, the gap between rich and poor continues to grow. Some have benefited from new technology and new trade opportunities; a few have become fabulously rich, while many others have begun a long and perilous climb into the middle classes. At the same time, poor farmers and poor urban workers often find themselves in even more desperate circumstances with no assurance of a livelihood. They live in a world of extreme poverty, subsisting on less than the equivalent of one dollar a day.

The world can eliminate this extreme poverty, if it has the will to do so, contends economist Jeffrey Sachs. Article 6 examines Sachs's plan to eliminate the most extreme forms of poverty. The challenges in this process are enormous. In some parts of the world, an unofficial form of slavery traps children and adults alike in servitude. Article 7 examines how this system of bondage operates behind the scenes in the sub-Saharan African country of Niger. Around the world, poor farmers and village dwellers are fleeing to burgeoning cities in hopes of better opportunities. All too often, the opportunities elude them. Article 8 looks at the case of rickshaw pullers in the capital of the country of Bangladesh and at their struggles to use this informal occupation as way to a better life.

Some who have gained enormous wealth in the global economy or great fame in our global culture have determined to take up the challenge of eliminating poverty. For its people of the year, *Time Magazine* chose Microsoft billionaire Bill Gates and his wife, founder of the Gates Foundation, and rock star Bono. Article 9 looks at how the three have worked together in schemes to address some of the most pressing needs of the world's very poor.

Globalization can also bring greater poverty and social disruption. In many places, women have born the brunt of the hardships. Article 10 explores how the economic crisis in Mexico has made women particularly vulnerable to violence. At the same time, some entrepreneurs have found innovative ways to use financing and global technology to benefit the world's poor, especially poor women. Article 11 looks at one such enterprise in South Asia that is improving the lives of poor rural women.

6.  Always With Us: Jeffrey Sachs's Plan to Eradicate World Poverty.
    John Cassidy. *New Yorker.* April 11, 2005.
7.  Born Into Bondage.
    Paul Raffaele. *Smithsonian.* September 2005.
8.  Pulling Rickshaws in the City of Dhaka: A Way Out of Poverty?
    Sharifa Begum and Binayak Sen. *Environment and Urbanization.* Vol. 17, No. 2. 2002.
9.  The Good Samaritans: Melinda Gates, Bono, and Bill Gates.
    Nancy Gibbs. *Time.* January 2, 2006.
10. Violencia Femicida: Violence Against Women and Mexico's Structural Crisis.
    Mercedes Olivera. *Latin American Perspectives.* Vol. 33, No. 2. 2006.
11. How One Company Brought Hope to the Poor.
    Marco Visscher. *Ode Magazine.* April 2005.

# CHAPTER 6

## Always With Us

*Jeffrey Sachs's Plan to Eradicate World Poverty*

John Cassidy

Economist Jeffrey Sachs proposes a plan to end extreme poverty in the world through careful investments in markets, health, and education.  He argues that rich nations have the means and obligation to assist the poorest.

On July 9, 1985, a thirty-year-old American economist named Jeffrey Sachs stepped off a plane in La Paz, Bolivia, high in the Andes, where the inflation rate was three thousand percent. Prices were rising so fast that on the streets of the capital people were frantically trading bags of depreciating pesos for dollars. Sachs, one of the youngest tenured professors in the history of the Harvard economics department, had established himself as an authority on inflation and international finance and was someone who, in his own words, "thought that I knew just about everything that needed to be known" about his subject.

It was Sachs's self-confidence that had earned him an invitation to Latin America. A few months earlier, during a seminar at Harvard on the Bolivian crisis organized by some Latin-American students, he had interrupted the speaker, strode to the blackboard, and announced, "Here's how it works." When he finished scribbling equations, a voice at the back of the room said, "Well, if you're so smart, why don't you come down to La Paz to help us?" Sachs laughed, but the speaker, Carlos Iturralde, a Bolivian businessman who later became his country's foreign minister, wasn't joking. Seven weeks after Sachs arrived in La Paz, some of his recommendations were implemented, and three years of hyperinflation came to an immediate end.

Thus began the twenty-year journey through the developing world which Sachs recounts in *The End of Poverty: Economic Possibilities for Our Time* (Penguin Press; $27.95). From Bolivia, where he acted as an economic adviser for several years, Sachs moved on to Poland and Russia, where he played a controversial role in the transformation from Communism to capitalism, and, most recently, to sub-Saharan Africa. For the past three years, Sachs has been leading the Earth Institute at Columbia University and directing the United Nations Millennium Project, a multinational task force of economists, scientists, and development experts. The Millennium Project recently published a plan to halve global poverty and hunger by 2015, a target that the world community adopted in September, 2000, at the U.N. Millennium Summit. The plan calls on rich countries to double their financial assistance to poor nations, something that Sachs insists is workable, affordable, and in the long-term interest of the developed world. "Ending poverty is the great opportunity of our time," he writes.

As Sachs points out, more than a billion people currently subsist on less than a dollar a day—the standard threshold for "extreme poverty." Every year, hundreds of thousands die of starvation, malnutrition, or diseases like AIDS and malaria; tens of millions of children perish in infancy. In the face of this ongoing catastrophe, this year the American government will extend to poor countries approximately fifteen billion dollars in aid, which is roughly a thirtieth of the Pentagon budget and about an eighth of one percent of the gross domestic product. . . .

In the absence of a natural disaster, such as the Asian tsunami, or a bloody civil conflict, such as the one in Sudan, the fate of the world's poor rarely attracts attention in this country. So it's greatly to Sachs's credit that he has been a gifted and tireless advocate; indeed, he may be the only economist to have published a book with a foreword by a rock star. ("His voice is louder than any electric guitar, heavier than heavy metal," writes Bono, the lead singer of U2.) But Sachs is also making some grand claims: "We can realistically envision a world without extreme poverty by 2025." . . .

In the summer of 1989, Sachs was in Warsaw advising the Polish reformers who had won a historic victory in parliamentary elections. At a late-night meeting, he and a colleague, David Lipton, sketched out some ideas for decontrolling prices immediately, stabilizing the currency, canceling foreign debts, and, eventually, privatizing state-owned enterprises. Jacek Kuron, one of the leaders of the Solidarity movement, told them to write up a plan. . . .

Sachs and Lipton worked through the night, and by dawn had completed a fifteen-page brief with a specific chronology of policy reforms. "It was the first time, I believe, that anyone had written down a comprehensive plan for the transformation of a socialist economy to a market economy," Sachs recounts. "Our proposal was for a dramatic, quick transformation." Some Polish economists advocated less radical changes, arguing that their country had neither the institutions nor the expertise necessary to handle unbridled capitalism, but on January 1, 1990, the government enacted the main elements of the Sachs-Lipton all-nighter as part of a new policy that was widely referred to as "shock therapy," a phrase Sachs now dismisses as a misleading "journalistic concoction." Freed from government control, prices soared, and many people saw their savings wiped out. Unemployment rose sharply, too, especially in the heavy industries that had provided most of Solidarity's support. Although Sachs's Polish critics claimed that their warnings had been vindicated, he argues that his strategy worked out well over time: "By 2002 Poland was 50 percent richer in per capita terms than it had been in 1990, and it had logged the most successful growth record of any post-communist country in Eastern Europe or the former Soviet Union."

If Sachs' s account of his time in Poland sounds a little self-serving, his account of his time in Russia,

where he advised the economic reformers who surrounded Boris Yeltsin when he came to power in the fall of 1991, is downright contentious. . . .

After the reform program was enacted, Russia experienced rampant inflation, a precipitous decline in industrial production, a surge in crime, an unprecedented fall in life expectancy, and the looting of the country's mineral wealth by well-connected businessmen, some of whom were gangsters. Sachs denies that these calamities had anything to do with the policies he espoused. "Most of the bad things that happened—such as the massive theft of state assets under the rubric of privatization—were directly contrary to the advice that I gave and to the principles of honesty and equity that I hold dear," he maintains. The responsible parties, in his view, included Viktor Gerashchenko, "whom I tagged at the time as 'the world's worst Central Bank governor'"; the International Monetary Fund, which failed to provide adequate support for the ruble and the United States government, which spurned Sachs's call for a Marshall Plan for Russia.

The fact is that in both Poland and Russia Sachs favored large-scale social engineering over gradual change and institution-building. . . .

Sachs returned to Harvard full time in 1994, but he also continued to travel widely as a consultant. For several years, he worked with the World Economic Forum, a pro-globalization group that organizes an annual conference in Davos, Switzerland. He wrote for an annual publication called the *Global Competitiveness Report,* in which he criticized big government and expounded the virtues of open markets. On the latter point, Sachs has been consistent. Although he now tips his hat to antiglobalization protesters who detest everything Davos stands for, commending them for "ending years of self-congratulation by the rich and powerful," he also regards them as fundamentally misguided. "By now the anti-globalization movement should see that globalization, more than anything else, has reduced the numbers of extreme poor in India by two hundred million and in China by three hundred million since 1990," he writes. "Far from being exploited by multinational companies, these countries and many others like them have achieved unprecedented rates of economic growth on the basis of foreign direct investment (FDI) and the export-led growth that followed."

The facts support Sachs: between 1990 and 2001, G.D.P. per capita rose by 5.5 percent a year in East Asia and by 3.2 percent a year in South Asia, and poverty fell sharply in both regions. Despite the claims of some analysts on the left, economic growth really is the best antipoverty strategy. If the rest of the developing world had matched the growth rates of China and India, victory over poverty would be in sight. Unfortunately, in sub-Saharan Africa, between 1900 and 2002, per capita income didn't rise at all, and the number of people living on less than a dollar a day increased by a third, to more than three hundred and thirty million. . . .

Why is Africa poor? Sachs argues that economists have generally paid too little attention to geographic factors. In Bolivia, three years into his career as an economic adviser, he met a World Bank consultant named David Morawetz, who pointed out that Bolivia was a landlocked country with high transport costs. As a result, it had succeeded only in exporting goods with a high value-to-weight ratio, such as silver, tin, and cocaine. Lower-value goods, such as foodstuffs, were not worth exporting once the cost of getting them to the market was taken into account. "Morawetz's point about Bolivia's geographical distress was truly (and incredibly) something new to me," Sachs recounts. "In all of my training, the ideas of physical geography and the spatial distribution of economic activity had not even been mentioned." Alerted to the importance of geography, Sachs decided that Africa's failure to develop was probably connected to the fact that much of the continent is hot, isolated, and ridden with tropical diseases. Starved of fertile soil, transport links, power, and adequate health care, much of the continent is stuck in "the worst poverty trap in the world."

He describes visiting a group of villages in the Sauri region of western Kenya, where AIDS has stricken thirty percent of the populace and the survivors don't have enough money for fertilizer or mosquito nets. "There are no cars or trucks owned or used within Sauri and only a handful of villagers said they had ridden in any kind of motorized transport during the last year," he writes. "Around half of the individuals at the meeting said that they had never made a phone call in their lives." With some relatively modest resources, Sachs says, a "clinical economist" could provide many of the things that Sauri desperately needs: a power line to a nearby town, a health clinic with a doctor and nurse, fertilizer, water-storage facilities, mosquito nets, a cell phone, a truck.

How much would all this cost? Sachs and his colleagues at Columbia's Earth Institute estimate the bill for getting the Sauri region up on its feet at three hundred and fifty thousand dollars annually, or about seventy dollars per inhabitant per year. "The benefits would be astounding," Sachs writes. "Decisive malaria control, a doubling or tripling of food yields with a drastic reduction of chronic hunger and malnutrition, improved school attendance, a reduction of waterborne disease, a rise in incomes through the sale of surplus grains and cash crops." . . .

He argues, persuasively, that aid ought to be extended in the form of grants, instead of loans which have to be repaid, and that it shouldn't be tied to specific expenditures. (Some donors have insisted that the money they give be spent on goods and services they export.) Ideally, aid should also be guaranteed by long periods. "In the past, donors often helped countries to build clinics, but then rejected the plea to help cover the salaries of doctors and nurses to help staff the clinics," Sachs notes. "The predictable result has been the construction of empty shells rather than operating health facilities."

Under the U.N. plan, financial assistance would be extended until 2015, as long as the recipients met certain performance targets. Health care, primary schooling, and other services for the poor would be provided free of charge, reversing the recent trend toward user fees, which the World Bank and the International Monetary Fund have encouraged in a misguided effort to improve efficiency. "The extreme poor don't have enough to eat, much less to pay for electricity or water or bed nets or contraceptives," Sachs observes.

He's surely right to emphasize spending on health care, direct poverty relief, and education. For one thing, rates of infection, malnutrition, and enrollment in schools are a lot easier to monitor than over-all economic progress. In Tanzania in 2001, for example, the government more than doubled the education budget and abolished user fees, using aid money to help meet the cost. Since then, the enrollment rate in primary schools has risen from sixty percent to ninety percent.

Yet, as the history of development policy suggests, there can be political dangers to overpromising, and Sachs, by placing so much emphasis on geography, underplays other reasons for Africa's stalled development. Most African countries, bequeathed arbitrary borders by their colonial heritages, are ethnically heterogeneous, and that has led to political problems, as groups compete for the spoils of government. Kenya, which contains about forty different ethnic communities, has been plagued by corruption and ethnic conflict, as have many African nations. Congo, Ivory Coast, Sierra Leone, and several other countries have been riven by what the development economist Paul Collier refers to as resource wars, in which rival ethnic groups compete for control of valuable natural resources.

Sachs, as he did in Poland and Russia, refuses to acknowledge that institutional failures could hobble his ambitious plans. "Africa shows absolutely no tendency to be more or less corrupt than any other countries at the same income level," he writes. Then he presents the results of a study that he and some colleagues carried out recently, using various indicators of quality of governance. Countries they judge to have "average" standards of governance include Chad, Republic of Congo, Eritrea, Rwanda, and Sierra Leone—all places that have recently experienced devastating civil conflicts.

Many African scholars, such as the Ghanaian economist George B. N. Ayittey, are far more willing to criticize their kleptocratic governments than Sachs is. Ayittey points out that aid money sometimes helps corrupt and incompetent regimes to remain in power. The World Bank and the I.M.F. extended nine loans to the tyrannical administration of Mobutu Sese Seko, who looted Zaire for decades, at one point taking personal control of an entire gold-mining region. Sweden and other Scandinavian countries supported Julius Nyerere's socialist regime in Tanzania, which almost destroyed the agricultural sector by dragooning scattered bushmen into collective farms.

Sachs also downplays the problem of misappropriated aid. Many African nations are so poor that under the U.N. plan they would probably receive annual aid payments equivalent to fifteen to twenty percent of their gross domestic product. Without adequate safeguards, one has to wonder how much of this money would end up helping the people it was supposed to reach. Sachs's plan calls for recipient governments to commit to good governance, it's true, but, once the money started flowing, these assurances would need to be supplemented with stringent external supervision.

. . . What Africa needs is one or two unequivocal success stories that would serve as models to reformers in other places and attract global investors. Among the strongest arguments for the U.N. anti-poverty plan is that it would offer help and encouragement to countries that have embarked on reform programs but are still struggling to break out of poverty traps. "The biggest problem today is not that poorly-governed countries get too much aid," Sachs notes, "but that well-governed countries get too little." Ghana, Kenya, and Ethiopia are good examples. Each of these countries has worked with the World Bank and the I.M.F. to introduce reforms but is also facing enormous challenges, such as AIDS and malaria and heavy debts.

Although a little humility would help his cause, Sachs, youthful still at fifty, must be commended for trying to hold rich nations to their promises, and for reminding his countrymen that military action is not the only way to export American values. It will be fascinating to see how he gets on with Paul Wolfowitz, President Bush's nominee to head the World Bank. . . .

In a few months, Wolfowitz may well be pressing politicians in rich countries to increase their aid budgets, including his former colleagues in the Bush Administration. In order to pay its share of the U.N. poverty plan, the United States would have to find another forty billion dollars a year by 2015. Sachs reminds us that merely reversing the President's first-term tax cuts for those earning more than half a million dollars a year would generate enough to meet this target. Here's another way to look at it: to pay for the extra spending, each American would have to contribute less than the cost of buying a cappuccino from Starbucks once a week. Aid is not a panacea, and, even if the funding Sachs wants were to materialize, his grandest objectives may well remain unfulfilled. But, targeted carefully, aid can reward responsible governments, encourage individual initiative, and alleviate suffering. Surely that's worth a cup of coffee.

---

## Questions

1. Why are the poorest places so poor, according to Sachs?

2. How does he propose that richer nations change this? Why should they do this?

---

# CHAPTER 7

## Born Into Bondage

Paul Raffaele

Slavery has not disappeared from the planet. Slavery takes different forms in various places. In the sub-Saharan African country of Niger, slavery is intertwined with ancient traditions and modern practices.

*Despite denials by government officials, slavery remains a way of life in the African nation of Niger.*

Lightning and thunder split the Saharan night. In northern Niger, heavy rain and wind smashed into the commodious goatskin tent of a Tuareg tribesman named Tafan and his family, snapping a tent pole and tumbling the tent to the ground.

Huddling in a small, tattered tent nearby was a second family, a man, a woman and their four children. Tafan ordered the woman, Asibit, to go outside and stand in the full face of the storm while holding the pole steady, keeping his tent upright until the rain and wind ceased.

Asibit obeyed because, like tens of thousands of other Nigerians, she was born into a slave caste that goes back hundreds of years. As she tells it, Tafan's family treated her not as a human, but as chattel, a beast of burden like their goats, sheep and camels. Her eldest daughter, Asibit says, was born after Tafan raped her, and when the child turned 6, he gave her as a present to his brother—a common practice among Niger's slave owners. Asibit, fearful of a whipping, watched in silence as her daughter was taken away.

"From childhood, I toiled from early morning until late at night," she recalls matter-of-factly. She pounded millet, prepared breakfast for Tafan and his family, and ate the leftovers with her own. While her husband and children herded Tafan's livestock, she did his household chores and milked his camels. She had to move his tent, open-fronted to catch any breeze, four times a day so his family would always be in shade. Now 51, she seems to bear an extra two decades in her lined and leathery face. "I never received a single coin during the 50 years," she says.

Asibit bore these indignities without complaint. On that storm-tossed night in the desert, she says, she struggled for hours to keep the tent upright, knowing she'd be beaten if she failed. But then, like the tent pole, something inside her snapped: she threw the pole aside and ran into the night, making a dash for freedom to the nearest town, 20 miles across the desert.

History resonates with countless verified accounts of human bondage, but Asibit escaped only in June of last year.

Disturbing as it may seem in the 21st century, there may be more forced labor in the world now than ever. About 12.3 million people toil in the global economy on every continent save Antarctica, according to the United Nations' International Labour Organization, held in various forms of captivity, including those under the rubric of human trafficking.

The U.S. State Department's annual report on trafficking in persons, released in June, spotlighted 150 countries where more than a hundred people were trafficked in the past year. Bonded laborers are entrapped by low wages in never-ending debt; illegal immigrants are coerced by criminal syndicates to pay off their clandestine passage with work at subminimum wages; girls are kidnapped for prostitution, boys for unpaid labor.

The State Department's report notes that "Niger is a source, transit, and destination country for men, women and children trafficked for the purposes of sexual exploitation and forced domestic and commercial labor." But there is also something else going on in Niger—and in Chad, Mali and Mauritania. Across western Africa, hundreds of thousands of people are being held in what is known as "chattel slavery," which Americans may associate only with the transatlantic slave trade and the Old South.

In parts of rural West Africa dominated by traditional tribal chieftains, human beings are born into slavery, and they live every minute of their lives at the whim of their owners. They toil day and night without pay. Many are whipped or beaten when disobedient or slow, or for whatever reasons their masters concoct. Couples are separated when one partner is sold or given away; infants and children are passed from one owner to another as gifts or dowry; girls as young as 10 are sometimes raped by their owners or, more commonly, sold off as concubines.

The families of such slaves have been held for generations, and their captivity is immutable: the one thing they can be sure of passing on to their children is their enslavement.

One of the earliest records of enslaved Africans goes back to the seventh century, but the practice existed long before. It sprang largely from warfare, with victors forcing the vanquished into bondage. (Many current slave owners in Niger are Tuareg, the legendary warlords of the Sahara.) The winners kept slaves to serve their own households and sold off the others. In Niger, slave markets traded humans for centuries, with countless thousands bound and marched to ports north or south, for sale to Europe and Arabia or America.

As they began exercising influence over Niger in the late 19th century, the French promised to end slavery there—the practice had been abolished under French law since 1848—but they found it difficult to eradicate a social system that had endured for so long, especially given the reluctance of the country's chieftains, the major slave owners, to cooperate. Slavery was still thriving at the turn of the century, and the chances of abolition all but disappeared during World War I, when France pressed its colonies to join the battle. "In order to fulfill their quotas each administrator [in Niger] relied on traditional chiefs who preferred to supply slaves to serve as cannon fodder," writes Nigerian social scientist Galy Kadir Abdelkader.

During the war, when rebellions broke out against the French in Niger, the chieftains once again came to the rescue; in return, French administrators turned a blind eye to slavery. Following independence in 1960, successive Nigerian governments have kept their silence. In 2003, a law banning and punishing slavery was passed, but it has not been widely enforced.

Organizations outside Niger, most persistently the London-based Anti-Slavery International, are still pushing to end slavery there. The country's constitution recognizes the United Nations' Universal Declaration of Human Rights (Article 4: "No one shall be held in slavery or servitude; slavery and the slave trade shall be prohibited in all their forms"), but the U.N. has done little to ensure Niger's compliance. Neither has France, which still has immense influence in the country because of its large aid program and cultural ties.

And neither has the United States. While releasing this year's trafficking report, Secretary of State Condoleezza Rice reminded Americans of President Bush's plea in a 2004 speech for an end to human trafficking, but the U.S. Embassy in Niger professes little on-the-ground knowledge of chattel slavery there. In Washington, Ambassador John Miller, a senior adviser to Rice who heads the State Department's Trafficking in Persons section, says, "We're just becoming aware of transgenerational slavery in Niger."

The Nigerian government, for its part, does not acknowledge the problem: it has consistently said that there are no slaves in Niger. Troubled by the government's denials, a group of young civil servants in 1991 set up the Timidria Association, which has become the most prominent nongovernmental organization fighting slavery in Niger. Timidria ("fraternity-solidarity" in Tamacheq, the Tuareg language) has since set up 682 branches across the country to monitor slavery, help protect escaped slaves and guide them in their new, free lives.

The group faces a constant battle. Last March, Timidria persuaded a Tuareg chief to free his tribe's 7,000 slaves in a public ceremony. The mass manumission was widely publicized prior to the planned release, but just days before it was to happen, the government prevailed upon the chief to abandon his plan.

"The government was caught in a quandary," a European ambassador to Niger told me. "How could it allow the release when it claimed there were no slaves in Niger?" . . .

Niger is three times bigger than California, but two-thirds of it is desert, and its standard of living ranks 176th on the United Nations' human development index of 177 countries, just ahead of Sierra Leone. About 60 percent of its 12 million people live on less than $1 a day, and most of the others not much more. It's a landlocked country with little to sell to the world other than uranium. (Intelligence reports that Saddam Hussein tried to buy yellowcake uranium from Niger have proved "highly dubious," according to the State Department.) A 2004 U.S. State Department report on Niger noted that it suffers from "drought, locust infestation, deforestation, soil degradation, high population growth rates [3.3%], and exceedingly low literacy rates." In recent months, 2.5 million of Niger's people have been on the verge of famine.

A Nigerian is lucky to reach the age of 50. The child mortality rate is the world's second worst, with a quarter of all children dying under the age of 5. "Niger is so poor that many people perish daily of starvation," Jeremy Lester, the European Union's head of delegation in Niamey, tells me.

And Niger's slaves are the poorest of the poor, excluded totally from the meager cash economy.

Clad in a flowing robe, Soli Abdourahmane, a former minister of justice and state prosecutor, greets me in his shady mud-house compound in Niamey. "There are many, many slaves in Niger, and the same families have often been held captive by their owners' families for centuries," he tells me, speaking French, the country's official language, though Hausa is spoken more widely. "The slave masters are mostly from the nomadic tribes—the Tuareg, Fulani, Toubou and Arabs."

A wry grin spreads across his handsome face. "The government claims there are no slaves in Niger, and yet two years ago it legislated to outlaw slavery, with penalties from 10 to 30 years. It's a contradiction, no?"

Moussa Zangaou, a 41-year-old member of Parliament, says he opposes slavery. He belongs to a party whose leaders say it does not exist in Niger, but he says he is working behind the scenes toward abolition. "There are more than 100,000 slaves in Niger, and they suffer terribly with no say in their destiny," he tells me. "Their masters treat them like livestock, they don't believe they are truly human."

I'm puzzled. Why does the government deny there is slavery in Niger, and yet, in the shadows, allow it to continue? "It's woven into our traditional culture," Zangaou explains, "and many tribal chieftains, who still wield great power, are slave owners and bring significant voting blocs of their people to the government at election time."

Also, the government fears international condemnation. Eighty percent of the country's capital budget comes from overseas donors, mostly European countries. "The president is currently the head of the Economic Community of West African States," Zangaou adds, "and he fears being embarrassed by slavery still existing in Niger."

In the meantime, slaves are risking terrible beatings or whippings to escape and hide in far-off towns— especially in Niamey, with a population of 774,000, where they can disappear. . . .

Niger's prime minister, Hama Amadou, is . . . insistent when we meet at his Niamey office, not far from the U.S. Embassy. He is Fulani and has a prominent tribal scar, an X, carved into his right cheek. "Niger has no slaves," he tells me emphatically.

And yet in July 2003, he wrote a confidential letter to the minister of internal affairs stating that slavery existed in Niger and was immoral, and listing 32 places around the country where slaves could be found. When I tell him I know about the letter—I even have a copy of it—the prime minister at first looks astonished and then steadies himself and confirms that he wrote it.

But still he denies that his country has slaves. "Try and find slaves in Niger," he says. "You won't find even one."

As I leave for Niger's interior to take up the prime minister's challenge, I am accompanied by Moustapha Kadi Oumani, the firstborn son of a powerful Tuareg chieftain and known among Nigerians as the Prince of Illéla, the capital of his father's domain. Elegant, sharp-minded and with the graceful command that comes from generations of unchallenged authority, he guides us by SUV to Azarori, about 300 miles northeast of Niamey and one of more than 100 villages under his father's feudal command.

Moustapha in boyhood was steeped in his tribal traditions, with slaves to wait on him hand and foot, but his exposure to their condition, and a few years studying in Italy and Switzerland, convinced him that no person should belong to another. Moustapha now works in the Department of Civil Aviation in Niamey, but he devotes much of his spare time working to end slavery in Niger and improve the living conditions of ordinary Nigerians. In December 2003, he freed all ten of the slaves he had inherited in a public ceremony at Tahoua, about 110 miles from Azarori. On the government's orders, police seized the audio- and videotapes of reporters and cameramen who were covering the event. "They didn't want people to know," says Idy, who was there for the BBC.

The number of slaves in Niger is unknown. Moustapha scoffs at a widely quoted Timidria survey in 2002 that put it at 870,363. "There was double counting, and the survey's definition of a slave was loose," he says. Anti-Slavery International, using the same data, counted at least 43,000 slaves, but that figure has also been questioned—as both too high and too low.

The countryside, facing a famine, looks sickly, and when the SUV pulls to the side of the road for a comfort stop, a blur of locusts clatter into the air from a stunted tree nearby. We arrive at Azarori (pop. 9,000) at mid-morning as several men and children—all slaves, Moustapha says—herd goats to pasture.

A stooped old man in a conical hat and purple robe tells me that he has worked hard for his owner for no pay since he was a child. Another man, Ahmed, who is 49, says that Allah ordained that he and his family are to be slaves through the generations. (Niger is 95 percent Muslim.) When I ask him to quote that command from the Koran, he shrugs. "I can't read or write, and so my master, Boudal, told me," he says.

Like most of the slaves I would meet, Ahmed looks well fed and healthy. "A slave master feeds his donkeys and camels well so they can work hard, and it's the same with his slaves," Moustapha says.

This may explain the extraordinary devotion many slaves insist they offer their masters in this impoverished nation, especially if they are not mistreated. I ask Ahmed how he would feel if his owner gave away his daughter. "If my master asked me to throw my daughter down the well, I'd do it immediately," he replies.

Truly?

"Truly," he replies.

Moustapha shakes his head as we sip the highly sugared bitter tea favored by the Tuareg. "Ahmed has the fatalistic mindset of many slaves," he says. "They accept it's their destiny to be a *bellah*, the slave caste, and obey their masters without question."

We journey to another village along dirt roads, framed by a sandy landscape with few trees but many mud villages. At one of them, Tajaé, an 80-year-old woman named Takany sits at Moustapha's feet by her own choice and tells how she was given to her owner as an infant. Her great-grandson, who looks to be about 6 years old, sits by her side. Like many other child slaves I see, he is naked, while the village's free children wear bright robes and even jeans. The naked children I see stay close to their relatives, their eyes wary and their step cautious, while the clothed children stroll about or play chase....

In late afternoon, we reach the outskirts of Illéla and enter wide, sandy streets lined with mud-house compounds. About 12,000 people live here, ruled by Moustapha's father, Kadi Oumani, a hereditary tribal chieftain with more than a quarter of a million people offering fealty to him. "My ancestor Agaba conquered Illéla in 1678 and enslaved the families of warriors who opposed him," Moustapha tells me. "Many of their descendants are still slaves."

Moustapha has surveyed the families of the 220 traditional chieftains in Niger, known as royal families, and found that they collectively own more than 8,500 slaves whose status has not changed since their ancestors were conquered. "When a princess marries, she brings slaves as part of her dowry," he tells me. He has caused trouble for his highborn family by opposing slavery, but shrugs when I ask if this worries him. "What worries me is that there are still slaves in Niger."

Moustapha's father sits on a chair in a mud-wall compound with a dozen chiefs perched cross-legged on the ground around him. Two dozen longhorn cattle, sheep and goats mill about, there for the Tuareg aristocrats to enjoy as a reminder of their nomadic origins. Kadi Oumani is 74 years old and wears a heavy robe and an open veil that reveals his dark, bluff face. Moustapha greets him with a smile and then leads me to the compound set aside for us during our visit.

For the next hour Moustapha sits serenely on a chair at the compound's far end, greeting clan leaders who have come to pay their respects. A special visitor is Abdou Nayoussa, one of the ten slaves Moustapha freed 20 months ago. Abdou's broad face marks him as a member of the local tribe conquered by Moustapha's ancestor.

"As a boy I was chosen to look after the chieftain's horses, feeding, exercising and grooming them," he tells me. "I worked hard every day for no pay, was beaten many times and could never leave Illéla because I belonged to Moustapha's family." His eyes—which never once meet Moustapha's—are dim with what I take to be pain. "At night I cried myself to sleep, thinking about my fate and especially the fate of the children I'd have one day."

Abdou still works as the chieftain's horse handler, for which he is given little pay, but he is now free to do what he wants. "The difference is like that between heaven and hell," he tells me. "When I get enough money, I'm going to Niamey and never coming back."

As the sky darkens, we eat grilled lamb and millet. Nearby a courtier sings an ancient desert tune. Moustapha's cousin Oumarou Marafa, a burly, middle-aged secondary school teacher, joins us. "He's a slave owner and not ashamed of it," Moustapha informs me.

"When I was younger, I desired one of my mother's slaves, a beautiful 12-year-old girl, and she gave her to me as a fifth wife," Oumarou tells me. "There was no marriage ceremony; she was mine to do with her as I wished."

Did that include sex? "Of course," he says. After a few years, he sent the girl away, and she married another man. But Oumarou still considers her his possession.

"When I want to sleep with her, she must come to my bed," he says without a hint of emotion.

I find this hard to believe, but Moustapha says it is true. "It's the custom, and her husband is too scared to object," he adds....

Next morning, Moustapha takes me to the 300-year-old mud-brick palace where his father, in a daily ritual, is meeting chiefs who have come to honor him. Inside, Kadi Oumani sits on a modest throne from which he daily delivers judgments on minor disputes, principally about land and marriages.

"There are no slaves in Niger," he tells me.

"But I've met slaves."

"You mean the bellah," he says in his chieftain's monotone. "They are one of the traditional Tuareg castes. We have nobles, the ordinary people and the bellah."

Just before dawn the morning after, I set out with Idy, my translator, to drive north more than 125 miles deeper into the desert near Tamaya, the home of Asibit, the woman who says she escaped from her master during the storm.

There, we pick up Foungoutan Oumar, a young Tuareg member of Timidria, who will guide us across 20 miles of open desert to wells where he says slaves water their masters' herds in the morning and late afternoon. Foungoutan wants to avoid meeting slave owners, especially Asibit's former master, Tafan, who he says recently used his sword to lop off the hand of a man in a dispute. But it's not necessarily Tafan's anger we wish to sidestep. "If we go to the tents of the slave masters, they'll know we've come to talk to their slaves, and they'll punish them," Foungoutan says.

The sand stretches to the horizon, and the sun already burns our skin even though it's just eight o'clock in the morning. There is no one at the first two wells we visit. "The slaves have already gone with the herds," Foungoutan says with a shrug. The third well, nudged by a cluster of trees, is owned by a man named Halilou, Tafan's brother.

Six children are unloading water containers from donkeys. The younger children are naked. When they see us, they scream and bury their heads in the donkey's flanks and necks. Shivering in apparent fear, they refuse to lift their heads or talk. Three women arrive balancing water containers on their heads, having walked the three miles from Halilou's tents. They turn their faces away from us.

Soon a middle-aged man appears with a naked child by his side. His face clouds when he sees us. "My master said he'll beat me if I talk to strangers," he says. He warns the others not to tell their master about us.

With some coaxing he says their master's name is Halilou and adds that they are all slaves in his camp. He says he has toiled for Halilou's family since he was a child and has never received any money. Halilou has beaten him many times, but the man shrugs off more talk of punishment and refuses to give his name.

Another man arrives, and the two of them begin drawing water from the well, helped by five donkeys hauling on a rope attached to a canvas bucket. They pour the water into troughs for the thirsty cows, sheep and goats and then fill the containers. As the women lead the water-laden donkeys back to their master's tents, the two men and children herd the livestock out into the desert to graze on the shriveled grass and plants that grow there.

At Tamaya, a small village hemmed in by desert, we find Asibit at her usual spot in the bustling marketplace where robed Tuareg, Fulani, Hausa and Arabs buy and sell livestock, foodstuffs and swords. "Many of these men own slaves," Foungoutan says. "I've reported them to the police, but they take no action against them."

When Asibit reached Tamaya on the morning after the thunderstorm, she was led to Foungoutan, who took her to the police. She made a formal complaint that Tafan was a slave owner, and the police responded by rescuing her children, including the daughter presented to Halilou. But Asibit says they left her husband with Tafan.

Asibit squats in the shade, making a drink from millet and selling it for the equivalent of 10 cents. She smiles easily now. "You can't understand what freedom is until you've been a slave," she says. "Now, I can go to sleep when I want and get up any time I want. No one can beat me or call me bad names every day. My children and grandchildren are free."

Freedom, however, is relative. For former slaves, the search for a place in Nigerian society is harsh. "Former slaves suffer extreme discrimination in getting a job, government services, or finding marriage partners for their children," says Romana Cacchioli, the Africa expert for Anti-Slavery International, speaking by telephone from the group's London headquarters.

The government is not likely to come forward to help ex-slaves on its own; to acknowledge ex-slaves would be to acknowledge slavery. And the government, lacking the power to confront the chieftains and fearing condemnation from the outside world, gives no signs of doing that.

Within Niger, Timidria remains the most visible force for change, but it, too, faces a long road: many Nigerian say they do not support the antislavery cause because they believe the group's president, Ilguilas Weila, has profited from his association with Western aid organizations. (Both he and Anti-Slavery International insist he has not.)

In April, the government arrested Weila and another Timidria leader in response to the failed release of the 7,000 slaves. Weila was freed on bail in June but is awaiting a ruling on whether there is enough evidence to try him. The charge against him amounts to fraud: he solicited funds overseas to fight slavery in his country, the government contends, but of course there are no slaves in Niger.

---

## Questions

1. What forms does slavery take in Niger, and why does it persist?

2. Why do you think the government of Niger continues to insist so strongly that slavery does not exist in the country?

---

*Source:* Born Into Bondage. Paul Raffaele. *Smithsonian.* September 2005. Reprinted by permission of the author.

# CHAPTER 8

## Pulling Rickshaws in the City of Dhaka

*A Way Out of Poverty?*

Sharifa Begum and Binayak Sen

In many parts of the world, poor displaced rural people seek a livelihood in rapidly growing cities. Often there are no jobs waiting for them, and the poor must make their own employment in the service sector and in low-skill ad hoc jobs that make up the informal economy. Rickshaw pulling is an example of this type of work in the crowded South Asian country of Bangladesh, whose capital of Dhaka will soon be among the world's most populous cities.

## I. Introduction

The cities of Bangladesh have been experiencing overwhelming population growth and extreme poverty. This is, in part, a result of rural poverty, which has led to the migration of poor people from rural to urban areas in search of a better life, better job opportunities and better social services. Most of these rural migrants are absorbed into the urban informal sector, in such activities as petty retail trade, transport, manufacturing, construction and domestic services. In this paper, we examine the condition of Dhaka's rickshaw pullers, a major occupational group in the urban informal sector, and discuss the viability of this livelihood as a strategy for responding to chronic poverty.

Five ideas constitute the central message of this study. They are summarized here and elaborated in the discussion below. First, urban rickshaw pullers in Dhaka come from very poor economic backgrounds consistent with the characteristics of chronic poverty. Second, rickshaw pulling provides a route for modest upward mobility for those chronic rural poor who come to the city for work. Third, the rickshaw pullers are susceptible to systematic health risks; deteriorating health, combined with health shocks, can impose a significant burden on the

urban poor, dragging down the pace of upward mobility during their lifetime. Fourth, rickshaw pulling represents an unsustainable livelihood, as the initial welfare gains taper off with length of involvement in the sector. As longitudinal data is lacking, this story has emerged from a comparison of younger, recent joiners and older, long-duration rickshaw pullers, as well as current and former pullers. Fifth, intergenerational mobility of rickshaw-puller households is constrained by very limited schooling and the poor range of occupational choices for children. Public policy has an important role to play in mitigating health shocks, as well as supporting targeted education for the urban poor in the informal sector.[1]

## II. Data

The study is based on a sample of 402 current rickshaw pullers and 98 former rickshaw pullers who, at the time of the survey (April–June 2003), were all living and working in Dhaka. A stratified sample was drawn at random from different points in the city, and all age groups were included.[2] Selected rickshaw pullers were interviewed using a more detailed structured questionnaire. The sub-sample of former rickshaw pullers (i.e., those who had been rickshaw pullers at some stage in their lives, but who were now engaged in another activity) was drawn from low-income neighborhoods on the basis of information provided by other individuals, including rickshaw pullers. They were interviewed using a shorter version of the questionnaire. Although the sample population represents both groups, this paper concentrates primarily on current rickshaw pullers, and information on former rickshaw pullers is only referred to, where necessary, to substantiate a point about rickshaw pullers or rickshaw pulling.

## III. Profile of Rickshaw Pullers and Their Families

The average age of the sample rickshaw pullers is around 38 years, with 53 percent falling in the 30–44-year-old age group and numbers dropping sharply after the age of 45. About 5 percent of the sample is aged 60 years or more. A negligible proportion is under the age of 20. The estimated average duration of rickshaw pulling for the sample rickshaw pullers is ten years. While some 61 percent have been pulling for fewer than ten years, a significant proportion (14 percent) has been pulling rickshaws for more than 20 years.

Most of the sample rickshaw pullers are married (87 percent), 11 percent are unmarried, and only 2 percent are widowed or divorced (although this is twice the estimated national figure).[3] In general, the rickshaw pullers come from very poor origins, both in terms of household human capital assets and physical capital assets.[4] In both respects, rickshaw pullers belong to one of the most deprived social categories. They are mostly uneducated (58 percent) or semi-educated, having never completed primary-level education (17 percent). Of the remaining 25 percent, only 2.5 percent reported having finished secondary school; all the others either completed primary school but did not continue (9 percent) or did not complete secondary education (13 percent).

Rickshaw pullers who have joined the occupation relatively recently (in the last five years) come from higher educational backgrounds than those who have been pulling rickshaws for 15 years or more, and these groups represent two socially distinct waves of migrants. Two-thirds of recent rickshaw pullers are uneducated or semi-educated, compared to 83 percent of the older generation of pullers. This difference is to be expected, given the rapid expansion of primary education in rural areas during the 1990s.

As many as 62 percent of the rickshaw pullers reported having no cultivable land at all, and another 22 percent reported having less than 50 decimals—the standard cut-off point in Bangladesh for defining functional landlessness. Housing status is also poor for the rickshaw pullers. Almost none of the pullers own a house in Dhaka, although 83 percent own a house in their home village. The younger rickshaw pullers, or those who joined the occupation in recent years, come from relatively better-off backgrounds than their older counterparts. Only 44 percent have no cultivable land at all, against 75 percent for those who joined the occupation more than 15 years ago. Among the recent pullers, 20 percent have more than 100 decimals of land, compared to 2 percent of the older generation. All recent rickshaw pullers own a house in their village, while only two-thirds of the older generation do so. This phenomenon of younger people from relatively better socioeconomic backgrounds migrating to cities and undertaking rickshaw pulling as an economic activity may reflect the growing problem of unemployment among rural youths. Of married rickshaw pullers, 19 percent have economically active wives. More than half of these wives work in garment factories, and about one-third work as maidservants.

More than 90 percent of the rickshaw pullers in Dhaka city came there straight from the villages. Substantial numbers of long-duration rickshaw pullers have lived in Dhaka city for significant periods, while recent rickshaw pullers tend to be recent migrants to the city and are likely to have made this move in search of a better livelihood. The average duration of residency in Dhaka city among the sample rickshaw pullers is 11 years. Of those who are married, about 60 percent live with their family, i.e., the entire family has migrated to the city.

Although few rickshaw pullers own a house in Dhaka, not all live in rented accommodation. Twenty-one percent live in rent-free accommodation, generally provided by the rickshaw owners and located in the rickshaw garages. Almost all the rickshaw pullers (93 percent) who live in Dhaka city with their families live in one-room houses, with an average of four persons living in that one room. Among those who live collectively, the average is 17 persons sleeping in a single room. Housing quality is very poor. Although the roofing material is corrugated tin in 95 percent of cases, wall materials are generally of a lower quality and in one-third of the houses consist of bamboo, polythene or similar low-quality materials. The recent joiners (less than five years) appear to live in houses with better-quality walls; only 5 percent of the houses of recent rickshaw pullers have poor-quality wall materials, compared to 49 percent for the older generation.

Almost all of the households of rickshaw pullers who live with their families have access to some urban amenities: 90 percent have electricity; 52 percent have gas facilities; 62 percent have access to tap water; 78 percent have bathroom facilities; 99 percent have latrine provision; and 61 percent have a separate kitchen. However, most of the facilities are shared and are rated as highly inadequate, especially water, sanitation and kitchen facilities. In terms of consumer durables, about 14 percent of the rickshaw pullers' houses have a chest of drawers; 36–46 percent have a table, chair, watch or clock; 87 percent have a bed (*chowki*) or cot; 23 percent have a working radio; and 15 percent have a working television.

Prior to migration to Dhaka city, 58 percent of the rickshaw pullers worked as casual day laborers, mostly in the agricultural sector. Previous studies show that the incidence of extreme poverty is highest among agricultural wage laborers,[5] so a large proportion of the sample rickshaw pullers appear to have come from the rural extreme poor. The next most commonly reported occupation was "rickshaw/van/pushcart driving" (20 percent). Few were engaged in farming (10 percent) or petty business (9.5 percent). About 5 percent had been children or students before migrating to Dhaka city, and only 4 percent had been unemployed. This pre-migration occupational profile suggests that the rickshaw pullers migrated to Dhaka not only in search of employment as such, but also for more remunerative occupations. This has been found to be true in general for the recent poor migrants to urban areas, particularly to the Dhaka area.[6]

For nearly 80 percent of the respondents, rickshaw pulling was the first economic activity after migrating to Dhaka; the remaining 20 percent were mostly day laborers and workers in the service sector. Rickshaw pulling thus seems to be the easiest available work option for rural migrants to Dhaka city. Indeed, several studies have noted that the most important or commonly held informal-sector occupation of rural migrants, particularly to Dhaka city, is rickshaw pulling.[7]

The average household size for rickshaw pullers is 4.5; but the average rickshaw puller supports five persons, including him. In other words, on average, an additional half person. Ninety-three percent of married rickshaw pullers have at least one living child, and 37 percent reported four or more living children. The educational profile of the rickshaw pullers' children is little better than that of their fathers. Among children aged 20+, 55 percent have no formal education at all, and another 16 percent have only an incomplete primary education. Thus, more than 70 percent of these adult children are likely to be semi-literate at best. The school attendance rate of children aged between 5 and 15 is only about 63 percent. Thus, it seems likely that this low level of educational attainment will continue. The school attendance rate was found to be lower among children living in Dhaka (58 percent) compared to those living in the villages (73 percent). This rural–urban gap exists even when age and work characteristics are taken into account. In general, there is a lack of targeted education programs for the urban poor compared to what is available to the rural poor. The higher cost of living in urban areas may also mean that children of the urban poor are more often required to work to supplement household income. The work-participation rate of rickshaw pullers' children in Dhaka city is higher than that for children who remained behind in the villages.

In terms of building human capital—which arguably is a key to overcoming poverty in the longer run[8]—the rickshaw pullers of Dhaka city do not seem to have any advantage over their rural counterparts. Moving themselves and their families to urban areas seems only to reduce the prospects for escaping poverty in the longer run, since children are more likely to remain uneducated. This intergenerational transfer of poverty can then "reverse" during the rickshaw pullers' later life, when children who have not escaped poverty remain largely unable to support their aging parents.

Nine percent of the 10–14-year-old children of the sample rickshaw pullers work regularly, and 2 percent do so on an irregular basis. In the 15–19-year-old age group, the figures are 40 percent and 11 percent, respectively; and for the 20+ age group, 56 percent and 6 percent, respectively. Involvement in work is relatively greater for male children, with 10 percent working regularly and 4 percent on an irregular basis in the 10–14-year-old group; 54 percent and 16 percent, respectively, in the 15–19-year-old age group; and 93 percent and 5 percent, respectively, in those aged 20+.

While the labor-force participation of adult children, particularly of sons, is quite satisfactory in the sense that almost all are employed regularly in some economic activity, occupational choice is poor. Given the educational background of adult children, this is to be expected. Three major economic activities, employing more than 80 percent of adult sons, are: skilled and semi-skilled labor (e.g. masonry and carpentry); wage work in the agricultural and non-agricultural sectors; and occupations such as rickshaw pulling and van/pushcart driving. These occupations provide neither sufficient income nor livelihood security. Working adult daughters of rickshaw pullers are almost wholly employed in garment factories (92 percent), with 4 percent working as domestic help. The occupational profile of the rickshaw pullers' adult children indicates little likelihood of upward mobility.

## IV. Characteristics of Rickshaw Pulling

Of the sample rickshaw pullers, only 13 percent own a rickshaw themselves and the remainder hire the vehicles. Longer-duration pullers are more likely to own their own rickshaw, and 18 percent are owner-pullers compared to 5 percent of recent joiners. However, a large majority of those who have been pulling rickshaws for more than 15 years still rent. This suggests that there are barriers to ownership and/or that a rickshaw is not perceived to be a sensible investment by the rickshaw pullers. The unsettled lifestyle, job changes and frequent visits to rural areas can make rickshaw ownership difficult for rural migrants. Space to keep a rickshaw is difficult to find and obtaining a rickshaw license can also pose formidable problems.

Of the sample, 92 percent pursue the occupation throughout the year. Only 7 percent undertake seasonal rickshaw pulling, and these are primarily recent joiners. Ninety-five percent work only as rickshaw pullers. More than 60 percent work every day of the week, 28 percent take one day off a week and fewer than 10 percent take more than one day off a week. Very few of the rickshaw pullers (about 10 percent) pull rickshaws on a "whole day" basis, working from early morning until night. The majority (61 percent) pull on a "full day" basis, hiring the rickshaw in the morning and returning it by five or six o'clock in the evening. A smaller group (29 percent) pulls on a "half day" basis (e.g. from morning until two o'clock in the afternoon). The amount of rent paid to the rickshaw owner generally depends on how long the rickshaw is hired for and its condition. Generally, it costs Tk50 (US$0.80) to rent a rickshaw for the "whole day," Tk40 for the "full day" and Tk30 for the "half day." On average, rickshaw pullers work for nearly 9.5 hours a day; about 60 percent pull rickshaws for more than 10 hours a day; and only 19 percent pull for fewer than 8 hours. Among recent joiners, 88 percent pull rickshaws for more than 10 hours a day, as opposed to 52 percent of the

middle-duration rickshaw pullers and 43 percent of long-duration ones. Presumably, the arduousness of the job restricts the number of hours that older, long-duration rickshaw pullers can work.[9]

It is estimated that the daily average income of a Dhaka city rickshaw puller is Tk143 (approximately US$2.38 in 2003), with 82 percent of sample rickshaw pullers earning Tk100–199 (approximately US$1.60–3.20). Those earning more than Tk200 a day are most likely to be "middle-duration" pullers. The average daily income varies little before 15 years of pulling, although it may increase marginally during this period, and thereafter it declines somewhat. Differences in income among rickshaw pullers are more marked across other occupational features than duration. As might be expected, the average daily income of the rickshaw pullers who work for a full day is more than those who work for half days, although nowhere near twice as much. Those who pull a rickshaw six or seven days a week earn about 20 percent more each day than those who work for five or fewer days a week. Those who work fewer days are also those who work less than 8 hours a day. Presumably, whatever prevents them from working longer hours—poor health, for example—also prevents them from working every day of the week.

Why do rural migrants accept rickshaw pulling as an occupation, despite its arduous nature? The most common reason, cited by 83 percent of the sample rickshaw pullers, is "easy entry," especially for men who are illiterate, unskilled and lacking capital. Other reasons include the regular flow of income, possibly not found in previous occupations, and the "promise of higher income." For more recent entrants, reasons such as "earning more money," "non-availability of suitable jobs" and "peer influence" were relatively more important in the decision-making process, while "regular flow of income" and "easy availability of the job" were the most important considerations for longer-duration pullers.

The survey of former rickshaw pullers suggests that the main reason for leaving the occupation was an inability to continue such arduous labor. Nearly 85 percent of the sample former pullers were physically unable to continue; a much smaller number (16 percent) left for a more remunerative occupation. Sickness (10 percent), accidents (5 percent) and age (1 percent) played a less significant role in the decision. Three-quarters of current, and more than 90 percent of former, rickshaw pullers mentioned physical exhaustion and fatigue as the main problems encountered in rickshaw pulling.

According to engineers, under "normal conditions" rickshaw pulling is not a highly difficult job, and an averagely fit man or woman should be able to work for several hours. But as soon as conditions depart from "normal," rickshaw pulling becomes something of a feat of endurance. A 10 mph wind doubles the power required to maintain the same speed; a slight gradient of 2 percent similarly doubles it. Worn tires, rough roads and repeated stopping and starting in busy traffic each raise the power required by up to 100 percent. A combination of adverse conditions can therefore raise the power required three- or four-fold. Considering that the maximum power output a person can sustain over several hours is around 0.4 horsepower, it is clear that in adverse conditions (which are "normal" for rickshaw pullers in Dhaka), rickshaw pullers have to work nearly as hard as Olympic athletes.[10] Being as physically fit as these athletes is an absurd proposition for rickshaw pullers, who are poor, often malnourished and living in unhealthy environments. Fatigue and exhaustion are the natural outcome of hours, days and years of rickshaw pulling for these men.

The physical exhaustion associated with rickshaw pulling restricts the pullers' capacity to pursue the occupation on a sustained basis. More than 80 percent of the sample rickshaw pullers who work half a day, and nearly 95 percent of those who work fewer than six days a week, report physical incapacity as the main reason for doing so. Those who work every day do so primarily to satisfy the daily subsistence needs of their families. Although the rural migrants may have been able to achieve some upward income mobility by taking on rickshaw pulling in Dhaka city, this enhanced income may not be enough to allow them a comfortable life. Children's education and daughters' marriages both became significantly important reasons for working every day for the longer-duration pullers.

## V. Household Income and Expenditure, and Other Indicators of Well-Being

For the sake of simplicity, the discussion on household income, expenditure, and other features relating to the well-being of the rickshaw pullers will focus on those who are ever-married, i.e., living in Dhaka with their families. The average monthly household income for this group of rickshaw pullers, taking into account all sources of income, is estimated at Tk4,591 and rises over time; the average monthly household income for recent joiners is Tk4,160; that for medium-duration pullers, Tk4,604; and that for long-duration pullers, Tk4,782. The average monthly per capita income is estimated at Tk1,073, with the highest being for medium-duration rickshaw pullers

(Tk1,109) and the lowest for long-duration ones (Tk920, or 17 percent lower). The incidence of income poverty within this group is nearly 18 percent, with 3 percent living in extreme poverty (60 percent of the income poverty line). As would be expected from the per capita income statistics, the incidence of poverty is highest among the long-duration rickshaw pullers. More than a quarter (27 percent) live in poverty, and more than 5 percent in extreme poverty. By contrast, only 10 percent of recent joiners live in poverty, and none in extreme poverty.

The income-based evidence suggests that, in general, the level of wellbeing among long-duration rickshaw pullers may be lower. Although we do not have any longitudinal data to prove this point conclusively, there is strong evidence that the limited upward mobility achieved by the young rural migrants through rickshaw pulling tapers off in later years, when they reach a certain stage in the occupation and/or a certain age. This cross-sectional contrast pertaining to the duration of rickshaw pulling as well as age may well reflect what happens over time to the rickshaw pullers. The income from rickshaw pulling for the current pullers diminishes over time by 5–10 percent, and per capita household income by 14–33 percent over a 15-year period, as measured across duration of rickshaw pulling and age of the pullers (Table 8.1). A comparison of household income for current rickshaw pullers with that of former rickshaw pullers, which is 9 percent lower, further reveals the long-term adverse effects of rickshaw pulling (Table 8.2). Per-capita income is also about 8 percent lower among former pullers. Exit strategies provide a route for upward mobility only for a few; only about one-third of former rickshaw pullers reported that they had moved to more remunerative occupations. Indeed, at the time of interview, 8 out of 98 former rickshaw pullers had no work or no regular employment from which to earn an income. These points support the earlier observation that those who abandoned rickshaw pulling and switched to another activity did so because they found pulling physically difficult rather than because they were moving to a higher-paid occupation. Notwithstanding the generally lower income, virtually none of the former pullers expressed any desire to go back to rickshaw pulling.

Who are the fortunate few who leave rickshaw pulling to enter higher-income jobs? Income variation over time for former rickshaw pullers throws some light on the issue. Those who had pulled for 5–9 years had the same average individual income as current rickshaw pullers who have been in the job for 5–14 years (the average.) Those who had pulled for fewer than 5 years, or more than 10 years, had significantly lower average

**Table 8.1**        Monthly household income of current rickshaw pullers by income source and duration of rickshaw pulling

|  | *Income in taka/duration of rickshaw pulling (years)* | | | |
|---|---|---|---|---|
|  | < 5 | 5–14 | 15+ | Total |
| Income from rickshaw pulling | 4,068 | 3,800 | 3,680 | 3,807 |
| Wife's income | – | 396 | 325 | 310 |
| Children's income | 53 | 308 | 597 | 358 |
| Land/other asset | 39 | 83 | 180 | 107 |
| Income from other family member | – | 17 | – | 9 |
| Total | 4,160 | 4,604 | 4,782 | 4,591 |
| Income per household member | 1,073 | 1,109 | 920 | 1,020 |
|  | *Percentage distribution* | | | |
| Income from rickshaw pulling | 97.8 | 80.7 | 76.3 | 81.7 |
| Wife's income | – | 8.4 | 6.7 | 6.7 |
| Children's income | 1.3 | 6.5 | 12.4 | 7.7 |
| Land/other asset | 0.9 | 1.8 | 3.7 | 2.3 |
| Income from other family member | – | 0.4 | – | 0.2 |
| Total | 100.0 | 97.8 | 99.1 | 98.6 |

*Note*: Information relates to month prior to data collection.

**Table 8.2**        Monthly household income of current and former rickshaw pullers by income source and age group

|  | *Income in taka/age group (years)* | | | |
|---|---|---|---|---|
|  | < 30 | 30–44 | 45+ | Total |
|  | *Current rickshaw puller* | | | |
| Income from rickshaw pulling | 3,778 | 3,928 | 3,599 | 3,807 |
| Wife's income | 270 | 340 | 270 | 310 |
| Children's income | – | 192 | 764 | 358 |
| Land/other asset | 65 | 92 | 148 | 107 |
| Income from other family member | 87 | – | – | 9 |
| Total | 4,200 | 4,552 | 4,781 | 4,591 |
| Income per household member | 1,325 | 1,063 | 894 | 1,020 |
|  | *Former rickshaw puller* | | | |
| Own income | 2,967 | 4,002 | 2,273 | 3,361 |
| Wife's income | 250 | 393 | 420 | 389 |
| Children's income | – | 37 | 791 | 274 |
| Land/other asset | – | 134 | 273 | 167 |
| Help | – | – | 32 | 10 |
| Total | 3,217 | 4,566 | 3,789 | 4,201 |
| Income per household member | 919 | 1,069 | 750 | 944 |

incomes than those of the matching current rickshaw pullers. There is a negligible difference between per capita and household incomes of former rickshaw pullers aged 30–44 and those of current rickshaw pullers in the same age group.[11]

At the same time, a similar proportion of former rickshaw pullers aged 30–44 live in poverty, as do current rickshaw pullers in the same age group. Poverty among older and younger former rickshaw pullers is significantly higher than among those still pulling. A similar pattern is observable for rickshaw pullers who left the occupation within 5–9 years, compared to those who abandoned the job earlier or later. Many of those who abandon rickshaw pulling relatively early—both in their rickshaw-pulling careers and in their lives—appear more likely to improve their lot through opting for another occupation. There are likely to be multiple reasons why an individual rickshaw puller would leave rickshaw pulling during that particular period, including opportunities and changes in household needs, but these probably combine with the realization that rickshaw pulling is not sustainable in the long term.

Those who abandoned the occupation relatively late are the worst off—even compared to current rickshaw pullers in the same age group.[12] Presumably, they have been compelled to abandon rickshaw pulling under desperate conditions, when it was difficult for them to engage productively in rickshaw pulling but also in other activities. Evidence suggests that a sizeable number had left rickshaw pulling when they had fallen sick, suffered an accident or simply became too old to sustain the drudgery of rickshaw pulling.

An analysis of household income reveals that, on average, a rickshaw puller contributes 83 percent towards total household income; a wife, 7 percent; children, 8 percent; and the remainder comes from assets owned by the family, such as land and rent from rickshaws. Although the rickshaw puller's income always forms the major share of total household income, its relative importance diminishes over duration of rickshaw pulling. Contributions by children increase over time (coinciding with an increase in age of the puller and his children). Increased children's contributions fully compensate for the declining income of the aging, long-duration rickshaw pullers, but it is not enough to protect the household from diminishing per capita income, due to an increase in the family size. In other words, younger children are unable to compensate for the increase in household expenditure that they represent.

The estimated monthly household expenditure of the Dhaka-based ever-married rickshaw puller is Tk4,081, with a per capita expenditure of Tk907.[13] A comparison of household income with household expenditure indicates that rickshaw-puller households in Dhaka generate, on average, a surplus of around Tk500 a month. Per-capita household expenditure, like income, declines with the duration of rickshaw pulling and is almost 10 percent lower in the long-duration pulling households than in recent-joiner households. Sixty percent of expenditure goes on food requirements and 22 percent on housing. The remaining 18 percent is divided among clothing, children's education, transport, loan repayments, rickshaw-related matters (such as repairs, fines and payments to the police) and health care. On average, about 3 percent of expenditure is sent to non-immediate family, a similar proportion to that spent on children's education or clothing. Rickshaw pullers' expenditure on asset acquisition is negligible.

According to rickshaw pullers, little is spent on entertainment and recreation, which challenges the commonly held belief that rickshaw pullers often go to watch movies. Even younger rickshaw pullers report spending almost nothing on entertainment, and only 3.5 percent of all pullers reportedly watch movies. Finally, while on average only about 0.4 percent of household expenditure goes to addictive substances, for some rickshaw pullers the practice can become a significant problem. It is important to note that the problems associated with self-reporting are likely to be especially acute when it comes to admitting to spending limited household income on entertainment or drugs. Hence, the amounts stated for these types of expenditure may be underestimated. Other indicators of well-being, including household savings, assets, food security status, levels of indebtedness and an ability to generate surplus from income, confirm the two key observations made earlier. First, the aspiring rural poor who migrate to Dhaka and take up rickshaw pulling achieve some upward economic mobility. Second, they remain vulnerable, as the initial benefits gradually taper off with duration of rickshaw pulling. In support of the first point, several indicators of well-being can be summarized here. Over a year-round period, 79 percent of rickshaw pullers' households eat three meals a day; 49 percent can generate some surplus from income; 43 percent have positive savings; and 48 percent have been able to acquire some form of asset from income they have earned. In rural areas, by contrast, only about 60 percent of households eat three meals a day, year round; only 14 percent save; and 24 percent sell some of their assets—in more than one-third of cases, for consumption purposes only.[14]

However, to substantiate the second point, the value for all these indicators declines over the duration of rickshaw pulling. For example, 82 percent of recent pullers' households eat three meals a day, compared to only 72 percent of long-duration pullers' households. Sixty-six percent of recent rickshaw pullers generate some surplus from income earned, compared to 39 percent for long-duration pullers; 66 percent of the former had some positive savings compared with 37 percent of the latter; and 53 percent of the former have acquired some assets compared to 43 percent of the latter. Even among rickshaw pullers who have savings, the amount held by the long-duration pullers is no higher than that of middle-duration pullers. Nor is the value of their assets higher than that of the other two groups of rickshaw pullers. Thus, while rickshaw pulling initially helps rural migrants to move out of poverty, it does not keep them out of poverty in the long run and on a durable basis. The most frequently acquired asset by rickshaw pullers is land, not rickshaws. Of those who reported some assets, 40 percent invested in land and 20 percent in rickshaws. In monetary terms, half of the money earmarked for acquiring assets is being spent on land, with 10 percent being spent on rickshaws. This suggests that rickshaw pullers do not consider rickshaw pulling (or owning) as a long-term livelihood strategy. Rather, they would prefer to return to land-based livelihoods and village life. It is also possible that they don't find it safe to invest in rickshaws; 29 percent of current and 42 percent of former pullers said that rickshaw theft was a major problem in their occupation.

About 60 percent of the sample rickshaw pullers report that they can secure a loan in case of urgent need; 34 percent are uncertain about the possibility, and 5 percent believe that they have no access to emergency credit. At the time of interview, 46 percent of the ever-married rickshaw pullers had an outstanding loan.[15] The estimated average loan is Tk5,535 for those who are actually in debt or, on average, two-thirds of their savings. The rickshaw pullers generally borrow money from informal sources. In two-thirds of cases, they received loans from friends, relatives, and neighbors, including rickshaw owners, and in one-third of cases from formal sources such as banks and NGOs. The major reasons for borrowing are asset acquisition, meeting daily needs and health care costs—in 85 percent of cases, loans are taken out for these purposes. For recent joiners and middle-duration pullers, loans are more often taken out for the health care needs of family members rather than for themselves; for long-duration pullers, the situation is markedly reversed, indicating their high burden of ill health.

## VI. Crises

Crises typically trigger the downward movement of poor households and individuals into further poverty. Information on crisis events was collected for the five-year period prior to the survey, during which time the sample rickshaw pullers experienced on average two crises. Only one-quarter had never experienced a crisis

during the reference period but the remaining three-quarters had experienced at least one crisis.[16] Recent joiners are less likely to have experienced a crisis in the last five years (64 percent) compared to long-duration pullers (85 percent).

Health crises, affecting both the rickshaw puller's own health and that of the family members, are the most frequently encountered type of crisis. Of the 75 percent of rickshaw pullers who had experienced at least one crisis, 67 percent had encountered a health-related crisis. The next most frequent type of crisis, experienced by 52 percent of pullers, relates to personal insecurity, and includes mugging, theft and robbery, household eviction, humiliation,[17] involvement with the police or the courts, physical violence (including rape), abduction and threats. The most frequent crisis of this type is rickshaw theft and "hazards relating to police or court." Financial crises that arise out of the marriage of a daughter or sister (including the provision of a dowry) and other social events, and maltreatment by in-laws leading to divorce have been experienced by about 16 percent of the rickshaw-puller households. "Misfortunes" such as a house fire, damage to a rickshaw as a result of an accident, or the accidental death of a household member were experienced by 9 percent of the rickshaw pullers' households, while natural disasters were experienced by only 3 percent. Except for natural disasters, the incidence of all other types of crises is highest among long-duration rickshaw pullers. On average, a rickshaw puller is required to spend more than Tk6,000 to mitigate a crisis. Overall, it is health shocks—and not the social ceremonies and dowries—that cost the rickshaw pullers most. This leads to severe resource depletion in the short term, with potentially extremely adverse long-term consequences for escaping the poverty trap.

## VII. Health Status of Rickshaw Pullers

Subjective perceptions about feeling healthy are an important ingredient in both human well-being and behavior. Data reveal that, on average, only about 60 percent of the sample rickshaw pullers "feel good" about their current health status, 20 percent feel "not so good" and another 20 percent feel "bad." Positive perceptions about health vary inversely with duration of rickshaw pulling. Nearly 70 percent of the recent joiners feel "good," compared with 42 percent of long-duration pullers. Among the latter, 27 percent feel "bad," while another 31 percent rated themselves as being in "not so good" health. These variations in feelings about their health status is, perhaps, the outcome of the combined effects of age and the drudgery of years of rickshaw pulling, and is linked also to the practice of working for fewer hours a day and/or fewer days a week by this group of older and long-duration pullers.

Two factors underlie subjective perceptions about health and well-being. One is the presence of some recognizable health problem, and the other relates to the general signs of "physical weakness." The latter is most frequently cited. About 80 percent mentioned physical weakness as a reason for feeling "bad," while "health problems" were mentioned by only 38 percent. Even among recent joiners, 85 percent noted "physical weakness" as a reason for "feeling bad." This supports the conclusion that irrespective of duration, rickshaw pulling is physically exhausting work. The situation worsens with the depletion of energy linked to the aging process and duration of pulling.

Before discussing morbidity, it is important to note that the data may significantly underestimate actual morbidity for rickshaw pullers, as only those pullers who were working were included in the survey. Rickshaw pullers who were at home due to illness or fatigue were excluded. Morbidity rates on the day of the survey were estimated to be 11.4 percent. The figure rises to 39 percent when the reference period is widened to the past month. Both these rates are higher than those documented for the rural poor.[18] Of sample rickshaw pullers, 28 percent had suffered from a major illness in the past five years, and about 40 percent had suffered chronic and/or intermittent ill health. As expected, the burden of ill health among long-duration rickshaw pullers is substantially higher than among recent joiners. On the survey day, about 22 percent of long-duration pullers were unwell compared to 2 percent of recent joiners. About half of the former are vulnerable to frequent sickness, compared to 37 percent of the latter and 23 percent of middle-duration rickshaw pullers.

Among sample rickshaw pullers, acute health problems arise primarily from a small number of conditions: colds and fevers; gastro-enteric problems including acidity and ulcers; aches and pains; and physical weakness. These problems account for 71 percent of the acute ailments suffered by rickshaw pullers. Chronic illness is also linked primarily to gastro-enteric problems, aches and pains, and physical weakness. The last two make up 43 percent of all chronic ailments, and are likely to be associated with rickshaw pulling itself. Hence, a significant part of the health vulnerability of the pullers may be related to occupational hazards. Rickshaw pullers consider their occupation to be largely responsible for their continued health problems. They consider that 78 percent of acute illnesses, 67 percent of repeat illnesses, and 70 percent of their major health problems are directly or indirectly connected to rickshaw pulling itself.

At first sight, access to health care by the rickshaw pullers seems to be quite high. Eighty-eight percent of cases of acute illness and almost all major illnesses receive some form of health care treatment. However, only in 77 percent of cases was the treatment received for acute illness perceived to be adequate. For those who are unable to access adequate health care (or any health care at all), financial reasons are mentioned as the main obstacle. The Dhaka city rickshaw pullers depend primarily on the private sector for health care. This may be an outcome of the lack of a primary health care network in urban areas.

It is well known that ill health can impose a significant economic burden on individuals and households in several ways, with particularly adverse consequences for the poor. The pathways from ill health to poverty operate through the direct costs of treatment and non-medical care, and the indirect costs of lost income (due to days missed and/or diminished productivity). The psychological costs on breadwinners and on family members can also be significant. The partial information that is available shows the extent to which ill health affects the households of rickshaw pullers. The average cost of treatment for an episode of illness is estimated to be Tk263 for an acute illness and Tk5,453 for a major illness. A rickshaw puller has to stop work, on average, for four days for each episode of acute illness, and for 44 days for each episode of major illness. If this income loss is taken into consideration, then the aggregate cost for an episode of acute illness would be about Tk863, equivalent to six days' income. For a major illness, the figure would be close to Tk12,000, equivalent to three months' income. Given the monthly savings potential of an average rickshaw-puller household, a major sickness can wipe out two years of savings. But more than half of pullers have no savings or assets at all, one-fifth are unable to secure three meals a day, half cannot generate any surplus from income, and a similar proportion has outstanding debt. Set against this, the average economic burden of ill health is considerable.

Rickshaw pullers generally meet the treatment costs for acute illness from current household income. Only in 6 percent of cases are they forced to incur debt. As might be expected, the situation is different for major illness or injury. To meet these costs, 30 percent of the sample rickshaw pullers had liquidated their savings, 16 percent had disposed of assets and 27 percent had incurred debt. Reduced physical capacity to work and the resulting negative effects on the income and non-income well-being of the household, are the most commonly mentioned effects. In total, it is estimated that almost one-fifth of all rickshaw pullers every five years, or 4 percent every year, may face reduced productivity after a major illness.[19] Combined with large-scale resource depletion as a result of a health crisis, decreasing productivity means an even greater chance that a rickshaw-puller household will become trapped in a downward spiral. This can also have significant negative effects on children's education, health and nutritional status, thus affecting the intergenerational development of human capital within a rickshaw puller's household.

## VIII. Concluding Remarks

Most rickshaw pullers come from very poor rural backgrounds and have found rickshaw pulling to be somewhat effective as a route out of poverty. Upon entering the city, rickshaw pulling appears to be a relatively easy livelihood option. An analysis of changing household fortunes over time suggests that those who remain in the occupation for a few years do attain a degree of modest upward mobility. Initially, the incidence of food poverty appears to be much less prominent among rickshaw pullers than among the rural extreme poor. The main advantage that a rickshaw puller has over an agricultural laborer is not so much a higher income but, rather, a regular income flow, which is missing for rural laborers working in an environment marked with high seasonality. When considering the capacity to save, to access credit and to acquire assets, the average rickshaw puller does appear to have a much better chance of escaping poverty than his rural counterpart.

However, although rickshaw pulling may provide an escape from extreme rural poverty, the high degree of susceptibility to crisis appears to be a serious obstacle to sustained upward mobility. An extraordinarily high proportion (75 percent) of rickshaw pullers reported having encountered at least one crisis in the last five years, with an average incidence of two major crises per household. Of these, two-thirds of the crises and almost half of the crisis-related expenses relate to health shocks. Health-related shocks are the single most important factor in downward mobility, and often originate from the nature

of rickshaw pulling itself. The level of morbidity, and the associated decline in the number of days and hours worked, increases with years of rickshaw pulling as well as with age. The average financial loss per health crisis is more than the average monthly household income. As a result, many liquidate savings and/or assets, and/or go into debt, especially to mitigate major illnesses and injuries related to road accidents. There is a very strong case for health interventions to help rickshaw pullers and their households cope with health shocks.

Thus, the initial trend of "modest upward mobility" is not sustained in the long run. Almost all economic and social indicators—including income poverty—appear to deteriorate with the length of involvement in rickshaw pulling. This is not just because of pullers' vulnerability to health shocks, as the unsustainability of rickshaw pulling as a livelihood is reflected in several further dimensions. First, the effort that pullers are able to put into pulling, in terms of time spent working, declines with the length of involvement in the occupation. As a result, both rickshaw pullers' own incomes and household per capita incomes decline. At the same time, the capacity to generate a surplus income for savings and asset acquisition is reduced, indebtedness rises, and both food and income poverty also rise. "Normal" circumstances for a Dhaka city rickshaw puller means having to work nearly as hard as an Olympic athlete, but in a context of poverty and malnutrition. This suggests that it is not only health shocks, or even aging, that create the conditions of unsustainability, but rather the way shocks and demography combine with a more gradual process of diminishing levels of energy and general well-being.

Policy interventions should focus on encouraging exit from rickshaw pulling at a relatively early stage of involvement, through programs that, for example, provide credit, training and information.[20] The data suggest that it is those "early-middle duration" rickshaw pullers (i.e., who have been in the occupation for 5–9 years and who are aged between 30 and 44) who have the best chance of finding alternative, more remunerative, jobs. Rickshaw pullers who have recently migrated from rural areas appear to have slightly better socioeconomic backgrounds and a higher human capital than their older counterparts, suggesting that they may be better able to succeed in alternative livelihoods. If, by reducing both health risks and associated costs, the savings and asset accumulation of rickshaw pullers could be raised while they were in their prime, at the peak of their productive capacity, then rickshaw pulling might offer a longer-term escape from poverty. Public health measures appropriate to rickshaw pullers may range from the enforcement of road safety regulations, to improved public provision of emergency health care and better coverage of urban primary health care systems so that rickshaw-puller households can access affordable treatment. Improved access to flexible credit, as well as some form of health insurance, may improve the pace of capital accumulation among this group of urban poor.

This case study of rickshaw pullers carries wider implications around issues of "pro-poor growth." As an ideological formulation, pro-poor growth can vary from "anything that is good for growth must be pro-poor" to "anything that is good for the poor here and now must be good for growth." Hence, traditionally there has been an emphasis on growth acceleration by any means, with an emphasis on labor-intensive sectors whenever possible. The present study, however, suggests that an analysis of the dynamic effects of labor intensity is crucial to understanding the actual pro-poorness of a growth process and in designing a better policy environment for the poor.

In the early 1990s, according to one estimate, the rickshaw sub-sector accounted for 34 percent of total value added in the transport sector, and about 4.5 percent of the national workforce depended on this sector for subsistence.[21] The importance of rickshaw pulling as a livelihood activity has increased over the past decade. In traditional informal sector literature, this process of rickshaw sub-sector growth would have been considered as a mass example of pro-poor growth, at least in the early stages of development in low-income countries. However, as has been implicitly argued throughout this study, such an assessment does not take into account the absence of a future market for long-duration pullers, who either have to abandon the activity for health reasons or persist on the margins of the sub-sector as part-time pullers. Paradoxically, easy entry and exit, labor intensity and intense competition—all the "positive" characteristics of the rickshaw market—lead to sub-optimal welfare outcomes from the perspective of private returns to labor invested in rickshaw pulling. In terms of social return, the promotion of such activities beyond a certain point in time represents a colossal loss, with immense human social suffering and a perpetuation of poverty.

## Questions

1. Why would someone choose rickshaw pulling as an occupation?

2. The rickshaw pullers are entrepreneurial, hard-working, and dedicated; why doesn't this lead to economic success?

## Notes

1. Several studies of rickshaw pullers have been carried out, but none have focused on the long-term health effects and resultant unsustainability of rickshaw pulling, as this study does. See, for example, Rashid, Selim (1978), "The rickshaw industry of Dhaka: preliminary findings," Research Report No 51, BIDS, Dhaka; also Masum, M. (1988), "Informal financial markets in rural Bangladesh: the case of rickshaws," Working Paper No 13, BIDS, Dhaka; and Gallagher, Rob (1992), *The Rickshaws of Bangladesh,* University Press Ltd, Dhaka.

2. The different points in the city that are covered include Mohammadpur Bery Badh, Mohammadpur Shia Masjid area, Mohammadpur town hall, Mohammadpur Krishi market, Asad Gate, Jigatala, Shamoly cinema hall, Shaymoli ring road, Sheorapara, Agaragaon market, Agargaon Planning Commission Office, Manik Mia Avenue, Bijoy Sharani, Dhaka zoo, Mirpur 1, 2, 10, 11, 13 and 14, Pallabi, College Gate, Farm Gate, Shahabag, Malibag, Elephant Road, New Market, Azimpur, Motijheel, Jatrabari, Lalbagh, Kamrangir Char, Sutrapur, Sadarghat, Khilgaon, Kamalapur railway station, Sabujbagh, Gabtali, Kachukhet, Ibrahimpur, Banani, Mahakhali, Bhashantek and other similar places.

3. Less than 1 percent of males over the age of 20 are widowed or divorced. See BBS (1994), *Statistical Yearbook of Bangladesh,* Ministry of Planning, Bangladesh.

4. Multiple asset and process indicators may be considered to ascertain whether a particular social category belongs to the most disadvantaged groups. For an application to Bangladesh data, see Sen, Binayak and Sharifa Begum (1998), "Methodology for identifying the poorest at local level," Technical Paper No 27, *Macroeconomics, Health and Development Series,* World Health Organization, Geneva.

5. An attempt to devise extra-poor-sensitive indicators, by emphasizing broad group characteristics rather than individual targeting, revealed that, among a host of tested variables, three stand out prominently. They are land, housing and occupation. In Bangladesh, it has been observed empirically that the poorest are agricultural laborers, those who reside in Jhupri, or those living in single-structure thatched homes with a maximum owned land area of 50 decimals. See reference 4, Sen and Begum (1998).

6. Afsar, Rita and M. Hossain (1992), "Urbanization and urban poor in Bangladesh: issues trends and challenges," BIDS (mimeo).

7. Siddiqui, K., S. Rowshan Qadir, S. Alamgir and S. Huq (1990), "The informal sector poor of Dhaka city" in Social Formation of the Dhaka City, University Press Ltd, Dhaka; also Centre for Urban Studies (CUS) (1983), "Slums in Dhaka city," University of Dhaka; and Begum, Anowara (1997), "The socioeconomic condition of the pavement dwellers of Dhaka city," Research Report No 150, BIDS, Dhaka.

8. Sen, Binayak (2003), "Drivers of escape and descent: changing household fortunes in rural Bangladesh," *World Development* Vol 31, No 3, pages 513–534.

9. Although for long-duration pullers age can be a barrier to putting in more hours, the length of time spent in the occupation also matters. Among rickshaw pullers in the same age group, the daily labor input in terms of hours worked declines noticeably the longer an individual has been pulling. However, in terms of weekly engagement, no decline is noted. Thus, a somewhat different dynamic may be at work. When the physical capacity of rickshaw pullers decreases the longer they have been pulling, this adversely affects their work

input and income potential. Thus the pressure to work every day to compensate for the daily income loss becomes greater.

10.  The British cycling record for 100 miles involved an average output of 0.44 horsepower over 3.75 hours. See reference 1, Gallagher (1992), pages 345–346.

11.  As only six former rickshaw pullers are in the under-30 age group, they are excluded from the present analysis.

12.  The mean duration elapsed since abandoning rickshaw pulling is 33 months for the 30–44 age group, and 48 months for the 45+ age group. The average duration of rickshaw pulling by former pullers was seven years for the 30–44 age group and 12 years for the 45+ age group.

13.  Information on monthly expenditure relates to the month prior to data collection.

14.  Nath, N. C. (1992), "Condition of the rural poor and operation of an anti-poverty programme [sic]: a household level analysis," mimeo, BIDS, Dhaka.

15.  For comparative purposes, the analysis in this section has been confined to ever-married rickshaw pullers who live in Dhaka with their families.

16.  The figure may be even higher depending on the accuracy of recall.

17.  This refers to incidents such as: severe insult by local powerful and/or law-enforcing people; dowry-related and other vio-

lence against women; divorce/abandonment of female household members; retrenchment from a job with no reason; unwarranted harassment by the police, etc.

18.  Ahmed, Kazi Saleh et al. (1997), "Morbidity and disability patterns of destitute households in rural Bangladesh, 1994 and 1995," *Monograph* Series No 4, BBS, Dhaka; also Begum, Sharifa (1996), "Health dynamics of poverty" in Hossain, Zillur Rahman et al. (editors), *The Dynamics of Rural Poverty, 1987–95,* BIDS, Dhaka (forthcoming).

19.  This estimate was arrived at based on figures denoting that 27.8 percent of sample rickshaw pullers had suffered from a major health problem in the five-year period; and of these, 70 percent had reported a reduced physical capacity to work. As previously noted, this is probably an underestimation, as the sample rickshaw pullers are working at present.

20.  Exit programs may also include measures that create disincentives for involvement in rickshaw pulling as a long-term occupational choice. This is, however, easier said than done. Recent restrictions on the movement of rickshaws on several streets of Dhaka are a case in point. Many pullers have voiced their resentment, citing a loss of income as a result of this measure. In terms of sequencing of measures, creating viable alternatives must precede disincentive measures.

21.  See reference 1, Gallagher (1992).

*Source:* Pulling Rickshaws in the City of Dhaka: A Way Out of Poverty? Sharifa Begum and Binayak Sen. *Environment and Urbanization.* Vol. 17 No. 2 2002. Reprinted by permission of International Institute for Environment and Development (IIED) and the authors.

# CHAPTER 9

## The Good Samaritans

### *Melinda Gates, Bono, and Bill Gates*

Nancy Gibbs

Bill Gates of Microsoft Corp. and his wife, Melinda, and Bono of the Irish rock band U2 would seem to have little in common, yet Time chose them together as persons of the year. They have embarked on a campaign of planned giving to benefit the world's poorest, especially in areas of disease and healthcare. Shared concerns have brought them together into a team that is trying to change the world's commitments to its poorest and sickest people.

These are not the people you expect to come to the rescue.

Rock stars are designed to be shiny, shallow creatures, furloughed from reality for all time. Billionaires are even more removed, nestled atop fantastic wealth where they never again have to place their own calls or defrost dinner or fly commercial. So Bono spends several thousand dollars at a restaurant for a nice Pinot Noir, and Bill Gates, the great predator of the Internet age, has a trampoline room in his $100 million house. It makes you think that if these guys can decide to make it their mission to save the world, partner with people they would never otherwise meet, care about causes that are not sexy or dignified in the ways that celebrities normally require, then no one really has a good excuse anymore for just staying on the sidelines and watching.

Such is the nature of Bono's fame that just about everyone in the world wants to meet him—except for the richest man in the world, who thought it would be a waste of time. "World health is immensely complicated," says Gates, recalling that first encounter in 2002. "It doesn't really boil down to a 'Let's be nice' analysis. So I thought a meeting wouldn't be all that valuable."

It took about three minutes with Bono for Gates to change his mind. Bill and his wife Melinda, another computer nerd turned poverty warrior, love facts and data with a tenderness most people reserve for their children, and Bono was hurling metrics across the table as fast as they could keep up. "He was every bit the geek that we are," says Gates Foundation chief Patty Stonesifer, who helped broker that first summit. "He just happens to be a geek who is a fantastic musician."

And so another alliance was born: unlikely, unsentimental, hard nosed, clear eyed and dead set on driving poverty into history. The rocker's job is to be raucous, grab our attention. The engineers' job is to make things work. 2005 is the year they turned the corner, when Bono charmed and bullied and morally blackmailed the leaders of the world's richest countries into forgiving $40 billion in debt owed by the poorest; now those countries can spend the money on health and schools rather than interest payments—and have no more excuses for not doing so. The Gateses, having built the world's biggest charity, with a $29 billion endowment, spent the year giving more money away faster than anyone ever has, including nearly half a billion dollars for the Grand Challenges, in which they asked the very best brains in the world how they would solve a huge problem, like inventing a vaccine that needs no needles and no refrigeration, if they had the money to do it.

It would be easy to watch the alliance in action and imagine the division of labor: head and heart, business and culture; one side brings the money, the other side the buzz. But like many great teams, this one is more than the sum of its symbols. Apart from his music stardom, Bono is a busy capitalist (he's a named partner in a $2 billion private equity firm), moves in political circles like a very charming shark, aptly named his organization DATA (debt, AIDS, trade, Africa) to capture both the breadth of his ambitions and the depth of his research. Meanwhile, you could watch Bill and Melinda coolly calculate how many lives will be saved by each billion they spend and miss how impassioned they are about the suffering they have seen. "He's changing the world twice," says Bono of Bill. "And the second act for Bill Gates may be the one that history regards more."

For being shrewd about doing good, for rewiring politics and re-engineering justice, for making mercy smarter and hope strategic and then daring the rest of us to follow, Bill and Melinda Gates and Bono are TIME's Persons of the Year.

As it happens, they have arrived at the right time, as America stirs itself awake from the dreamy indifference with which the world's poor have forever been treated. In ordinary times, we give when it's easy: a gesture, a reflex, a salve to conscience. The entreaties come on late-night TV from well-meaning but long-discarded celebrities who cuddle with big-eyed children and appeal to pity and guilt. Maybe we send off a check, hope it will help someone somewhere stay alive for another day. That is not the model for the current crusaders or the message for these extraordinary times.

This was already a year that redefined generosity. Americans gave more money to tsunami relief, more than $1.6 billion, than to any overseas mission ever before. The Hurricane Season from Hell brought another outpouring of money and time and water bottles and socks and coats and offers of refuge, some $2.7 billion so far. The public failure of government to manage disaster became the political story of the year. But the private response of individuals, from every last lemonade stand to every mitten drive, is the human story of 2005.

"Katrina created one tragedy and revealed another," Melinda Gates said in a speech after the hurricane. "We have to address the inequities that were not created by the hurricanes but exposed by them. We have to ensure that people have the opportunity to make the most of their lives." That just about captures the larger mission she and her husband have embraced. In the poorest countries, every day is as deadly as a hurricane. Malaria kills two African children a minute, round the clock. In that minute a woman dies from complications during pregnancy, nine people get infected with HIV, three people die of TB. A vast host of aid workers and agencies and national governments and international organizations have struggled for years to get ahead of the problem but often fell behind. The task was too big, too complicated. There was no one in charge, no consensus about what to do first and never enough money to do it. In Muslim parts of Ethiopia, aid workers can't talk to teenage girls about condoms to prevent AIDS; but in Tanzania they're encouraged to. How you cut an umbilical cord can determine whether a baby risks a fatal infection, but every culture has its own traditions. They cut with a coin for luck in Nepal and a stone in Bolivia, where they think if you use a razor blade the child will grow up to be a thief. There is no one solution to fit all countries, and so the model the Gates Foundation and Bono have embraced pulls in everyone, at every level. Think globally. Act carefully. Prove what works. Then use whatever levers you have to get it done.

The challenge of "stupid poverty"—the people who die for want of a $2 pill because they live on $1 a day— was enough to draw Gates away from Microsoft years before he intended to shift his focus from making money to giving it away. He and Melinda looked around and recognized a system's failure. "Those lives were being treated as if they weren't valuable," Gates told Fortune in 2002. "Well, when you have the resources that could make a very big impact, you can't just say to yourself, 'O.K., when I'm 60, I'll get around to that. Stand by.'"

There have always been rich and famous people who feel the call to "give back," which is where big marble buildings and opera houses come from. But Bill and Melinda didn't set out to win any prizes—or friends. "They've gone into international health," says Paul Farmer, a public-health pioneer, "and said, 'What, are you guys kidding? Is this the best you can do?'" Gates' standards are shaping the charitable marketplace as he has the software universe. "He wants to know where every penny goes," says Bono, whose DATA got off the ground with a Gates Foundation grant. "Not because those pennies mean so much to him, but because he's demanding efficiency." His rigor has been a blessing to everyone—not least of all Bono, who was at particular risk of not being taken seriously, just another guilty white guy pestering people for more money without focusing on where it goes. "When an Irish rock star starts talking about it, people go, yeah, you're paid to be indulged and have these ideas," Bono says. "But when Bill Gates says you can fix malaria in 10 years, they know he's done a few spreadsheets."

The Gates commitment acts as a catalyst. They needed the drug companies to come on board, and the major health agencies, the churches, the universities and a whole generation of politicians who were raised to believe that foreign aid was about as politically sexy as postal reform. And that is where Bono's campaign comes in. He goes to churches and talks of Christ and the lepers, citing exactly how many passages of Scripture ("2,103") deal with taking care of the poor; he sits in a corporate boardroom and talks about the role of aid in reviving the U.S. brand. He gets Pat Robertson and Susan Sarandon to do a commercial together for his ONE campaign to "Make Poverty History." Then he heads to Washington, where he stops by a meeting of House Democrats to nuzzle them about debt relief before a private lunch with President George W. Bush, whom he praises for tripling aid to Africa over the past four years. Everyone from Republican Senator Rick Santorum to Hillary Clinton used Bono's October concert as a fund raiser. "He knows how to get people to follow him," Stonesifer says. "We are probably a good complement. We're more likely to give you four facts about the disease than four ways that you can go do something about it."

Bono grasps that politicians don't much like being yelled at by activists who tell them no matter what they do, it's not enough. Bono knows it's never enough, but he also knows how to say so in a way that doesn't leave his audience feeling helpless. He invites everyone into the game, in a way that makes them think they are missing something if they hold back. "After so many years in Washington," says retired Senator Jesse Helms of North Carolina, whom Bono recruited to his cause, "I had met enough well-known people to quickly figure out who was genuine and who was there for show. I knew as soon as I met Bono that he was genuine. He has absolutely nothing to gain personally as a result of his work. In fact, he has opened himself to criticism because he has been willing to work with anyone to find help for these children who have taken his heart."

This is not about pity. It's more about passion. Pity sees suffering and wants to ease the pain; passion sees injustice and wants to settle the score. Pity implores the powerful to pay attention; passion warns them about what will happen if they don't. The risk of pity is that it kills with kindness; the promise of passion is that it builds on the hope that the poor are fully capable of helping themselves if given the chance. In 2005 the world's poor needed no more condolences; they needed people to get interested, get mad and then get to work.

---

## Questions

1. Why would the world's richest corporate executive and his wife come together with a rock musician to work on global poverty?

2. What do Bill and Melinda Gates and Bono hope to change through their combined efforts? Are they succeeding?

---

*Source:* The Good Samaritans: Melinda Gates, Bono, and Bill Gates. Nancy Gibbs. *Time*. January 2, 2006. Reprinted by permission.

# CHAPTER 10

## Violencia Femicida

### *Violence Against Women and Mexico's Structural Crisis*

Mercedes Olivera

**Translated by Victoria J. Furio**

Accounts of murdered women in Mexico have made newspaper headlines in both Mexico and the United States. This article argues that these are not just random acts of violence, but are rooted in economic changes that are destroying rural livelihoods and making the poor ever more desperate.

*The World Bank and IMF, two grindstones of the same mill, imposed the violence of the free market on us.... In such a "democracy," who's really in charge?*

—Eduardo Galeano

Women are being murdered in Mexico at an alarming rate. Since the 1990s this rate has increased so dramatically—in direct relation to the expansion of neoliberalism—that, under pressure from feminists, the government has finally had to recognize it as a national problem. It can be viewed as an expression of the country's current crises of governability, internal security, and respect for human rights.

Although there have been episodes of multiple murders of women, femicides, linked to particular regions, as in the case of Ciudad Juárez, for example, at this point it is a pathology that has spread throughout Mexico. In 2002 there were more than 5,000 cases nationally (Lagarde, 2005), and the number may reach 8,000 by the end of 2005. For the most part, the victims are women of childbearing age murdered with guns or knives, but many are also beaten, burned, or poisoned. The fact that the perpetrators are so rarely punished and that the

number and the viciousness of crimes against women continue to increase reveals the government's political incapacity to deal with this kind of crime.

Many of these killings are carried out by unknown assailants. Others occur in public security actions. In the majority of cases, however, women are murdered by someone known to them or related through work, family, or romantic involvement. According to the World Health Organization, 70 percent of the women murdered throughout the world in 2002 were victims of their husbands or lovers (Urías, 2005). Their bodies, often found on the street, show the brutality carried out against them: a large percentage are beaten and tortured before their deaths.

With the Mexican congressional representative Marcela Lagarde, I view femicide as but the extreme end of a range of violations of women's human rights—a direct and extreme expression of economic, political, social, and gender violence that is structural in nature.[1] Much of this generalized violence is exerted against women for being women—that is, it is misogynous.

Violence against women, an expression of male power, is present in various forms and degrees throughout their lives. As a naturalized part of the culture, symbols, institutional functioning, and cultural prescriptions, it shapes identities and internalizes subjectivities. In all societies the cultural models for being a woman assign positions to women that subordinate them to the personal and institutionalized power of men, creating real and symbolic inequalities. These inequalities are expressed in direct or hidden messages, discriminatory actions and excluding omissions, lack of resources, limits on freedom and coercion, objectification, exploitation, self-depreciation, feelings of guilt and shame, deception, and false justifications. In all these situations violence against women progressively develops from insinuations, offensive comparisons, harassment, threats, verbal intimidation, abuse, irresponsibility, betrayals, and abandonment to beatings, forced sex, rape, and persecution. It even appears in other realms such as counterinsurgency and war.

From this perspective, femicide and femicidal violence can be identified as specific forms of gender violence, which is defined by the United Nations as a mechanism of domination, control, oppression, and power over women (UN, 1979). Although gender violence does not always result in murder, it does increase the possibility of it. Gender violence is a constant violation of the human rights of women and girls. Its presence in the home, on the street, in the community, in the workplace, in government, church, and organizations and within couples allows tension and hatred to build up and reaffirms and reproduces gender relations of domination/subordination. In this article, I analyze briefly some of the structural causes of recent violence against women in Mexico. Taken together, they demonstrate the failure of the neoliberal system to provide either development or a model of democracy in our country.

Having defined femicide and femicidal violence as a direct expression of the structural violence of the neoliberal social system, we could pursue its causes in the political realm or in the ways in which individuals have been divided and battered by the violent dynamics of social transformation. Putting the neoliberal mandates into practice through institutionalized patriarchal power, Mexico's so-called political class and its business and financial sectors have undermined and violated both society's and individuals' rights, interests, and needs. In the case of women, one outcome of the processes on both levels has been murder.

At the same time as we consider the increase in violence against women, we must also take into account the increase of violence within families and personal violence in general. These are the other side of the systemic violence of the neoliberal social structure, which creates a social ecology in which men are driven to hypermasculinity, exaggerating the violent, authoritarian,

aggressive aspects of male identity in an attempt to preserve that identity. The counterpart of these attitudes is found in the subordinate positions of women in relation both to men and to institutionalized masculine power. In the face of neoliberalism's increasing demands, the dysfunction and obsolescence of these stereotypes is ever more evident. The disturbances they have always produced in personal relations are inflamed by the current social violence. Conflicts within couples and families as masculine domination is brought into question and delegitimized steadily increase the levels of violence and, of course, the risk of murder. These conflicts are multiplied under the pressure produced by unemployment, poverty, social polarization, alcoholism, and insecurity, among the many other problems that fill daily life with tension.

## Neoliberal Dynamic, Economic-Political Crisis, and Violence Against Women

The United Nations committee that recently investigated the murders and disappearances of women in Ciudad Juárez and Chihuahua concluded that they had to be seen not as isolated cases but as a product of a "situation of violence in a structurally violent society" (UN, 2003). It therefore recommended "combating criminality concurrently with the structural causes of gender violence, including domestic, intrafamilial and public incidents such as sexual abuse, homicides, kidnapping and disappearances." Its report associates these cases with the high density of the cities bordering the United States and with the establishment of maquilas and the predominance in them of poorly paid female workers. The lack of job opportunities for men, the report states, "has changed the traditional dynamics of relations between the sexes . . . creating a situation of conflict towards women because [the changes in employment patterns] have not been accompanied by a change in either traditional patriarchal attitudes and mentalities or the stereotyped vision of the social roles of men and women" (CEDAW, 2005: 7–11).

Indeed, poverty, unemployment, the disintegration of the peasant economy, and migration—all more acute since the Salinas government (1988–1994) accelerated neoliberal policies—are, along with the national crisis of governability, the most important structural causes of the increase in violence against women. Boltvinik and Hernández Laos (2000; Boltvinik, 2000) maintain that in 2000 more than 75 percent of the country's population was poor or extremely poor. According to a recent survey, this figure now exceeds 80 percent (Boltvinik, 2005).

Although official sources recognize only between 45 percent and 52 percent as poor, a survey by the Organization of American States (OAS) concludes that Mexico, Brazil, and Colombia form a "triangle of extreme poverty" in Latin America because, in addition to high rates of poverty, they demonstrate insufficient progress with regard to the "reduction of maternal mortality (which is as high as Africa's) and unemployment, the provision of universal primary education and sanitation, and environmental sustainability." This situation is the result of the intense social polarization brought about by neoliberalism, which has deepened historical inequality and fostered corruption and inefficiency in governments that maintain oligarchic, authoritarian, and patriarchal social structures even though they are now disguised as democracies (OAS, 2005).

In Mexico, where neoliberal policies are applied dogmatically, favoring national and transnational companies and financial institutions at all costs, President Vicente Fox has adopted a discourse that systematically denies the exasperating social realities experienced by the population, among them marginalization; social, legal, and political exclusion in both urban and rural areas; and a critical absence of human rights. The government reports that the economy has grown by 3.4 percent a year and that poverty has been reduced in this six-year period by 6.1 percent. This is something of an illusion, however, because in fact we have barely returned to the levels of poverty that existed before the crash of 1995. Moreover, the growth described refers only to the macroeconomic level. What poverty reduction there is in rural areas is actually due to the transfer of resources by government assistance programs and to remittances from the United States, both of which are used more for consumption than for investment.[2] Consequently, according to the United Nations Development Program, Mexico is among the countries in Latin America with the *least* improvement in human development in recent years, with barely 1.3 percent growth in per capita income between 1990 and 2003 (UNDP, 2005). During this same period real salaries remained stagnant, while unemployment increased from 600,000 in 2000 to 1,027,000 in 2005 and inequality increased to the point that "5 percent of the income from the richest households would be enough to pull 12 million Mexicans out of poverty, reducing the national poverty rate from 16 percent to 4 percent" (González and Vargas, 2005).[3] And, of course, bad as inequality and marginalization are in central and northern Mexico, they are much more severe in the south, where there is a high percentage of indigenous people and peasants.

Growth in industrial production and exports is also somewhat fictitious, since most of it comes from the maquiladoras, with little value added, minimal technology transfer, and volatile capital investment. Meanwhile, petroleum production is on the point of collapsing, both because of the rapid exhaustion of reserves accelerated by demand from the United States and because of the use of the profits to cover the country's current expenditures rather than for reinvestment (González and Vargas, 2005).

The widespread poverty that results from these conditions has forced women to join the labor market under conditions of great inequality and vulnerability, basically because of their lack of training[4] and freedom of movement and because the jobs to which they have access are in services and the informal economy, with low and unreliable incomes.[5] Many women work 10-to 12-hour days in domestic service, restaurants, and small factories without any guarantees or benefits. The flexibilization of labor—the growth of temporary, informal work—throughout the economy has facilitated an increase in the exploitation of women, in the process feminizing poverty, access to jobs, and exploitation. According to a national survey, in 2005 95.38 percent of women considered economically active were employed in informal jobs in services and sales or some combination of the two. One-fourth of those in sales were self-employed in small establishments and the rest worked for others, although not all received salaries (INEGI, 2005). Poverty and marginalization have also forced women into prostitution or criminal gangs.

The massive integration of women into the labor force in search of a wage has effectively destroyed the traditional model of a sexual division of labor without changing the collective imaginary that women are dependent on men and that their obligations are in the home. In addition to working for wages, women continue to bear the responsibility of domestic chores, child care, and the organization of daily life, forcing them into double and triple work days. But women are also questioned and made to feel guilty on the neighborhood and the community level and through the discourse of the right-wing government, which, for example, holds them responsible for juvenile delinquency. Supposedly, by "opting" to work outside the home, women are "neglecting their maternal obligations." Beyond ignoring men's responsibilities, this discourse deflects attention from the fact that violence and unemployment are a failure of government.[6]

The contradictions between the vision and the reality of being a woman not only affect the situation and subjectivity of women but cause a crisis in the images men have of themselves. The reason for this is that the changes in women's situations often lead them both to become fuller citizens and to develop gender consciousness. The fact that women acquire and manage their own resources troubles many men, especially in cases in which a woman's income is greater than that of her partner or in which the woman has decided on separation. For many men the stereotypical self-image of the *macho* makes it difficult to accept roles that are inferior either objectively or symbolically to those of their mates. It is not uncommon in this situation for men to direct their aggression against their wives and children. Men's insecurity under these circumstances is often the cause of abandonment, divorce, and murder.

One symptom of the breakdown in traditional families and the increase in women's responsibilities and work outside of the home is the large and growing percentage of households headed by women, almost 40 percent in 2005. This one figure brings together the employment crisis, the absence of fathers in the lives of children, and the redefinition of feminine roles. At the same time, changes in women's economic situation, while they may increase individual women's possibilities of self-determination, do not thereby lead to the elimination of subordinate gender and class status. The reason for this is that the cultural and economic contexts in which these changes are occurring are not yet themselves changing. These contexts are deeply embedded in our individual and social ways of being (what Bourdieu [1999] calls *habitus*), and altering them will involve a more profound transformation.

Meanwhile, in addition to the economic distress of the middle class and the poor, there is the fact that the peasant model of production is breaking down, forcing a wave of rural workers to migrate to the United States. Several factors have contributed to this, almost all of them related to the implementation of neoliberal policies. The privatization of communal lands (*propiedad social*), which became possible only with the changes to Article 27 of the Constitution in 1992, has been promoted in recent years through the Programa de Certificación Agraria (Agrarian Certification Program— PROCEDE), particularly in the north and central regions of the country, where large tracts of arable land have been urbanized or rented for agro-industrial production. In addition to defining boundaries and dividing the land of each *ejido* or community, PROCEDE has permitted placing individual titles for plots in the names of family heads, mostly men. Women have in general been excluded despite the fact that most of them work the land and that under the ejido regimen the plots were considered family property.

Nationally, women with personal rights to land constituted only 16.31 percent of holders of ejido and communal land in 2001 (INEGI, 2001). Most were widows who were holding the land until their eldest sons, heirs to the title, came of age. The women recognized by PROCEDE, however, are even fewer. According to the 2005 *Registro Agrario Nacional* (2005), in Chiapas, for example, between January 1993 and May 2005, women held land rights in only 14.25 percent of the communal units and 11.74 percent of the ejidos. In all, barely 0.7 percent of communal landowners and 3.4 percent of ejido owners are women.

Despite the fact that they have no rights as titleholders, in general women manage family plots when their husbands migrate. This of course adds to their burdens, because even though they may hire others to help work the land, they remain responsible for cultivating and harvesting it. Even worse, many migrants sell their family plots to pay for their travel and the services of a "coyote" to get them to the United States. Women and children in these cases are even more dependent on men's remittances, which are, of course, always at risk as men are captured and expelled from the United States, lose their lives in the attempt to cross the border, or after months or years of absence start new families in the "States." With migrants now tending to stay two years or more in the United States, wives left behind essentially become single mothers, which places great stress on them and their children (Bartra, 2005).[7]

Finally, privatization has extended to public services. Reduction in health services is felt in the quality of life of most Mexicans and is statistically detectable in, for instance, the relative increase in maternal and infant mortality (UNDP, 2005). Given lack of resources and prenatal care, population growth, which continues to be high in rural sectors (3.6 percent), occurs at the expense of women's health, evidenced by their rapid aging and high morbidity rates. Public education has also suffered, and even public higher education has ever fewer resources for scientific and technological development.

## Violence and Ungovernability

The economic crisis has given rise to various types of social violence. One of these arises from the existence of guerrillas whose movements have repeatedly been violently repressed. The massacre that most tragically illustrates this official violence occurred in 1997 in Acteal, Chiapas, where a paramilitary force trained by the army attacked a group of more than 50 people, most of them women and children, suspected of supporting the Zapatistas. Refugees from surrounding hamlets, the victims were trapped and murdered in a Catholic chapel. After the slaughter, the assassins mocked the symbols of maternity by hacking the women's breasts with machetes and extracting the fetuses from those who were pregnant (Olivera and Cárdenas, 1998).

Beyond Chiapas, terror is also the objective of the army's permanent militarization of Guerrero and Oaxaca, typically in close coordination with state police. The destruction of villages, cornfields, and harvests, as well as harassment, the threat of sexual violence, jailings, disappearances, and the killing of men and women—all almost always unpunished—have served to generate and perpetuate a climate of fear. In the face of such terror, thousands of campesinos have fled their land; poverty, illness, and intrafamilial violence have increased; and women have seen their freedom of movement curtailed (SIPAZ, 2005). But, surprisingly, official violence has also stimulated women as well as men to defend their villages, even blocking the army's entrance to their communities with their bodies on occasion, as recently happened in Xo'yep, Chiapas (Speed, 2000). Counterinsurgency strategies have also taken the form of development programs competing for adherents with the organized resistance groups, predictably leading to internal divisions and confrontations within communities.

Meanwhile, so-called organized social violence has also become a crisis for the government despite the significant expenditure to combat it. Much is spent, for instance, in fighting the drug cartels, which in recent years have been at war among themselves over distribution zones and control of points of entry into the United States. Thousands of deaths have resulted. Narcocorruption is so great that official security structures have had to be continually replaced as gang members penetrate or bribe the police. Recently (September 2005) several top police officials, including the federal director of Public Security, died in a suspicious helicopter crash that many in the media and the public believe to have been caused by drug gangs. Some researchers and journalists now believe that Mexico has become like Colombia in the sense that the narcos have practically become a parallel power. President Fox and the government have tried to conceal the extent of the violence, but it has surpassed all their efforts. Indeed, the murders of women that first attracted attention to femicide as a national problem were those of Ciudad Juárez, which many journalists and activists believe may be related to the powerful drug cartels along the U.S.-Mexican border.

The proliferation of violent youth gangs is also associated with poverty, unemployment, narco-trafficking, and the lack of prospects for young people. Such gangs have become a permanent threat to young women in particular, especially on the borders and in the larger urban centers. The increase in rapes, robberies, and kidnappings puts young women at constant risk, with very little institutional protection. Misogyny is a recurrent trait of the gangs' violations of women's human rights. In Chiapas, for example, the state with the second-highest rate of murders of women after Chihuahua, many of the bodies found exhibit the marking "MST" or just "S" carved somewhere on the body as a terrifying insignia of the border gang Mara Salvatrucha.

In recent years, one of the pretexts for direct U.S. intervention in Mexico has been the struggle against insecurity and violence, which always employs violent means in return. President Fox was recently pressured to broaden the scope of Mexico's own border patrols and accept a program of joint activity with U.S. officers in the border areas of Chihuahua, Sonora, and Tamaulipas. However, in addition to the serious crime problems that were used to justify these actions, these are also the crossing points for undocumented migrants, men and women who are almost as often victims of institutional crime as of offenses committed by common criminals.

The last element that contributes to insecurity and impunity throughout the country is a nonfunctional justice system. NGOs and government institutions alike report that murders of women, wherever they occur, are rarely treated with professionalism by prosecutors and judges. Not only are most cases inadequately investigated and documented, but the justice system's treatment of the families affected is truly inhuman (Lagarde, 2005). While punishing those who commit these murders might not stop them from occurring, it might serve as a deterrent.

The justice system's deficiencies in this regard have forced us to recognize that no one is even sure of the number of murders in Mexico in general. This recognition has led Congress to establish the Special Commission on Femicide, chaired by the feminist Representative Marcela Lagarde. Over the past several months this commission has brought together a significant number of feminists from around the country to conduct an investigation in the 11 states with the highest incidence of murders of women. The results, along with proposals for public policies to resolve the problem, are expected by the end of 2005 (for preliminary data, see Comisión Especial, 2005). The problem is so deep, however, that in order to make progress the women of Mexico need to participate in building a different world, one without violence, sexism, or oppression, and to do that we must struggle against the neoliberal system that has invaded our lives.

---

## Questions

1. What are neoliberal policies, and how are they changing Mexican economy and society, according to the author?

2. How is this disruption related to violence against women?

---

## Notes

1. Gender violence against women is considered here to be any act directed at the feminine sex that may result in injury or physical, sexual, or psychological suffering, including threats of such acts, coercion, or arbitrary deprivation of liberty either in public or in private life. These acts constitute violence even when their origin lies in custom or the personal characteristics of those who commit them (Feministas de Chiapas, 2004).

2. More than 8 million Mexican migrants work in the United States and, despite the existing salary discrimination, send remittances to Mexico that will approach US$20 billion in 2005 (Bartra, 2005).

3. The report suggests that one of the reasons that neoliberalism has had less success than expected in Mexico is that the last three governments lowered trade barriers too quickly.

4. On a national level in 2000, 11.7 percent of women 15 and older had no education. A little more than 50 percent of women had some schooling, but only 9.4 percent had managed to get higher education. The poorest states had much lower rates. For example, in Chiapas 28 percent of the women have had no education, and only 4.5 percent have had higher education (INEGI, 2005).

5. Such discrimination strongly affects peasant and indigenous women in particular. In Chiapas, for example, many indigenous women make craft products that they may sell directly to consumers but more typically sell through middlemen who retail them in tourist markets in Mexico or even abroad. Although there are some cooperatives that export in the solidarity market, most artisans barely recover their investment in materials, much less the value of their labor.

6. See the conclusions of the Congreso Mundial de la Familia, held in Mexico City in 2004 with government sponsorship (*La Jornada*, February 4, 2004).

7. See the articles in this issue by Delgado Wise, Ruiz, and Barkin for more on the causes and effects of the changes in the rural economy.

## References

Bartra, Armando. 2005 "Cuando los hijos se van: Dilapidando el 'bono demográfico.'" *Masiosare: Suplemento de La Jornada*, no. 402, August 4.

Boltvinik, Julio. 2000 "Debate, desigualdad y pobreza." *La Jornada*, April 28.

Boltvinik, Julio. 2005 "Aumentó la pobreza en la actual administración." *La Jornada*, September 18.

Boltvinik, Julio and E. Hernández Laos. 2000 *Pobreza y distribución del ingreso en México*. Mexico City: Siglo XXI.

Bourdieu, Pierre. 1999 *Razones prácticas: Sobre la teoría de la acción*. Barcelona: Ed. Anagrama.

CEDAW (Convention on the Elimination of All Forms of Discrimination against Women). 2005 *Informe de México*. New York: United Nations. http://www.un.org/womenwatch/daw/cedaw/cedaw32/CEDAW-C-2005-OP.8-MEXICO-S.pdf.

Comisión Especial sobre los Feminicidios en la República Mexicana. 2005 "*Documentos para la investigación, elaborados por el Comité Científico, Congreso de la Unión*." MS, Mexico City.

Feministas de Chiapas. 2004 "Posicionamiento contra la violencia en SCLC." San Cristóbal: Centro de Derechos de la Mujer/Mujer Centroamericana/Kinal/Mujeres Independientes.

González, Roberto and Rosa Vargas. 2005 "Baja pobreza rural, pero crece la desigualdad." *La Jornada*, August 25.

INEGI (Instituto Nacional de Estadística, Geografía e Informática). 2001 *Propiedades sociales y ejidatarios, según disposición de parcelas y sexo: VIII Censo Ejidal, Resumen Nacional por Entidad*. Aguascalientes, Mexico.

INEGI. 2005 *Encuesta nacional de ocupación y empleo 2005*. Aguascalientes.

Lagarde, Marcela. 2005 *Por la vida y la libertad de las mujeres: Primer informe sustantivo de las actividades de la Comisión Especial para Conocer y Dar Seguimiento a las Investigaciones Relacionadas con los Feminicidios en la República Mexicana y a la Procuración de Justicia Vinculada*. Mexico City: Cámara de Diputados, Congreso de la Unión, LIX Legislatura.

OAS (Organization of American States). 2005 *Objetivos del desarrollo del milenio: Una mirada desde América Latina y el Caribe*. Mexico City: Comisión Económica para América y el Caribe.

Olivera, Mercedes and Guadalupe Cárdenas. 1998 "Violencia estructural hacia las mujeres," in *Reclamo de las mujeres ante la violencia, la impunidad y la guerra*. San Cristóbal.

Registro Agrario Nacional. 2005 *Documentos y superficie certificada y/o titulada del 01/01/2005 al 18/05/05*. Tuxtla Gutiérrez.

SIPAZ. 2005 "Guerrero: Un mosaico de esperanza sobre un muro de impunidad." *Informe SIPAZ* 10 (2).

Speed, Shannon. 2000 "Mujeres indígenas y resistencia de género a raiz de Acteal: Las acciones dicen más que las palabras," in Mercedes Olivera (ed.), *Identidades indígenas y género*. Tuxtla Gutiérrez: Facultad de Ciencias Sociales, Universidad Autónoma de Chiapas.

UN (United Nations). 1979 *Declaration on the elimination of violence against women*. General Assembly Resolution no. 48/104. Geneva.

UN 2003 *Diagnóstico sobre la situación de los derechos humanos en México*. Mexico City.

UNDP (United Nations Development Program). 2005 *Informe sobre el desarrollo humano*. New York.

Urías, Tania. 2005 "El Salvador: Las mujeres también son víctimas." http://www.elsalvador.com/hablemos/2005.

---

*Source*: From Olivera, Mercedes (2006). Violencia Femicida: Violence Against Women and Mexico's Structural Crisis. *Latin American Perspectives* Vol. 33, No. 2. Reprinted with permission from Sage Publications, Inc.

# CHAPTER 11

## How One Company Brought Hope to the Poor

Marco Visscher

Bangladesh is a country beset with deep poverty and massive unemployment. It would not seem a good place to market cell phones, especially to the poor. Yet cell phones have become one example of unusual business opportunities that can empower low-income people with new sources of information, opportunity, and income.

The battle against poverty has gained a surprisingly effective ally: business. By treating the poor like clients and consumers, they are accepted into the global economy. As a result, they are ultimately given the chance to prosper. . . .

She had never talked on the telephone before she bought her first Nokia. How is it possible, she must have thought four years ago, to talk to someone who is somewhere else using this tiny little thing. . . . That same mobile telephone has become Anju Monwara Begum's constant companion. It goes where she goes.

Except just now. A neighbor is using her cell phone to find out how her family in Sri Lanka is doing in the aftermath of the tsunami.

But hang on a second. This is Bangladesh, just about the poorest country in the world. We're standing here on the muddy sand paths of Kalampur, a village with a population of 2,000 families—mostly farmers—50 kilometers (31 miles) outside the capital Dhaka. Have these people also been overtaken by the modern creed that you have to be reachable anywhere, anytime?

No, that's not it. Begum is simply earning money. She is actually a walking telephone booth, making her phone available to other villagers. When her neighbor has finished with her call, Begum will look to see how much she owes. She charges the villagers the market rate: 6 taka, around 7 euro cents (9 cents U.S.), a minute for a domestic call, half that for calls made within the district

or even less during off-peak hours. Begum pays half this amount to the telephone company. The difference is her income: around 200 takas, or 2.5 euros ($3.20 U.S.), a day, which is at least twice the average income in Bangladesh, and comparable to some office jobs in the city.

The country currently has around 100,000 women like Anju Monwara Begum spread throughout 50,000 villages out of its total of 68,000, which has helped open access to the outside world for some 100 million Bangladeshis. She took out a loan from Grameen Bank, the world's first and largest microcredit bank, which she used to buy the mobile telephone that has hooked up her village to the rest of the world. It means, for example, that people can boost their earning potential because they now have access to information that was previously difficult to come by.

Combating poverty with mobile telephones. Has any large telecom company in Europe considered raising used mobile phones for the poor people in Bangladesh? No. This radical idea is an example of a company that saw an opportunity to make a profit—for its shareholders yes, but also for the country.

Begum and the other women are like billboards for GrameenPhone, the country's largest mobile telecom company, founded in 1996. GrameenPhone is an unprecedented success story. In Bangladesh, a fixed telephone line is an uncommon luxury only afforded to an elite few in cities. The company had expected to have around 70,000 subscribers by 2002, but already had 100,000 two years earlier in 2000. It reached the one million mark in 2003. Today, it has some 2.5 million subscribers around the country.

Until the end of last year, GrameenPhone's success has required an investment of 230 million euros ($300 million U.S.). In 2001, the company reported its first profit back of 22 million euros ($29 million U.S.) on a turnover of 77 million euro ($100 million U.S.). Since then, the company's profitability has steadily improved. By 2003 the company had booked a net profit of 58 million euros ($75 million U.S.) and currently has 62 percent of the Bangladeshi mobile phone market.

GrameenPhone was not the first and is not the only mobile telephone provider operating in a poor country, but it is the first and—so far—the only one offering such large-scale service outside the cities. And this is noteworthy, because the telephone companies in developing countries are often in the hands of the government and serve only the urban elite. But this company's motto is that good business and good development can go well hand in hand.

GrameenPhone is not your typical exploiter of cheap labor in the developing world. For example, the company offers free health care and sports facilities to its 1,000-odd employees. By Bangladeshi standards, "revolutionary" is the only accurate word to describe its parental leave policies, the opportunities for women and the degree of staff input in decision-making. Moreover, a portion of the profits is invested in public initiatives to enhance people's lives, such as hiring day laborers to work cleaning up and beautifying the median strips of highways.

Who in heaven's name came up with the crazy idea that it's profitable to operate a mobile telephone company in this land of poverty, hunger and natural disasters? Enter Iqbal Quadir, born and raised in Bangladesh until he left to study in the United States and is now a fellow at Harvard University where he taught graduate classes on development the last three years. He worked in New York for a company that manages money for major investors until one day, back in 1993, when the computer network went down. He couldn't work all day and thought back to a day when, as a 13-year-old boy, he had walked from his village to another one to get medicines only to discover they were out of stock. And this was another such lost day. Then . . . the brainwave of his life hit him . . . .

If he could have known as a boy that the medicines were not available, he could have spent his day more productively. If he just could have found out before walking all that way, he could have spent the day studying. The young Quadir came from a wealthy family that had temporarily fled the commotion in the city during the 1971 War of Independence. But there are 130 million people living in his small country, the vast majority of whom struggle to survive every day. If they waste their day walking to the doctor, it means they can't work in the rice fields, or milk the cow—in short, that they can't earn money.

The lives of poor people are full of inconvenience associated with isolation and a lack of information. Farmers, for example, sell their products to an unscrupulous middleman who cheats them with an unreasonably low price, when a simple telephone call would have enabled them to find out what the market prices are or what prices the competitors are offering. . . .

It was 1994. Bangladesh had the lowest number of telephones per capita in the world: one phone per 300 inhabitants, with a significant chance that the one they had didn't work. Anyone living in the city who applied for a phone would have no grounds to complain if he got it within a year. Back then, mobile telephones were only seen in the most industrialized countries and even there, you paid a lot of money for one. What Chowdhury was trying to say was that he didn't have a lot of faith in Quadir's idea. And he was by no means the only one.

But Iqbal Quadir knew that a telephone call was definitely going to be cheaper than the value people lose by not being able to connect with others. Wasted time is a huge cost for everyone and poor people should not waste time, he believed—time is at least one resource they have the same amount of everyday as rich people do. In addition, Quadir knew a thing or two of what, back then, was referred to as the "new economy." One: the costs of software and hardware decrease as volume rises. Two: the value of a product increases when greater numbers of people use it. After all, the more people who have a phone, the more there are who can be called. Quadir foresaw spectacular price declines—and was proven right. Now you can buy a mobile telephone for 50 euros ($65 U.S.). . . .

Quadir had set his sights on a successful company. He discovered that Bangladesh's government was planning to issue licenses for mobile telephony—probably because the government civil servants underestimated its potential and because the World Bank had refused to extend a loan to Bangladesh government for this sector.

The next step was to find a Western telecom company, a partner Quadir needed to realize his crazy plans. Thanks to an investment from Josh Mailman—a New York businessman and the founder of the Social Venture Network, which encourages companies with socially and ecologically progressive goals—Quadir set up Gonofone Development, whose only aim was to achieve what ultimately became known under the name GrameenPhone. Quadir traveled all over the world looking for support for his business plan. After many rejections, he discovered the ideal partner in Norway: Telenor, the country's largest telephone service provider, which was then a state-owned company. At one time, the Norwegian government started a development program in Bangladesh to lay a 1,800-kilometer fiber optic cable network along the country's railway tracks. This was a good place to start in building a network of mobile transmission towers as well. . . .

While Quadir was trying to convince a foreign telephone company, he looked for a second partner for the distribution of the phones. He was drawn to Grameen Bank who knew village life in Bangladesh like no other as it issues small loans to landless villagers throughout the country. This commercial bank is internationally renowned, as is its founder Muhammad Yunus, the visionary whose microcredit model has been imitated in over 100 countries since the 1970s and whose service record impressed Tormod Hermansen.

Initially, Quadir found Grameen disinterested. We're a bank, we provide a service, why would we want to get involved in the telephone business? The cooperation only got off the ground when the idea emerged to issue loans to current, reliable customers who would then use the mobile telephones to earn money in their village as an income generating enterprise. This "telephone lady"—Grameen Bank's experience is that women are better able than men to repay their loans—would get a 50 percent discount on the airtime tariff. With the money she earned she could repay the bank, perhaps in as little as a year. She could run her own small business, be independent, and, thanks to her income, increase her status in her own family and in society. This is because every villager would be dependent on her to use the phone: not an insignificant detail in a culture in which social standing is reserved for men. . . .

To help form a partnership with Telenor, Grameen Bank established Grameen Telecom. This non-profit arm of the bank was given the responsibility of purchasing calling minutes in bulk, handling administrative processing and collecting on calls made by all the owners of the Village Phone, as the program in the villages was dubbed. This saves money for GrameenPhone, which now sends out a single phone bill for its 100,000 Village Phone customers. While these women only represent a marginal proportion of the company's total customer base (4 percent), the telephones are used much more often than those of the average subscriber in the city and calls are more often placed to family abroad. As a result, these telephone ladies account for 25 percent of GrameenPhone's monthly turnover now. . . .

The first telephone call made via GrameenPhone on 26 March 1997 involved the former prime ministers of Bangladesh and Norway, Sheikh Hasina and Thorbjørn Jagland, as a symbol of the unique cooperation between the two countries. After the statesmen had verified that it was 32 degrees Celsius in Dhaka and the same in Norway, except below freezing, they hung up.

And then, ring, ring, the mobile telephone rang in the office of Prime Minister Hasina. Laily Begum, a resident of Patira just outside Dhaka, was on the line. Her husband was a day laborer and she had turned to Grameen Bank for help a few years earlier. From her first loan of 4,500 taka, around 50 euros ($65 U.S.), she bought a cow. She was able to repay what she owed with the proceeds from the milk. Three loans and three repayments later, Begum had pulled her family out of poverty. The bank had now approached her to become the country's first telephone lady. Her children, who are at school, would help her figure out the instructions.

Eight years later Laily Begum, together with her husband, now owns five different types of shops and a restaurant. They earn a whopping 13,000 taka (165 euros or $212 U.S.) a month, a fortune that has given them status in their community. Begum has even become nationally renowned; she is living proof that information technology can free a family from poverty. Begum is now in talks with Grameen Telecom about setting up an internet service in her village.

But the figures also tell another story. Laily Begum initially earned double what she is now making with her telephone. But now that there is competition—from other telephone ladies and other companies—her earnings fell quickly. In other villages, competition has led to similar drops in income. In Kalampur, Anju Monwara Begum, who was the first in this village, has already trained three competitors to use the cell phone, only to have one of them scour the village actively—and successfully—to poach her customers.

Will the success of mobile telephones end in a downward spiral? No, according to Abdul-Muyeed Chowdhury, director of BRAC, Bangladesh's largest and widely respected development organization. "More telephones means that more people will be more accessible," he calculates while sitting in his office sandwiched between Dhaka's fanciest neighborhood and a slum. "More competition means lower prices and that means that more people can call, and therefore have more opportunities to make economically useful phone calls." In other words, the decrease in income of a few telephone service owners is cancelled out by the increasing economic activity and growing wealth of many others. . . .

After years in which a doubling of the number of subscribers and profits was not unusual, a new era appears to be dawning for GrameenPhone. While it has always been able to remain well ahead of the competition in the Bangladeshi mobile telephone market—including Aktel, CityCell and Sheba—a formidable competitor is waiting in the wings. BTTB, the state-owned fixed-line monopoly, has started a mobile phone project, Teletalk, which is expected to enter the market anytime now. And a number of other companies have also purchased mobile telephone licenses in an effort to take their share of the spoils.

How will GrameenPhone respond? By offering new, innovative high-quality services, says a self-confident Aas who refrains from offering details. The price war will likely be concentrated in the bigger cities among customers with the most money to spend—customers that GrameenPhone has faithfully served for years. The area of concern is mainly the urban middle class, which will be tempted by new, affordable telephones that are not equipped to accept SIM cards from other telephone companies. . . .

Is a solution to combating poverty being developed here in Bangladesh—often called the "world's basket case"? Is business the right instrument? For Quadir, the answer is yes. He thinks part of the problem lies in the way poor countries are looked at. "In the West we establish companies to solve our problems," he says. "When they are not appropriate, we establish non-profits. But in developing countries people refer to the same type of organizations as non-governmental organizations. Why is that? Perhaps because in developing countries they think the government is the most suitable body to tackle a problem in an organized way. But look at the wealthy countries. There, entrepreneurs, investors, employees, consumers—collectively, citizens—have the power to require their governments to be supportive of their productivity. But in poor countries, the state has too much power. The best way to change that is to strengthen the hands of the citizens. GrameenPhone's handsets are doing that, literally."

The four mobile telephones in the village of Kalampur won't suddenly make the village a hotbed of economic growth. But they can help individuals to move ahead and it's likely that this effect will eventually benefit the community as a whole. But don't forget that Bangladesh's per capita yearly income is 280 euros ($360 U.S.): the shape of the economy only allows small steps to be made in the right direction.

Ibrahim Muhammad is someone who is taking these steps. Anju Monwara Begum's telephone in Kalampur offers him the prospect of a better price for the fertilizer he sells. "I always went to the same market, just down the road, to sell my fertilizer," the 22-year-old Muhammad explains. "But sometimes the prices are a little higher in a village that is further away. Now I always call first to find out what the prices are in the area." For him, the difference may be no more than a few extra takas in profit, but it means that Muhammad has a little more money after deducting his costs for the phone calls and longer trip to the market.

When we go to say good-bye, Muhammad wants me to know he doesn't just use the phone for business. He falls silent for a moment and looks down. "Sometimes, when my girlfriend is at her parent's house a couple of villages away," he says, "I'll call her too."

---

## Questions

1. Why would a company want to try to sell cell phones to the poor, and why would the poor want to buy them?

2. How have cell phones brought new opportunities? Could this model apply to other products and businesses?

---

*Source:* How One Company Brought Hope to the Poor. Marco Visscher. *Ode Magazine.* April 2005. Reprinted by permission.

# PART III

# EDUCATION

Education can be a means to a better life, but only if it is widely available and affordable and if it is the doorway to new opportunities. Education is also more than just a means to a better livelihood; it can also open the door to new awareness and help us understand the changing world around us.

Article 12 examines the right of everyone to an education and the complexities inherent in this simple-sounding idea. Article 13 contends that globalization requires a new kind of education, and that global learning is vital for all of us. Dreams of education can be dashed, however, when not supported. Article 14 looks at the challenges a young black man faces in realizing his educational and vocational dreams in South Africa.

12. The Right to Education in a Globalized World.
    Ronald Lindahl. *Journal of Studies in International Education*. Vol. 10, No. 1. Spring 2006.

13. Breaking Down Notions of Us and Them: Answering Globalization With Global Learning.
    Angelo Carfagna. *FDU Magazine*. Spring 2006.

14. A Would-Be Pilot, Hitting Turbulence on the Ground.
    Michael Wines. *The New York Times*. April 30, 2005.

# CHAPTER 12

## The Right to Education in a Globalized World

Ronald Lindahl

Is education a basic human right? United Nations declarations have repeatedly said it is. But how much education and of what kind and for whom? This article highlights the idea of global human rights and what that means for our understanding of education. It also shows the complexities of getting quality education to everyone and debates the nature of education itself.

Taken separately, both components of the title of this article, the "right to education" and "globalized world" are highly controversial topics. The interaction of these two issues produces even more complex issues. Is education truly a universal right? What implications does globalization have for education and, more specifically, for the right to education? These are the primary questions addressed in this article. There are obviously no definitive answers to many of these questions; instead, the author's aim is to raise and clarify issues that should be at the heart of ongoing policy discussions around the world.

## Is Education a Universal Right?

On the surface, this seems to be an easy question with which to begin this discussion; however, such a perspective is deceptive. Human rights are generally attributed to two sources: *natural* rights and *legal* rights. The concept of natural rights derives from ancient and medieval religious beliefs that people should organize their society in accordance with the rules of nature (i.e., God; *The Columbia Encyclopedia,* 2001). During the 1600s, philosophers expanded these beliefs to espouse that individuals have natural rights of which they cannot be deprived by individuals or societies (Hobbes, 1651/1982; Locke, 1690/1986). Hasnas (1995) noted that in all these

writings about natural rights, the rights delineated were *negative* rights, or rights of autonomy for the right holder. There were no *positive* rights, rights that entitle the right holder to be provided something by another individual or society, as would be the case of a right to education. He did observe, however, that a more contemporary, albeit less accepted, view avowed that natural rights also include some positive rights, a view promoted by utilitarian philosopher Jeremy Bentham (1789/1988).

Because societies recognize the inherent merit of providing specific positive rights (e.g., welfare, health care, education), the arguments regarding natural rights can be put to rest by declaring them to be legal rights. Although most human rights declarations and covenants approach education as a natural right, they seek to define and codify it as a legal right.

Article 26 of the United Nations' (UN) 1948 *Universal Declaration of Human Rights* states, "Everyone has the right to education," and most nations are signatories to this Declaration. The concept of education as a fundamental legal right is further supported by the UN's 1959 *Convention on the Rights of the Child,* the seventh principle of which states, "The child is entitled to receive education, which shall be free and compulsory, at least in the elementary stages." Article 13, Clause 2 of the UN's (1966) *International Covenant on Economic, Social, and Cultural Rights* extends this commitment to education as a fundamental right, including the universal right to a free and compulsory primary education, secondary and technical education available and accessible to all, with a progressive movement toward this being free to all and higher education being accessible to all "on the basis of capacity," with a progressive movement toward being free as well. Most recently, the September 2000 *United Nations Millennium Declaration* commits all 189 UN member states to achieving the eight Millennium Development Goals by 2015. Among these are goals for expanding and improving early childhood care and education, ensuring that all children have access to a free and compulsory primary education of good quality, achieving a 50% reduction in levels of adult literacy (especially among women), achieving gender equality in primary and secondary education, and improving all aspects of the quality of education (World Education Forum, 2000).

However, substantial evidence exists that despite these covenants and declarations, education is not universally recognized as a legal right. In his 1944 State of the Union Address, President Franklin D. Roosevelt recognized that education was not a right in the United States and called on the American public to accept it as such, more through national commitment than through legal means (Sunstein, 2004, p. B9). More than half a century later, Beach and Lindahl (2000) documented that education still does not enjoy legal status as a right in many states within the United States nor has that nation ratified the *International Covenant on Economic, Social, and Cultural Rights* (UN, 1966). Similarly, other nations, including China, have refused to sign the *International Covenant on the Rights of the Child* (Hallak, 1999) and other documents attempting to define education as a legal right.

With a worldwide estimate of 125 million children not enrolled in school, the majority of whom are girls, and with 40% of African children receiving no education (Global Campaign for Education, 2003, p. 1), it is also evident that education is not a de facto right. Statistics from the UN Statistics Division (2004a) show that in 1999, only 27.3% of age-eligible Angolan children were enrolled in primary school, with similarly low figures for Madagascar (35.1%), Rwanda (39.1%), and Mozambique (42.7%). Pakistan's girls-to-boys ratio, even in primary schools, was only 0.55 to 1 in 2000, followed by Yemen at a ratio of 0.60 to 1 and Chad, at 0.63 to 1. These ratios get considerably more prejudicial at the secondary and tertiary education levels, as in many other nation states (for similar findings, see Education for All, 2004).

Despite these de jure and de facto conditions arguing against the existence of a universal right to education, there may well be a general global sentiment that education, indeed, should be a universal right (Devidal, 2004; International Commission on Education for the 21st Century, 1992; Matsuura, 2002; UN Educational, Scientific, and Cultural Organization [UNESCO], 2005; World Education Forum, 2000). Implicit in this right is the principle of universal equity in relation to the right to education.

If education is considered a fundamental human right (see Spring, 2000, 2001), it is essential to recognize that it is a positive right, not merely a liberty or negative right. Devidal (2004) listed three obligations related to such positive rights:

- to not interfere with anyone's enjoyment of the right,
- to ensure that others do not interfere with anyone's enjoyment of the right, and
- to provide the necessary conditions for the enjoyment of the right

Assuming that education is, or will soon be, recognized as a human right, two questions follow: What conditions are necessary for the enjoyment of the right and who should provide these conditions? This can only be answered in context, and the current and projected future context is one of globalization.

## Globalization and the Right to Education

Globalization is generally viewed as encompassing a broad range of economic, social, cultural, and political issues (Bhagwati, 2004; Coyle, 2001; Friedman, 2000; "Globalization—the 21st Century Version," 2001; Petrella, 1996; Stiglitz, 2003) that arise from multinational markets and flows of capital, labor, goods, and information (Astiz, Wiseman, & Baker, 2002). One of the simplest, yet most useful, definitions comes from Spring (2001), who defined global flow as "a conglomeration of ideas, technology, media and money that envelops the world" (p. 8). Singh (2004) condensed the many definitions of globalization into two key concepts, "time-space compression" and "global consciousness" (p. 103). A. T. Kearney, Inc. and the Carnegie Endowment for International Peace publish an annual Globalization Index ("Measuring Globalization," 2004) based on the extent to which nations (a) are economically integrated through trade, foreign direct investment, portfolio capital flows, and investment income; (b) use the Internet, host Internet sites, and employ secure servers; (c) engage in international trade and tourism, international telephone calls, international remittances and personal transfers; and (d) hold memberships in international organizations, make personnel and financial contributions to UN Security Council missions, ratify international treaties, and engage in government transfers.

Neo-liberal critiques of globalization often view the phenomenon as a modern form of colonialism, with roots in the international actions of ancient Rome, the Spanish Conquistadores, and the British Empire (for interesting discussions of the analogy between globalization and colonialism, see "Globalization—the 21st Century Version," 2001; Verzola, 1998; see also Devidal, 2004; Hill, 2003; Martinez & Garcia, 1997; Rikowski, 2003; Woolman, 2001). The legitimacy of this analogy is debated, as is the inevitability of globalization's growing influence on the world (International Forum on Globalization, 2002). However, statistics abound similar to those cited by British Chancellor of the Exchequer Gordon Brown in his 2000 speech (see Ryan, 2000), in which he stated that in the past three decades, world trade increased 15-fold, international capital 13-fold, and foreign investment 50-fold. With statistics like these, it is little wonder that the general consensus remains that globalization may well be the most powerful force shaping the world in the present and foreseeable future. Much as education shifted significantly in countries when their paradigm moved from agrarian to industrial, the conditions necessary to satisfy the right to education will be affected by globalization.

## Defining the Right to Education in a Globalized World

Determining what conditions are necessary for the enjoyment of the right to education in a globalized world is a highly complex task. Dale (2000) posited a series of questions that can be useful in deriving an operational definition of the right to education: "Who gets taught what, how, by whom, and under what conditions and circumstances?" (p. 29). Hallak's (1999) advocacy for issues of quality, access, efficiency, equality, gender, and relevance must also be considered but can readily be subsumed under Dale's overarching framework.

### Who Gets Taught?

If one accepts education as a universal human right, the response to this question is straightforward and clear. Every human being has the right to education,

regardless of his or her circumstances. Hallak's (1999) issues of access, equality, and gender become moot.

However, this question also implies the need to define the quantity of education that satisfies the right; this is a far more complex question to answer. The expected number of years students will be engaged in formal schooling varies greatly from nation to nation. In Burkino Faso the average length of schooling is only 2.8 years; similarly, in Djibouti it is only 3.9 years. These low expectations are contrasted with 16.7 years in Finland and 16.8 in Australia (UN Statistics Division, 2004b). However, these figures refer only to the typical school-age population in those nations, which is only a portion of the people who would be affected by a universal right to education. The UN Educational, Scientific, and Cultural Organization (UNESCO) estimated that some 860 million people worldwide (20% of adults older than age 15) are illiterate, with two thirds of those being women (UNESCO, 2003). Furthermore, adult literacy rates (and definitions) vary greatly by country, with 70% of adult illiterates being concentrated in sub-Saharan Africa, South and West Asia, the Arab States, and North Africa. Burkina Faso (12.8%) and Mali (19%) showed very low adult literacy rates, especially when contrasted to Latvia, Slovakia, Slovenia, and Uruguay's rates of 99.7% (UNESCO, 2004). Education for All (2004, p. 1) provides very similar data but introduces such issues as the fact that in 30 of the 91 reporting nations, survival rates to grade 5 are less than 75% and a child in sub-Saharan Africa can only expect 0.3 years of pre-primary schooling, whereas in North America and Western Europe, this expectation rises to 2.3 years.

With the ever-increasing rate of technological, scientific, and social change in the world, perhaps the right to education must extend beyond basic literacy to lifelong learning (Trustees of Education 2000, 1997); however, no statistics are available that even attempt to measure lifelong learning and lifelong educational opportunities around the globe. This is further complicated by the recognition that much of human learning takes place outside of schools (see Howley, 2001, p. 17; Trustees of Education 2000, 1997), which makes it more difficult to plan, monitor, or measure.

Clearly, there is no consistent answer regarding the quantity of formal and informal schooling that would satisfy the right to education. However, the amount of education provided represents only a small portion of the operational definition of the right to education. It is equally, or more, important to examine what should be taught and, by inference, learned.

## What Should Be Taught?

With the shift to a knowledge-based economy and heavy reliance on technology, location, natural resources, or even military power are no longer as important as human capital (Czinkota & Kotabe, 1998; Friedman, 2000; Lindahl & Mays, 2001; Peters, 2001; Ryan, 2000; Thurow, 1996). However, human capital cannot be measured merely in terms of quantity of education; the content of that education is an essential consideration, as is the quality of that education (Education For All, 2004).

Dale (2000) laid out two competing paradigms for education in a globalized world. First, the Common World Educational Culture previews a highly homogenized educational curriculum worldwide, reflecting the economic, social, and cultural homogenization resulting from globalization. Second, the Globally Structured Agenda for Education would be based on general knowledge, skills, and dispositions required by the globalized economy, modified and complemented by local and regional cultures, circumstances, histories, politics, and needs. Of these two, the latter paradigm seems more appropriate and more probable (see Lapayese, 2003; Woolman, 2001).

Boufoy-Bastic (2002) posited that the curriculum must reflect the sociocultural values of society and may be either humanistic, individually sensitive, or economically driven, with a social development orientation. Similarly, Woolman (2001) proposed that schooling must be diversified to reflect every aspect of the culture, social context, values, and differing life contexts, such as rural versus urban life. Like thoughts were presented by Lapayese (2003, p. 493) in her review of three recent books on global citizenship, especially with regard to the inherent tensions between local and global dynamics. It would also appear obvious that education must vary to some extent among individuals; for example, learning, physical, or emotional disabilities may well result in different educational needs.

Within Dale's (2000) Globally Structured Agenda for Education paradigm, the International Commission on Education for the 21st Century recognized that for education to be at the heart of both the individual and the community in a globalized world, it must teach knowledge, skills, and dispositions in four basic areas:

- learning to live together in the global village,
- learning to know (including both broad, general knowledge and in-depth knowledge in a few specific areas),

- learning to do (including preparing for the unforeseeable future), and
- learning to be (including such areas as aesthetics, responsibility for community goals, reasoning, and creativity).

This is not particularly far from the curriculum proposed by Hanvey (1975), who began his vision of a globalized curriculum with the need for *perspective consciousness,* which he defined as individuals recognizing that their personal views and interpretations are not necessarily shared by others around the world. He complemented this with a call for four specific domains to be included in educational curricula: (a) state-of-the-planet awareness, (b) cross-cultural awareness, (c) knowledge of global dynamics, and (d) awareness of human choices. Considerable overlap exists between Hanvey's ideas and those of Case (1993), who advocated a curriculum incorporating both the existing knowledge, skill, and disposition base as well as (a) both universal and cultural values and practices, (b) global interconnections, (c) present worldwide concerns and conditions, (d) origins and past patterns of worldwide affairs, and (e) alternative future directions in worldwide affairs.

As Heidi Hayes Jacobs noted, "There's a need for both *timeless* curriculum content and *timely* content" (Perkins-Gough, 2003–2004, p. 13). Jacobs went on to discuss the need for the curriculum to include such things as citizenship education, national heritage, global studies, ethical considerations in science, environmental planning, earth science, space science, the life sciences, physical science, a language-oriented math curriculum, media literacy and criticism, and the arts. This list was not intended to be exhaustive, but it does reflect the complexity of the issue of what content areas constitute the definition of the right to education.

Pigozzi (2004) extended this discussion even more precisely and prescriptively, stating that education, as a right, must include the knowledge, skills, values, and processes that constitute primary education, including such areas as reading and writing; mathematics; basic science, including natural science, social science, and life skills; rights and responsibilities; numeracy and literacy; social skills; life skills; core (global) values such as respect, honesty, and responsibility; an understanding of the right to privacy; and conflict resolution.

Hallak (1999) presented a very similar curriculum but included such issues as cultural diversity, knowledge of oneself and one's rights, international concerns and experiences beyond national boundaries, how to live together, economics, international law, human rights, and sustainable development. The International Commission on Education for the 21st Century (1992) added such curricular areas as how to search for peace, democracy, alleviation of poverty, population control, and health. Peters (2001) noted that learning related to the economics of abundance, de-territorialization of the state, importance of local knowledge, and information technology are essential in a globalized world.

However, many difficult decisions must be made in relation to curriculum if the right to education is truly to be satisfied in a globalized world. The International Commission on Education for the 21st Century (1992) described some of the many tensions that will underlie such a curriculum. Among these, they listed the following:

- global versus local,
- universal versus individual,
- traditional versus modern,
- long-term versus short-term,
- competition versus equality of opportunity,
- expansion of knowledge versus human beings' capacity to absorb that knowledge, and
- spiritual versus material.

Lindahl, Obaki, and Zhang (2003) explored the theme of inherent tensions between local and global dynamics and probed curriculum issues on an even more specific level, arguing for the need for education in a globalized world to preserve unique social and cultural heritages and traditional knowledge systems and languages (also see Spring, 2004) while offering everyone a relatively standardized curriculum of knowledge, skills, and dispositions very much in alignment with those discussed above (also see Braslavsky, 2000).

## How Should Students Be Taught?

Dale's (2000) guiding question on curriculum is not merely about what is taught, it also is concerned with how students are being taught and how they are learning. Again, the social and economic environment of globalization has a distinct influence in this area. Economic and social environments are moving from the industrial age emphasis on deference to a need for workers who show personal responsibility and creativity, basic skills, the ability to be self-starting, quick thinking, the ability to work with others, strong verbal skills, good problem-solving and decision-making skills, the ability to go

beyond their own expertise, and the ability to learn something in one situation and apply it in another that is significantly different (The 21st Century Learning Initiative, 1998; Trustees of Education 2000, 1997).

Hargreaves (2000) highlighted a very similar series of abilities that students need to function effectively in a knowledge-management-based world. These included the following:

- meta-cognitive skills;
- the ability to access, select, and evaluate knowledge;
- the ability to develop and apply various forms of intelligence;
- the ability to work and learn effectively and in teams;
- the ability to create, transpose, and transfer knowledge;
- the ability to cope with ambiguous situations and problems;
- the ability to learn to redesign themselves and their careers; and
- the ability to choose and fashion relevant education and training.

Pigozzi (2004) commented that for the right to education to exist, children must be in environments free from mental and physical violence, must be free to express themselves openly and participate fully, and must be given dignity. Their education must be child-centered and appropriate to their developmental levels and linked to their own experiences.

The implications for education are both obvious and challenging. Many instructional/learning paradigms that were effective and efficient for transmitting the knowledge, skills, and dispositions needed for industrial economies will not produce these desired, or needed, results. In some ways, education for a globalized world may more resemble the old African forms of education, which focused on social responsibility, work orientation, morality, and spiritual values and which integrated character building, intellectual training, manual activities, and physical education through student involvement, observation, imitation, and participation (Woolman, 2001). Clearly, the use of emerging information and communication technology can help play a role in shifting the teaching/ learning paradigm, but the majority of the change will probably occur through realignment of teacher education programs, redesign of instructional materials, and reconceptualization of what teaching/learning methods are most appropriate.

## Under What Conditions and Circumstances Should Education Be Provided?

To this point, discussion in the professional literature has barely considered the issue of quality as it relates to the right to education. Yet while visiting schools in Cartagena, Colombia recently, the author of this article quickly noted vastly different levels of student engagement in learning between those attending expensive private schools and those in the public or even much-less-expensive private schools. Was it because only the expensive private schools provided air conditioning to shelter students from the sweltering heat? Was it because those students in the expensive private schools had access to nutritious meals that were unavailable to their less fortunate counterparts? Was it because the expensive private schools employed teachers with degrees from top national and international universities, often including graduate degrees, whereas their counterparts in poorer schools had far less education? Similarly, while visiting schools in the highlands of central Ecuador, this author was aghast at the high rates of teacher absenteeism, which province-level officials attributed to the extremely low levels of teacher compensation in the region. Class sizes of more than 60 students are not uncommon in some schools in India and Latin America, yet many states in the United States have enforced limits of 20 or less. Schools in Cuba often lack such basics as lights, paper, duplicating equipment, and textbooks (Lindahl & Mays, 2001), a far cry from the technology and educational-stimulus-rich classrooms of most of Europe and North America. In Nepal, poor households devote an impressive 29% of their non-food expenditure to schooling, yet many of these children do not learn to read, write, or do basic sums because of the poor quality of the schools in which they are enrolled (Global Campaign for Education, 2002a, p. 4). In short, what quality levels are implicit in a universal right to education and what resources are essential to providing those quality levels? To what extent can or should these vary from one educational system, or culture, to another, yet still fulfill the right to education?

Yin (2003) discussed the need for quality assurance in education. It seems apparent that there is not yet a global consensus on the qualities of inputs and processes needed for the right to education to be realized. Embedded in the definition of that right to education are such questions as: How should teacher quality be measured, and how important is it to the provision of the right

to education? What teacher preparation is minimally necessary? What physical resources are essential in the operational definition of the right to education? Reaching universal consensus on the answers to these questions promises to be a difficult task, for education has long been dependent on such contextual variables as culture, time frame, and socioeconomic conditions (Farrell & Papagiannis, 2002). In part, the answers to these questions depend heavily on the last of Dale's (2000) guiding questions: Who should provide the right to education?

## By Whom Should Education Be Provided in a Globalized World?

Rousseau's (1662/1968) concept of a social contract would assign this responsibility to a government on the basis that people willingly surrendered part of their liberty rights to better secure their other rights, which would by implication include the right to education. Worldwide, in 1998 (latest data reported), nations spent an average of 4.5% of their gross domestic product (GDP) on education, although the least-developed nations spent only an average of 2.9% of their GDP on education. As a percentage of total public expenditures, education ranged from a low of 7.1% in Zambia to 33.1% in Senegal (Roberts, 2003). These percentages relate only to relative effort to provide education; the disparities between the per capita GDP (and per pupil educational expenditures) in industrialized nations and developing nations are enormous.

However, governments are not the only sponsors of education; there are also many private funds used to purchase education worldwide. For example, in Jamaica in 1999 (latest data available), 2.8% of the GDP was spent from private funds on primary and secondary education, with a similar high level of private funding found in Paraguay (2.7%). In India, even slum dwellers are investing their meager funds into private education (Waldman, 2003). Virtually no private funds were spent on primary or secondary education in Sweden, Finland, or Norway (World Bank, 2004), yet these three nations' levels of education are among the highest in the world because of high levels of government expenditures on education. For higher education in 1998 (latest data available), 2.07% of the Republic of Korea's GDP was in private education expenditure, with other high levels shown in such countries as Thailand (1.74%) and the United States (1.33%) (World Bank, 2004). Again, these percentages merely show patterns of private versus public provision of education; disparities in per capita GDP greatly distort the relationship of percentages of GDP and per-pupil expenditures among nations.

The role of nation-states, including the provision of education, is changing considerably. As of 1995, the World Bank has advocated the decentralization of education, shifting responsibility from the public to the private sector (Desmond, 2002; World Bank, 1995). The World Bank assumes that developing nations can cover approximately 80% of their nation's educational costs, but Education for All (2004) projected that developing nations will be able to cover only a small portion of these costs. Thurow (2000) contended that governments are becoming platform builders that invest in infrastructure, including education, to allow their citizens to participate in the globalizing world. Davies and Hentschke (2002) found that, in many cases, the role of government is changing from being a direct provider of education to one of regulator of the education industry. Both Verzola (1998) and the People's Conference Against Globalization (2002) decried the trend for governments to yield responsibilities to private enterprises. Medovoi (2002) agreed, noting that nation-states are finding themselves losing control and less able to regulate living standards and the welfare of their citizens.

For the past decade, the World Bank has called for developing nations to cover 80% of the costs of providing a free, universal primary education, although this may not be a feasible target economically (Global Campaign for Education, 2002b, p. 12). The World Bank recognizes that many governments cannot provide the necessary funding for education and suggests that the private sector may have to become the primary provider; the implications of this, however, are not positive for a universal right to education. To date, the globalization movement has increased economic inequities rather than reduced them; privatization might introduce yet further inequities into the fulfillment of a universal right to education.

Although the Global Campaign for Education (2002b) challenges, in the ideal, governments with the provision of a free, quality education to every child, it also calls for international donors to provide a minimum of $5 billion per year to enhance educational access and opportunities in poorer nations. It calls for rich nations and international institutions to increase their aid to education in poor nations to at least 10% of their total aid budgets (p. 3). The Global Campaign for Education (2003, pp. 30–31) also investigated the percentage of gross national income that the 22 richest nations in the world (based on 2001 economic data) gave to poorer nations for basic education. Luxembourg was the most generous, giving 0.3%, but the United States gave only 0.2% and Greece gave only 0.1%. By way of comparison, the United States' donation of $196 million to basic education pales in comparison with the $167 billion it spent for occupation and rebuilding in Iraq and Afghanistan during 2003 (Public Broadcasting Service, 2003). Ongoing patterns like this prompted the Center for Global Development and Foreign Policy Journal (2004) to conclude, "In the end, no wealthy country lives up to its potential to help poor countries. Generosity and leadership remain in short supply" (p. 54). Recognizably, private giving and aid from nongovernmental organizations often exceed formal governmental aid, as in the recent case of aid to tsunami victims in Indonesia, Sri Lanka, and Thailand; however, such sources are too inconsistent to be counted on for guaranteeing the right to education worldwide.

There is little argument in the professional knowledge base that worldwide education is essential to both the production and consumption aspects of globalization and for people to be able to make informed choices affecting their lives (Global Campaign for Education, 2002b). However, the exigencies and conditions of globalization may occasion a shift from the traditional pattern of government-provided education supplemented by small percentages of wealthy families purchasing private education for their children.

In many sectors, globalization has already brought about a shift in power and institutional patterns (see Waks, 2003), with multinational corporations gaining considerably more influence and with the nation-states losing many of their traditional powers and roles. To illustrate this shift in power and the concomitant need for highly educated populations across national borders, of the 100 largest economies in the world, 51 are corporations (based on a comparison of corporate sales and country GDPs) (Anderson & Cavanagh, 2000, p. 1). The 200 largest corporations' sales are greater than the combined economies of all nations, except the largest 10 (Anderson & Cavanagh, 2000, p. 2). There are more than 63,000 transnational corporations worldwide, with 690,000 foreign affiliates (CorpWatch, 2001, p. 1). Ninety-nine of the 100 largest transnational corporations are from the industrialized nations (Anderson & Cavanagh, 2000, p. 1). At the same time, many nation-states have ceased to exist or have become radically fragmented. Thurow (2000) noted that the former Yugoslavia has become five different states, whereas the former Union of Soviet Socialist Republics has split into 15, Czechoslovakia has split into two nations, Spain may well split into three, and with 10,000 ethnic groups in Africa constantly vying for power, nation-states may not be as stable as they are typically viewed to be.

Education has not been totally immune to these shifts in power and responsibility. Hill (2003) discussed the marketization of school systems in Britain, the United States, Australia, and New Zealand, viewing this process as ideological and policy offensives by neo-liberal capital. Hatcher (2001, 2002) expressed similar concern that, in Britain, private national and transnational companies own, run, and govern schools (see also Hatcher & Hirtt, 1999). Hill interpreted these patterns in the provision of schooling as leading to a loss of national and global equity, a loss of democracy, and a loss of critical thought.

Both Rikowski (2003) and Devidal (2004) voiced great concern that the General Agreement on Trade in Services (GATS), which arose from the 1986 to 1994 Uruguay Round of talks and which is binding for the 144 members of the World Trade Organization, is facilitating the transformation of education into a huge globalized market. Both offered examples from the increasing cross-border supply of education, the consumption of education abroad, direct foreign investment in education, and the growing international penetration of educational service providers. Rikowski assessed the European Union as having no restrictions for all privately funded educational services, many of which are used throughout the EU's public schools. Woolman (2001) vividly summed up his concerns on this pattern: "Dependency on textbooks, curriculum designs, teachers, and priorities from external sources that cannot be translated into locally relevant forms of education should be abandoned" (p. 43).

Outsourcing of jobs to other nations has recently become a major concern in relation to globalization. The U.S. Department of Labor and Forrester Research, Inc. projected that in the United States, by 2015, 3.3 million such jobs will be handled by workers in other nations, representing more than $136 billion of wages (and accompanying income taxes) lost to the United States (Mangan, 2004, p. A13). However, as Drezner (2004, p. 26) noted, during this same time period, and largely attributable to globalization, 22 million new jobs will be added to the U.S. economy, representing a large net gain in jobs and income. The implications of outsourcing for the right to education are significant. With the outsourcing of many midlevel clerical jobs (e.g., call centers and billing centers) to places such as India and the Philippines, many U.S. workers must retrain and gain skills in areas in which they can be more wage competitive. Education systems that used to prepare people for this level of employment cannot assume that these jobs will ever return; an entirely different set of skills and dispositions may need to be developed in the future. A decade ago, the *maquiladora* manufacturing plants of northern Mexico provided abundant labor in clothing manufacturing and electronic assembly plants; today, many of those jobs have migrated to Asia, where wages are even lower than in northern Mexico. Again, education and training must prepare Asians for these new jobs and prepare Mexicans with the skills and dispositions for new types of employment.

Beyond outsourcing, the emigration and immigration of educated workers is another issue linking globalization and education and influencing governments' willingness to provide that education. For example, Hong (2003, p. 1) calculated that 70% of South Korea's adults in their 20s and 30s wanted to emigrate to another country; 42.3% of these said that their motivation was to provide better education for their children and 31.4% cited current unemployment problems in South Korea. South Korea is by no means unique in this regard; in developing nations, the lure of economic and educational opportunities available in more industrialized nations is very strong. Despite a burgeoning worldwide demand for Filipino nurses, nursing programs are being forced to close in great numbers in the Philippines because of a shortage of qualified instructors, for these instructors have migrated to countries such as the United States and Canada, where they are readily employable as nurses at salary levels far above their salaries as instructors in the Philippines. Even physicians and dentists are leaving the Philippines to take jobs abroad as nurses to further their own financial prospects and opportunities for emigration (Overland, 2005).

In short, there are several potential providers of education in a globalized world. Governments have traditionally been the primary providers of education to their own citizenry. With people beginning to work in global economies and live in a globalized culture, perhaps the traditional pattern is no longer the most feasible or appropriate. Multinational corporations hold far more wealth than most governments and depend on educated workers and consumers worldwide. Despite their vested interest (and possibly ability) to provide for a universal right to education, they presently do not view this as a corporate responsibility, although an increasing number of corporations are moving into the educational arena for profit motives. In most nations, families have subsidized governmental expenditures on education, but with income disparities rising as globalization occurs, relying on familial wealth to provide education would seem to negate any concept of equity in education as a universal right. Asking governments of rich nations to share their wealth with poorer nations has not proven to be a politically feasible means of providing the right to education worldwide, and relying on private charity or nongovernmental institutions appears too uncertain to guarantee the right either.

## Conclusion

Does education exist as a fundamental human right? The argument of this article is that, in many nations, it does not, either legally or de facto. There is, however, an increasing general global discernment that education should be a human right.

Even for those who claim that education is a human right (e.g., the signatories to the 1948 Declaration of Human Rights; the 1958 Convention on the Rights of the Child; the 1966 International Covenant on Economic, Social, and Cultural Rights; and the 2000 UN Millennium Declaration), defining that right has proved to be an elusive, if not impossible, task. Several of the later documents have adopted pragmatic approaches to the right to education, calling for progressively free, universal primary education. Is this truly a fulfillment of a universal right to education? What jobs and futures are available today to people with only primary education? Can sufficient skills be learned in such a short span of time for education to become anything more than a sorting mechanism for the labor force (see Carnoy & Levin, 1985)? What resources and other quality-control issues are inherent in the right to education? What curriculum is needed to fulfill that right?

The era of globalization in which the world is currently embroiled further complicates the issue of a universal right to education. How universal is that right? Does it transcend national borders, much as today's economy often transcends those borders? Do citizens, governments, or other organizations within a nation-state have any obligation to provide for education beyond the borders of that state? Does a globalized economy imply a globalized corporate responsibility for guaranteeing the positive right to education? What role do national and ethnic cultures play in operationally defining the right to education versus the role of a globalized economy and culture? What curriculum is necessary for education to be an enabling right that provides access to jobs, security, and other fundamental rights?

In short, this article raises many more important questions than it answers. How will these questions be answered? Perhaps a clue can be found in the words of Eleanor Roosevelt, who asked in a 1958 speech on human rights, "Where, after all, do universal human rights begin?" She answered her own question, "In small places, close to home, so close and so small that they cannot be seen on maps of the world" (quoted in Hoff-Wilson & Lightman, 1984, p. xix). The time has come for the right to education to become a focus of discussions and actions in these "small places" across the globe.

### Questions

1. Do you believe that education is a basic human right? If so, how much education?

2. Whose responsibility is it to provide this education: national governments, local communities, parents, or the world community? What arguments are offered in the article?

## References

Anderson, A., & Cavanagh, J. (2000, December 4). *Top 200: The rise of corporate global power.* Retrieved February 1, 2005, from http://www.corpwatch.org/issues/PID.jsp?articleid=377

Astiz, M. F., Wiseman, A. W., & Baker, D. P. (2002). Slouching towards decentralization: Consequences of globalization for curricular control in national education systems. *Comparative Education Review, 46*(1), 66–88.

Beach, R. H., & Lindahl, R. A. (2000). Can there be a right to education in the United States? *Equity and Excellence in Education, 33*(2), 5–12.

Bentham, J. (1988). *The principles of morals and legislation.* Amherst, NY: Prometheus Books. (Original work published 1789)

Bhagwati, J. (2004). *In defense of globalization.* Oxford, UK: Oxford University Press.

Boufoy-Bastic, B. (2002, March 25–28). *Slow cultural approach versus radical materialistic change: Making the school curriculum responsive to globalization in small island countries.* Paper presented at the International Conference on Problems and Prospects of Education in Developing Countries, Bridgetown, Barbados. (ERIC Document Reproduction Service No. ED465680)

Braslavsky, C. (2000). The education system of the nineteenth century: The direction, trends and tensions of curriculum reforms in the twenty-first century. In *Capacity-building for curriculum specialists in East and South-East Asia* (pp. 6–10). Geneva, Switzerland: International Bureau of Education. (ERIC Document Reproduction Service No. ED469231)

Carnoy, M., & Levin, H. M. (1985). *Schooling and work in the democratic state.* Palo Alto, CA: Stanford University Press.

Case, R. (1993). Key elements of a global perspective. *Social Education, 57,* 320.

Center for Global Development and Foreign Policy Journal. (2004, May/June). Commitment to Development Index. *Foreign Policy,* pp. 46–56.

*The Columbia Encyclopedia* (6th ed.). (2001). Natural rights. Retrieved February 1, 2005, from http://www.bartleby.com/65/na/natrlrig.html

CorpWatch. (2001, March 22). *Corporate globalization fact sheet.* Retrieved February 1, 2005, from http://www.corpwatch.org/issues/PID.jsp?articleid=378

Coyle, D. (2001). *Paradoxes of prosperity: Why the new capitalism benefits all.* Mason, OH: Thomson Texere.

Czinkota, M. R., & Kotabe, M. (1998). Emerging issues. In M. R. Czinkota & M. Kotabe (Eds.), *Trends in international business: Critical perspectives* (pp. 269–270). Cambridge, MA: Blackwell Business.

Dale, R. (2000, Fall). Globalization and education: Demonstrating a "common world educational culture" or locating a "globally structured educational agenda"? A comparative approach. *Educational Theory, 50*(4), 21–43.

Davies, B., & Hentschke, G. C. (2002, June). Changing resource and organizational patterns: The challenge of resourcing education in the 21st century. *Journal of Educational Change, 3*(2), 135–159.

Desmond, C. (2002, April 1–5). *The politics of privatization and decentralization in global school reform: The value of equity claims for neoliberalism at the World Bank and in El Salvador.* Paper presented at the annual meeting of the American Educational Research Association, New Orleans, LA. (ERIC Document Reproduction Service No. ED468518)

Devidal, P. (2004, September). Trading away human rights? The GATS and the right to education: A legal perspective. *Journal for Critical Education Policy Studies, 2*(2). Retrieved February 1, 2005, from http://www.jceps.com/print.pho?articleID=28

Drezner, D. (2004, May/June). The outsourcing bogeyman. *Foreign Affairs, 83*(3), 22–34.

Education For All Global Monitoring Team. (2004). *Education for all, 2005: The quality imperative.* Paris: UN Educational, Scientific, and Cultural Organization (UNESCO).

Farrell, R. V., & Papagiannis, G. (2002, March 6–9). *Education, globalization, and sustainable futures: Struggles over educational aims and purposes in a period of environmental and ecological challenge.* Paper presented at the Annual Comparative and International Education Society meeting, Orlando, FL. (ERIC Document Reproduction Service No. ED470963)

Friedman, T. L. (2000). *The lexus and the olive tree.* New York: Anchor.

Global Campaign for Education. (2002a, May). *A quality education for all: Priority actions for governments, donors, and civil society* (A briefing paper). Retrieved February 1, 2005, from http://www.campaignforeducation.org

Global Campaign for Education. (2002b, August). *Education now to build a better future* (A briefing paper for the Johannesburg World Summit). Retrieved February 1, 2005, from http://www.campaignforeducation.org

Global Campaign for Education. (2003, November). *Must try harder: A "school report" on 22 rich countries' aid to basic education in developing countries.* Retrieved February 1, 2005, from http://www.campaignforeducation.org

Globalization—the 21st century version of colonialism. (2001, February 6). *The Daily Monitor (Addis Ababa).* Retrieved February 6, 2001, from http://allafrica.com/stories/200102060080.html

Hallak, J. (1999, November). *Globalization, human rights, and education.* Paris: UNESCO, International Institute for Educational Planning.

Hanvey, R. G. (1975). *An attainable global perspective.* New York: The Center for War and Peace Studies. (ERIC Document Reproduction Service No. ED 116993)

Hargreaves, D. (2000). *Knowledge management in the learning society.* Paris: Organisation for Economic Co-operation and Development.

Hasnas, J. (1995). Are there derivative natural rights? *Public Affairs Quarterly, 9*, 215–226.

Hatcher, R. (2001). Getting down to the business: Schooling in the globalized economy. *Education and Social Justice, 3*(2), 45–59.

Hatcher, R. (2002). *The business of education: How business agendas drive Labour policies for schools.* London: Socialist Education Association.

Hatcher, R., & Hirtt, N. (1999). The business agenda behind Labour's education policy. In M. Allen et al. (Eds.), *Business, business, business: New Labour's education policy.* Brighton, UK: Institute for Education Policy Studies.

Hill, D. (2003, March). Global neoliberalism, the deformation of education and resistance. *Journal for Critical Education Policy Studies, 1*(1). Retrieved February 1, 2005, from http://www.jceps.com/index.php?pageID=article&articleID=7

Hobbes, T. (1982). *Leviathan.* Baltimore, MD: Penguin. (Original work published 1651)

Hoff-Wilson, J., & Lightman, M. (1984). *Without precedent: The life and career of Eleanor Roosevelt.* Bloomington: Indiana University Press.

Hong, S. (2003, September 18). Majority of 20s, 30s wish to emigrate. *The Korea Herald.* Retrieved February 1, 2005, from http://yaleglobal.yale.edu/display.article?id

Howley, C. (2001). *School administration and globalization.* Lanham, MD: ERIC Document Reproduction Service. (ERIC Document Reproduction Service No. ED461176)

International Commission on Education for the 21st Century. (1992). *Learning: The treasure within.* Retrieved February 1, 2005, from http://www.unesco.org/delors/

International Forum on Globalization. (2002). *Alternatives to economic globalization: A better world is possible.* San Francisco: Berrett-Koehler.

Lapayese, Y. V. (2003). Toward a critical global citizenship education. *Comparative Education Review, 47*(4), 493–501.

Lindahl, R. A., & Mays, R. O. (2001). The challenges of globalization for Cuba and its educational system. *Educational Planning, 13*(2), 34–54.

Lindahl, R. A., Obaki, S., & Zhang, S. (2003, Spring). Curriculum planning for a globalized world. *International Journal of Educational Reform, 12*(2), 159–169.

Locke, J. (1986). *The second treatise on civil government.* Amherst, NY: Prometheus Books. (Original work published 1690)

Mangan, K. S. (2004, May 14). This political hot potato is a course in demand. *The Chronicle of Higher Education,* pp. A12-A13.

Martinez, E., & Garcia, A. (1997, January 1). *What is neoliberalism? A brief definition for activists.* Retrieved February 1, 2005, from http://www.corpwatch.org/issues/PID.jsp?articleid=376

Matsuura, K. (2002, February 9). Education, an essential human right. *Le Figaro.* Retrieved February 1, 2005, from http://portal.unesco.org/educaiton/en/ev.php_URL_ID=197766&URL_DO=DO

Measuring globalization: Economic reversals, forward momentum. (2004, March/April). *Foreign Policy,* pp. 54–69.

Medovoi, L. (2002). Globalization as narrative and its three critiques. *The Review of Education, Pedagogy, and Cultural Studies, 24,* 63–75.

Overland, M. A. (2005, January 7). A nursing crisis in the Philippines. *The Chronicle of Higher Education, 51*(18), A46-A48.

People's Conference Against Globalization. (2002). Delhi Declaration and decisions and action plan. *The Review of Education, Pedagogy, and Cultural Studies, 24,* 193–207.

Perkins-Gough, D. (2003, December–2004, January). Creating a timely curriculum: A conversation with Heidi Hayes Jacobs. *Educational Leadership, 61*(4), 12–17.

Peters, M. (2001). National education policy constructions of the "knowledge economy": Towards a critique. *Journal of Educational Enquiry, 2*(1), 1–22.

Petrella, R. (1996). Globalization and internationalization: The dynamics of the emerging world order. In R. Boyer & D. Drache (Eds.), *States against markets: The limits of globalization* (pp. 62–83). London: Routledge.

Pigozzi, M. J. (2004). *Implications of the Convention of the Rights of the Child for Education Activities Supported by UNICEF.* New York: UN International Children's Educational Fund. Retrieved June 2, 2004, from http://www.unicef.org/teachers/learner/crc_impl.htm

Public Broadcasting Service. (2003, November 3). Senate approves $87 billion for Iraq, Afghanistan efforts. *OnLine NewsHour.* Retrieved February 1, 2005, from http://www.pbs.org/new shour/updates/supplemental_11-03-03.html

Rikowski, G. (2003, March). Schools and the GATS enigma. *Journal of Critical Education Policy Studies, 1*(1). Retrieved February 1, 2005, from http://www.jceps.com/index.php?pageID=article &article ID=8

Roberts, J. (2003, April). *Poverty reduction outcomes in education and health: Public expenditure and aid.* London: Overseas Development Institute.

Rousseau, J.-J. (1968). *The social contract* (Maurice Cranston, Trans.). New York: Penguin. (Original work published 1662)

Ryan, T. (2000, September). *The new economy's impact on learning.* Bath, UK: 21st Century Learning Initiative. Retrieved February 1, 2005, from http://www.21learn.org/acti/treconomics.html

Singh, P. (2004). Globalization and education. *Educational Theory, 54*(1), 103–115.

Spring, J. (2000). *The universal right to education: Justification, definition, and guidelines.* Mahwah, NJ: Lawrence Erlbaum.

Spring, J. (2001). *Globalization and education rights: An intercivilizational analysis.* Mahwah, NJ: Lawrence Erlbaum.

Spring, J. (2004). *How educational ideologies are shaping global society: Intergovernmental organizations, NGOs, and the decline of the nation-state.* Mahwah, NJ: Lawrence Erlbaum.

Stiglitz, J. E. (2003). *Globalization and its discontents.* New York: Norton.

Sunstein, C. R. (2004, June 11). We need to reclaim the second Bill of Rights. *The Chronicle of Higher Education,* pp. B9–B10.

Thurow, L. C. (1996). *The future of capitalism: How today's economic forces will shape tomorrow's world.* New York: William Morrow.

Thurow, L. C. (2000, July). Globalization: The product of a knowledge-based economy. *Annals of the American Academy of Political & Social Science, 570,* 19–32.

Trustees of Education 2000. (1997, May). *A proposal to Prime Minister Tony Blair.* Bath, UK: 21st Century Learning Initiative. Retrieved February 1, 2005, from http//www.21learn.org/publ/tonyblair.html

The 21st Century Learning Initiative. (1998, November). *The strategic and resource implications of a new model of learning: A policy paper.* Bath, UK: Author. Retrieved February 1, 2005, from http://www.21learn.org/publ/ publ.html

United Nations (UN). (1948, December 10). *Universal Declaration of Human Rights* (G.A. Res. 217A [III]). New York: Author. Retrieved February 1, 2005, from http://www.un.org/cyber schoolbus/humanrights/resources/universal.asp

UN. (1959, December 10). *Convention on the Rights of the Child* (G.A. Res. 1386 [XIV]). New York: Author. Retrieved February 1, 2005, from http://www.un.org/cyberschoolbus/humanrights/ resources/child.asp

UN. (1966). *The International Covenant on Economic, Social, and Cultural Rights* (G.A. Res. 2200A, 21 UN GAOR, Supp. [No. 16] 49, UN Doc. A/ 6316). New York: Author. Retrieved February 1, 2005, from http://www1.umn.edu/humanrts/instree/b2esc. htm

United Nations Educational, Scientific, and Cultural Organization (UNESCO). (2003, September 8). *International Literacy Day: Good news in four high population countries* (Press Release No. 2003–55). Paris: Author. Retrieved February 1, 2005, from http://portal.unesco.org/en/ev.php

UNESCO. (2004, March). *Literacy and non-formal education section: Youth (15–24) and Adult (15+) literacy rates by country and by gender for 2000–2004.* Paris: Author. Retrieved February 1, 2005, from www.uis.unesco.org/TEMPLATE/html/Exceltables/ education/View_Table_Literacy_04March04 .xls

UNESCO. (2005). *Mandate of the International Commission on Education for the 21st Century.* Paris: Author. Retrieved February 1, 2005, from http://www.unesco.org/delors/mandate.html

UN Statistics Division. (2004a). *Millennium indicators.* New York: Author. Retrieved February 1, 2005, from http://unstats.un. org/unsd/mi/mi_series_results.asp?rowId=589

UN Statistics Division. (2004b). *Indicators on education.* New York: Author. Retrieved February 1, 2005, from http://unstats.un.org /unsd/demographic/social/education.htm

Verzola, R. (1998, February 2–6). *Globalization: The third wave.* Paper presented at the international conference, "Colonialism to Globalization: Five Centuries after Vasco de Gama," New Delhi, India. Retrieved June 2, 2004, from http://www.corpwatch.org/ issues/PID.jsp?articleid=1569

Waks, L. J. (2003). How globalization can cause fundamental curriculum change: An American perspective. *Journal of Educational Change, 4*(4), 383–418.

Waldman, A. (2003, November 15). India's poor bet precious sums on private schools. *The New York Times.* Retrieved November 17, 2003, from http://www.nytimes.com/2003/11/15/international /asia/15INDI.html

Woolman, D. C. (2001). Educational reconstruction and post-colonial curriculum development: A comparative study of four African countries (Special 2001 Congress Issue). *International Education Journal, 2*(5), 27–46. Retrieved February 1, 2005, from http://www.flinders.edu.au/education/iej

World Bank. (1995, March 31). *Priorities and strategies for education: A World Bank sector review* (Report No. 14461). Washington, DC: Author.

World Bank. (2004). *World Bank education statistics database.* Washington, DC: Author. Retrieved February 1, 2005, from http://www1.worldbank.org/ education/edstats/

World Education Forum. (2000). *The Dakar framework for action: Education for All: Meeting our collective commitments.* Paris: UNESCO.

Yin, C. C. (2003). Quality assurance in education: Internal, interface, and future. *Quality Assurance in Education: An International Perspective, 11*(4), 202–214.

*Source:* The Right to Education in a Globalized World. Ronald Lindahl. *Journal of Studies in International Education.* Vol. 10, No. 1. Spring 2006. Reprinted by permission of Sage Publications.

# CHAPTER 13

## Breaking Down Notions of Us and Them

### *Answering Globalization With Global Learning*

Angelo Carfagna

Globalization can bring people together in new ways. It can also lead to misunderstanding, confusion, and hostility. The author argues that the best response to this challenge is global learning that breaks down the barriers, real or imagined, that divide people.

If, as Fairleigh Dickinson University (FDU) President J. Michael Adams observed, "Globalization is altering every dimension of our lives," the question becomes, "What should we do differently?" Adams asked, "Particularly for those of us concerned about educating the next generation of citizens and leaders, what do we need to do to develop the necessary skills, insights and understandings?"

That question aptly set the stage for a two-day conference on "Developing Global Competencies in Higher Education," held at Fairleigh Dickinson's College at Florham April 4 and 5. Designed to foster a dialogue among educators about global education and global citizenship, the program was sponsored by the University's Office of Interdisciplinary, Distributed and Global Learning and the Internationalization Collaborative of the American Council on Education (ACE)—and supported by a grant from the AT&T Foundation.

Speakers included Adams, current and former United Nations ambassadors; a sociology professor who has written two books on globalization; a leading international advocate from ACE; a veteran study-abroad administrator; key members of FDU's global education efforts, particularly faculty involved in using technology to bring the world to the classroom; and members of the University's innovative Global Virtual Faculty program.

More than 75 college faculty and administrators from East Coast universities, including 18 FDU faculty and staff, attended the conference.

## A Need for Global Citizenship

"Responding to globalization means adopting a global view," Adams suggested. "It means becoming a global citizen. With globalization has come a greater realization that our fates are now linked. A world view must be adopted with a sense of and sensitivity to today's interconnections, to our shared destinies and to the magnificent differences among us."

Describing the expansion of the global economy and the global challenges that necessitate cooperation, Adams said, "Becoming a citizen of the world is an economic, practical and moral imperative. Our only hope for peace in this world is through education and global citizenship."

Making a similar case was Ahmad Kamal, president of The Ambassador's Club at the United Nations and former ambassador of Pakistan to the United Nations. Pointing out that globalization is part of a much longer historical process, he said, "Globalization is all about a shrinking world. It is about acting on a stage that is a single home rather than divided into nationalities."

Kamal, who was instrumental in developing the University's U.N. Pathways Lecture Series and who teaches several courses at FDU, said the most important first step to meeting global challenges was to improve Americans' knowledge of geography. His second suggestion was to avoid what he called the "disease of self-centrism." He explained, "Each of us believes, 'I am the center of the world.' But there is much more of the world outside of you and it is your duty to search for what the rest of the world can bring you. Global education is an exciting invitation to explore this rich world."

Fairleigh Dickinson University Assistant Professor of Philosophy and Political Science Jason Scorza pointed out that, while some are skeptical of the notion of global citizenship, it's an entirely conceivable concept. "Citizenship at its root means being a full and equal member of a community, with all the rights and responsibilities of a full and equal member, and hopefully, the capabilities and skills necessary to both fulfill one's responsibilities and enjoy one's rights. From this perspective, we can imagine ourselves as citizens of any number of different kinds of communities—including the global community."

President Adams, who has inspired a mission of providing a global education at FDU, was asked about what specifics should be introduced to help transform a learning environment. He answered, "It's less about making particular changes than it is about how you view what you're doing. You need to view education as a process and take advantage of the resources you have, but the real issue is how you view what you're trying to do. The specifics will flow from that new mindset."

Madeleine Green, vice president and director of ACE's Center for Institutional and International Initiatives, said she has learned that, to provide successful international initiatives, leadership plays a strong role and the "faculty make it happen." She further pointed out that institutions must address why they are doing this, and resources must be identified and aligned. Also, supporting structures are needed, and partnerships must be created with businesses and institutions abroad. It's not a quick process, she added, instead it's "a long-distance run."

Unfortunately, according to Green, "there is more rhetoric than reality" on today's college campuses. She encouraged those in the audience to start the conversation on their campuses. Noting that recent surveys reveal public support for and student interest in international programs, she said "we need to figure out how to tap it."

## Defining the Skills

What should global education instill and what skills are needed by global citizens? Among those tackling the questions was Scott Sernau, an associate professor and chair of the department of sociology and anthropology at Indiana University, South Bend. Sernau is the author of, among other books, *Bound: Living in the Globalized World.* Echoing Adams and Kamal, Sernau framed the subject in the context of globalization. He stated that globalization has long been driven by the three Cs: commerce, control and curiosity—which reflect the three dimensions of globalization: economics, politics and culture. Despite some potential setbacks for globalization, these underlying processes "are not going away."

Sernau referred to a list of nine goals for globally competent learners developed by the American Council on International Intercultural Education. The globally competent learner, 1) is empowered by the experience of global education to help make a difference in society; 2) is committed to lifelong, global learning; 3) is aware of diversity, commonalities and interdependence; 4) recognizes the geopolitical and economic interdependence of the world; 5) appreciates the impact of other cultures on American life; 6) accepts the importance of all peoples; 7) is capable of working in diverse teams; 8) understands the nonuniversality of culture, religion and values; and 9) accepts responsibility for global citizenship.

But this is just a start, he emphasized. Educators need to provide more than just a taste of global learning. "Global education will really have arrived when it's not just a specialty course tacked onto the curriculum but when every course has global elements to it. It needs to permeate our courses."

Among other skills mentioned by Sernau are some new ones (Internet skills, how to find and assess information), some old ones (world history and geography) and some timeless skills (intercultural communication, how to communicate with those from different backgrounds and most importantly, how to listen to other perspectives).

But to fully define the skills needed, he emphasized, would require a cross-cultural dialogue. "This can't be defined by American academicians deciding what our students need to learn about the world. It has to emerge from a global conversation."

## Encouraging Study Abroad

Facility with foreign languages would be important to emphasize, suggested both Sernau and Kendall Brostuen, dean of the Institute for International Studies at Lock Haven University of Pennsylvania. Brostuen, who has overseen 28 student and faculty exchange programs in 20 countries, gave special significance to the role of study-abroad programs. "One cannot truly understand the subtleties of another culture without first having been a part of it."

He said educators should go beyond just endorsing study-abroad programs as wonderful opportunities and make it clear "that the institution itself fully expects that students will engage in an international experience."

One of the conference's keynote speakers, H.R.H. Prince Zeid Ráad Al Zeid Hussein, permanent representative of Jordan to the United Nations, went a step further and recommended students study and work in other parts of the world.

In his address, "Education in the Multilateral World," the ambassador discussed the tension between the local and the global in a globalized world. "The challenge before us, therefore, is our need to remain true to our locality yet without prejudice to our developing a broader understanding of the wider human family, and our place in it, and its place in the universe. Only, therefore, through the provision of a formal education that's both broad and specific will we succeed."

## Conclusions Reached

We return to the question of what exactly are global competencies? In concluding dialogues, breakout sessions involving all the attendees created specific reports fusing the various definitions and practices addressed during the event.

One group concluded that global competencies boiled down to the "knowledge, attitudes and skills that equip students to live and to work in a globally interdependent world and exercise the rights and responsibilities of global citizenship."

Another session broke down the essence of global competencies into the following parts:

- recognizing that you are a full member of a global community;
- understanding how your actions impact others and how others' actions impact you;
- having an attitude that is respectful of the diversity of human experience;
- being aware of the value and limitations of specific identities and being unafraid to go beyond them;
- possessing the ability to imagine and/or experience yourself in another time and space;

- and recognizing the interconnectedness of economic, social, political and environmental systems.

Among the many recommendations endorsed by the groups were having an institutional commitment to global education, thinking beyond and across disciplinary lines, empowering faculty to infuse global issues throughout the curriculum, enlarging student experiences, offering faculty incentives, using non-U.S. source material, emphasizing the importance of study abroad and international internships and using "whatever pedagogical means necessary to unglaze students' eyes."

Several challenges in the delivery of a global education were raised, including resistance from colleagues and the lack of time to prepare and incorporate global lessons into the curriculum. (For full group reports, see www.globaleducation.edu.)

## The FDU Experience

As the host institution, Fairleigh Dickinson University was able to showcase a number of its global education efforts. Its unique distance-learning initiative requires every undergraduate to take one distance-learning course per year and features Global Virtual Faculty—scholars and practitioners from around the world who engage students in online discussions about global issues. (FDU recently became one of 11 universities nationally awarded special recognition from ACE and AT&T for its use of technology as a tool for internationalization.)

Building on those experiences, Fairleigh Dickinson faculty presented "The Role of Technology in Creating Global Competencies," moderated by Jason Scorza, with Walter Cummins, professor emeritus of English; Nandita Ghosh, assistant professor of English; and Francis Ingledew, associate professor of English and comparative literature and director of special programs, University Core Program.

Scorza, who co-created two of FDU's online courses for the distance-learning initiative, cautioned that, while technology can help provide a global education, there are also dangers. "The Internet at its best can be a magnificent classroom but at its worst it's an open sewer. It misinforms as much as it educates."

Similarly, while Ingledew observed that the "Web opens up to students a quantitatively different experience from the traditional classroom," it demands significant attention, and we must guard against the illusion that the world is so easily found at our fingertips.

Walter Cummins shared with the audience examples of student online exchanges across cultures in a course, Nobel Literature, that he developed with a fellow FDU faculty member. "These kinds of exchanges are breaking down notions of us and them. They would not be possible without the technology."

Nandita Ghosh, who is teaching an online course using Global Virtual Faculty, says these scholars and practitioners "are giving me and my students a sense of interconnectedness" with the rest of the world. She adds that they challenge common assumptions and provide a real sense of the cultural differences that exist in the world.

Four GVF members (seven in total attended the conference) took their turns at giving presentations. In a session titled "Global Education Around the Globe," Nilufer Bharucha (India), Viorela Ciucur (Romania), Tomas Chuaqui (Chile) and John Lennard (United Kingdom) discussed how their countries viewed global education and their experiences with Fairleigh Dickinson's distance-learning initiative.

Ciucur said that, as her involvement deepened, she could see students' horizons expand and see them become more conscious of themselves as global citizens.

## The Dialogue Continues

Fairleigh Dickinson was the first ACE Internationalization Collaborative member to host a regional meeting exploring global learning. The collaborative is an invitational forum with approximately 45 colleges and universities committed to advancing internationalization.

"We're proud that ACE chose to partner with us and recognized us as playing a leading role in offering a global education," said Michael Sperling, associate provost for interdisciplinary, distributed and global learning. "It was a very lively couple of days, and we all learned a lot."

Sperling said the University would be active in upcoming events with the ACE Internationalization Collaborative and perhaps host another global education conference in the future. "We hope to continue to be a leader in bringing together educators who are interested in sharing ideas about global education and making it real on their campuses."

---

### Questions

1. How can globalization lead to both greater information about the world and greater hostility and misunderstanding?

2. What are the elements of global learning that can bridge such misunderstanding? What skills are needed to be global citizens?

---

*Source:* Breaking Down Notions of Us and Them: Answering Globalization with Global Learning. Angelo Carfagna. *FDU Magazine.* Spring 2003. Reprinted by permission of Fairleigh Dickinson University.

# CHAPTER 14

## A Would-Be Pilot, Hitting Turbulence on the Ground

Michael Wines

Young people have career dreams all over the world, but the obstacles to achieving those dreams can be very high. The story of James and his dream of becoming a pilot shows the many challenges encountered in pursuing an education in a poor community in South Africa.

Masjaing, South Africa—In a part of the world where so many young people never get off the ground, 17-year-old James Mokoena wants to be a pilot.

He will fly a fighter jet, but not just to wage aerial battles. Africa is full of hungry people and people sick with malaria, he said. Many of them need a James Mokoena to bring them food and medicine.

"I haven't been in a plane," he said, but dismissively. "I want to be in a plane for four, five years, and to know that I am in that plane—me. That I, James, am driving it."

He is standing outside his cement-stuccoed house, a four-room box on a dirt road in this township of about 30,000 on the Lesotho border. Inside is a single bed for him, three brothers and a sister. His mother is ill. His father never got past the sixth grade. Everything here fairly shouts that James's dream is folly.

Except James himself. Two years ago, having completed his elementary years at the township primary school, he walked the mile from Jasjaing to Fouriesburg, the far wealthier town on the other side of the highway. There, he announced that he wanted a better education than he could get at Masjaing's uninspiring local high school, from which few students ever graduate, and that he wished to enroll in the eighth grade.

"I asked him whether he realized there were school fees to be paid, and he said his father would pay them," said Irina Grice, the principal at Fouriesburg Intermediate School. "His father came, but oh, his clothes were torn, and he was very, very poor.

"But the father said, 'The child chose, and he wants to be in this school.'"

One in three of South Africa's 37 million blacks live in townships like Masjaing, slums built to keep them away from white people when they are not mining whites' coal or cleaning whites' houses. Of those township dwellers over age 15, well over half are jobless. Of those with jobs, about 6 in 10 earn less than $250 a month. The townships are economic and social sinkholes, poverty traps in a nation where the rich-poor gap is among the widest on earth.

Jeremane Mokoena—he calls himself James, he said, because he dislikes his first name—wants out of Masjaing. He wants out of the underclass that apartheid created and into the world of opportunity that apartheid's demise has opened up for other, luckier youths.

Few of his friends here—boys idling on the dusty soccer pitch and clustered on gravel street corners, clueless about how impending manhood will shut off their escape route—have the pluck for the journey James so clearly craves. For those who do try, success is rare. Failure, and consignment to a life in society's cellar, is crushing.

Slim, with a shy, if broad smile and a tendency to look away when talking, James resembles anything but a pioneer. But nobody should underestimate his grit.

His father, 44-year-old Petrus Mokoena, is James's unlikely inspiration. A gaunt man in threadbare blue coveralls and a fluorescent red jacket, he works a split shift for the Masjaing (pronounced mush-a-ENG) sanitation department, collecting trash in the predawn hours, catching some sleep, then collecting more trash in the afternoon.

For this, Mr. Mokoena earns under $300 a month. Fouriesburg Intermediate wanted $40 for tuition. Mr. Mokoena paid it. Apartheid, he said, kept him an indentured and ignorant laborer on a white-owned farm his entire youth.

"I want James to see that not to go to school is a bad thing," said Mr. Mokoena, speaking in Sotho, his only language. "I want him to speak English and to write English."

Forty dollars is no small sacrifice. Ms. Grice said she once asked James why he was doing poorly in one subject. "He said, 'I can't finish off the work before it's dark, and we don't have electricity,'" she said.

"So I said to him, 'It's possible to study by candlelight.' And he said, 'We don't have any candles.'"

It is James, the one with a shot at a future, who has become the family's center of gravity.

Petrus Mokoena passes many evenings drinking Lesotho beer. His wife MaDibeo, silent and vacant-eyed in her mysterious illness, has left a hole in the household and a gnawing fear in her children's bellies. Tiny 7-year-old Mampho and her 9-year-old brother Thabiso now demand James's attention instead of hers. So do the cleaning and cooking.

James's handsome older brother Dibeo, 19, spent four straight years in the ninth grade at Ypokaleng High, the school James escaped.

That leaves 13-year-old Joseph, as charismatic and quick-witted as James is quiet and deliberative, as perhaps his brother's closest companion.

There are girls, of course, and James said he was somewhat interested. But "if I had a girlfriend, I couldn't think as well," he said. "I don't have a girlfriend so that I can focus."

In truth, James has few close friends. Awkward and shy, he is in transit between worlds, and not really comfortable in either.

Some evenings, Mr. Mokoena frets over the cost of his son's schooling and how James, now the household's

most educated member, is moving beyond his rough-hewn father.

"My father told me that since I was in this school, I was beginning to lose my culture," James said. "That I am becoming a white person. That I don't eat with my hand; I eat with a fork."

But each weekday night for the last two years, as Mr. Mokoena left to collect trash, he took a pen with him to mark his time sheet. And when he returned about 6 a.m., just as James began to stir in his crowded bed, he gave his son the pen to use that day at school.

Then James donned his Fouriesburg uniform and walked the mile to his other world.

Rigidly Afrikaner and all-white under apartheid a decade ago, the Fouriesburg school has since become almost all black. Most white students stampeded to prep schools when apartheid ended; the current student body consists mostly of better-off blacks and a few whites who cannot afford private schooling.

James was neither. "He has the worst situation, in that the children tend to look down on him and see him as really poor," said Mick Andrew, a 67-year-old English literature teacher and the closest thing James has to a mentor.

James made a show of sloughing off their ostracism. "Most of the time, at school, I don't do things for fun," he said. "I come, I do what I have to do, and I go home."

At home, he studied. When he first came to the school, in January 2003, his grades were abysmal, in part because of his poor English. In his first term, he failed five subjects. In his second, he failed only English.

Fouriesburg classes end at the ninth grade. As the December end of term loomed last year, James made elaborate plans to enroll in the 10th grade at a private school in Tweeling, 75 miles to the north. James said his father would pay tuition. He could help, he said, by selling candy and drinks.

"I chose this school because I wanted to be far away," he said. "This place is away, but it's not far. Tweeling is far away."

But his dream exceeded his grasp: what James really needed was a scholarship, and his grades did not merit one. When the new term began in January, James attended Breda High School some 10 miles from Fouriesburg. It was the only school James could afford that would take him in.

"Very often, the bright ones can get out in some way," Mr. Andrew said. "Someone will see they have a future. James hasn't progressed very well at school, and that makes it even more difficult for him."

Ismail, another Masjaing ninth grader who was James's best friend at the Fouriesburg school, agreed. "I told him," he said, "'If you're going to be a pilot, you're going to have to study harder.'"

## Questions

1. What are the main obstacles that make it difficult for James to realize his dream?

2. What would it take for more children in James' family and community to succeed in school?

# PART IV

# CONFLICT

The face of war is changing. Old terrors lessen as new ones emerge. Our international news is so dominated by stories of conflict that at times one has a sense of nothing but a world of struggle. Increasingly the world's violent conflicts are not between countries but within countries between factions: religious, partisan, ideological, regional, and economic. Yet in an era of political globalization, civil and sectarian conflict often soon involve international intervention, sometimes from major powers such as the United States, Great Britain, or France, and often involving multinational coalitions, including forces operating under command structures such as NATO, the African Union, and the United Nations. Hope that a "new world order" following the Cold War would lead to a peace dividend have given way to fears that new violence will bring terrible new costs in lives and resources. At the same time, diplomats and peace scholars seek new ways of containing the world's tendency toward violence and of finding alternative ways of maintaining order while giving voice to the oppressed and the displaced.

Unrest is not limited to any one part of the world. Many locations in the United States, Canada, Australia, and across Western Europe have become much more diverse through new immigration. Often this process proceeds smoothly, but with new faces can come new suspicions and resentment. Article 15 looks at France's struggle to include a growing Muslim minority and the resentments over that process that led to unexpected rioting. Torture has been widely practiced by regimes around the world, but it was often seen as the domain of dictatorships and rogue states. More recently the treatment of prisoners in the so-called "war on terrorism," especially by the United States, has drawn new international concern. Article 16 examines the debates on what is acceptable to combat possible terrorism.

Article 17 looks at one of the world's long-standing troubled nations, the country of Haiti. At various times, the United States, France, and the United Nations have intervened to try to bring some form of stability and democratic government to the small, impoverished country. The article explores what is possible and what is not as the world community wonders whether and how to be involved in trouble spots. Article 18 reconsiders the idea of international security and what it means in an era of globalization. Article 19 examines one particular problem that much of the world has overlooked: the plight of people who are not international refugees, but who are displaced within their own country by war and conflict.

Common questions that thread through each of these articles are: what are basic human rights and what is the responsibility of the international community in protecting those rights?

Many countries, not the least including the United States, struggle with how to protect civil rights and liberties while still protecting citizens from threats both internal and external. The question of human rights and civil liberties in times of war is a very old one, but new types of conflict have demanded that the global community consider new dilemmas of rights, peace, and security.

15. France: The Riots and the Republic.
    Graham Murray. *Race and Class*, Vol. 47, No. 2. 2006.

16. Torture: The Struggle Over a Peremptory Norm in a Counter-Terrorist Era.
    Rosemary Foot. *International Relations*, Vol. 20, No. 2. 2006.

17. Peace and Democracy for Haiti: A UN Mission Impossible?
    Sebastian von Einsiedel and David M. Malone. *International Relations*, Vol. 20, No. 2. 2006.

18. Globalization and the Study of International Security.
    Victor D. Cha. *Journal of Peace Research*, Vol. 37, No. 3. 2000.

19. The Biggest Failure: A New Approach to Help the World's Internally Displaced People.
    Ray Wilkinson. *Refugees,* Vol. 4, No. 141. 2006.

# CHAPTER 15

## France

### *The Riots and the Republic*

Graham Murray

Many countries in Europe are struggling with how to integrate new immigrants into their society. Often the newcomers have very different social and religious attitudes and traditions from the majority in the host country. They may also face resentment and hostility, and discrimination that hides under claims of equal opportunity. These problems erupted into riots in urban France that shocked the nation.

It is France's Hurricane Katrina. The recent uprising (November 2005) of disenchanted youths that swept across France left parts of the country damaged and shocked. The government saw fit to invoke a state of emergency law, allowing the imposition of curfews, and deployed thousands of police reservists and paramilitary CRS in a desperate endeavor to quell the violence. Meanwhile, the European Union has agreed to a €50 million aid package to help France repair the damage caused by the rebellions. But perhaps more poignantly—and this is where the Katrina analogy is apposite—the events exposed the misery of the country's ethnic minority communities and the inherent racism that prevails throughout this land of *liberté, égalité, fraternité*. Many Francophiles (and Francophobes for that matter) have expressed consternation and shock that the birthplace of *la Déclaration universelle des droits de l'homme* (the universal declaration of the rights of man) has become the setting of a rebellion by an underclass of have-nots.

Be warned. Members of Britain's ethnic minority communities arriving in France should put back their watches by about thirty years. For those too young to have experienced the blatant racism of the 1970s, be prepared for a shock; for the rest, brace yourselves for some reminders of the past. This is a country where a foreign name on a CV will seriously undermine your chances of getting a job; where landlords still instruct estate agents to find white tenants; where *pâtissiers* sell chocolate-covered cakes called *tête de nègre* (negro's head) and whose inhabitants apologetically describe their poor English as *petit-nègre*. Where on television virtually everyone is white—except in the many cliché-ridden documentaries about *les Islamistes*. And where, in the chic white Parisian *arrondissements* (boroughs), African and Asian women push and carry expensively dressed white infants as they accompany them to and from school.

## The Two Frances

Whether you arrive in one of the capital's two airports or at the Euro-star terminus of Gare du Nord, you will immediately see men and women from France's diverse ethnic minority communities. For the most part, they will be cleaning and driving and cleaning and pushing and cleaning and serving. Not that different from elsewhere perhaps; except that for the rest of your stay—particularly in the heart of the capital and, above all, if you are here on business—these people will be doing little else. Cleaning and pushing, cleaning and emptying, cleaning and digging, cleaning and carrying. If you are here on business, do not be surprised if the company you are visiting is almost exclusively white. Except for the cleaners, of course. In scenes evocative of the Ken Loach film *Bread and Roses*, in which foreign janitors clean the plush offices of corporate America, women and men from France's ethnic minorities vacuum and tidy the offices and boardrooms of corporate France. And the country's highly lauded health service is virtually held together by workers of African origin, who usually do the menial undesirable tasks that French whites refuse. The case of a private clinic in the capital's chic 8th *arrondissement* illustrates this fact perfectly and is, in its own way, allegorical of modern France. The patients are largely white, middle-class Parisians who seek more comfortable and personalized health care than they would find in the large impersonal state hospitals. Since some of the special treatment and extra comforts such as private rooms with cable television are not reimbursed by *la Sécurité sociale*, the patients hold top-up health insurance policies that they have either paid for themselves or have received from their employers. What goes on within the walls of this clinic gives us a close-up view of what has been termed "the two Frances": surgeons, whose fees exceed the approved national health service limits, sit next to their patients and reassure them that "everything went perfectly." Meanwhile, black and Arab women and men administer medicine, take blood pressure, serve meals, clean lavatories, wash floors, change beds and help patients find their TV remote controls. And, when they have finished, most of them will probably have to take a bus, the metro and a train before they finally reach their flat on an isolated council estate a long way from the 8th *arrondissement*–and a long way from white, middle-class France with its posh clinics and expensive surgeons.

But while North Africans and blacks are allowed to do the jobs that nobody else wants to do, less laborious and better paid positions are rarely open to them. When graduates from France's ethnic minority communities try to reach the offices and boardrooms of French companies, they find themselves trapped in something akin to those strange glass pyramids in front of the Louvre: a prism of glass ceilings where refracted colors become white. In a bid to expose the racist recruitment policies of French companies, the anti-racist organization SOS Racisme sent two identical CVs to a range of companies. Qualifications, professional experience and knowledge—everything about the CVs—were identical except the names of the fictitious candidates; one being French and the other foreign. The outcome was sadly predictable: the lack of interest in the foreign candidate was stupefying. Not for the first time, corporate France had

been exposed. Even France's leading financial newspaper, *Les Echos*, recognized that "in order to justify their reluctance to employ youths from the suburbs, employers stigmatize their lack of qualifications. But prejudice, stereotypes and xenophobia are just as responsible."[1] It is little wonder that, while overall unemployment for French university graduates stands at 5 percent, the figure for graduates from France's North African communities is over 26 percent.[2] Even President Chirac, in his address to the nation in the wake of the uprisings, was forced to acknowledge the problem of the CVs that "finish up in the wastepaper basket because of the name or the address of the candidate."[3]

But Chirac made no mention of the fact that France's ethnic minorities are severely underrepresented among the country's civil servants and functionaries. And, as for ethnic minority representation in political life, it is virtually non-existent.[4] A gathering of the mayors of the Seine-Saint-Denis *département* (administrative area), where the uprisings began, illustrates this perfectly. After their emergency meeting about the disturbances, the municipal leaders posed for television cameras. Every single one of them was white. The country's powerful trade unions are not much better. The very thought of a French Bill Morris, the black former leader of the UK's Transport and General Workers' Union, is surreal in a country whose syndicates are almost entirely white and, in some cases, are known to actively block the recruitment of non-whites. Even the president of France's version of the UK's Commission for Racial Equality—la Haute Autorité de Lutte Contre les Discriminations et pour l'Egalité—is a white, middle-aged male. An industrialist and former chairman of Renault, Louis Schweitzer is indeed a bizarre choice to head an organization whose mission it is to promote racial equality in the workplace. But, then again, not even token blacks exist in France.

## Housing

As the recent '*émeutes*' (riots) have demonstrated, African and Asian communities in France have been (strategically?) housed in dreary council estates in the suburbs. And, when you talk about suburbs in France, you are not talking about sleepy leafy towns with nice parks and posh schools. With a few notable exceptions, *les banlieues* (suburbs) are, more often than not, dull and isolated places where unemployment can reach 40 percent. Scattered through the towns themselves are the ubiquitous post-war apartment blocks—rather ugly edifices, whether they be council or privately owned. In the more leafy areas there are *pavillons*, houses owned largely by white families. And then there are the council estates. The first of these were thrown up in the 1960s to house poor whites, including *les pieds-noirs*, the French colonials who fled northern Africa after the Algerian war of independence. Concrete monstrosities, sometimes stretching miles, were also erected to accommodate '*les immigrés*' who had been encouraged to come to France to provide urgently needed manual labor. It is on and around these council estates that the recent uprisings took place. During the disturbances, many of the French asked: "Why are they destroying their own neighbourhoods [*sic*]—their own schools and gymnasiums?" Take a look at a map and the answer becomes clear: to target more significant symbols of the state would have meant taking a couple of buses and a commuter train in order to first reach them. Which is why, at the height of the uprisings, the police kept a close eye on all major entry points to the French capital and perhaps why some railway stations were actually closed.

Of course, keeping the have-nots away from city centers has been common practice in France for many years. Take the case of Aubervilliers in the now infamous Seine-Saint-Denis *département*. A documentary film made just after the Second World War laid bare the poverty and neglect of the town where, as Jacques Prévert wrote, "children dive head-first into the oily waters of misery where pieces of old cork and dead cats float."[5] Today, the youths of Aubervilliers speak of revolt. "If one day we get organised [*sic*], we'll have grenades, explosives and Kalashnikovs. We'll gather at the Bastille and there'll be war." Such anger is hardly surprising given the second-class status of France's ethnic minorities.

## Poverty and Disenfranchisement

The roots of the recent uprisings in France are not dissimilar to those that sparked the events of Notting Hill (1976), Brixton (1981), Handsworth (1985) and Los Angeles (1992). The institutional racism plus police harassment minus jobs equation is certainly the same. But there are some French specificities which are difficult to ignore.

To begin with, the recent uprisings in France were truly multi-ethnic, with North African, black and even white youths rising up as one disenfranchised underclass. While the vast majority of these youths were indeed North African and black, it was poverty and despair that united them as much as ethnicity and color. And so determined has France been to suffocate the identity, culture and religion of its ethnic minority communities that it has inadvertently and unwittingly created communities which have become united in their misery and now in resistance. Indeed, within these communities, any potential divisions arising from ethnicity are more often than not cancelled out by shared experiences of unemployment, discrimination, police harassment, shitty housing and no future. Having witnessed the humiliation and exploitation of their parents, many of whom have lost their jobs and been unable to find new employment, North African and black youths have now come together in a shared struggle against poverty and hopelessness. And, as nobody has taken the time to listen to these youths, destroying cars, schools and shops has been the only way that they could advance this struggle. Writing in *Le Monde* about the recent events in the suburbs, Philippe Bernard observed that the youths involved in the rebellions

> are mostly French citizens who are smashing things up in order to make themselves heard. Whether they desire it or not, their actions are political . . . [Like the farmers, trade unions and students, they] know that for 25 years the politicians and the media have only taken them seriously when they carry out acts of violence.[6]

And if the disturbances in France spread so rapidly across the country and through so many different communities, it is because the youths who rose up are as much casualties of globalization as they are victims of state racism. Globalization means that factories that once employed their parents are disappearing; racism means that the remaining jobs are given to whites. Indeed, if unemployment reaches 40 percent in some of the country's deprived suburbs, it is not unconnected to the fact that many of the factories that once required cheap foreign labor are now moving to the other side of the world in search of even cheaper foreign labor. So a Tunisian who came to France to work in the French car industry has now been thrown on the scrap heap because French industry has gone to Tunisia or Slovakia or south-east Asia. Global economic "realities" mean that the factories and workshops that were previously situated in the French suburbs are scattered across the world. The globalization of French business may well be one factor leading to violent rebellion, but this is apparently a small price to pay compared to the savings that French companies can make: whereas in France car workers earn €20 an hour, their counterparts in Slovakia and Romania are paid just €5 an hour and €1 an hour respectively.[7]

That the recent uprisings were inevitable is a serious indictment of the failure of the French to tackle—indeed even to recognize the existence of—racial oppression and discrimination. Compared to Britain and the US, the lack of progress in combating racism in France is particularly shocking. The Haute Autorité de Lutte Contre les Discriminations et pour l'Egalité only became operational in 2005, a quarter of a century later than the British Commission for Racial Equality. Two American historians recently noted that the advances made by African-Americans in the United States are

> alas still inconceivable in France, where a minority presence among the ruling political and economic classes is conspicuously absent, where police harassment is often practised [sic] with impunity and where discrimination in employment and housing is a daily reality for those French deemed to be of immigrant background.[8]

## Policing

Then there are the police. There are notorious levels of harassment and brutality; there are deaths in police custody, as elsewhere, but there is also a specifically French factor that should act as a warning to the advocates of national identity card schemes. Just as the notorious "sus" laws and stop and search methods of the British police outraged Britain's black communities in the 1980s, repetitive identity checks of France's ethnic minority youths have only served to further alienate and antagonize the very people whose *assimilation* the authorities claim to desire. Verbal interaction between the police and non-white youths is often initiated by the inevitable "show me your papers, please." But while "sus" was eventually discredited due to the flimsy pretexts being used to apply it, an identity check is just an identity check. Another specifically French issue concerns the language employed by the police. Even the authorities are now acknowledging that the not uncommon police practice of addressing non-white youths with the condescending "*tu*" rather than the more respectful "*vous*" undermines police-community relations. And overtly racist police language is still a problem in a country

which has, according to anti-racist campaigners, refused to deal with the taboo subject of police-community relations. Speaking in the aftermath of the recent uprisings, a spokesman for the organization Devoirs de Mémoire (Duty to Remember) referred to the problem of police-officers who, on apprehending blacks and North Africans, "imitate monkey cries and call Arabs 'wogs.'"[9]

## The Far Right and the Philosophers

While the extreme Right has fueled the fires of racism in Britain, it has not (yet) been really legitimized politically and endorsed electorally as it has been in France. When, in the first round of the 2002 presidential elections, Jean-Marie Le Pen of the Front National obtained the second highest number of votes after Jacques Chirac and secured his presence in the second round, there was disbelief and virtual unanimity that such results were deplorable. Except that the figures speak for themselves: almost 20 percent of voters had endorsed the ideology of the far Right by voting for Le Pen and (in considerably lower numbers) for his rival Bruno Mégret. France's ethnic minorities may justifiably ask how they are supposed to assimilate into, and adopt the values of, a society whose electorate votes in such high numbers for the racist Right. And they may understandably wonder how many of these people hold positions of responsibility, whether it be in the human resources departments of companies and institutions, the police force, the education system, the health service.

Although ultimately Le Pen lost the 2002 elections to Chirac, it can be argued that it is the ideology of the Front National that has prevailed. Indeed, the success of the far Right in 2002 seems to have accelerated the subliminal "LePen-isation" of French political discourse, with issues such as *l'insécurité, l'immigration, l'Islam radical* and *les travailleurs clandestins* ("illegal workers") acquiring the same ubiquity in electioneering-speak as "jobs, education and health." So that targeting "*les immigrés*" has become politically expedient. The French Right (and some on the Left) seem to have reached one conclusion as to how to deal with the ideas of Le Pen: "If you can't beat them, emulate them." The inflammatory language of Interior Minister Nicolas Sarkozy, which many blame for igniting the disturbances, is reminiscent of the provocative outbursts of Le Pen. Sarkozy's reference to "scum" (*racaille*) in the housing estates provoked condemnation from many, but the interior minister's popularity subsequently increased by 11 percent according to an Ipsos-Le Point opinion poll. Moreover, according to the same poll, Sarkozy had become the most popular political figure in France, with some 63 percent of those interviewed backing him and 68 percent condoning his handling of the uprisings.[10] An analysis of President Chirac's much-awaited "*Déclaration aux Français*," on 14 November 2005, intended to reassure the French people in the wake of the recent uprisings, confirmed this trend towards "LePen-isation." The chronological order of the issues that the French president chose to address in his speech indicated how the state intended to respond to the uprising: repression of violence, parental responsibility and immigration were the themes that Chirac immediately raised. Some two minutes into his pronouncement, he got around to acknowledging the problems of racism and discrimination. But, then again, this is the same Chirac who, in 1991, spoke of the French people being driven mad by the noise and the smells emanating from the homes of their foreign neighbors.

While the "LePen-isation" of French politics has encouraged this racist discourse, a more recent phenomenon has also contributed to the lurch to the Right. In recent years, and particularly since September 11, a number of French intellectuals have adopted views which are strikingly similar to those of the American neoconservatives. Indeed, these right-wing philosophers and commentators adhere to many of the beliefs and values of the "neocons": the Huntington "clash of civilizations" theory, the threat of Islamic fundamentalism, the menace of urban violence and the necessity of defending western culture and values. The American Right may have boycotted French produce for a couple of years, but little do its adherents realize that an increasingly influential group of French intellectuals is ready to speak out against anti-Americanism and "political correctness." Indeed, so similar are the views of these French *intellos* to those of the American neocons that this Gallic new Right has been labeled *les néoréacs*, the neo-reactionaries.

That a group of French philosophers should hold such reactionary views is perhaps surprising but not, one might think, particularly alarming. What threat can a bunch of thinkers and writers possibly represent, particularly as they wield no political power? But such a view underestimates the extent to which philosophers and other intellectuals can influence French society. Let us not forget that one of France's biggest selling daily newspapers, *Libération*, was founded by Jean-Paul Sartre. For in France, no television debate or newspaper analysis of any of the great questions of the moment would be complete without the contribution of a Glucksmann,

a Finkielkraut or a Lévy. And, surreal as it may sound, the presence of a philosopher is practically mandatory on election night television discussions. Even lighthearted chat shows occasionally invite these cerebral superstars to share their views with the prime-time public. This used not to matter, since the views of French philosophers were almost always characterized by progressive and humanistic analyses; anyone who has read Fanon's *The Wretched of the Earth* will have been impressed with Sartre's brilliant preface. But along with a growing number of other French intellectuals and political figures, today's philosophers are unashamedly expressing the kinds of views which, once upon a time, would have been confined to the extreme Right. Indeed, the French magazine *Le Nouvel Observateur* recently warned that the discourse of *les néoréacs* risked exacerbating the divisions in French society.[11]

Interviewed by the Israeli newspaper *Haaretz* about the recent uprisings, philosopher Alain Finkielkraut is quoted as saying that blacks and Arabs were involved in an "anti-Republic pogrom": "They tell us that these neighbourhoods [*sic*] are neglected and the people are in distress. What connection is there between poverty and despair, and wreaking destruction and setting fire to schools? I don't think any Jew would ever do a thing like this." Finkielkraut's views on Islam confirm the spiritual rapprochement between the French *néoréacs* and American neocons:

> Why have parts of the Muslim-Arab world declared war on the West? The Republic is the French version of Europe. They, and those who justify them, say that it derives from colonial breakdown. Okay, but one mustn't forget that the integration of the Arab workers in France during the time of colonial rule was much easier. In other words, this is belated hatred. Retrospective hatred.[12]

Another philosopher, André Glucksmann, claimed that the uprisings were a manifestation of "nihilism" and pure hate, and defended Nicolas Sarkozy's use of the word "scum" to refer to the undesirable elements in the council estates. And Pascal Bruckner, also a philosopher, recently wrote about "the impossibility of having a debate about radical Islam, immigration and nationalism without being branded a fascist." But then this is the Pascal Bruckner who, over twenty years ago, denounced "anti-white racism." [13] Meanwhile, an expert on Russia, Hélène Carrère d'Encausse, told the Russian media that if so many African children were loitering around in the street it was because "*beaucoup de ces Africains sont polygames*" (many of these Africans are polygamists).[14] That such things are being said by such "respectable" figures explains why their comments now seem to be having an impact on government policy. Alain Finkielkraut was quoted by Haaretz as saying: "Now they teach colonial history as an exclusively negative history. We don't teach any more that the colonial project also sought to educate, to bring civilisation [*sic*] to the savages."[15] Under threat of legal action from the anti-racist organization Mouvement contre le Racisme et pour l'Amitié entre les Peuples, Finkielkraut subsequently claimed, having read the French translation of his comments, not to "recognize" himself in the words attributed to him, and denied outright having made the "bring civilisation [*sic*] to the savages" comment. He nevertheless accepted, with certain qualifications, other remarks attributed to him by *Haaretz*.

Whatever Finkielkraut's exact words were, the historically revisionist views implicit in such discourse are becoming progressively more acceptable. *Le Nouvel Observateur* recently ironically pointed out that such *néoréac* thinking is "so marginal, heretic, that it figures . . . in a law recently voted by the French parliament."[16] It is indeed the case that Finkielkraut's views seem to be mirrored in the controversial "Law of 23 February 2005," which stipulates that "school syllabuses recognise, [*sic*] in particular, the positive role of the French presence overseas, notably in North Africa."[17] On 29 November 2005 (less than a month after the uprisings) the French parliament voted to preserve this controversial law. So, as French intellectuals sanitize French colonial history, the state follows suit.

## Republican Values

In fact, France's *néoréacs* have strong foundations on which to build their pernicious ideas. For example, there is the anachronistic and, in practice, xeno-racist French ideal of *l'indivisibilité de la République*. Anachronistic because this principle was born out of the French revolution and pertained to federalist tendencies of that time which threatened to split the country. Xeno-racist because the French see precisely the same threat as emanating now from ethnic minority communities. An apparent unwillingness to acknowledge that modern France is multiracial and multicultural engenders a justified feeling of rejection and exclusion among the country's ethnic minorities. France's vision of itself is

both entrenched in its past and skewed by an obsession with 'republican values" and *les gloires nationales*; the national glories that it arrogantly puts on display at every available occasion. Events such as Britain's Black History Month are unimaginable in a country where many still employ the generic *les immigrés* to refer to black people (French citizenship notwithstanding). The more enlightened French acknowledge that something is wrong. Analyzing the reasons for the failure of Paris to clinch the 2012 Olympic Games, some will cite Luc Besson's picture-postcard view of the city as part of the problem, pointing out that the Eiffel Tower, Jean-Paul Belmondo and Catherine Deneuve neither reflect modern multiracial France nor encapsulate the Olympic spirit. Others will agree that, although they loved the French blockbuster *Le Fabuleux Destin d'Amélie Poulain*, it was rather odd that the character played by comedian Jamel Debbouze should be called Lucien, as if a foreign-sounding name, just like the airbrushed-out graffiti, would have spoilt the beautiful scenes of Montmartre. Indeed, the Besson film and *Amélie Poulain* are symptomatic of the French mindset: that France will always be France with French values and customs and a proud history; that *les immigrés* must assimilate by embracing the culture, language and traditions of *La République*.

This perhaps explains why candidates for French nationality are asked whether they read foreign newspapers and why; once they become French, they are encouraged to adopt French-sounding names. In fact, such is the paranoia around all that is non-French, that *la naturalisation* can be a humiliating exercise in which applicants are subjected to a French variation on nose-measuring. And, if the analogy sounds rather harsh, consider the case of a North African lawyer who, having finally reached the interview stage of her application for French nationality, was asked how many times a week she ate couscous; how often she visited Morocco; what nationality most of her friends were; and even which newspapers she read. Or there were the cases of a Tunisian applicant, who was required to justify his two visits to Mecca, and a Serbian researcher, who was asked which language she spoke with her family.[18] And then there is color. In 1997, the journal *Migrations Société* reported that between 35 percent and 50 percent of blacks had their nationality applications turned down; the figure for North Africans was 20 percent, while only 8 percent of applicants from southern Europe failed to obtain French nationality. In an exposé of the inequity of the naturalization process, journalist Maurice T. Maschino pointed out that small details "affect the big decisions, and it is not rare for an over-obvious foreignness (the wearing of a jellaba or hijab), a religious practice automatically categorised [*sic*] as fundamentalist, family links outside France, to provoke an adjournment of the application." Maschino concludes that such practices are "absurd, mean, often illegal—any excuse is acceptable in order to keep the foreigner at bay." [19] So when applicants for French nationality are interrogated about their visits to Morocco, their provocative headwear, their couscous and foreign newspapers and their pilgrimages to Mecca, it is not the legacy of the revolution that is at work, but what Sivanandan has previously defined as "a new state racism that promises to safeguard the patriot nation from the shadow enemy within." [20]

## The French *Modèle d'intégration*

The French declare proudly that their *modèle d'intégration* is the antithesis of Britain's multicultural society, which is caricatured as a multitude of ethnic and religious ghettos. For example, a commentator on the highbrow France Inter radio station, giving his personal view of the enduring troubles, indirectly equated British *multiculturalisme* with apartheid. Indeed, the term "*communautarisme*" is routinely used to ascribe negative connotations to multiculturalism and the recognition that minority ethnic communities may have distinct identities. Such a concept is anathema in a country that resolutely refuses to look itself in the mirror. In spite of the recent uprisings, politicians and intellectuals have been staunchly defending the virtues of the French *modèle d'intégration*. Politicians assert that they will never tolerate Anglo-Saxon-style *communautarisme* and will always strive for *l'assimilation*. "France is not a country like others. We will never accept that fellow citizens can live separately, with different chances and unequal futures," Prime Minister Dominique de Villepin told the French parliament in the wake of the recent troubles. The fact that this statement can only be interpreted as an oblique rejection of Anglo-Saxon *communautarisme* is evident in the syntax: notice how "live separately" takes precedence over "different chances and unequal futures." That France's ethnic minorities already do live in separate ghettos did not seem to have occurred to de Villepin.

Take even the language used to refer to communities. There is, at best, a strange coyness—an evasiveness—with regard to how to describe the ethnic minorities in France. While slang such as "*les beurs et les blacks*"[21] is now common in colloquial French, the establishment shies away from appellations which might promote any sense of a community identity other than that of the French republic itself. Indeed the very terms communauté, minorités ethniques and noir seem to be treated with caution. Ambiguous and patronizing anachronisms in the vein of "*les personnes issues de l'immigration*" (persons of immigrant origin), "*les jeunes des quartiers difficiles*" (youths from difficult areas) or even "*les personnes de couleur*" (people of color) appear to be more acceptable terminology. If this reluctance to speak clearly and accurately about ethnic minority communities is at best coyness, it is at worst a deliberate negation of their very existence. Not exactly on the level of Golda Meir's "there is no such thing as a Palestinian people" but more a collective denial that France has become, de facto, a multiracial society.

## The Failure of the Left

Furthermore, when, as is currently the case, minority ethnic communities become part of *l'actualité* (current affairs) and politicians, social commentators and—as this is France—philosophers engage in deep debate about what to do, the linguistic intransigence becomes pure farce: we are over ten days into the disturbances and Ségolène Royal, a Socialist Party high-flyer, is being questioned by a panel of journalists about the burning *banlieues*. One journalist refers to the minority communities who live in the affected areas. The debate instantly stalls as Madame Royal admonishes his choice of language. 'But what should we call them?' the journalist retorts in exasperation. "They are French," Madame Royal replies. One is tempted to reply that German Jews were also German! That Madame Royal is a member of the French Socialist Party, indeed the likely Socialist candidate for the 2007 presidential election, is of little surprise, since the French Left is as culpable as the Right of failing to address the specific problems faced by the country's ethnic minorities. American historians Diamond and Magidoff pointed out that

> the programme [of the French Left] which aims to improve economic equality without taking into account the painful question of racial and ethnic inequality can only offer a partial and unsatisfactory response to this problem . . . Paralysed [*sic*] by the fear of *communautarisme a' l'américaine*, the French Left has systematically refused to acknowledge the racial dimension of social inequalities.

Diamond and Magidoff note that those youths who took part in the recent uprisings are "way ahead of the French Left [since] the riots represent a political mobilisation [*sic*] around racial identity which is not about to go away."[22] So, just as American identity politics made the mistake of focusing on race to the exclusion of class, the French Left has done exactly the opposite by concentrating on class while ignoring race.

And, even after the recent uprisings, in which black and North African youths figured so prominently, the French Left and the rest of the political class continue to employ woolly and vague language to describe those who set the suburbs alight. The generic term that everyone is using in the aftermath of the rebellions is "*les jeunes*" (the youths), which is a conveniently vague term that conjures up images of hooligans and yobs and elicits a "boys will be boys" reaction. Equally, "*les jeunes*" suggests a problem with a disenchanted generation rather than a rebellion based on race and (under)class. And it is this obdurate, dogmatic and blinkered view of French society that so hinders its ability to deal with events like the recent uprisings. For this is a nation of intellectuals, statisticians and mathematicians where statistics pertaining to ethnicity and religion barely exist. How to even start to respond to the disenchantment of France's ethnic minorities when basic information about educational performance, unemployment and homelessness is virtually non-existent?

## Colonial Legacy

If the French intellectual class is casuistic when it refers to ethnic minorities, it is particularly taciturn about the roots of the racism that permeates French society; namely French colonialism and the Algerian war of independence. Given the recent uprisings, one might assume that discussions and debates about the unrest would place it in an historical context. Yet, if you tune into one of France's more intellectual radio stations in order to gain some insight, you will be disappointed. For serious analysis about the Algerian legacy, you will probably have to turn to the foreign media. In a recent discussion about the French uprisings on American radio, the journalist Robert Fisk pointed out that it was

> impossible to see the crisis in Algeria today, the crisis in France today, without going back to the war of independence ... And you've got to realise [*sic*] that the wounds of that war were never healed. The

*pieds-noirs* have never forgiven the Algerians for throwing them out, effectively, of the country. And one of the things we're not talking about now, but which we should be, is that many of the areas where this violence is taking place around Paris and other large French cities, are areas where lower middle-class French people who were *pieds-noirs* [from Algeria] now live.[23]

We could also add to Fisk's observation the reflection that the extreme Right in France draws a significant proportion of its support from these *pieds-noirs*.

And when the French do refer to Algeria, it is, as we have seen, often part of a historical revisionism that portrays French colonialism as intrinsically altruistic and self-sacrificing. There is, for example, the alarming sight, in a number of French towns, of monuments glorifying the notorious Organisation de l'Armée Secrète (OAS), whose savage activities in Algeria remain a stain on the French conscience. In his analysis of the recent uprisings, Philippe Bernard pointed out that until "a truthful discourse about colonialism" replaces the emphasis on the "positive role of the French [colonial] presence" in the Law of February 2005, "the youths in the poor neighbourhoods, [*sic*] who have read neither Frantz Fanon nor Che Guevara, will continue to feel how the weight of this history still affects the attitudes of others towards them."[24] Indeed, the government's decision to impose curfews in response to the recent uprisings is itself indicative of the historical legacy that lingers over France: such drastic measures were only made possible thanks to a 1955 law that allows the declaration of a state of emergency in parts, or all, of France. The law was originally passed to deal with Algerians fighting for the independence of their country.

## Secularism and Islamophobia

Some of the roots of the recent unrest in France unquestionably lie in the country's hysterical obsession with secularism and an associated state-sanctioned Islamophobia. The separation of religion and state is one of those *valeurs républicaines* which everyone has been referring to since "*les émeutes*." But secularism in France seems to be going horribly wrong. Indeed, *la laïcité* (secularism) seems to have become a form of fundamentalism itself which discriminates against the country's Muslims. Numerous politicians and intellectuals claim that Islam, France's second religion, is incompatible with *les valeurs républicaines*. The rights and dignity of women are typically cited as examples of the incompatibility of Islam with *les valeurs républicaines*. Yet this is a country where images of naked women (advertising everything from yogurt to perfume) are on display wherever you go and on whatever television channel you watch. And where wife-beating has become a national epidemic, with six women dying at the hands of their husbands every month.[25] Such is the scale of *la violence conjugale* that the government recently launched an information campaign about the problem.

The infamous law which prevents Muslim girls from wearing the hijab in school and the refusal of the authorities to grant the building of urgently needed mosques are tantamount to a stranglehold on French Muslims. And since Islam is both a faith and a culture, a stranglehold on the former will inevitably suffocate the latter. That this should breed resentment and discontent is hardly surprising. The stigmatization of Islam in France means the subjugation of the vast majority of its ethnic minority communities. But it is in France's schools and colleges, where Muslim girls are forbidden to wear headscarves in the name of secularism, that a pernicious Islamophobia is taking hold. As Liz Fekete has pointed out, "In France, the paranoia about the hijab is taking on the dimensions of a modern witch hunt."[26]

It is the first day back to school after the summer holidays. Muslim schoolgirls, threatened with exclusion from school, have agreed to take off their headscarves and to wear bandanas, smaller headbands which reveal more of their necks and ears. As they enter the school, the girls are scrutinized from head to toe lest they be wearing an item of clothing that breaks the non-religious dress code. A girl with a bandana is stopped by the headmaster. "It's covering your ears," he complains. "I want to see your ears." He also finds fault with the girl's dress, a fashionable sari-style item worn by many Parisian women last year. Having endured this ordeal with remarkable patience, the girl is eventually allowed to enter the school. What her state of mind must be, one can only imagine. To make matters worse, already sitting behind her desk, having entered the school without raising anyone's eyebrow, is a non-Muslim girl in a low-cut t-shirt which reveals much of her ample bosom. The treatment meted out to Muslim schoolgirls arguably represents a French variation on the notorious stop and search practices that provoked Britain's black communities to rebel in the 1980s. And the message to young women is clear: covering your head is demeaning and antithetical to women's rights and freedoms, while

displaying your body in an ostensibly sexual fashion is okay. Even the French women's movement apparently shares this viewpoint: Muslim girls participating in a women's march through Paris are harangued by their white "sisters" who declare that their headscarves are "shameful."

A genuinely secular state, as Sivanandan has pointed out, "should ensure the same range of choices to all its citizens, excepting only that these do not cut across the range of choice of any other citizen."[27] And "while European governments should certainly uphold the rights of girls or women forced to wear the hijab against their will, they should not use state power to force on any individual a dress code, whether culturally or religiously determined."[28]

If this French secularism is provocative and unjust, it is also inconsistent. For in an Orwellian way, some in France are more secular than others. While Muslims are forced to obey the rules of the secular state schools, Catholic children are free to attend the thousands of state-supported Catholic schools that are paradoxically an important pillar of France's education system. And there are also Jewish schools and Protestant schools. These private establishments are often used as a haven for parents wishing to keep their children out of state schools that are considered too "*populaire*" (a euphemism for lower-class and/or non-white). Hence a French sociologist's description of the French education system as "*apartheid scolaire*."[29] And the asymmetrical nature of French *laïcité* is also manifest in the country's iniquitous treatment of places of worship. While the churches and synagogues that decorate towns and cities benefit from financial support from the state, mosques have no such funding, and planning permission for their construction is frequently refused. Friday prayers often take place in insalubrious flats, basements and cellars. Muslim leaders plead with the government to treat their religion on an equal par with Christianity and Judaism. "Islam needs to be practised [*sic*] in dignity and serenity," they try to explain.[30] In the wake of the uprisings, a contributor on Radio France pointed out that it is hardly surprising that some young Muslims "don't believe in the Republic" when the authorities in cities like Nice continue to block the construction of mosques. The mayor of Nice, Jacques Peyrot, defended his refusal to grant planning permission for a mosque in the language of the far Right: "Faced with urban violence and the rise of radical Islam, it is not the right time to establish a place of Islam right in the heart of Nice."[31] If France wishes to encourage *l'assimilation*, it is going about it in rather a strange way: what better way to alienate and "radicalize" its ethnic minorities than to continually ghettoize them as aliens and outcasts? Meanwhile, the Chief Rabbi of France, Joseph Sitruk, recently announced the establishment in France of a national rabbinical tribunal. In an interview in *Actualité Juive*—a weekly magazine for France's Jewish community—the Chief Rabbi stated that the tribunal would be presided over by a prominent Israeli, Rabbi Mordehai Gross, who apparently speaks no French. He also expressed his hope that the national *Beth Din* (rabbinical court) would be competent to deal with conflicts between individuals, explaining: "What I would like is, when two Jews are involved in a dispute, that they would get used to the idea of going to the *Beth Din* . . . We have to learn to deal with problems between ourselves."[32] So this is *égalité*: while France's Jewish community is allowed to set up Jewish courts, Muslim schoolgirls cannot even wear the hijab.

Of course, the law banning "oversized" religious symbols in all state schools is pure sleight of hand. Anyone with a basic understanding of the world's religions knows that, outside of the church and synagogue, the Christian crucifix and the Jewish skullcap are hardly comparable with the Muslim hijab or the Sikh turban. And the French authorities know this too. It is no coincidence that the law regarding religious symbols has had virtually no impact on Christians and Jews. Because, contrary to the outwardly secular image that France likes to project of itself, French society is in reality very much a Judeo-Christian one. To understand this is to comprehend the subtext of French 'secularism': the upholding of western Judeo-Christian values which are perceived to be under threat from Islam. And this must be done on the grounds that Islam is not compatible with 'our' values; that it is out of sync with European civilization. So that the French republican values, born out of the revolution, appear to have become French Manichaean values. Just listen to the French talk about the prospect of Turkey joining the European Union: most make no mention of the country's lamentable track record on human rights—it is Turkey's 'incompatibility' with European Judeo-Christian culture that gets them het up. Indeed, an opinion poll conducted in 2003 found that some 62 percent of those questioned considered Islamic values to be "incompatible with those of the Republic."[33] Then again, the question put to those polled, "Do you feel that the values of Islam are compatible with the values of the French Republic?" was hardly going to elicit a positive response.

That the attachment of the adjective "secular" to the phrase "French republican values" creates an oxymoron is illustrated in Alain Finkielkraut's recent comments in his interview with *Haaretz*. Referring to the French uprisings, the French philosopher claimed that the problem is that most of these youths are blacks or Arabs, with a Muslim identity. Look, in France there are also other immigrants whose situation is difficult—Chinese, Vietnamese, Portuguese—and they're not taking part in the riots. Therefore, it is clear that this is a revolt with an ethno-religious character. . . . These are very violent declarations of hate for France. All of this hatred and violence is now coming out in the riots. To see them as a response to French racism is to be blind to a broader hatred: the hatred of the West, which is deemed guilty of all crimes. France is being exposed to this now. . . . [The riots] are directed against France as a former colonial power, against France as a European country. Against France, with its Christian or Judeo-Christian tradition.[34]

So, there we have it, spelled out clearly: the uprisings in France are an assault on French Judeo-Christian traditions. It is no surprise then that Finkielkraut is a staunch defender of the ban on the hijab in French schools; his vitriol illustrates clearly that the French *valeurs républicaines* have become imbued with what Sivanandan has identified as a populist anti-Muslim culture that has spread throughout the West since September 11.[35] Except that by the time "9/11" came around, the French already had a patent pending on populist anti-Muslim culture, thanks to the Paris bombings of the 1990s and the legacy of Algeria. The French media have played a not insignificant role in feeding this Islamophobia: television news reports of horrific massacres in Algeria, allegedly carried out by Islamic extremists, have been "coincidentally" run before or after reports about the hijab "problem" in France and sensationalist documentaries about *les Islamistes* are the regular fodder of French TV viewers. The title of a recently published study of Islamophobia in France makes clear where much of the problem lies: *La Construction Médiatique de l'Islamophobie en France, 1975–2005*.[36]

## The Response to the Uprisings

At the time of writing, discussions in the wake of the uprisings suggest that the French have still not got the message. As noted earlier, in his reaction to the disturbances, President Chirac prioritized parental responsibility, law and order and immigration. Others on the Right have blamed polygamous and/or large Muslim families, proposing that child benefits should be withdrawn from such families, as well as from those whose children are found guilty of participating in the uprisings. And rap music is also being held responsible, with 153 members of the French parliament asking the justice minister, Pascal Clément, to consider taking legal proceedings against seven different rap groups whose lyrics are allegedly "anti-white" and incite a hatred of France.[37] Daniel Mach and Jean-Paul Garraud, members of the French parliament, are proposing that it should become a criminal offense to "attack the dignity of France and the state." Garraud is also pushing for a law which would mean that recently naturalized citizens found guilty of committing a criminal offense would be stripped of their French nationality.[38]

Prime Minister de Villepin has warned against overheated language, but has also spoken of "measures to incite parents to fulfill their responsibilities." On 18 November 2005, de Villepin announced that the state of emergency would be maintained into the beginning of 2006. And Nicolas Sarkozy, the interior minister, pledged that foreigners convicted of involvement in the disturbances would be deported, a move which, according to a CSA opinion poll, was supported by 55 percent of the French.[39] Sarkozy is widely expected to run in and win France's next presidential election in 2007, a prospect which France's ethnic minorities will hardly relish since the interior minister has not only reiterated his provocative references to the "scum" in the council estates, but has qualified his words as "perhaps a little weak."[40]

Many do recognize the problems of racism, discrimination and poverty, but the language they use indicates that they are not willing to tackle them. "We must defend *les valeurs républicaines*," you will hear them chant. It's a mind-numbing mantra and the more they chant it, the more hollow, demagogical and ambiguous it sounds. In the light of the disturbances, the political discourse has been decorated with a thousand clichés: *fracture sociale, fracture urbaine, la République, la France pour tous, l'ordre républicain, l'intégration, la solidarité*. These hackneyed phrases and platitudes seem to be part of the problem. Words not action. Just as SOS Racisme's "don't touch my pal," lapel badges did not prevent skinheads from throwing a North African youth into the Seine on the same day that the Front National was holding its annual rally in Paris. Just as the slogan "*liberté, égalité, fraternité*" does not prevent African families, forced to live in squats, from being burnt to death in suspicious fires.

In his "*Déclaration aux Francais*," President Chirac spoke of "the discrimination that weakens the very foundations of our Republic" and promised that acts of discrimination would be punished. But Chirac offered no real hope to France's have-nots, although he did address them personally in his speech: "I want to say to the children of the difficult neighbourhoods [*sic*] that whatever their origins, they are all daughters and sons of the Republic."[41] Were it not so long, it would look good on a lapel badge.

---

## Questions

1. What are the different factors that led to the riots among immigrants in France?

2. Do you believe the answer to the tensions lies in greater assimilation, in greater multiculturalism, or something else?

# References

1. *Les Echos* (7 November 2005).
2. Cited in BBC News, "French Muslims face job discrimination" (2 November 2005) at <http://news.bbc.co.uk/1/hi/world/europe/4399748.stm>.
3. "Déclaration aux Français de Monsieur Jacques Chirac, Président de la République" (14 November 2005).
4. There appears, for example, to have been just one black deputy in the national parliament, Kofi Yamgnane, elected for Finistère in 1997.
5. Jacques Prévert, *Aubervilliers* (1946).
6. Philippe Bernard, "Banlieues: la provocation coloniale," *Le Monde* (18 November 2005).
7. "Renault: la tactique de la tête de pont," *L'Expansion* (27 October 2004).
8. Andrew Diamond and Jonathan Magidoff, "A gauche, le racial impensé," *Libération* (30 November 2005).
9. *Le Monde* (20–21 November 2005).
10. *Le Monde* (17 November 2005).
11. *Le Nouvel Observateur* (17 December 2005).
12. *Haaretz* (17 November 2005).
13. *Le Nouvel Observateur*, op. cit.
14. Ibid.
15. *Haaretz*, op. cit.
16. *Le Nouvel Observateur*, op. cit.
17. Diamond and Magidoff, op. cit.
18. *Le Monde Diplomatique* (June 2002).
19. Ibid.
20. Cited in Hazel Waters, "Editorial," *Race & Class* (Vol. 46, no. 1, 2004), p. 1.
21. The phrase "*les beurs*" is used to refer to French-born youths of north African heritage.
22. Diamond and Magidoff, op. cit.
23. *Democracy Now* (9 November 2005).
24. Bernard, op. cit.
25. *Télérama* (No. 2915, 23 November 2005).
26. Liz Fekete, "Anti-Muslim racism and the European security state," *Race & Class* (Vol. 46, no. 1, 2004), p. 26.
27. Ibid.
28. Ibid.

29. G. Felouzis, F. Liot and J. Perroton, *L'Apartheid Scolaire: enquête sur la ségrégation ethnique dans les collèges* (Paris, Seuil, 2005).

30. Fouad Alaoui, *L'Express* (10 January 2005).

31. *Le Monde* (12 November 2005).

32. *Le Monde* (27–28 November 2005).

33. Le Point (16 May 2003).

34. *Haaretz*, op. cit.

35. Cited in Waters, op. cit.

36. Thomas Deltombe, *La Construction Médiatique de L'Islamophobie en France, 1975–2005* (Paris, La Dé couverte, 2005).

37. *Le Monde* (25 November 2005).

38. *Le Nouvel Observateur*, op. cit.

39. *La Tribune* (20 November 2005).

40. *Le Monde* (21 November 2005).

41. "Déclaration . . . de . . . Jacques Chirac," op. cit.

*Source*: France: The Riots and the Republic. Graham Murray. *Race and Class*. Vol. 47, No. 2. 2006. Reprinted by permission of Institute of Race Relations.

# CHAPTER 16

## Torture

### *The Struggle Over a Peremptory Norm in a Counter-Terrorist Era*

Rosemary Foot

It would seem that one thing on which the world community might agree is that torture is unacceptable. Yet many debates remain about just what is torture and about what can properly be done to both protect human rights and to protect innocent people from the dangers of terrorism. The Bush administration has chosen to carefully redefine what constitutes torture in ways that are very controversial in the world.

As many of those associated now or in the recent past with the University of Wales at Aberystwyth have recognized, while E. H. Carr offered a "corrective to the exuberance of utopianism," that correction prompted him to develop a position that acknowledged the connections between two apparently opposing approaches to world politics—realist and utopian thought. Carr believed humankind to be capable of progress—indeed was someone who believed that through a process of incrementalism or accumulated "reformist steps" human beings could create a better world.[2] Carr makes reference to what he calls the ordinary person's assumptions about international morality, stating: "Some recognition of an obligation to our fellow men as such seems implicit in our conception of civilization." He goes on: "All agree that there is an international moral code binding on states," one aspect of which is the "obligation not to inflict *unnecessary* death or suffering on other human beings, i.e., death or suffering not necessary for the attainment of some higher purpose which is held, rightly or wrongly, to justify a derogation from the general obligation."[3]

There are obvious resonances between some of the arguments that have become current in the contemporary return to torture and Carr's reference to the "derogation from the general obligation" to attain a "higher purpose," as will become clear later on. This is so even though the legal prohibition against torture has the status of a peremptory humanitarian norm. That is, it is considered binding on all states and no derogation under any circumstances is permitted.[4] As Henry Shue wrote in his classic essay of 1978: "No other practice except slavery is so universally and unanimously condemned in law and human convention."[5] While the practice of torture has been widespread, until recently it had come to be understood that no representatives of the state could openly admit that they would use torture for fear of being removed from office and of having their state ostracized by "civilized" nations.[6]

Why, then, given the rhetorical, moral and legal status of this prohibition, is torture being debated, contemplated and even resurrected as an unsavory and allegedly necessary course of action in this counter-terrorist era? As Manfred Nowak, the UN's Special Rapporteur on

---

*Note:* This article is a revised and expanded version of the E. H. Carr Memorial Lecture given at the University of Wales, Aberystwyth, 13 October 2005.[1]

Torture, put it to the UN Commission on Human Rights in April 2005: For the first time since World War II, this important consensus of the international community [the prohibition against torture] seems to have been called into question by some governments in the context of their counterterrorism strategies." [7] What have been some of the consequences of this questioning of the prohibition? In recognition that the torture convention allows for no derogation because torture has been recognized as a most profound violation of human dignity, I ask too what efforts are being made to restore the status of this humanitarian norm. [8]

The argument unfolds in four main sections. Inevitably, much of the discussion about torture's contemporary return has to focus on developments in the United States and surrounding US action since September 11, 2001. The first section introduces the main contours of that debate in the United States, legal and otherwise. A second section, moving beyond discussion of America, provides a brief historical review of some of the conditions under which torture has been used in the past and then the process by which it has (or is it had?) become regarded as beyond the pale for civilized states. This provides a deeper understanding of the reasons for the current use of torture, linking its present prevalence to the desire of state authorities, and especially the United States, to demonstrate a capacity for effective and ruthless action in a counter-terrorist era. Next, I suggest some of the ways in which this heightened attention to counter-terrorist action has contributed to the weakening of this prohibition against torture in other parts of the world, before turning, in a fourth section, to an exploration of the attempts that are being made to reverse this weakening of the anti-torture norm. The role of institutions—domestic as well as global—and the discursive opportunities they offer to help restore the prohibitions against the use of torture and other forms of abuse are a particular focus here. In my conclusion I argue that, for its own counter-terrorist purposes, the US executive branch has been attempting to reduce the scope of what is meant by torture and degrading treatment, as well as to define a category of detainee who can be subjected to coercive methods of interrogation. Nevertheless, other actors have been arguing against these attempts, making their cases on prudential, moral or legal grounds.

## Torture After 9/11

That torture has been resurrected as a course of action and subject of debate hardly needs elaboration. [9] While

President George W. Bush did state on June 26, 2004, the UN International Day in Support of Victims of Torture, that "the United States reaffirms its commitment to the worldwide elimination of torture" and that "Freedom from torture is an inalienable human right, and we are committed to building a world where human rights are respected and protected by the rule of law." [10] This statement came after much evidence of behavior and discussion that had appeared to contradict it. As early as October 21, 2001, a *Washington Post* article reported FBI agents outlining their frustrations over the refusal of suspects to provide information and suggesting they might have to use pressure to get those details. [11] On November 5, 2001, a *Newsweek* article appeared entitled "Time to Think About Torture." [12] In January 2003, *The Economist* published a cover story entitled "Is Torture Ever Justified?" [13] Two professors of law, Alan Dershowitz from Harvard and Sanford Levinson from Texas Law School, have recommended in Dershowitz's case the "limited administration of nonlethal torture supervised by judges," or more equivocally in Levinson's to the need for a debate "over the possibility that torture, at least in some carefully specified circumstances, might be a 'lesser evil' than some other 'greater evil' that menaces society." [14]

The infamous Bybee memorandum of August 1, 2002, written for Alberto R. Gonzales when he was Legal Counsel to the US President, set out to justify the torture of detainees and to protect from prosecution those that might engage in it. As summarized by Sir Nigel Rodley, Bybee tries to argue that the relevant legal treaties (such as the Geneva Conventions, the CAT and the International Covenant on Civil and Political Rights [ICCPR]) do not apply to these detainees; what the US interrogators want to do or are doing does not constitute torture (i.e., the pain inflicted has to be as great as that associated with organ failure or even death); and, moreover, international law is not directly enforceable in US courts. In addition, Bybee discusses the President's Commander in Chief role, arguing that it provides him with overriding power to "ensure the security of the United States in situations of grave and unforeseen emergencies" by means that he sees fit. [15] And although this 2002 memorandum was withdrawn in June 2004, and on December 30, 2004, formally replaced in an opinion offered by Daniel Levin, the Acting Assistant Attorney General of the Office of Legal Counsel, the reaction of some is that Levin's statement "represents the minimum possible cosmetic emendation of the Bybee Memo" since it still offers a narrow definition of torture, avoids discussion of the necessity defense, and evades the Commander in Chief question and the President's ability to authorize torture. [16]

The implication is that the US executive branch has been seeking to reinterpret and weaken the anti-torture norm as it has come to be understood. And elsewhere too, even in other consolidated democracies such as Canada, France, Germany, the Netherlands, Sweden and the UK, we have witnessed the unsettling of legal and moral prohibitions.[17]

## The Legal and Moral Abolition of Torture—The Historical Process

Investigation of the long historical process culminating in the 1984 UN CAT offers us some pointers as to why we have returned to a struggle over this peremptory norm in global politics, and how this return might be resisted. The exploration also alludes to the strong association between torture and terrorism in the period of modern statehood.

Over the millennia, torture has been used for four main reasons.[18] First, at some historical junctures, political agents have acted on the belief that there is a category of subhuman. For example, in Greek and Roman times it was assumed that torture was the only means to ensure that slaves told the truth. There are obvious reminders here of the behavior of Nazi interrogators, experimenters and exterminators, and of the consequences of resort to the typology of "savage" or "barbarian."[19]

Secondly, the place of confession as a means of establishing guilt has been strongly associated with the use of torture. A twelfth-century legal revolution in Europe required conviction only if guilt was certain. In the absence of full certainty, a confession had to be extracted, most frequently through the use of torture. With confession established as the "queen of proofs," torture became commonplace and technically became disassociated from the status of the accused or the gravity of the crime. Torture remains commonplace in countries where there is no presumption of innocence, combined with undeveloped forensic and other such skills, including the arts of interrogation.[20] Shue, writing in 1978, reminds us of the "reputed informal motto of the Saigon police, 'If they are not guilty, beat them until they are.'"[21]

Thirdly, there is the relationship between torture and power. According to Michel Foucault, torture in a time of unconstrained royal power had an important reconstitutive function. In the public display of mind-numbing cruelty, the sovereign could demonstrate his "unrestrained presence," and the "absolute power of life and death" through punishment that was "both personal and public."[22]

Finally, with the advent of modern statehood, political dissent—including the use of terrorist tactics and political assassination—led to torture's use for deterrent or intimidation purposes or to acquire information, even in states where it had previously been outlawed. Though torture had formally been abolished in Russia in 1801, the terrorist attacks on the Russian state of the late nineteenth century saw its deadly return.[23] Torture was also widespread under twentieth-century colonial, fascist and totalitarian governments, and secretly endorsed as a method in democratic states for fighting the Cold War.[24]

Reversing this tide has been difficult, complex and incomplete. The major factors leading to torture's legal abolition have involved functional changes in society and in the relations between leaders and led, together with the gathering power of moral argument. For example, the abolition of torture in Europe in the eighteenth and early nineteenth centuries came in part through changes to the European law of proof. It also related to the development of new forms of punishment and places of control, alongside the capacity of the state to finance via taxation those new places of incarceration. The shift to popular sovereignty removed the need to demonstrate royal power through the enactment of public punishment. Moreover, the horrific nature of public executions (as well as their excessive use) was serving only to generate political revolt.[25] The state needed to offer alternatives, with institutions such as the factory, prison, school and military performing the necessary controlling functions. And when a crime had taken place, the galley, the workhouse and the practice of transportation offered—for a time—alternative forms of punishment for dealing with it.

Significant too, however, were the writings of Enlightenment thinkers. Cesare Beccaria in 1764 argued with great lucidity and directness against torture on the grounds of its immorality and because it risked the torment of the innocent and that the guilty would go free provided they could resist the pain. As he put it, torture was "a sure way to acquit robust scoundrels and to condemn weak but innocent people."[26]

Such moral reasoning was revived especially strongly at the global level after World War II, leading to the development of an international legal norm. The contempt shown for human rights during that war underpinned the creation of several human rights treaties and declarations, and advanced the protections for combatants and non-combatants in wartime. Article 5 of the 1948 Universal Declaration of Human Rights was the first international code to state that "No one shall be subjected to torture or cruel, inhuman or degrading treatment or punishment." This statement reappeared in one of the core human rights conventions, the ICCPR, first opened for signature in 1966, as well as in the African Charter and the European and American conventions. The 1949 Geneva Conventions also prohibited physical or mental torture and other forms of coercion.

However, it took the birth of an international human rights NGO—Amnesty International—in 1961, before serious attempts were made to focus specifically on the scourge of torture and to expose the extent to which it was still being practiced.[27] Its widespread use in two formerly democratic states boosted Amnesty's anti-torture campaign. The military coup in Greece in May 1967, which led to the severe beating of those suspected of subversion and dissent, resulted in actions taken against Greece by Scandinavian governments and the Netherlands through the Council of Europe—clear instances where the combination of non-state actors and enlightened states could work in tandem to expand the areas of moral concern. Another military coup, this time in Chile in September 1973, again enhanced the potency of Amnesty's arguments. It particularly boosted the organization's membership base in the United States (from 3,000 to 50,000 members between 1974 and 1976).[28] Chile helped Amnesty's cause for other reasons, too. The coup displaced not only the leadership of a country member of the non-aligned movement but also a socialist government. Moreover, a US hand was seen to be behind the overthrow of the country's leader, Salvador Allende. This made certain states more receptive: you could be both anti-torture and against a US-installed Pinochet regime.

Over one million people in 85 countries signed Amnesty's petition calling on the UN General Assembly to outlaw torture's use, and in December 1975 the UN General Assembly adopted a Declaration on Torture. Nine years later, in March 1984, the UN Commission on Human Rights adopted the CAT, which came into force after obtaining the required number of signatures two and a half years later. Today there are 141 state parties.[29] The formulation of that Convention took the combined forces of global and domestic civil society, certain non-major states, and the UN in order to ensure that, once the norm had emerged, it next was codified, and finally implemented—at least to the extent of state ratification of an international treaty and the marrying of that treaty's provisions with domestic law. (As noted earlier, actual practices have often fallen well short of expressed intentions.) Political bargaining and challenges to democratic identities favored its emergence too.

This cursory survey of the history of torture and its legal abolition points to several possible reasons for its resurrection in a more open form since 9/11. It also suggests from where the most important sources of resistance to this opening are likely to come. The designation of certain peoples as of lesser status, or as not fully human; the priority given to the security of the sovereign or of the state over that of the individual; the types of conditions under which evidence is acquired which influences the means adopted for determining guilt; and the necessity to be seen to punish in order to demonstrate overwhelming power and to deter opposition to those in power have all played roles in keeping torture alive over the millennia. And, on the other side, the anti-torture norm embedded in law and in state and inter-state institutions, and the activism of those who stand outside the control of the executive arm of the state, have worked in mutually reinforcing ways to mount a challenge to torture. The abolition of torture, viewed as a process, shows a complex interaction between expanding areas of normative concern, state interest and moral and functionalist arguments, each propelling the other forward at certain crucial junctures.

In explaining torture's return since September 11, and in particular the widespread nature of the debate that it has engendered, David Luban has argued persuasively that this owes much to its claimed association with the gathering of intelligence about future events, a relationship to which I have not so far given much emphasis. Even some liberals can stomach this return, he argues, because unlike confession which is "backward-looking," intelligence gathering looks forward and is "to forestall future evils like terrorist attacks." Under these circumstances torture becomes divorced from cruelty and when used "to gather intelligence and save lives seems almost heroic."[30]

Luban goes on to make a forceful case for why this represents a "dangerous delusion," but clearly he is right to argue that this type of reasoning has been powerful in resurrecting the debate and justification of torture even among liberals in the period since the terrorist attacks of September 2001. My argument, though, is intended to emphasize behavior and debate that goes beyond liberal reasoning and the points Luban articulates so persuasively. What we are witnessing is the resurrection of some of these other time-honored functions of torture— particularly those related to the demonstration of power and its usage against "enemies of the state" both to deter and to intimidate. These older functions of torture have been given a new lease on life.

## Torture, Power and Reputation

I want to illustrate this in reference to what I have referred to elsewhere as competing reputations in world politics since September 11.[31] By reputation I am referring to the embodiment in states, international organizations, non-state actors or individuals of certain durable characteristics.[32] The two competing reputations I refer to are first, a commitment to the protection and promotion of human rights—particularly prevalent in the 1990s—and second, to the demonstration of an effective, even ruthless, capacity to promote a counter-terrorist agenda.[33]

At the end of the twentieth century it was understood, as Michael Ignatieff put it, that human rights had become the "dominant moral vocabulary in foreign affairs,"[34] and that the ability of a state to exercise sovereignty over territory and people was no longer enough—that sovereignty as responsibility was the newly emergent understanding. Jack Donnelly described it as the establishment of a new standard of civilization in which membership in international society depended on the extent to which governments observed human rights standards.[35] No one questioned whether human rights should be a part of foreign policy. We were still fighting over which rights to promote on which occasions and about how best to promote human rights. But the expectation that global actors would—indeed should–be concerned about human rights in any part of the world where they might be being abused was broadly understood. It was in this climate that torture came to be established as illegal and publicly condemned as a moral outrage.

Since September 2001, however, the preeminence of this reputation of human rights protector or defender has been undermined. In some other ways, it has been recast: especially in the cases of the US and UK governments, human rights have been used to legitimize coercive regime change in Iraq outside the justification associated with a supreme humanitarian emergency. A new and valued reputation is one of effectiveness in dealing with suspected terrorists, including the ability to pass regulations that strengthen the central authority of the state, police air, sea and land borders, arrest terrorist suspects, focus on their interrogation rather than trial, and investigate more fully those seeking asylum or to migrate. In the case of the United States, this has gone beyond trying to demonstrate effectiveness and embraces a reputation for ruthlessness in dealing with the terrorist threat: as Steven E. Miller puts it, the US has adopted "a 'win through intimidation' strategic outlook."[36] Walter Russell Mead refers to it as the triumph of the Jacksonian tradition in the American way of war. As Mead puts it: the Bush administration "believed that it was more important to frighten and deter potential enemies than to reassure friends. If the good guys had to be scared in order to make sure the bad guys knew you were

serious, so be it."[37] This particular reputation has been projected via demonstrations of military and technological strength, images of the subjugation of the enemy, statements that some in detention do not deserve humane treatment, and regularly reported indications of abuse of suspect detainees.

Is that not the implication of the US release of photographs distributed around the world of those held captive at the US naval base at Guantanamo Bay, prisoners in cages in orange overalls crouching before US marine commanders, blindfolded and shackled? As John Mackinlay has written: these "damning prisoner photographs were not taken by a paparazzo camera commando, but by US Marine photographers for a Republican home audience that wants to see the boot of retribution being applied."[38] The audience was, of course, much larger than that, and presumably it was meant to interpret that graphic visual evidence as (to use Foucault's terms) the absolute sovereign demonstrating its "unrestrained presence," the "absolute power of life and death" through punishment that is "both personal and public"; and at a minimum as a *political* version of military "shock and awe" tactics, above all to demonstrate mastery over the enemy and to try to intimidate would-be terrorists, their sympathizers or other opponents. The intelligence value of many of those held at Guantanamo has always been questionable; thus deterrence and control seemed to be primary motives. Reinforcing the impact of these photographs and film clips have been the multiple statements by CIA agents and others that detainee abuse, outsourced or not, is taking place.[39]

More directly still, the US Attorney General, Gonzales, in the course of his confirmation hearings in January 2005, despite all the ongoing controversy about US treatment of detainees at Guantanamo, Abu Ghraib and Bagram, in response to Senate questions informed in writing US Senators that "cruel, inhuman and degrading treatment of detainees is forbidden to interrogators only within U.S. territory." And both he and then National Security Adviser Condoleezza Rice, when asked why the "Bush administration fought off restrictions (passed by a 96–2 Senate vote) which 'would have explicitly extended to intelligence officers a prohibition against torture or inhumane treatment, and would have required the C.I.A. as well as the Pentagon to report to Congress about the methods they were using,'" replied that this was done "to deny protection to people who are not entitled to it."[40]

This "torture culture" (Luban's phrase) had earlier been given license by the President who made the statement that the Geneva Conventions did not apply either to Al Qaeda or Taliban detainees, except that "as a matter of policy" (i.e., not "as a matter of law") they would be treated humanely, "including those who are not legally entitled to such treatment." As Rodley has put it: "With those few words, the highest authority in the United States has taken the position that some persons held in connection with an armed conflict have no legal right to be treated humanely."[41] Other senior administration officials were to reinforce Bush's sentiments, his Secretary of Defense Rumsfeld saying of the detainees at Guantanamo: "I do not feel even the slightest concern over their treatment. They are being treated vastly better than they treated anybody else over the last several years and vastly better than was their circumstance when they were found."[42] All such statements reinforce the sense that the Bush administration intends a weakening of humanitarian norms and a reduction in their scope.

## Global Consequences

The consequences of this US adjustment to its "valued reputation" for other countries' behavior are also devastating for the torture norm. My focus will be on Asia,[43] although there are many other instances of abuse that could be drawn upon, including those that further implicate the Western world. I refer to two main developments: first, some parts of the US administration have tried to project rights-abusing states instead as important partners; and, second, there is emulation of US rhetoric and behavior, frequently for politically opportunistic reasons, on the part of a number of governments. (In amended and new anti-terrorist legislation, for example, terrorism is frequently defined in dangerously wide-ranging ways.)

Uzbekistan, for example, and prior to the 2005 announcement of US expulsion from bases in that country, had been described not as (or not only as) a human rights abuser of the severest kind, but—to quote Rumsfeld (again) in February 2004—"a key member of the coalition's global war on terror" that has offered "stalwart support" in the anti-terrorist campaign.[44] Malaysia, previously criticized for its abuse of detainees, and indiscriminate and blatantly political uses of its Internal Security Act (ISA), has since been described as a model, moderate, predominantly Islamic country in Southeast Asia that is a "beacon of stability in the region."[45] Governments such as these have regularly received symbolic and material support from the US administration, either in the form of summits in Washington, high-level meetings in their own countries, or economic and military aid.

Secondly, since 9/11 politically opportunistic behavior has been rife throughout Asia: for example, Uzbek security forces in May 2005 used indiscriminate force against civilians in Andijan, killing possibly between 200 and 700 people, on the grounds that these were groups linked with international Islamist terrorism. Subsequently, a widespread crackdown on those trying to expose the brutality led to indefinite detention, coercion of the families of those who fled the country, and scripted confessions on government-controlled television.[46] China has moved with alacrity to designate its problems with opposition and independence groups in Xinjiang, Tibet and elsewhere as part of the global anti-terrorist campaign. In September 2004, Beijing held what it described as an anti-terror exercise in Lhasa, involving joint operations among the army, police, paramilitary forces and militia, for no obvious security reason.[47] Malaysian officials have tried to resist domestic calls for reform of the country's ISA on the twin grounds that it chimes with the US Patriot Act and the US administration now supports rather than criticizes it.[48] A Human Rights Watch report on those 100 or so detained since August 2001 under Malaysia's ISA on suspicion of links with terrorist activity concluded that they have suffered serious abuse. Even more tellingly, if these detainees failed to cooperate with Malaysian authorities, they were threatened with being sent to US detention facilities at Guantanamo—an indication of the latter's perceived high place in the hierarchy of the abuse of personal security rights.[49]

Pan-Asian and domestic human rights organizations have stated that the abuse of personal security rights has been rising "exponentially across Asia." Human rights defenders are under threat and some have lost their lives.[50] What is happening in Asia (and in other regions of the world) is an indication of how unrestrained many governments believe themselves to be when the most powerful state in the international system elevates counter-terrorist action above other values. Torture and other forms of abuse become commonplace and often more openly so. Shue has put this in succinct form: "We have no guarantee that a precedent of refraining from torture will be followed by others, but we can be sure that a precedent of engaging in torture will be followed." He goes on:

> Torture seems to be the ultimate in efficiency, the shortcut to end all shortcuts. It is difficult enough to resist when you would be the exception if you gave in. When you would simply be following the leader, the precedent is irresistible.[51]

Thus, the relationship between power and norms appears, on this reading, to vindicate a realist interpretation of world politics, at least to the extent that US power appears to have given it the capacity to shape global agendas and to expose the hollowness at the heart of even a so-called obligatory norm. In the Bush administration's efforts to reinterpret the torture norm for strategic reasons, it has weakened its constraining effects not only on US service and other official personnel, but apparently elsewhere in the world as well.

## The Power of the Anti-Torture Norm?

What, then, of the power of norms—and the power of a peremptory norm at that? The discussion in this fourth section is meant to clarify in what ways and by what means the normative prohibition against the use of torture has maintained some residual constraints on behavior. With respect to the United States, I argue that, while separation of powers has been important in this regard (and may over time become more so), at this stage it has not been enough to make a critical difference. Its proper functioning seems to be dependent on the work of US domestic and transnational human rights NGOs, the persistence of individual political figures, and the existence of UN human rights mechanisms, all of which have pointed to past legal and other commitments, or have drawn on US rhetoric in support of rights to expose the normative gap between words and action. These types of criticisms become more potent still in the context of a US counter-terrorist strategy that is just not working and may be making matters far worse.[52]

Why do I argue that US institutions on their own are not enough to address the breaching of the torture norm? After all, it is the case that the US administration did withdraw the August 2002 Bybee memo, it did submit its Second Periodic Report to the Committee against Torture on May 6, 2005 (some three and a half years late), and it did begin that report with a rousing statement that "Torture is wrong no matter where it occurs, and the United States will continue to lead the fight to eliminate it everywhere."[53]

Nevertheless, US officials, including the US Attorney General, continue to make a distinction between the severest forms of torture and the rest of the behavior that they want to define as cruel, inhuman and degrading treatment. This is so even though the CAT prohibits all these forms of behavior and much jurisprudence has raised the standards when it comes to the protection of

detainees.[54] The US Constitution itself rules out cruel and unusual punishment to induce confession and this Article has been interpreted as coincident with the prohibitions outlined under the CAT. Moreover, some of these US officials (notably the US Vice President) have also argued that aliens held overseas are not subject to the prohibitions against inhuman treatment. (According to Amnesty, the US has held some 70,000 detainees outside the country since September 2001.[55]) And while some US military personnel have been brought to book, no single high-level figure has taken responsibility for the abuses, and those convicted have generally been given light sentences.[56]

True, the US court system has played a role in reining in some of the circumstances that have contributed to the abuse, then Supreme Court Justice, Sandra Day O'Connor, writing the majority opinion in June 2004 that overturned the Bush administration's claim that those held in Guantanamo are beyond US law.[57] However, again we cannot afford to be too sanguine. According to a leading US constitutional lawyer, Owen Fiss, those decisions involving the Padilla, Hamdi and Rasul cases (two of whom were American citizens at the time of their arrest[58]) did less than they should have. For example, Fiss describes the interpretation in the Padilla case as an "act of judicial cowardice," pragmatic and parochial in intent. The Supreme Court Justices decided the outcome on the narrow basis of jurisdiction, not in the spirit of a constitution that projects the ideals of the nation.[59]

There have, too, been several US Defense Department-appointed commissions of enquiry into the abuses at Abu Ghraib and elsewhere.[60] But welcome though these are, as Joseph Lelyveld has put it:

> For all the genuine outrage in predictable places over what was soon being called a "torture scandal"—in legal forums, editorial pages, letter columns—the usual democratic cleansing cycle never really got going. However strong the outcry, it wasn't enough to yield political results in the form of a determined Congressional investigation, let alone an independent commission of enquiry.[61]

The Senate Judiciary Committee, meeting in June 2005, explained it thus, its chair stating:

> It may be that it's too hot to handle for Congress, may be that it's too complex to handle for Congress, or it may be that Congress wants to sit back as we customarily do . . . But at any rate, Congress hasn't acted.

That Judiciary Committee hearing elicited a number of important statements, including one from the Vermont Democrat, Senator Patrick Leahy, who issued a blistering attack on US detention policy; but he also referred, in anguish, to the Senate standing "idly by," watching the spreading "stain" of Guantanamo.[62]

In the autumn of 2005 this congressional inertia started to be overcome. As the US Congress finished its business in August 2005, the executive pulled the defense appropriations bill from consideration because Republican Senator John McCain of Arizona, Senator Lindsay Graham of South Carolina (a former military judge), and Senator John Warner of Virginia and chair of the Senate Armed Services Committee, had appended amendments setting standards for the treatment of prisoners in US military detention facilities. They, together with Republican Senator Susan Collins of Maine, also included an amendment that would prohibit cruel, inhumane or degrading treatment of prisoners.[63] On October 5, the Senate voted 90–9 to support these amendments that are intended to make binding use of the "US Army Field Manual on Intelligence Interrogations."[64] They are also designed to reinforce the ban on cruel, inhuman or degrading treatment of detainees.[65]

As we await the outcome of this particularly revealing and potentially consequential battle between the executive and legislative branches, we are relying predominantly on certain key individuals, and on domestic[66] and transnational civil society groups to keep the anti-torture norm alive. These groups are aided, as in the 1970s and 1980s—but this time with some stronger, formal, institutional backing—by UN institutions such as the Office of the UN High Commissioner for Human Rights, the UN Secretary-General, and the thematic rapporteurs that have presented information on various forms of abuse to the UN Commission on Human Rights.

To give just a few of the examples of UN activism in this area: the UN's Counter-Terrorism Committee (CTC), set up under UN Security Council resolution 1373 towards the end of September 2001, began with a statement from its first chair that the body was "not a tribunal for judging states," which among other things meant that it would not test whether state reports on the counter-terrorist measures they were developing were consistent with human rights standards. That particular "hands-off" approach has been left behind following lobbying and statements from several in the UN with human rights competencies.[67] The CTC has now had a staff expert on human rights, humanitarian law and refugee law appointed to it. The UN High Commissioner's office in Geneva has produced a "Digest of Jurisprudence of the

UN and Regional Organizations on the Protection of Human Rights while Countering Terrorism" which, among other matters, clarifies the concept of nonderogable rights under UN and regional human rights conventions. It states categorically:

> This publication will help policy makers, including government officials, parliamentarians, judges, lawyers and human rights defenders, in developing counter-terrorism strategies that are fully respectful of human rights.[68]

No government can claim to be in ignorance of its obligations. A final example refers to the pressure from five independent special rapporteurs of the United Nations Commission on Human Rights, mounted since early in 2002, to gain private access to those held in detention in Guantanamo. So far, the Bush administration has refused this group's request that interviews with detainees be conducted in private and thus the visit has not gone ahead. The expectations of the rapporteurs are, however, that US compliance with the full terms of reference will eventually be agreed.[69]

These UN bodies have traditionally relied on the fact-gathering activities of the major human rights NGOs, given the paucity of their own resources. The NGOs—domestic and transnational—indeed have been active in reminding governments, the UN and others that there is a sense of impunity abroad that has to be addressed. The UN is providing a platform for normative debate as well as information about the legal requirements that states have entered into when signing treaties such as the UN CAT. In addition, having asked states to report to the CTC (and all 191 have done so, many on more than one occasion), that reporting offers opportunities for civil society groups to highlight lapses (potential and actual) in state behavior and areas of concern. The UN's human rights bodies and NGOs, in particular, have played important roles in trying to ensure that the two reputations previously referred to are in contention, and that the international human rights regime that has been built up painstakingly, over several decades, retains some visibility and relevance at a time when it is under attack.

## Conclusion

Are we witnessing, then, the inevitable overwhelming of a peremptory humanitarian norm at a time of heightened national and global insecurity, or can we conclude that, despite the difficulties being faced by those concerned about maintaining protections for core human rights, "struggle" remains a more accurate description? The US NGO Human Rights First, together with the Carter Center believes the latter to be so. They claimed in August 2005 that there is:

> a growing international consensus that violating human rights in the name of countering terrorism is counterproductive, which in turn has induced increasing references by governments to human rights and freedom as key elements of a strategy designed to promote peace and security.[70]

There is some truth to this statement, although there is certainly no room for complacency, and it will take a huge effort to regain lost ground. Nevertheless, despite overwhelming US material power, the Bush administration has not been able simply to cast aside the anti-torture norm. It can, however, continue its efforts to reinterpret it in ways which suggest its intention is not to clarify the CAT's use in operational circumstances but primarily to find ways of violating it.

Efforts to counter this are mounting, however. Prudential or instrumental reasons of the kind promoted in that Human Rights First statement (that violations of rights are counterproductive) are showing up more frequently as the struggle progresses, including the idea that US behavior undermines the prospect that other states will lend their support to coalition operations and that abusive forms of treatment, rather than deterring oppositional and terrorist acts, appear to be engendering new ones. Neither control nor deterrence nor a demonstration of overwhelming sovereign power appears to be having the intended effects.

Instrumentalism or prudential reasoning, though, is only a part of the story of resistance. Moral reasoning has been resurrected too and is available to examine for its intrinsic worth, or, when voiced by governments that have been engaging in abuse, can be exploited as a means of underscoring the normative gap between rhetoric and behavior. International reminders of the legal arguments and of the previous delegitimization of the act of torture resonate particularly strongly in the context of the Bush administration's own claims that it is engaged in the promotion of freedom, human rights and democracy. The statements of influential US individuals such as Senator McCain, who has actually had to endure being tortured, complements this international and self-induced pressure. In Wilsonian rather than Jacksonian language, McCain—a supporter of the 2003 military intervention in Iraq—has made both the prudential and the moral argument. As he stated to his senatorial colleagues in July 2005:

> We are Americans, and we hold ourselves to humane standards of treatment of people no matter how evil or terrible they may be. To do otherwise . . . undermines our security, but it also undermines our greatness as a nation. We are not simply any other country. We stand for something more in the world—a moral mission, one of freedom and democracy and human rights at home and abroad. . . . The enemy we fight has no respect for human life or human rights. They don't deserve our sympathy. But this isn't about who they are. This is about who we are.[71]

Such a statement might have one unfortunate effect in that it reinforces the "us versus them" argument. Moreover, it may not have much influence on perceptions of America outside the United States. Nevertheless, it is couched in terms which carry weight inside the country. The US executive branch does not have the discursive field to itself, the struggle with McCain and other like-minded groups and individuals showing that its attempts to reinterpret the norm have not been wholly persuasive.

In that finding, we have a continuing place for what Carr described as recognized moral obligations, a place for morality in any world order. It is a reminder too of the continuing force of the Melian reply to the Athenian claim that the "strong do what they have the power to do and the weak accept what they have to accept." In counseling both prudence and respect for humanity, Melos stated:

> It is at any rate useful that you should not destroy a principle that is to the general good of all men—namely, that in the case of all who fall into danger there should be such a thing as fair play and just dealing. . . . And this is a principle which affects you as much as anybody, since your own fall would be visited by the most terrible vengeance and would be an example to the world.[72]

## Questions

1. For years the United States has denounced the use of torture in the world. Why has the Bush administration sought to redefine what is torture and what is acceptable interrogation?

2. Do you believe there is ever reason to use "coercive methods" in trying to get information from a prisoner?

# Notes

1. For their astute comments on earlier versions of this article, and useful suggestions for additional reading, I would like to thank Alan Angell, Tim Dunne, Andrew Hurrell, Adam Roberts and Henry Shue. The discussions at Aberystwyth immediately after the lecture and during the following day were enormously stimulating and helpful. Of course I remain responsible for any errors and inconsistencies that remain.

2. Michael Cox, "Introduction" to E. H. Carr, *The Twenty Years' Crisis* (reissued Basingstoke: Palgrave, 2001), p. xxiii; "reformist steps" from Ken Booth, "Security in Anarchy: Utopian Realism in Theory and Practice," *International Affairs,* 67(3), July 1991, pp. 527–45. See also Michael Cox (ed.), *E. H. Carr: A Critical Appraisal* (Basingstoke: Palgrave, 2000); Charles Jones, *E. H. Carr and International Relations: A Duty to Lie* (Cambridge: Cambridge University Press, 1998).

3. Carr, *Twenty Years' Crisis* (2001 ed.), p. 141.

4. The definition of torture contained in Article 1 of the 1984 Convention Against Torture and Other Cruel, Inhuman or Degrading Treatment or Punishment (CAT) is "any act by which severe pain or suffering, whether physical or mental, is intentionally inflicted on a person for such purposes as obtaining from him [*sic*] or a third person information or a confession, punishing him for an act he or a third person has committed or is suspected of having committed, or intimidating or coercing him or a third person, or for any reason based on discrimination of any kind, when such pain or suffering is inflicted by or at the instigation of or with the consent or acquiescence of a public official or other person acting in an official capacity. It does not include pain or suffering arising only from, inherent in or incidental to lawful sanctions." Article 2(2) states, "No exceptional circumstances whatsoever, whether a state of war or a threat of war, internal political instability or any other public emergency, may be invoked as a justification of torture."

5. Henry Shue, "Torture," *Philosophy and Public Affairs,* 7(2), Winter 1978, p. 124.

6. The various forms of denial used in reference to uses of torture, and many instances of the use of denial, are discussed in Stanley Cohen, *States of Denial: Knowing about Atrocities and Suffering* (Cambridge: Polity Press, 2001).

7. "Statement of the Special Rapporteur on Torture, Manfred Nowak to the 61st Session of the UN Commission on Human Rights," 4 April 2005, available at http://www.unhchr.ch/huricane/huricane. nsf/ (accessed 12 May 2005).

8. In an extension of the Kantian argument that torture represents total disrespect for humanity and in addition carries the weight of a "distinctive kind of wrong," see David Sussman, "What's Wrong with Torture?" *Philosophy and Public Affairs,* 33(1), January 2005, pp. 1–33. Sussman, in arguing for what distinguishes interrogational torture from, for example, the violence of war or police action, states: "Torture does not merely insult or damage its victim's agency, but rather turns such agency against itself, forcing the victim to experience herself as helpless yet complicit in her own violation." Thus, "water-boarding," "a technique that involves repeated partial drownings," used by US officials on some suspect terrorist detainees, and which is otherwise quite common as a form of torture elsewhere in the world, involves "not just the agony of inhaling water, but the hopeless struggle against one's own desperate urge to breathe that precedes it. Not only does the victim find himself hurt by his body, but he also finds himself to be the one hurting his body as well, in some way

pushing it against itself. The relationship of torturer to victim is thus replicated in the victim's own consciousness of himself as an embodied agent. In the most intimate aspects of his agency, the sufferer is made to experience himself not just as a passive victim, but as an active accomplice in his own debasement" (pp. 23, 30). (Sussman gives several other such examples.) Grasping this idea of complicity brings us closer to understanding the humiliation experienced by the torturer's victim.

9. The story of the abuse at Abu Ghraib began to break in November 2003 with photographs being released to the *Washington Post* and the CBS news program *Sixty Minutes II* in April 2004. In May the International Committee of the Red Cross (ICRC) report of February 2004 was leaked to the *Wall Street Journal.* Before the breaking of the Abu Ghraib story, however, several press reports indicated that "rendition" of suspects to countries that routinely torture was taking place, together with the use of "stress and duress techniques" on those who were held in US detention facilities in Afghanistan and at Guantanamo Bay. See William Schulz, *Tainted Legacy: 9/11 and the Ruin of Human Rights* (New York: Thunder's Mouth Press, 2003), pp. 157–8. The ICRC report can be found in Mark Danner, *Torture and Truth: America, Abu Ghraib, and the War on Terror* (London: Granta, 2004), and Karen J. Greenberg and Joshua L. Dratel (eds.), *The Torture Papers: The Road to Abu Ghraib* (New York: Cambridge University Press, 2005).

10. Annex 2 to the "Second Periodic Report of the United States of America to the Committee Against Torture," submitted 6 May 2005, US Department of State.

11. Alan Dershowitz, *Why Terrorism Works* (New Haven, CT: Yale University Press, 2002), p. 134.

12. Jonathan Alter, "Time to Think about Torture," *Newsweek,* 5 November 2001.

13. *The Economist,* cover story, 11–17 January 2003.

14. Sanford Levinson (ed.), *Torture: A Collection* (Oxford: Oxford University Press, 2004), p. 24. Elaine Scarry offers a powerful critique of the Dershowitz argument in this collection. See "Five Errors in the Reasoning of Alan Dershowitz," chapter 15. Jean Bethke Elshtain in the same volume (chapter 4) also puts forward a strong argument against Dershowitz but in favor of "torture lite," which she defines to include (p. 85), via a quotation from Mark Bowden, as: "sleep deprivation, exposure to heat or cold, the use of drugs to cause confusion, rough treatment (slapping, shoving or shaking), forcing a prisoner to stand for days at a time or sit in uncomfortable positions, and playing on his fears for himself and his family." All these methods are illegal under the Geneva Conventions. Similar, though less severe, activities were once investigated and outlawed in the UK. In 1972, the Minority Report of a three-man committee of Privy Councillors, charged to decide whether the existing authorized interrogation procedures in Northern Ireland—such as wall-standing, hooding, noise and manipulation of diet and sleep—required amendment, pleaded for a return to the more humane interrogation standards adopted during the Second World War and which came to be reflected in the 1949 Geneva Conventions. These recommendations were accepted by Prime Minister Edward Heath in March 1972. See Adam Roberts, "Is There a Distinctive British Approach to the Law of Armed Conflict?" paper given at the conference on "UK Perspectives on the Law of Armed Conflict," St Antony's College, Oxford, 30 June–2 July 2004, pp. 18–19 of manuscript.

15. Memorandum for Alberto R. Gonzales, Counsel to the President, from Jay S. Bybee, Assistant Attorney General, 1 August 2002, reprinted in full in Danner, *Torture and Truth,* pp. 115–66, and see

pp. 146–9 for the Commander in Chief argument. Sir Nigel Rodley, "Torture in the 21st Century," the William J. Butler Lecture on International Law, given to the Urban Morgan Institute for Human Rights at the University of Cincinnati College of Law, 23 September 2004.

16. David Luban, "Liberalism, Torture, and the Ticking Bomb," *Virginia Law Review,* 91, 2005, p. 1457; and Amnesty International, *Guantanamo and Beyond: The Continuing Pursuit of Unchecked Executive Power,* May 2005, p. 38 of printer-friendly version, available at http://web.amnesty.org/library (accessed 18 July 2005). The Levin memo is available at http://www.usdoj.gov/olc/dagmemo.pdf (accessed 8 June 2005).

17. See, for example, Human Rights Watch, *Still at Risk: Diplomatic Assurances No Safeguard against Torture,* 15 April 2005, which discusses renditions, removals and deportations by a number of Western governments to countries that routinely torture. See www.hrw.org (accessed 16 June 2005). The British government has tried to negotiate agreements that provide protection against human rights abuse where a suspected foreign militant deemed a threat to the British public is deported to his country of origin. In the case of Egypt, its National Council for Human Rights rejected a UK proposal that it act as monitor of the treatment of those so deported, believing that role to be impossible adequately to fulfill. See William Wallis, "Egypt Human Rights Body rejects UK's Extradition Proposal," *Financial Times,* 21 September 2005, p. 11. The French army officer, Paul Aussaresses, has had his book, which sets out the case for torture during the Algerian resistance struggle, reprinted in March 2002 and again in February 2005. See *The Battle of the Casbah: Terrorism and Counter-Terrorism in Algeria 1955–1957* (New York: Enigma Books, 2005). See too the references to the circumvention of the CAT in the 2005 report of the "independent expert on the protection of human rights and fundamental freedoms while countering terrorism," Robert K. Goldman, esp. pp. 18–20. Commission on Human Rights, 61st Session, "Promotion and Protection of Human Rights," E/CN.4/2005/103, 7 February 2005.

18. Particularly helpful to this section is Edward Peters, *Torture* (Oxford: Blackwell, 1985); Matthew Lippman, "The Development and Drafting of the United Nations Convention Against Torture and Other Cruel, Inhuman or Degrading Treatment or Punishment," Boston College, *International and Comparative Law Review,* XVIII(2), 1994, pp. 275–335; Michel Foucault, *Discipline and Punish: The Birth of the Prison* (London: Penguin Books, 1977); V. A. C. Gatrell, *The Hanging Tree: Execution and the English People 1770–1868* (Oxford: Oxford University Press, 1994); and John H. Langbein, *Torture and the Law of Proof: Europe and England in the Ancien Regime* (Chicago: University of Chicago Press, 1977). Luban discusses the "Five Aims of Torture," adopting a somewhat different set from mine, in "Liberalism," pp. 1429–40.

19. US Vice-President Richard Cheney asked a few days after September 11, 2001 whether other countries were going to stand with America on the side of freedom, democracy and civilization, "or are they going to stand with the terrorists and the barbarians." Quoted in Schulz, *Tainted Legacy,* p. 58.

20. Torture is also promoted and validated where confession evidence achieved via torture is accepted in legal proceedings, even where one's own state officials do not do the actual torturing—one reason for the importance of the current debate about "outsourcing" torture and the "rendition" of terrorist suspects.

21. Shue, "Torture," p. 135.

22. Foucault, *Discipline and Punish,* p. 48. Elaine Scarry's argument about the relationship between pain and power should also be remembered here. See *The Body in Pain* (Oxford: Oxford University Press, 1985).

23. Walter Laqueur associates the birth of modern terrorism with the flogging in Russia in 1878 of a political prisoner. In response, Vera Zasulich shot the man who ordered the flogging, General Trepov, the police chief of St. Petersburg. Walter Laqueur, *The Age of Terrorism* (London: Weidenfeld and Nicolson, 1987), p. 33, and also quoted in Adam Roberts, "The 'War on Terror' in Historical Perspective," *Survival,* 47(2), Summer 2005, pp. 110–11. Note, however, that this implies a definition of terrorism that goes beyond the intentional killing of civilians. Torture's association with terrorism, and with political and other forms of dissent, including in its most violent form civil war, has always been apparent. Of all the factors that the quantitative studies show as being strongly influential in leading governments into sanctioning torture, civil war and political rebellion, which may include the use of terrorist acts, carry a great deal of the explanatory weight. Steve C. Poe, C. Neal Tate and Linda Camp Keith, "Repression of the Human Right to Personal Integrity Revisited: A Global Cross-National Study Covering the Years 1976–1993," *International Studies Quarterly,* 43, 1999, pp. 291–313.

24. For one example of the latter see the National Security Archive Electronic Briefing Book no. 122, which discusses two CIA interrogation manuals from the 1960s and 1980s which outline coercive techniques, later described in 1992 as "offensive and objectionable." See http://www.gwu.edu/~nsarchiv/NSAEBB/NSAEBB122/ (accessed 12 October 2005).

25. Public hanging was not deemed equivalent to torture, but reactions to the form it took fed into the same search for alternative methods of punishment. Public hanging was abolished in England in 1868. See Gatrell, *The Hanging Tree.* Gatrell argues that "if there was any single reason why executions were hidden behind prison walls from 1868 onwards it was because the crowd's sardonic commentaries could no longer be borne. Too often that despised crowd denounced justice as murderous in itself" (p. viii). He describes the "latent premiss of this book that humane feelings prevail when their costs in terms of security or comfort are bearable" (p. 12).

26. Cesare Beccaria, *On Crimes and Punishments,* trans. David Young (Indianapolis: Hackett Publishing Co., 1986), p. 29. By the end of the century there were about 60 editions available in multiple languages. See also Marcello Maestro, *Cesare Beccaria and the Origins of Penal Reform* (Philadelphia: Temple University Press, 1973).

27. Ann Marie Clark, *Diplomacy of Conscience: Amnesty International and Changing Human Rights Norms* (Princeton, NJ: Princeton University Press, 2001).

28 William Korey, *NGOs and the Universal Declaration of Human Rights* (New York: St Martin's Press, 1998), p. 169; Margaret E. Keck and Kathryn Sikkink, *Activists Beyond Borders: Advocacy Networks in International Politics* (Ithaca, NY: Cornell University Press, 1998), pp. 90–1. The Chilean government, in November 2004, made public the official report of the National Commission on Political Imprisonment and Torture (Spanish text available at www.comisiontortura.cl). It prompted the government of President Ricardo Lagos to offer lifelong pensions to the more than 28,000 people tortured by agents of Pinochet's military government. See http://newsvote.bbc.uk/mpapps/pagetool/print/news.bbc.co.uk/2/hi/americas (accessed 28 September 2005).

29. Status of Ratifications of the Principal International Human Rights Treaties, office of UNHCHR, available at http://untreaty.un.org/english/access.asp (accessed 26 January 2006).

30. Luban, "Liberalism," p. 1436.

31. Rosemary Foot, "Human Rights and Counter-terrorism in Global Governance: Reputation and Resistance," *Global Governance,* 11(3), July-September 2005, pp. 291–310.

32. Thus, in the field of strategic studies, military alliances can have or can build a reputation for treating their mandates seriously and for standing firmly in support of other alliance members. Economic actors are said to be particularly interested in building a reputation for trustworthiness because this helps to induce cooperation, thereby lowering transaction costs in the future. For Amnesty, a reputation for impartiality, consistency, accuracy and a high level of expertise are crucial to sustaining the prominence of its role in global governance. On reputation, see, among other works, Jonathan Mercer, *Reputation and International Politics* (Ithaca, NY: Cornell University Press, 1996).

33. Ian Clark makes a point somewhat similar to this. He argues that the rhetorical commitment to a good governance reputation—that is, a commitment to democratic self-determination and the promotion of human rights—has become paramount in the post-Cold War era. But he also notes that we live in normatively unsettled times and that rightful membership of international society and rightful conduct have "fallen increasingly out of alignment." See Ian Clark, *Legitimacy in International Society* (Oxford: Oxford University Press, 2005), pp. 188–9, 233.

34. Michael Ignatieff, "Is the Human Rights Era Ending?" *New York Times,* 5 February 2002, p. A25.

35. Jack Donnelly, "Human Rights: A New Standard of Civilization?" *International Affairs,* 74(1), January 1998, pp. 1–23.

36. Miller writes: "Washington's response to September 11 was governed by a fervent belief in a 'win through intimidation' strategic outlook that viewed U.S. primacy as decisive; gave high priority to military strength; assumed that vigorous displays of U.S. power would send beneficial coercive messages that would cow enemies; and judged that hostile regimes who refused to cooperate should (and could) be crushed." Steven E. Miller, "Terrifying Thoughts: Power, Order, and Terror After 9/11," *Global Governance,* 1( 2), 2005, p. 256.

37. Walter Russell Mead, *Power, Terror, Peace and War: America's Grand Strategy in a World at Risk* (New York: Knopf, 2004), p. 115. Andrew Hurrell also notes what is "most dramatically visible in the case of the US [is] the idea that the overriding moral responsibility of the political leader is to his or her political community, and not to some notion of a world community." Andrew Hurrell, "'There Are No Rules' (George W. Bush): International Order after September 11," *International Relations,* 16(2), 2002, p. 202.

38. John Mackinlay, "Vulnerable," *The World Today,* March 2002, p. 16.

39. Some of the statements have come in the form of leaks and have clearly occurred in order to stop the practice of torture in US detention facilities; but it is not hard to find statements such as that of one US national security official to a *Washington Post* reporter: "If you don't violate someone's human rights some of the time, you probably aren't doing your job." Dana Priest and Barton Gellman, "U.S. Decries Abuse but Defends Interrogations," *Washington Post,* 26 December 2002, p. A1.

40. Luban, "Liberalism," p. 1458. See also Douglas Jehl and David Johnston, "White House Fought New Curbs on Interrogations, Officials Say," *New York Times,* 13 January 2005, p. A1; Eric Lichtblau, "Gonzales Says Humane-Policy Order Doesn't Bind C.I.A.," *New York Times,* 19 January 2005, p. A17 and discussed at note 57, p. 2100 of Diane Marie Amann, "Abu Ghraib," *University of Pennsylvania Law Review,* 153, 2005, pp. 2085–141. Rice's replacement, Stephen Hadley, during a

CNN interview on 13 November 2005, refused to rule out torture in all circumstances because of the responsibility to protect the American people from terrorist attack. See http://transcripts.cnn.com/TRANSCRIPTS/0511/13/le01.html (accessed 27 November 2005).

41. Rodley, "Torture in the 21st Century," pp. 4–5.

42. Stated 15 January 2002 and quoted in Roberts, "War on Terror," p. 111.

43. For a more detailed discussion see Rosemary Foot, "Collateral Damage: Human Rights Consequences of Counterterrorist Action in the Asia-Pacific," *International Affairs,* 81(2), March 2005, pp. 411–25.

44. See http:usinfo.state/gov/pol/terror/texts/04022501.htm, 25 February 2004 (accessed 28 February 2004). In 2002, then UN Special Rapporteur on Torture, Theo van Boven, visited Uzbekistan. On leaving the country, he told a news briefing that torture was "systemic" in the country and that the types of torture regularly employed by the police and security services included "beatings, electric shocks, immersing the victim's head in water, and suffocation by plastic bags." "Uzbekistan: UN Rapporteur says Torture 'Systemic,'" Radio Free Europe/Radio Liberty, 6 December 2002, available at http://www.rferl.org/nca/features/ (accessed 20 January 2003). A *Sunday New York Times* report by Don Van Natta Jr., "U.S. Recruits a Rough Ally to be a Jailer," noted on 1 May 2005, section 1, p. 1, that there was "growing evidence that the United States has sent terror suspects to Uzbekistan for detention and interrogation" with one intelligence official estimating that the number sent "was in the dozens."

45. "Mahathir Welcome in United States as Washington Shifts Focus," Associated Press, 15 April 2002.

46. C. J. Chivers, "Rights Group Describes Brutal Uzbek Crackdown," *International Herald Tribune,* 20 September 2005, p. 4.

47. Reuters, "China Holds Anti-Terror Exercises in Tibet," 12 September 2004.

48. "US Understands Reason for ISA, Says Rais," *Bernama,* 11 May 2002; "Malaysia's Abdullah Rules out Abolition of Internal Security Act," Foreign Broadcast Information Services—East Asia, Daily Report, 16 June 2002.

49. Human Rights Watch, *In the Name of Security: Counterterrorism and Human Rights Abuses under Malaysia's Internal Security Act,* May 2004, available at http://www.hrw.org/reports/2004/Malaysia/0504 (accessed 20 January 2005). See also Human Rights Watch, *Detained Without Trial: Abuse of Internal Security Act Detainees in Malaysia,* available at http://hrw.org/reports/2005/malaysia0905/ (accessed 2 December 2005).

50. Foot, "Collateral Damage," p. 415.

51. Henry Shue, "Responses: The Debate on Torture," *Dissent,* Summer 2003, p. 90.

52. Moreover, states that have an interest in criticizing the human rights element in US foreign policy (China, for example) find it useful to publicize these breaches of the norm because such publicity further exposes the gap between US moral claims and its actual behavior. See the March 2005 paper by the Information Office of the State Council of the People's Republic of China, which began its annual critique of the US human rights record with the statement: "In 2004 the atrocity of US troops abusing Iraqi POWs exposed the dark side of human rights performance of the United States." Section VI produces graphic evidence often drawing on Western press reports. See "The Human Rights Record of the United States in 2004," 3 March 2005, available at http://english.people.com.cn/200503/03/eng20050303_175406.html (accessed 26 January 2006).

53. Furthermore, where the Uzbek government is concerned, the State Department line seems to have won out over that of Defense: since the events at Andijan, the US has repeated the need for an international investigation. This criticism contributed to the Uzbek decision in July 2005 to close the US military base at Karshi-Khanabad.

54. Susan Marks and Andrew Clapham, "Torture," in *International Human Rights Lexicon* (Oxford: Oxford University Press, 2005), p. 367.

55. Amnesty International, *Guantanamo and Beyond*, table at p. 2.

56. See Appendix 1 of Amnesty International's *Guantanamo and Beyond*.

57. She wrote: "It is during our most challenging and uncertain moments that our nation's commitment to due process is most severely tested. It is in those times that we must preserve our commitment at home to the principles that we fight [for] abroad." *Financial Times*, 29 June 2004, p. 10.

58. On the condition that he renounce his American citizenship, Hamdi was returned to Saudi Arabia. See Amann, "Abu Ghraib," p. 2099.

59. Jose Padilla, a US citizen and the so-called "dirty bomb" suspect, was first arrested at O'Hare Airport, Chicago, having come from Pakistan. He was then transferred to a naval brig in Charleston, South Carolina. As Fiss puts it, "The Supreme Court failed to address the lawfulness of Padilla's detention in any way. The Court simply ruled that Padilla's lawyer had filed the habeas petition in the wrong district court." Owen Fiss, Professor of Law at Yale Law School, HLA Hart Memorial Lecture, "The War Against Terrorism and the Rule of Law," given at Oxford, 10 May 2005, in Examination Schools, pp. 5–6 of manuscript (forthcoming in the *Oxford Journal of Legal Studies*). David Cole writes: "In practice . . . the government has most often at least initially sacrificed *noncitizens'* liberties while retaining basic protections for citizens. . . . But as Hamdi's and Padilla's cases illustrate, what we do to foreign nationals today often paves the way for what will be done to American citizens tomorrow." See his *Enemy Aliens: Double Standards and Constitutional Freedoms in the War on Terrorism* (New York: New Press, 2003), pp. 4–5. On 23 November 2005 it was reported that the Bush administration had decided to charge Padilla with less serious crimes because of the abusive interrogation techniques used against the two senior members of Al Qaeda who had incriminated him. Douglas Jehl and Eric Lichtblau, "Shift on Suspect is Linked to Role of Qaeda Figures," *New York Times*, 24 November 2005, available at http://www.nytimes.com/2005/11/24/politics/24padilla.html (accessed 25 November 2005).

60. The findings of many of these enquiries are contained in Danner, *Torture and Truth*, and Greenberg and Dratel, *The Torture Papers*.

61. Joseph Lelyveld, "Interrogating Ourselves," *New York Times* (magazine), 12 June 2005, available at http://www.nytimes.com/2005/06/12/magazine/12TORTURE (accessed 12 June 2005). This is not to suggest that there are not some damning passages in, for example, the Taguba and Schlesinger reports.

62. "Pentagon Officials Defend Practices at Guantanamo Prison," *New York Times*, 15 June 2005, available at http://www.nytimes.com/aponline/national/AP-Guantanamo-Congress (accessed 15 June 2005); United States Senate, Committee on the Judiciary, "Detainees," 15 June 2005, available at http://judiciary.senate.gov/hearing (accessed 17 June 2005).

63. William Fisher, "It's that Pesky Prisoner Abuse Scandal Again," Inter Press Service News Agency, 2 August 2005, available at www.ipsnews.net/news/ (accessed 3 August 2005). Several retired US military personnel supported this action. Writing to Senator McCain on 25 July 2005, they argued that the 'abuse of prisoners hurts America's cause in the war on terror, endangers U.S. service members who might be captured by the enemy, and is anathema to the values Americans have held dear for generations.' Available from Human Rights First at http://action.humanrightsfirst.org/ct/EpwDzBS1Du8W/ (accessed 21 September 2005).

64. This 1987 manual states: "The use of force, mental torture, threats, insults, or exposure to unpleasant and inhumane treatment of any kind is prohibited by law." It goes on: "the use of force is a poor technique, as it yields unreliable results, may damage subsequent collection efforts, and can induce the source to say whatever he thinks the interrogator wants to hear."

65. "HRF Applauds Passage of Senator McCain's Proposals to End Prisoner Abuse," available at http://www.humanrightsfirst.org/us_law/etn/mccain/index.asp (accessed 7 October 2005). An apparent agreement between President Bush and Senator McCain has been thrown in doubt by a subsequent presidential statement claiming he would interpret the amendment "in a manner consistent with the constitutional authority of the president." This prompted a strong repudiation from Senator McCain. Elisabeth Bumiller, "For President, Final Say on a Bill Sometimes Comes after the Signing," *New York Times*, 16 January 2006, p. A11.

66. Human Rights First, for example, has been giving much publicity to Senator McCain's efforts.

67. In September 2002, High Commissioner Mary Robinson submitted a "Note to the Chair of the Counter-Terrorism Committee: A Human Rights Perspective on Counter-Terrorist Measures," which urged the CTC "to have in view continually certain fundamental principles which are essential to keeping the struggle against terrorism consistent with respect for human rights." The late Sergio Vieira de Mello spoke before the CTC in October 2002. He stated that the best and only way to defeat terrorism was by respecting human rights, promoting social justice and democracy, and upholding the rule of law. See http://www.un.org/Docs/sc/committees/1373/ohchr (accessed 20 July 2005).

68. http://www.un.org/Docs/sc/committees/1373/human_rights.html (accessed 20 July 2005). The Digest was updated in 2005 and before that had a second press run. UN Commission on Human Rights, 61st Session, "Promotion and Protection of Human Rights," 16 December 2004, E/CN.4/2005/100. At the UN Summit in September 2005 the UN Security Council passed resolution 1624 which requires states to report to the CTC on legal measures to be adopted to deal with the incitement of terrorism, but this time adding "in accordance with international law, in particular international human rights law, refugee law, and humanitarian law." See UN Security Council S/Res/1624 (2005), 14 September 2005. However, such a resolution is clearly open to abuse by governments willing to justify its use against those voicing legitimate dissent.

69. "Rights Experts 'Deeply Regret' United States Refusal of Terms for Fact-Finding Mission to Guantanamo," United Nations Press Release, 18 November 2005, available at http://www.unhchr.ch/huricane/ (accessed 27 November 2005); "Press Conference on Response Received from United States on Access to Guantanamo Bay Detention Facilities," 1 November 2005, United Nations Press Conference, available at http://www.un.org/News/briefings/docs/2005/051031_Guantanamo.doc.htm (accessed 27 November 2005).

70. Human Rights First and the Carter Center, "Global and National Trends Affecting the Protection of Human Rights," Atlanta, 5–7 June 2005, via email.

71. "Statement of Senator John McCain Amendment on Army Field Manual," 25 July 2005, available at http://mccain.senate.gov/ (accessed 12 October 2005). He also stated that the "Army Field Manual authorizes interrogation techniques that have proven effective in extracting life-saving information from the most hardened enemy prisoners. It also recognizes that torture and cruel treatment are ineffective methods, because they induce prisoners to say what their interrogators want to hear, even if it is not true, while bringing discredit upon the United States."

72. Thucydides, *History of the Peloponnesian War,* trans. Rex Warner (London and New York: Penguin Classics, 1972), p. 402.

*Source:* Torture: The Struggle Over a Peremptory Norm in a Counter-Terrorist Era. Rosemary Foot. *International Relations*, Vol. 20, No. 2. 2006. Reprinted by permission of Sage Publications.

# CHAPTER 17

## Peace and Democracy for Haiti

### *A UN Mission Impossible?*

Sebastian von Einsiedel and David M. Malone

Restoring peace and democracy in troubled countries where the rule of law and civil authority have broken down is one of the most difficult tasks that the United Nations faces. United Nations' efforts at peacebuilding in Haiti have met many struggles and setbacks. The United Nations continues to try to find strategies to bring peace to troubled areas without incurring huge risks and the possibility of greater violence.

## Introduction

In 2004, Haiti's fortunes executed a full circle. Shortly after leading the celebrations marking Haiti's bicentennial anniversary of its independence in February 2004, Jean-Bertrand Aristide, three time president of Haiti, was swept from power by violent rebellion. Aristide's departure and the preceding turmoil, the culmination of a political and economic crisis that had festered for years, provoked first a US and French military intervention, which was shortly thereafter replaced by a UN peacekeeping force to restore order and create the conditions for long-term stability and democracy.

These unhappy developments are all the more striking for following intense international involvement in Haiti's affairs throughout the 1990s. In particular, the United Nations engaged in a broad range of activities in support of democracy in Haiti, including election monitoring in 1990, UN Security Council (UNSC) mandated sanctions in 1993–4, a naval blockade in 1993–4, Security Council-authorized use of force in 1994 to restore democratically elected president Aristide, and a major peacekeeping operation in 1994–6, subsequently reduced to a small international police force aimed at building a domestic police capacity.

The case offers the first, and to date only, instance of the Security Council authorizing the use of force to effect the restoration of democracy within a member state. Unlike in a number of other situations, democratic processes were not seen as a means of national reconciliation, nor were elections seen as a mechanism to anchor fragile peace agreements. Rather, democratic rule was asserted as the goal in and of itself.

The Haiti file reveals themes present in many other of the UN's efforts to address internal crises following the end of the Cold War: promotion and monitoring of human rights; concern over the humanitarian plight of a civilian population affected by political turmoil; a desire to bring to justice those responsible for gross human rights violations; and an effort at peacebuilding through national economic development. . . .

## Lead-Up to the First UN Intervention

When Haiti in February 1990 sought assistance from the Organization of American States (OAS) and the United Nations for elections, the challenges to genuine democracy in Haiti were immense. Ever since gaining independence from French colonial rule in 1804, Haiti has been unable to establish a stable political system. The tradition of "one man rule" flourished through a system of institutional corruption. The US occupation, which lasted from 1915 until 1934, failed to produce a more responsive governing system. The notoriously brutal Duvalier dynasty, ruling Haiti from 1957 until 1986, was the culmination of almost two centuries of misrule. Haiti thus became a prime example of what William Reno has labeled a "shadow state," in which the rule of law is replaced by personal rule and privatization of state assets, in which the ruler, often propped up by a superpower patron, had no interest in nurturing taxable autonomous economic actors, and instead preyed on their own population.

Yet the elections in December 1990, monitored by the UN and the OAS, unfolded well, bringing to power a young Roman Catholic priest and partisan of liberation theology, Jean-Bertrand Aristide. Aristide's government made serious efforts to address the country's formidable challenges, with uneven skill and results. However, faced with numerous obstacles, Aristide's exercise of power became increasingly personalized and authoritarian. On September 29, 1991, Raoul Cédras, the commander of Haiti's armed forces, fearing mass revenge violence against the protagonists of the former regime, overthrew his government.

From his exile in Venezuela, Aristide successfully mobilized the international community, notably through the OAS and the UN. An OAS trade embargo imposed on Haiti only a few weeks after the coup produced some early pressure, but "exemptions" covering supplies for US-owned local industries severely undermined the effectiveness of the sanctions. Meanwhile, large numbers of Haitians took to the seas, threatening to engulf Florida with boat-going refugees.

Stopping short of coercive measures, the UN at the time relied on diplomatic action led by the Secretary-General's Group of Friends (initially Canada, France, the United States and Venezuela) and the Secretary General's special envoy to Haiti. Together they laid the groundwork for the deployment in early 1993 of a much-praised joint OAS/UN human rights monitoring mission, known as the International Civilian Mission in Haiti (MICIVIH).

By mid-1993, consensus emerged among the Friends that UN mandatory sanctions were required to nudge Cédras, and on June 16, 1993, the Security Council unanimously adopted Resolution 841, imposing a universal embargo on weapons, oil and petroleum products against Haiti. The sanctions succeeded in inducing Cédras to move to the negotiating table with Aristide, leading on June 27, 1993 to the Governor's Island

Agreement (GIA). The GIA foresaw successively a new civilian government, the suspension of sanctions, the deployment of UN peacekeepers, an amnesty, the retirement of Cédras and the return of Aristide.

In spite of the GIA's uneven application, the Security Council suspended the sanctions against Haiti and plans proceeded for a UN force, the UN Mission in Haiti (UNMIH), with US, Canadian and French troops at its core. However, upon the arrival of the USS *Harlan County* in Port-au-Prince harbor on October 11, carrying the bulk of the US and Canadian UN peacekeepers, thugs in the pay of the de facto regime prevented the landing of the troops. The US, still in shock over the death of 18 US Army Rangers eight days earlier in Mogadishu, on October 12, without consultation with the UN, ordered the *Harlan County* to depart Haitian waters. From this astonishing failure of nerve at least one lesson was learned: when the UN in 1994 prepared for UNMIH redeployment, roughly ten times more military personnel were planned than in 1993.

The Security Council responded by reimposing sanctions and ordering a naval blockade on Haiti. The naval blockade, on its surface a very strong measure, in fact signaled desperation following the collapse of the Governor's Island Agreement. The blockade could not be effective, due to Haiti's extensive land border with the Dominican Republic (which did not enforce the sanctions). However, the humanitarian and economic costs of the embargo were to prove lastingly crippling for Haiti with the poor hardest hit.

Aristide now turned his attention to Washington DC, where he lobbied hard for a surgical military intervention to restore him to power. Implicitly threatening further floods of Haitian refugees on Florida's shores, and successfully rallying Democratic members of Congress, Hollywood royalty, and influential NGOs, Aristide, with much of the quality media in the US on his side, managed to pressure the Clinton administration to tighten the screws on the de facto government in Port-au-Prince. The sanctions regime was strengthened, and on July 31, 1994, the Security Council adopted Resolution 940, authorizing a US-led multinational force (MNF) under Chapter VII, followed, once a "secure and stable environment" had been established, by a Chapter VI UN Peacekeeping Operation.

The adoption of Resolution 940 was groundbreaking in several respects. It marked the first time the United States had sought UN authority for the use of force within its own hemisphere. The resolution was also unprecedented in authorizing force to remove one regime and install another within a member state. By

September 15, 1994, the Pentagon had recruited 19 countries with a total of 2000 troops to join a 20,000 strong US force within the MNF.

When word arrived in Port-au-Prince on September 18 that US military aircraft were preparing to take off for Haiti, the Haitian military leadership agreed to leave. The MNF thereupon deployed smoothly, accompanied by the small UN team charged with monitoring it. On October 16, the Security Council lifted sanctions and the blockade the day after Aristide's return to Haiti.

## Peacekeeping and Peacebuilding

Following Aristide's return, the UN faced a number of new challenges in Haiti. The most pressing problem was that of institution-building in order to achieve a sustainable democracy. In the short term, credible elections needed to be held to a bewildering range of national offices. Fears of violence in Haiti following Aristide's return initially proved unfounded. He worked to promote calm, going out of his way to consult members of the economic elite, who might have preferred a return to the old order, but could no longer count on the armed forces to secure this end.

In January 1995, the US MNF force commander certified a "secure and stable environment" and the handover from the MNF to UNMIH comprising 6000 troops and almost 800 civilian police officers took place in March. UNMIH's mission was to provide security, stabilize the country, create a new police force and to professionalize the Haitian armed forces. . . .

The first peaceful transfer of power through what international observers agreed were free and fair elections in February 1996 constituted a significant step towards bringing democracy to Haiti, even though René Préval, Aristide's hand-picked successor, was largely dependent on him for his political legitimacy. The UNMIH operation itself, which ended in June 1996, was also seen as a success, which, in the highly positive final report of the US contingent in UNMIH, was attributed to two main factors: (a) there was a clear mandate from the Security Council, facilitating effective planning and resource allocation; and (b) there was plenty of time to pull the force together (from July 31, 1994 to March 31, 1995), creating the conditions essential for a smooth transition between the multinational intervention force and the follow-on UN peacekeeping force.

While UNMIH was a success on its own terms, the UN's broader peacebuilding efforts failed. Establishing a new police force respecting human rights and immune to politicization proved a difficult and slow process.

Disaffection among former army personnel and the continued existence of paramilitary networks kept the security situation fragile. And the archaic state of the judicial system and poor economic prospects were aggravated by a years-long political impasse that followed the legislative elections of April 1997.

The mandate of UNMIH's three follow-up missions—the UN Support Mission in Haiti (UNSMIH) from June 1996 to July 1997; the UN Transition Mission in Haiti (UNTMIH) from July 1997 to November 1997; and the UN Civilian Police Mission in Haiti (MIPONUH) from November 1997 to March 2000—became increasingly narrow. The central task, carried out by 300 international civilian police (CIVPOL), remained to assist the government of Haiti to establish and train an effective national police force. However, the successive UN missions were also encouraged to coordinate the activities by the UN system to promote institution-building, national reconciliation and economic rehabilitation in Haiti. At the same time the military peacekeeping dimension gradually receded and after the last UN military personnel were withdrawn upon the completion of UNTMIH's mandate in November 1997, the UN's presence on the ground was purely civilian. . . .

Failure to resolve the crisis through negotiations led President Préval in January 1999 to declare the lawmakers' and most of the country's mayors' terms expired and to rule by decree. This move made him one of only nine elected officials in the whole of Haiti. The achievements of "Operation Restore Democracy" seemed to be lying in ruins.

The political crisis dealt a further blow to the country's already dismal economy. In 1995, Haitian per capita gross domestic product (GDP), at $242.1, was by far the lowest in the Western Hemisphere. Haiti ranked only 159 out of 174 in the 1998 UNDP's global Human Development Index. Investment failed to materialize given the uncertain political and security situation. What modest signs of life the economy showed in 1995 and 1996 were due entirely to massive infusions of foreign assistance, but donors rapidly grew disenchanted with Aristide's political and economic management priorities. . . .

The security situation also deteriorated as the political crisis proceeded. While in early 1998 the Secretary-General could still report that "most instances of lawlessness do not appear to have a political motivation," the numerous murders and attempted murders of human rights activists and high-profile political figures or their relatives in 1999 made it clear that political violence was on the rise. . . .

The UN's task of creating a police force from scratch took place in a particularly adverse environment. The HNP suffered from a severe lack of resources. The mushrooming drug trade, which according to one estimate increased fourfold in 1997–8, offered a potent incentive for corrupt behavior. Deportation of 300 or so Haitian criminals annually from the US did not help. Finally the lamentable local judicial system continued to impede the HNP's efforts to combat crime and clearly judicial reform had not kept pace with the building of the HNP.

Moreover, police reform was only insufficiently complemented by efforts to reform the penal and the judicial system. The fact that in 1999, 80 percent of the prison population was in pretrial detention (a third of these prisoners having been held for over a year) underscored the justice system's ongoing weakness. While considerable international financial assistance was made available for such reforms the Haitian government failed to follow through on its commitment to broad reforms.

## An Exit Strategy?

Throughout 1999, nervousness increased over the scheduled end of the UN's peacekeeping presence. General elections in Haiti were scheduled for the end of the year and the Secretary-General and others feared that withdrawing MIPONUH during the election period might undermine security at a particularly sensitive moment. However, China had never overcome its reservations toward the mission and some Council members expected that the Chinese would veto any renewal. Russia was also lukewarm, at best, and both countries had abstained when MIPONUH was extended the last time for a full year term in November 1998. However, had the US thrown its weight behind an extension of MIPONUH, this might have been agreed. But in the US, support for any involvement in Haiti was also gradually waning, and Washington was increasingly frustrated with "Mr. Préval's passivity and Mr. Aristide's duplicity." In mid-1999, the Pentagon decided that the US should pull out the remaining 500 soldiers, who were performing nation-building tasks outside the UN mission, saying that it had been unable to create stability in Haiti. In January 2000, almost all US soldiers left the country and thus ended an almost six-year military presence in Haiti. Republicans in Congress used every opportunity to undermine the Clinton administration's efforts to support Haiti, for instance sitting on funding for MICIVIH, which was slated to start its phaseout. Moreover, Haitians themselves were unhappy with any continued foreign military presence on their soil, which reinforced the view of those Council members who began to see the situation in Haiti

as more a matter of development than a question of international peace and security. . . .

In May 2000 general elections finally took place, after the polling date had been rescheduled four times. Although the vote itself was surprisingly peaceful it only resulted in further dissension over what was widely considered a flawed method of calculating the election results, and the electoral mission of OAS quit in protest.

Just as Aristide was elected as president for a second time, Secretary-General Kofi Annan recommended the termination of MICAH when its mandate expired in February 2001. He contended that the climate of instability made it inadvisable to extend the mission, but funding constraints certainly played a role. Indeed, by March 2000 no voluntary contributions had been received for the MICAH trust fund and the mission had therefore begun its mandate on March 16 without any of the substantive staff necessary for the implementation of its mandate. The pullout came at a time when the "human rights situation in Haiti was more worrying than at any time since the 1994 return to democracy." The UN then turned back the lead international role in addressing Haiti's political problems to the OAS. . . .

## Lessons Learned?

A key question is whether the resources the UN (and the international community more broadly) invested and the strategies it applied in Haiti during its interventions in the 1990s were adequate and appropriate to the highly ambitious goal of building a stable democracy and functioning state institutions in an endemically impoverished country, deprived of democratic traditions and rule of law. Three sets of broad lessons can be drawn from this period.

First, in an environment characterized by extremely weak state institutions and self-serving local leaders, a more sustained and intrusive international presence is required. Building state institutions from scratch in a profoundly divided country takes time and needs to be underpinned by a prolonged international security presence and stable flows of foreign aid. . . .

Second, Haiti confirms the findings of several comparative studies on international peacebuilding efforts in the 1990s that have suggested that one of the most urgent tasks of any post-conflict operation should be the demobilization of soldiers and the reintegration of combatants. Indeed, the experience in Haiti—as well as more recently in Iraq—shows that one of the greatest blunders in peacebuilding is to disband an entire army without first disarming its soldiers and putting in place a solid reintegration scheme. (Heavily armed unemployed young men represent an explosive ingredient for any society.) The international community should either strongly have discouraged Aristide from disbanding the army or have provided Haiti with meaningful disarmament, demobilization and reintegration (DDR) assistance. . . .

Third, none of the strategies of the international community had a more lastingly negative impact than the OAS and UN sanctions regimes—notwithstanding the fact that the latter did produce a negotiated settlement in the aftermath of SCR 841 in June 1993. Indeed, even the porous and ineffective OAS sanctions "triggered a trend that eventually led to the elimination of 300,000 jobs in the formal employment sector by the time sanctions were lifted in 1994." As a result, according to estimates by the World Bank, Haiti's per capita GDP shrank by up to 30 percent during those years—economic costs that UN and other multilateral actors were later unable to counteract. Adding insult to injury, the sanctions significantly enriched the de facto regime.

Alongside the Iraq sanctions regime, admittedly much more severe in its humanitarian impact, the Haiti case reinforced the UN's growing ambivalence toward mandatory economic sanctions. In a major example that the UN is indeed capable of occasionally learning from its mistakes, the Security Council has never again resorted to such crude measures and it has since developed and refined targeted sanctions, mostly in the form of travel and financial embargoes.

Much more controversial, however, is the proposition that the Haiti sanctions episode calls into question the doctrine of the use of force as last resort that is only legitimate once all other measures have failed. Indeed, increasing pressure slowly and incrementally before employing force allows the target to adapt and devise coping strategies, making later coercion all the more difficult. Unfortunately, such is the aversion to the use of force that the Security Council is more inclined toward the imposition of sanctions, even draconian ones, than toward credible threats of military force. Against a relatively weak adversary, the threat of force would have stood a much better chance of bringing the de facto regime to heel after the coup.

## Renewed Crisis and Intervention

. . . In early 2004, following the celebrations commemorating the bicentennial anniversary of Haiti's independence, anti-Aristide protests grew and became more violent. Armed conflict broke out in the city of Gonaïves and quickly spread to other cities. Local militia groups took control of provincial capitals and closed in on Port-au-Prince. Without an army, and with declining public support, the government was unable to resist the advance of well-armed groups. The Haitian National Police almost completely collapsed.

Amidst the turmoil, the OAS Council called upon the UN Security Council to take all the necessary and appropriate urgent measures to address the deteriorating situation in Haiti and Caribbean Community (CARICOM) submitted a formal request to send troops to "end the spiral of violence." However, there was no appetite in the Council to put the deeply compromised Aristide regime on life support. Last-minute mediation offers and diplomatic initiatives spearheaded by CARICOM and supported by the OAS, the US, France, Canada and the Bahamas were rejected by the opposition, which did not see much to be gained from negotiating with the crumbling Aristide government. Soon it became clear that Aristide's forces could not stem the tide. Overcoming their disagreements over the 2003 Iraq crisis, and disregarding the fact that Aristide was democratically elected, the US and France joined forces to exert pressure on Aristide to step down. Ten years after the US brought Aristide back to power through the threat of military force, it was Washington that played an important role in removing him. Haiti had gone full circle. . . .

## Rebuilding a Failed State

The UN was saddled with challenges far more daunting than in 1995. Three indicators are instructive. In the 2005 Freedom House index, ranking countries according to democratic liberties, Haiti was listed near rock-bottom and second to last among all post-conflict countries. In *Foreign Policy* magazine's 2005 Failed State Index, Haiti was listed as the tenth most likely country to collapse, the presence of thousands of peacekeepers notwithstanding. And finally, the 2004 Transparency International Corruption Perception Index ranked Haiti dead last on its list of 145 countries.

With widespread poverty and hunger, record unemployment rates, high crime and gang violence, many Haitians have lost hope for a better future after ten years of failed peacebuilding efforts. Already adverse humanitarian circumstances were aggravated when a series of tropical storms hit Haiti in 2004, burying entire cities in mud and killing thousands. Moreover, while the 1994 intervention brought back to power a democratically elected leader, who at the time enjoyed widespread support among Haiti's population, Aristide's successor in 2004, Gérard Latortue, an international technocrat installed to govern the country until elections were to be held in late 2005, never enjoyed such legitimacy, and lacked the political support to carry out much-needed political and economic reforms. Caribbean leaders, furious over the course of events in Haiti, seen by them and many others as undermining democratic order in their region, demanded a United Nations-led investigation into the events leading to Aristide's ouster (an initiative that was successfully blocked by the US and France) and never granted recognition to the transitional government in Port-au-Prince. Not surprisingly, Haitian support for the international presence seems much weaker than in the 1990s.

Moreover, the UN mission is haunted by a repeat of history. In 2004, intervening forces once again failed to systematically disarm militias—admittedly a daunting task that carries the risk of further inflaming an already volatile situation on the ground. Haiti's fledgling police force, whose strength shrank from 5000 prior to the crisis to a mere 2500 during the violent uprising, are sometimes outnumbered and generally outgunned by the well-armed militias and gangs (estimated to be around 25,000 strong) that continue to take advantage of the security vacuum prevalent in Haiti today. Belatedly, the Haitian government, with UN help, has started to address these problems, initiating efforts in October 2004 to reintegrate former officers of the Haitian army.

An even more fundamental challenge for Haiti is its dramatic loss of human capital over past decades. A 2005 World Bank report points out that 80 percent of Haitians who have college degrees live outside their country. While remittances sent home by the Haitian diaspora comprise a large portion of international aid transfers, the lack of skilled Haitians to build up state institutions presents a severe development challenge. . . .

Looking from afar, it is also hard to discern a political strategy that promises to bridge the paralyzing divides in Haitian politics and society. Having been repeatedly postponed, parliamentary and presidential elections finally took place in early February 2006, but these cannot serve as an exit strategy; rather, they need to be viewed as merely a first step in a long process of helping to establish legitimate sustainable government. Unfortunately, in the recent past, elections in Haiti have mainly served to polarize political life, and disputed election results have repeatedly triggered political crises. . . .

As in the 1990s, international efforts in 2004 and 2005 failed to address the lack of consensus between the country's different sectors on fundamental social and economic goals and on the means for achieving them. To the distress of the Group of Friends, Aristide remains the most potent political force within Haiti, and the reascendance to the presidency of his former close associate René Préval, might spell a potential further challenge to international assistance should Aristide somehow return to Haiti and resume pulling the strings of government (of which today there is no evidence). . . .

## The New Peacebuilding Template

In creating the High-level Panel on Threats, Challenges and Change in late 2003, Kofi Annan had in mind not only acute new worries about terrorism, weapons of mass destruction and unilateralist impulses, but also the Security Council's failure, and that of the UN more broadly, to see through the extended peacebuilding efforts required to allow war-torn countries to move toward sustainable peace. The UN's inability to prevent Liberia and Haiti defaulting back to violence, in spite of considerable investments in both by the international community, highlighted research findings that suggest that fully half of the countries that emerge from civil war relapse into conflict within five years.

While the UN's track record where major peace operations were deployed is better than widely supposed—one study found that seven of eight cases remain at peace today—a UN internal report indicated that between 1988 and 2003 countries where a post-conflict UN field mission was established were just as likely to revert to war as countries with no UN presence.

The High-level Panel's research staff identified several weaknesses in UN peacebuilding capacity, most prominently inadequate coordination across the UN and its agencies, the international financial institutions and bilateral donors; lack of the international community's long-term attention to post-conflict cases and a particular attention deficit disorder of the Security Council; absence of strategic thinking underpinning peacebuilding efforts, reflected in a tendency toward a "laundry list" approach; and a lack of priority to the vital task of institution building, exacerbated by inflexible financing mechanisms that fail to address medium term institutional needs. One study found that resources tend to decline precisely when state capacity to manage and administer them gains traction in the medium term (three to seven years post-crisis).

Against this background, the High-level Panel recommended the creation of an intergovernmental Peacebuilding Commission, complemented by a Peacebuilding Support Office within the UN Secretariat and a Peacebuilding Fund. These recommendations were later endorsed and then refined by the Secretary-General, and adopted by 191 heads of state and government at the 2005 World Summit in New York. . . .

## How Relevant to Haiti?

How would the UN's new machinery for peacebuilding actually aim to help a country like Haiti, and is it likely to succeed? First, special representatives of the UN Secretary-General (SRSGs), such as the energetic Juan Gabriel Valdés in Haiti, will doubtless welcome access to a planning tool for quick-impact local projects and longer-term development programming that can support their political strategies. Local UNDP offices will be able to help in the design of projects to ensure that they make a degree of developmental sense.

The Commission could also serve as a focal point for mobilizing much larger sums required for long-term development as complementary follow-on to peacebuilding strategies. As matters stand, ad hoc meetings of donors and "core group" or "friends" countries, such as several organized at the UN in mid-2005, at US instigation, often have trouble achieving concrete outcomes. . . .

The Haiti case since 1990 demonstrates that local actors matter critically in the success of UN mediation and peacebuilding activities. In 1994, the international community supported to the hilt Jean-Bertrand Aristide's restoration to power in circumstances still unique to international relations. The UN could certainly have done better in many respects, but this is one case in which the UN was able to summon not only the political will but also very significant resources necessary to help the Haitians help themselves. It is also a case in which the international community was fairly well coordinated, both politically and in terms of technical and developmental assistance. The UN was poorly repaid. Adhering to established patterns of Haitian political life, Aristide and his opponents reverted to "winner-takes-all" strategies, precluding compromise or any serious commitment to national interests. In these circumstances, the conditionality that donor governments and institutions attempted to use as leverage for better policies failed miserably. International interveners have not developed alternative strategies. The Haitian political community has squandered not only considerable international goodwill but also the huge resources poured into its stabilization in the years 1994–7. Myopic, self-serving Haitian leadership plunged the country back into a crisis both familiar and desperately sad.

For these and other reasons, a number of Haiti watchers and international security mavens have advocated turning the country into an international protectorate, an idea also openly debated in the Haitian media. Even though Haiti would appear, like Somalia or Liberia, to be an attractive test-case for new forms of international trusteeship, any such project would be risky and very expensive. . . .

Ultimately, Haitians of all stripes, resident in the country and in Haiti's impressive diaspora, must assume responsibility for their country's future rather than hoping that the UN can solve the country's multiple and complex problems for them. Their positive engagement is a sine qua non of future multilateral success in Haiti. Haitian politics need to move beyond posturing to political entrepreneurship in the public interest.

It is only when national authorities and international ones genuinely cooperate with each other, as was the case in East Timor and as is often the case in Afghanistan, that international efforts pay off. Thus it would be a mistake to see the Peacebuilding Commission and related UN machinery as a "silver bullet." But if the UN and other international actors critical to Haiti's recovery are met halfway by Haiti's new government in 2006, the growing international understanding of what is required for effective peacebuilding (including long-term engagement), and the UN's new machinery suggest that Haiti's prospects need not be seen as hopeless.

---

## Questions

1. What policies and interventions have the United Nations, the United States, and France tried to bring peace and stability to Haiti?

2. What efforts seem most hopeful in restoring peace to violent and troubled countries?

---

*Source:* Peace and Democracy for Haiti: A UN Mission Impossible? Sebastian von Einsiedel and David M. Malone. *International Relations,* Vol. 20, No. 2. 2006. Reprinted by permission of Sage Publications.

# CHAPTER 18

## Globalization and the Study of International Security

Victor D. Cha

Globalization, with its rapid movement of people, products, and ideas around the world, can often be at odds with a desire to maintain national identity and security. A major challenge for this century will be how countries deal with the pressures of globalization as they try to maintain both physical and non-physical security for their citizens.

## Introduction

At the threshold of the 21st century, two topics have dominated the study of international relations in the USA: globalization and the "new" security environment after the end of the Cold War. The latter has been the object of intense debate, largely dominated by those arguing about the relative importance of structural, institutional, and cultural variables for explaining the likelihood of global or regional peace. The former dynamic has been discussed so widely in scholarly and popular circles that it has reached the ignoble status of "buzzword," familiarly used by many to refer to some fuzzy phenomenon or trend in the world, but hardly understood by any. This essay explores how the processes of globalization have fundamentally changed the way we think about security. In spite of the plethora of literature on security and globalization, there is relatively little work written by US security specialists that interconnects the two. In the case of security studies, this has been in no small part because the field remains entrenched in the "food fight" of competing realist, liberal, and constructionist research programs. In the case of the globalization literature, this has stemmed from a relatively stronger focus on the social and economic process of globalization. The "new" security environment in the 21st century will operate increasingly in the space defined by the interpenetration between two spheres: globalization and national identity.

## Security and Globalization

Globalization is best understood as a spatial phenomenon. It is not an "event," but a gradual and ongoing expansion of interaction processes, forms of organization, and forms of cooperation outside the traditional spaces defined by sovereignty. Activity takes place in a less localized, less insulated way as transcontinental and interregional patterns crisscross and overlap one another.

. . . As Guehenno noted, globalization is defined not just by the ever-expanding connections between states measured in terms of movement of goods and capital but the circulation and interpenetration of people and ideas (Guehenno, 1999: 7). It affects not only external sovereignty choices but also internal sovereignty in terms of relations between the public and private sectors (Reinicke, 1997). Contrary to popular notions of globalization, this does not mean that sovereignty ceases to exist in the traditional Weberian sense (i.e., monopoly of legitimate authority over citizen and subjects within a given territory). Instead, globalization is a spatial reorganization of production, industry, finance, and other areas which causes local decisions to have global repercussions and daily life to be affected by global events . . . In short, the nation-state does not end; it is just less in control. Activity and decisions for the state increasingly take place in a post-sovereign space (Reinicke, 1997; Rosenau, 1996). In this sense, globalization is both a boundary-broadening process and a boundary-weakening one (Rosenau, 1996: 251).

Much of the literature on globalization has focused on its economic rather than security implications. In part, this is because the security effects of globalization often get conflated with changes to the international security agenda with the end of Cold War Superpower competition. It is also because, unlike economics where globalization's effects are manifested and measured everyday in terms of things like international capital flows and Internet use, in security, the effects are inherently harder to conceptualize and measure. To the extent possible, the ensuing analysis tries to differentiate globalization from post-Cold War effects on security . . .

## Agency and Scope of Threats

The most far-reaching security effect of globalization is its complication of the basic concept of "threat" in international relations. This is in terms of both agency and scope. Agents of threat can be states but can also be non-state groups or individuals. While the vocabulary of conflict in international security traditionally centered on interstate war (e.g., between large set-piece battalions and national armed forces), with globalization, terms such as global violence and human security become common parlance, where the fight is between irregular substate units such as ethnic militias, paramilitary guerrillas, cults and religious organizations, organized crime, and terrorists. Increasingly, targets are not exclusively opposing force structures of even cities, but local groups and individuals (Buzan, 1997a: 6–21; Klare, 1998: 66; Nye, 1989; Väyrynen, 1998; Waever et al., 1993). . . .

Globalization widens the scope of security as well. As the Copenhagen school has noted, how states conceive of security and how they determine what it means to be secure in the post-World War era expand beyond military security at the national level. Globalization's effects on security scope are distinct from those of the post-Cold War in that the basic transaction processes engendered by globalization—instantaneous communication and transportation, exchanges of information and technology, flow of capital—catalyze certain dangerous phenomena or empower certain groups in ways unimagined previously. In the former category are things such as viruses and pollution. Because of human mobility, disease has become much more of a transnational security concern. Global warming, ozone depletion, acid rain, biodiversity loss, and radioactive contamination are health and environmental problems that have intensified as transnational security concerns precisely because of increased human mobility and interaction (Matthew & Shambaugh, 1998; Väyrynen, 1998; Zurn, 1998). . . .

Globalization has ignited identity as a source of conflict. The elevation of regional and ethnic conflict as a top-tier security issue has generally been treated as a function of the end of the Cold War. However, it is also a function of globalization. The process of globalization carries implicit homogenization tendencies and messages, which in combination with the "borderlessness" of the globalization phenomenon elicits a cultural pluralist response.

At the same time, globalization has made us both more aware and less decisive about our motivations to intervene in such ethnic conflicts. Real-time visual images of horror and bloodshed in far-off places transmitted through CNN make the conflicts impossible to ignore, creating pressures for intervention. On the other hand, the hesitancy to act is palpable, as standard measures by which to determine intervention (i.e., bipolar competition in the periphery) are no longer appropriate, forcing us to grope with fuzzy motivations such as humanitarian intervention.

## Nonphysical Security

Globalization has anointed the concept of non-physical security. Traditional definitions of security in terms of protection of territory and sovereignty, while certainly not irrelevant in a globalized era, expand to protection of information and technology assets. For example, Nye and Owens (1998) cite "information power" as increasingly defining the distribution of power in international relations in the 21st century. In a similar vein, the revolution in military affairs highlights not greater firepower but greater information technology and "smartness" of weapons as the defining advantage for future warfare.

These nonphysical security aspects have always been a part of the traditional national defense agenda. Indeed, concerns about the unauthorized transfer of sensitive technologies gave rise to such techno-nationalist institutions as COCOM during the Cold War. However, the challenge posed by globalization is that the nation-state can no longer control the movement of technology and information (Simon, 1997). Strategic alliances form in the private sector among leading corporations that are not fettered by notions of techno-nationalism and driven instead by competitive, cost-cutting, or cutting-edge innovative needs. The result is a transnationalization of defense production that further reduces the state's control over these activities.

More and more private companies, individuals, and other non-state groups are the producers, consumers, and merchants of a US $50 billion per year global arms market (Klare & Lumpe, 1998). The end of the Cold War has certainly been a permissive condition for the indiscriminate, profit-based incentives to sell weapons or dual-use technologies to anybody. But globalization of information and technology has made barriers to non-state entry low and detection costs high. Moreover, while enforcement authorities still have the benefit of these technologies, two critical developments have altered the equation: (1) Absence of discrimination: over the past two decades the private sector, rather than the government, has become the primary creator of new technologies, which in essence has removed any relative advantages state agencies formerly possessed in terms of exclusive access to eavesdropping technology, surveillance, and encryption. Governments once in the position of holding monopolies on cutting edge technologies that could later be "spun off" in the national commercial sector are now consumers of "spin-on" technologies. (2) Volume and variety: the sheer growth in volume and variety of communications has overwhelmed any attempts at monitoring or control (Mathews, 1997; Freedman, 1999: 53).

## Propositions for Security Behavior

If nonphysical security, diversification of threats, and the salience of identity are key effects of globalization in the security realm, then how might this translate in terms of a state's foreign policy? . . .

## Intermestic Security

First, the globalization and security literature asserts but does not elaborate on how security decisions increasingly take place outside the traditional purview of sovereignty. Globalization creates an interpenetration of foreign and domestic issues that national governments must recognize in developing policy. One example of this "intermestic" approach to security policy might be an acceptance that the transnationalization of threats has blurred traditional divisions between internal and external security (Katzenstein, 1996a). The obverse would be the frequency with which a state adheres to "delimiting" security, formulating and justifying policy on the basis of "national security" interests rather than universal/global interests (Moon Chung-in, 1995: 64). Examples of the former are European institutions such as Interpol, TREVI, and the Schengen Accord, which represent an acknowledgment that domestic issues such as crime, drug-trafficking, terrorism, and immigration increasingly require transnational cooperation. . . .

## Multilateralism

Second, the globalization literature acknowledges that security is increasingly conceived of in post-sovereign, globalized terms, but does not delineate how the modes of obtaining security should change. As noted above, globalization means that both the agency and scope of threats have become more diverse and non-state in form. This also suggests that the payoffs lessen for obtaining security through traditional means. Controlling pollution, disease, technology, and information transfer cannot be easily dealt with through national, unilateral means but can only be effectively dealt with through the application of national resources in multilateral fora or through encouragement of transnational cooperation. As UN Secretary-General Kofi Annan intimated, US bombing of targets in Sudan in retaliation for terrorist bombings of two US embassies in Africa is a unilateral piecemeal approach far inferior to concerted global efforts at denying terrorists sanctuaries, financing, and technology and encouraging their extradition and prosecution.

Thus one would expect globalized security processes reflected in a state's striving for regional coordination and cooperative security. It should emphasize not exclusivity and bilateralism in relations but inclusivity and multilateralism as the best way to solve security problems. At the extreme end of the spectrum, globalization might downplay the importance of eternal iron-clad alliances and encourage the growth of select transnational "policy coalitions" among national governments, nongovernmental organizations (NGOs), and individuals specific to each problem (Reinicke, 1997: 134). . . .

## Bureaucratic Innovation

The globalization literature has not done justice to the role bureaucratic innovation plays in response to the new challenges of globalization. On this point, indeed, the literature has not kept pace with the empirics. For example, in the USA, the Clinton Administration created the position of Undersecretary for Global Affairs, whose portfolio included environmental issues, promotion of democracy and human rights, population and migration issues, and law enforcement (Talbott, 1997: 74). In a similar vein, the US State Department's Foreign Service Institute now has a new core course for FSOs on narcotics-trafficking, refugee flows, and environmental technologies (Talbott, 1997: 75). In May 1998, the Clinton Administration put forward its first comprehensive plan to combat world crime, identifying drug-trafficking, transfer of sensitive technology and WMD, and trafficking of women and children as threats to the USA (*Washington Post,* 1998). One might also expect to see foreign service bureaucracies placing greater emphasis on international organizations and NGOs in terms of representation, placement, and leadership if these are recognized as the key vehicles of security and politics in a globalized world.

Implicit in each of these examples is the trend toward greater specialization in the pursuit of security. As globalization makes security problems more complex and diverse, national security structures need to be re-oriented, sometimes through elimination of anachronistic bureaucracies or through rationalization of wasteful and over-lapping ones. In the US system, for example, while combating the spread of weapons of mass destruction is widely acknowledged as a key security objective in the 21st century, various branches of the government operate autonomously in dealing with these threats. Hence, there are greater calls for renovation and coordination to eliminate the overlap, inefficiency, and lack of organization among State, Defense, Commerce, Energy, CIA, and FBI in combating proliferation.

Another trend engendered by the security challenges of globalization is greater cross-fertilization between domestic law enforcement and foreign policy agencies. This relationship, at least in the USA (less the case in Europe), is at worst non-existent because domestic law enforcement has operated traditionally in isolation from national security and diplomatic concerns, or at best is a mutually frustrating relationship because the two have neither inclination nor interest in cooperating. States that understand the challenges of globalization, particularly on issues of drug-trafficking, environmental crimes, and technology transfer, will seek to bridge this gap, creating and capitalizing on synergies that develop between the two groups. . . .

One of the longer-term effects of specialization and cross-fertilization is that security also becomes more "porous." Specialization will often require changes not just at the sovereign national level, but across borders and with substate actors. "Boilerplate" security (e.g., dealt with by "hard-shell" nation-states with national resources) becomes increasingly replaced by cooperation and coordination that may still be initiated by the national government but with indispensable partners (depending on the issue) such as NGOs, transnational groups, and the media. The obverse of this dynamic also applies. With globalization, specialized "communities of choice" (e.g., landmine ban) are empowered to organize transnationally and penetrate the national security agendas with issues that might not otherwise have been paid attention to (Guehenno, 1999: 9; Mathews, 1997). . . .

## Strategies and Operational Considerations

Finally, the literature on globalization is notably silent on the long-term impact of globalization processes on time-tested modes of strategic thinking and fighting. In the former vein, the widening scope of security engendered by globalization means that the definition of security and the fight for it will occur not on battlefields but in unconventional places against non-traditional security adversaries . . . [W]hen states cannot deal with these threats through sovereign means, they will encourage a multilateralism and cooperation at the national, transnational, and international levels. However, the nature of these conflicts may also require new ways of fighting, that is, the ability to engage militarily with a high degree of lethality against combatants, but low levels of collateral damage. As a result, globalization's widening security scope dictates not only new strategies (discussed below) but also new forms of combat. Examples include incapacitating crowd control munitions such as blunt projectiles (rubber balls), nonlethal crowd dispersal cartridges, "stick 'em" and "slick 'em" traction modifiers, or "stink" bombs. "Smart" nonlethal warfare that incapacitates equipment will also be favored, including rigid foam substance, and radio frequency and microwave technologies to disable electronics and communications (CFR Task Force, 1999).

Regarding strategy, as the agency and scope of threats diversifies in a globalized world, traditional modes of deterrence become less relevant. Nuclear deterrence throughout the Cold War and post-Cold War eras, for example, was based on certain assumptions. First, the target of the strategy was another nation-state. Second, this deterred state was assumed to have a degree of centralization in the decision-making process over nuclear weapons use. Third, and most important, the opponent possessed both counterforce and countervalue targets that would be the object of a second strike. While this sort of rationally based, existential deterrence will still apply to interstate security, the proliferation of weaponized nonstate and substate actors increasingly renders this sort of strategic thinking obsolete. They do not occupy sovereign territorial space and therefore cannot be targeted with the threat of retaliation. They also may operate as self-contained cells rather than an organic whole which makes decapitating strikes at a central decision-making structure ineffective. In short, you cannot deter with the threat of retaliation that which you cannot target.

Governments may respond to this in a variety of ways. One method would be, as noted above, greater emphasis on the specialized utilization of whatever state, substate, and multilateral methods are necessary to defend against such threats. A second likely response would be greater attention and resources directed at civil defense preparation and "consequence" management to minimize widespread panic and pain in the event of an attack. A third possible response is unilateral in nature. Governments may increasingly employ pre-emptive or preventive strategies if rational deterrence does not apply against non-state entities. Hence one might envision two tiers of security in which stable rational deterrence applies at the state-state level but unstable pre-emptive/preventive strategies apply at the state-non-state level.

## Conclusion

What then is the "new" security environment in the 21st century that the globalization/security literature must strive to understand? It is most likely one that sits at the intersection of globalization and national identity. In other words, as globalization processes complicate the nature of security (i.e., in terms of agency and scope), this effects a transformation in the interests that inform security policy. Globalization's imperatives permeate the domestic level and should be manifested in some very broad behavioral trends or styles of security policy. Manifestations of this transformation are inclinations toward intermestic security, multilateralism, and bureaucratic innovation and specialization.

However, it would be short-sighted to expect that all states will respond similarly. In some cases, policies will emerge that directly meet or adjust to the imperatives of globalization, but in other cases the policy that emerges will not be what one might expect to linearly follow from globalization pressures. The latter outcomes are types of anomalies that offer the most clear indications of the causal role of domestic factors in the "new" security environment (Desch, 1998: 158–160); however, these alone only highlight national identity as a residual variable (i.e., capable of explaining only aberrations) in the "new" security environment. One would expect, therefore, that the former outcomes would be as important to process-trace: If policy adjustments appear outwardly consistent with globalization but the underlying rationale for such action is not, then this illustrates that the domestic-ideational mediation process is an ever-present one. The new security environment would therefore be one in which globalization pressures on security policy and grand strategy are continually refracted through the prism of national identity.

**Questions**

1. In what ways does globalization undermine a country's sense of security?

2. How do countries and international organizations try to maintain international security?

## References

Arquilla, John & David Ronfeldt, 1996. *The Advent of Netwar.* Santa Monica, CA: RAND.

Betts, Richard, 1998. "The New Threat of Mass Destruction," *Foreign Affairs* 77(1): 26–41.

Bracken, Paul, 1998. "America's Maginot Line," *Atlantic Monthly* 282(6): 85–93.

Brown, Michael, ed., 1995. *Perils of Anarchy: Contemporary Realism and International Security.* Cambridge, MA: MIT Press.

Brown, Seyom 1998. "World Interests and the Changing Dimensions of Security," in Klare & Chandrani (4–5).

Buzan, Barry, 1997a. "Rethinking Security After the Cold War," *Cooperation and Conflict* 32(1): 5–28.

Buzan, Barry; Ole Wæver & Jaap De Wilder, 1997b. *Security: A New Framework for Analysis.* Boulder, CO: Lynne Reinner.

Carter, Ashton & William Perry, 1999. *Preventive Defense: A New Security Strategy for America.* Washington, DC: Brookings Institution.

CFR Task Force, 1999. *Nonlethal Technologies: Progress and Prospects.* New York: Council on Foreign Relations.

Cha, Victor, 1997. "Realism, Liberalism and the Durability of the U.S.-South Korean Alliance," *Asian Survey* 37(7): 609–622.

Cha, Victor, 1998. "Defining Security in East Asia: History, Hotspots, and Horizon-Gazing," in Eun Mee Kim, ed., *The Four Asian Tigers.* San Diego, CA: Academic Press (33–59).

Chipman, John, 1992. "The Future of Strategic Studies' Beyond Grand Strategy," *Survival* 34(1): 109–131.

Cohen, Eliot, 1996. "A Revolution in Warfare," *Foreign Affairs* 75(2): 37–54.

Corcoran, Elizabeth, 1998. "A Bid to Unscramble Encryption Policy," *International Herald Tribune,* 13 July.

Crossette, Barbara, 1998. "Clinton Urges World Action on Terror," *New York Times* (online edition), 22 September.

Desch, Michael, 1998. "Culture Clash: Assessing the Importance of Ideas in Security Studies," *International Security* 23(1): 158–160.

Deudney, David, 1990. "The Case Against Linking Environmental Degradation and Security," *Millenium* 19(3): 461–476.

Falk, Richard, 1997. "State of Siege: Will Globalization Win Out?" *International Affairs* 73(1): 123–136.

Falkenrath, Richard, 1998. "Confronting Nuclear, Biological and Chemical Terrorism," *Survival* 40(4): 43–65.

Freedman, Lawrence, 1998a. "International Security: Changing Targets," *Foreign Policy* 110: 56.

Freedman, Lawrence, 1998b. *The Revolution in Strategic Affairs,* Adelphi Paper 318, Institute for International Security Studies. Oxford: Oxford University Press.

Freedman, Lawrence, 1999. "The Changing Forms of Military Conflict," *Survival* 40(4): 51–52.

Freeh, Louis J., 1997. "The Impact of Encryption on Public Safety," statement before the Permanent Select Committee on Intelligence, US House, 9 September, Washington, DC.

Friedman, Thomas, 1999. *The Lexus and the Olive Tree.* New York: Farrar, Straus, & Giroux.

Godson, Roy, 1997. "Criminal Threats to US Interests in Hong Kong and China," testimony before the Senate Foreign Relations Committee, East Asian and Pacific Affairs Subcommittee, 10 April, Washington, DC.

Goldblatt, David; David Held, Anthony McGrew & Jonathan Perraton, 1997. "Economic Globalization and the Nation-State: Shifting Balances of Power," *Alternatives* 22(3): 269–285.

Gray, Colin, 1992. "New Directions for Strategic Studies: How Can Theory Help Practice," *Security Studies* 1(4): 610–635.

Guehenno, Jean-Marie, 1999. "The Impact of Globalization on Strategy," *Survival* 40(4): 7.

Haas, Richard, 1995. "Paradigm Lost," *Foreign Affairs* 74(1): 43–58.

Held, David, 1997. "Democracy and Globalization," *Global Governance* 3:253.

Hoffman, Bruce, 1997. "Terrorism and WMD: Some Preliminary Hypotheses," *Nonproliferation Review* 4(3): 45–53.

Huntington, Samuel, 1999. "The Lonely Superpower," *Foreign Affairs* 78(2): 35–49.

Katzenstein, Peter, 1996a. *Cultural Norms and National Security.* Ithaca, NY: Cornell University Press.

Katzenstein, Peter, ed., 1996b. *The Culture of National Security.* New York: Columbia University Press.

Katzenstein, Peter, 1998. "Regional Security Orders: Europe and Asia," unpublished paper presented at the European Security Working Group, Georgetown University, 11–14 February.

Kirchner, Emil & James Sperling, 1998. "Economic Security and the Problem of Cooperation in Post-Cold War Europe," *Review of International Studies* 24(2): 221–237.

Klare, Michael, 1998. "The Era of Multiplying Schisms: World Security in the Twenty-First Century," in Klare and Chandrani (59–77).

Klare, Michael & Yogesh Chandrani, eds., 1998. *World Security: Challenges for a New Century.* New York: St. Martin's.

Klare, Michael & Lora Lumpe, 1998. "Fanning the Flames of War: Conventional Arms Transfers in the 1990s," in Klare & Chandrani (160–179).

Laird, Robbin & Holger Mey, 1999. "The Revolution in Military Affairs: Allied Perspectives," *McNair Paper 60.* Washington, DC: National Defense University.

Layne, Christopher, 1997. "From Preponderance to Offshore Balancing: America's Future Grand Strategy," *International Security* 22(1): 86–124.

Leatherman, Jaime & Raimo Väyrynen, 1995. "Conflict Theory and Conflict Resolution: Directions for Collaborative Research Policy," *Cooperation and Conflict* 30(1): 53–82.

Lebow, Richard Ned & Thomas Risse-Kappen, eds., 1995. *International Relations Theory at the End of the Cold War.* New York: Columbia University Press.

Lipshutz, Ronnie, ed., 1995. *On Security.* New York: Columbia University Press.

Lynn-Jones, Sean, ed., 1993. *The Cold War and After: Prospects for Peace.* Cambridge, MA: MIT Press.

Mandelbaum, Michael, 1999. "Is War Obsolete?" *Survival* 40(4): 20–38.

Mathews, Jessica, 1997. "Power Shift," *Foreign Affairs* 76(1): 50–66.

Matthew, Richard & George Shambaugh, 1998. "Sex, Drugs, and Heavy Metal: Transnational Threats and National Vulnerabilities," *Security Dialogue* 29(2): 163–175.

Mittelman, James, 1994. "The Globalisation Challenge: Surviving at the Margins," *Third World Quarterly* 15(3): 427–443.

Moon Chung-in, 1995. "Globalization: Challenges and Strategies," *Korea Focus* 3(3): 64.

Mueller, John, 1989. *Retreat from Doomsday: The Obsolescence of Modern War.* New York: Basic Books.

Nye, Joseph, 1989. *The Contribution of Strategic Studies: Future Challenges,* Adelphi Paper 235. London: IISS.

Nye, Joseph & William Owens, 1998. "America's Information Edge," *Foreign Affairs* 75(2): 20–36.

Ohmae, Kenichi, 1993. "The Rise of the Region State," *Foreign Affairs* 72 (Spring): 78–87.

Reinicke, Wolfgang, 1997. "Global Public Policy," *Foreign Affairs* 75(6): 127–138.

Rosenau, James, 1996. "The Dynamics of Globalization: Toward an Operational Formulation," *Security Dialogue* 27(3): 18–35.

Rosenau, James, 1998. "The Dynamism of a Turbulent World," in Klare and Chandrani (21-23).

Ruggie, John, 1997. "The Past as Prologue? Interests, Identity, and American Foreign Policy," *International Security* 22(1): 89–125.

Schmitt, Eric, 1999. "Panel Urges Plan to Curb Proliferation of Weapons," *New York Times,* 9 July.

Shearer, David, February 1998. *Private Armies and Military Intervention,* Adelphi Paper 316. New York: International Institute for Strategic Studies.

Shinn, James, ed., 1996. *Weaving the Net: Conditional Engagement with China.* New York: Council on Foreign Relations.

Silverstein, Ken, 1997. "Privatizing War," *The Nation,* 28 July.

Simon, Denis Fred, ed., 1997. *Techno-Security in an Age of Globalization.* New York: M. E. Sharpe.

Sullivan, Kevin & Mary Jordan, 1999. "High-Tech Pirates Ravage Asian Seas," *Washington Post,* 5 July.

Talbott, Strobe, 1997. "Globalization and Diplomacy: A Practitioner's Perspective," *Foreign Policy* 108:69–83.

Thomson, Janice, 1996. *Mercenaries, Pirates, and Sovereigns: State-Building and Extraterritorial Violence in Early Modern Europe.* Princeton, NJ: Princeton University Press.

Van Creveld, Martin, 1991. *The Transformation of War.* New York: Free Press.

Väyrynen, Raimo, 1998. "Environmental Security and Conflicts: Concepts and Policies," *International Studies* 35(1): 3–21.

Wæver, Ole; Barry Buzan, Marten Kelstrup & Pierre Lemaitre, 1993. *Identity, Migration and the New Security Agenda in Europe.* London: Pinter.

Walt, Stephen M., 1991. "The Renaissance of Security Studies," *International Studies Quarterly* 35(2): 211-239.

*Washington Post,* 1998. "Clinton Plan Targets World Crime Threat," 11 May.

Zurn, Michael, 1998. "The Rise of International Environmental Politics: A Review of the Current Research," *World Politics* 50(4): 617–649.

---

*Source:* Globalization and the Study of International Security. Victor D. Cha. *Journal of Peace Research,* Vol. 37, No. 3. 2000. Reprinted by permission of Sage Publications.

# CHAPTER 19

## The Biggest Failure

### *A New Approach to Help the World's Internally Displaced People*

Ray Wilkinson

Since its beginnings in the years after the Second World War, the UNHCR, the UN refugee agency, has been working to find safe haven and eventual safe return for the world's refugees fleeing crises and trouble spots around the globe. The world's biggest failure in this effort may have been in ignoring the plight of internally displaced persons, those people who have had to flee their homes but have not crossed international borders. A new approach targets the needs of these people.

The attacks often begin at dawn—gunmen on horseback, camels and battered military vehicles, sometimes accompanied by aircraft and helicopters—swooping down swiftly against an undefended village. "They killed my husband in front of me," a recent survivor of one attack recalled. "They threw me to the ground and raped me. They took one of my children away. I have not seen him again. They burned the village and killed all of my neighbors before leaving."

The young mother crawled away from the carnage and with her surviving four children spent several weeks with virtually no food, water or shelter stumbling toward the comparative safety of the neighboring state of Chad from her home in the Darfur region of Africa's largest nation, Sudan.

There are literally thousands of similar atrocity stories circulating at any one time in the region. In a tragic escalation of the conflict, for the first time an officially established camp for displaced persons was attacked in September. Thirty-four persons were slaughtered including at least one man whose hands were tied behind his back and who was then dragged to his death behind a horse, Wild West style.

They were among the latest victims of a decades old dispute between black African farmers and Arabic nomadic communities for sparse natural resources which flamed into full conflict in 2003, when marauding bands of militia, some reputedly backed by the central government in Khartoum and others proclaiming themselves champions of the farmers, began plundering one of the most desolate and inhospitable regions of the world.

In the ensuing chaos, anywhere between 180,000 and 300,000 civilians were killed or died of war-related wounds and disease. Two million persons fled their towns and villages.

Former U.S. Secretary of State Colin Powell called the campaign of murder, loot and rape by one of the protagonists, the so-called *janjaweed* or "devils on horseback," as nothing less than genocide. John Prendergast from the advocacy International Crisis Group described the *janjaweed* as a "grotesque mixture of the mafia and the Ku Klux Klan" and said "a government-made hurricane had hit Darfur."

The situation was so dire at times that the gunmen often turned their guns on aid workers and their precious supplies. "There is nothing left to loot but the foreigners' convoys," one local tribal leader said.

## Why the Difference?

Sudan's nightmare confronted humanitarian agencies such as United Nations High Commissioner for Refugees (UNHCR) with their biggest and most complex ongoing emergency.

But it also highlighted a troubling and intractable problem which the international community has grappled unsuccessfully with for years—why millions of civilians similarly affected by war or other persecution are often treated so differently—some receiving major assistance and others virtually none at all?

An estimated 200,000 Sudanese civilians escaped the fighting by fleeing into Chad. Once they had reached a neighboring state, they came under the protection of global refugee conventions which entitled them to legal protection, shelter, food and water, rudimentary though the help was at times.

But the bulk of the civilian victims, men, women and children who remained in Sudan, faced an infinitely more dangerous future, still under the sway of their own government and militia supporters rather than international treaties and with no automatic right to any help from outside organizations.

Those civilians and millions of others scattered around the globe, lumped together under the clumsy bureaucratic acronym of IDPs, or internally displaced persons, were left to suffer and die in silence for many months as Khartoum sealed its borders and refused to allow aid or aid workers into the region.

When the government finally relented, the outside world was appalled at the human destruction it discovered. "We failed these people for too long," Jan Egeland, the United Nations Emergency Relief Coordinator and effectively the world's leading humanitarian bureaucrat, said later. "While over the years we have managed to save millions of lives, our response system has [also] been plagued by severe gaps. The needs of the internally displaced were often the first to fall between the cracks."

UNHCR High Commissioner António Guterres added that "We have too often been too late with too little support." The treatment of people internally displaced by conflict, he said, "has been the biggest failure of the international humanitarian community."

But if nothing else, the Darfur conflict now acted as a wake-up call, according to Egeland, and forced the world to once again confront the issue of people effectively abandoned within their own countries and denied their basic human rights. He determined, along with U.N. agencies, the Red Cross and other organizations, to re-examine the whole approach toward people like the Sudanese civilians who had "fallen between the cracks" and remained trapped in their desert hell holes.

## How Did We Get Into This Mess?

Politicians, journalists and the general public routinely label all civilians who flee persecution or war simply as refugees, a word which has become an easy catchall to describe anyone displaced from their homes either through war, persecution or even natural calamity, as happened during the catastrophic Asian tsunami, the earthquake in Pakistan and in the wake of hurricane Katrina which lashed the United States.

Given this oversimplified approach, it is difficult for the world to understand or accept that a Sudanese family who successfully reached Chad can be treated so differently from another family who fled from the same village at the same time and which is living only a short distance away, but inside Sudan.

The reasons are manifold—partly political, partly historical and massively influenced by the thorny issues of national sovereignty and the changing nature of conflict.

The current refugee regime was established in the wake of World War II with the creation of the UNHCR and the adoption of the 1951 Geneva Refugee Convention. The definition of a refugee was spelled out precisely—as a person who "owing to a well-founded fear of being persecuted for reasons of race, religion, nationality, membership of a particular social group, or political opinion, is outside the country of his nationality."

For most of the last half of the 20th century, many innocent victims of war and persecution fitted neatly into this category.

In the post Cold War era, however, the very nature of conflict and the predicament of displaced persons began to change.

Wars between conventional armies increasingly were overtaken by internal civil conflicts involving government forces, militias, religious extremists and outright terrorist groups.

Almost unnoticed at first, millions of innocents became war victims, often deliberately targeted by one or more sides carrying guns, but unlike earlier persecuted peoples, with nowhere to run and often no one to help them. For these people, there was no international safety net in place.

It was not until the closing years of the last century that the world began to appreciate the enormity of the unfolding IDP nightmare.

When U.N. Secretary-General Kofi Annan addressed the General Assembly for the last time in the old millennium, he proposed a radical departure from the way governments and agencies had been handling the problem. Effectively, he urged member states to put aside their most jealously guarded powers—sovereignty and the sanctity of national borders—in the higher interests of protecting hapless civilians caught up in war.

"Nothing in the [U.N.] Charter precludes a recognition that there are rights beyond borders," he told delegates. "There is no doubt that enforcement action is a difficult step to take. It often goes against political or other interests, but there are universal principles and values which supersede such interests, and the protection of civilians is one of them."

He suggested that the U.N., via the Security Council, should be able to intervene directly, even in internal conflicts, authorizing more preventative peacekeeping missions, enforcing existing international humanitarian and human rights laws and imposing sanctions such as arms embargoes against recalcitrant states.

The reaction, predictably, was mixed. While the Netherlands insisted that respect for human rights had become "more and more mandatory and respect for sovereignty less and less stringent," China noted that though "such arguments as 'human rights taking precedence over sovereignty' seem to be in vogue these days" respect for national sovereignty and noninterference in internal affairs were "the basic principles governing international relations."

As a new century dawned, Refugees magazine (No. 117) called the unfolding drama "The HOT issue for a new millennium."

## Twenty-Five Million People in Need

Halfway across the world from the desert wastes of Darfur and the fleeing mother and her children, in the hot dry uplands of northeastern Colombia, Alicia (not her real name) faced a more insidious and prolonged form of harassment and persecution than the Sudanese civilians subject to lightning raids by the gunmen on horseback.

Alicia's "mistake" was to start a cooperative for small farmers trying to grow crops other than coca and thus escape the drug wars involving government forces and rival armed groups which had helped plunge the country into four decades of war.

Shortly after the project began, the wreaths also started arriving . . . every day for a month. . . Alicia's name spelled out in large gold letters on the garish red ribbons. Killings followed, of friends and colleagues murdered in the most brutal fashion. The warning to Alicia was clear.

She abandoned her home and fled, as millions of other Colombians have done over the years, the outside world rarely aware of or concerned about this almost silent exodus.

Each time Alicia found a refuge, her tormentors found her and she was forced to move again.

Eventually, after years on the run across Colombia, she arrived in Soacha, a filthy shantytown of poor housing, few basic services and little law and order, but still only a few miles from downtown Bogotá, the country's capital. The majority of Alicia's neighbors had similar histories, abandoning their villages and towns because of the fighting and other forms of persecution and seeking safety in the anonymity of a big city slum.

Today, every big city in Colombia has a Soacha, belts of poverty ringing affluent centers where uprooted peoples live in dire poverty, where there are few police or military and where many remain at the mercy of those same armed groups from which they fled in the first place.

"They are in their own country, yet they cannot avail themselves of the protection of the state," says Roberto Meier, the Representative in Colombia of UNHCR which recently opened a "safe house" in Soacha to provide help to Alicia and her neighbors.

The Colombian woman and the Sudanese mother who was raped and whose husband was murdered in front of her, are among a staggering 25 million people in some 50 countries whose villages and towns have been destroyed, families killed or broken up, who have few possessions, often no shelter, little physical protection and who are constant prey to men with guns, either in uniform or with no allegiance at all except to a local warlord.

This figure compares to 9.2 million refugees worldwide.

More than half of this IDP population is in Africa, six million in Sudan alone, the largest single group of displaced persons in the world. There are 3.7 million victims of conflict displaced in the Americas, the bulk of them in Colombia, the second largest IDP global population.

Similar numbers are scattered around Asia and the Pacific and even in Europe.

It is a population in constant flux and motion. In 2004, an estimated three million people became newly displaced because of conflict, principally in Sudan, the Democratic Republic of Congo and Uganda.

But an equal number of civilians returned to their old homes in the same period, one million people to Democratic Congo, 900,000 to Angola and other large populations to Liberia and the Sudan.

Thus in the often schizophrenic IDP world, in Congo and Sudan at least, millions of people were on the move in both directions, either fleeing parts of those countries ravaged by ongoing war or returning to other, peaceful areas and virtually at the same time.

Throughout this constant swirl of movement and to-ing and fro-ing, the overall global IDP population remained relatively constant at an estimated 25 million during the first years of the new millennium. In comparison, the numbers of refugees continued to drop modestly in the same period.

## Softly-Softly

As the scope of the IDP problem exploded, steps were taken to address the issue.

In the wake of Gulf War I and then in the Balkans during the 1990s, governments, humanitarian agencies and donors intervened, financially, politically and with resources on the ground, to help the millions of people trapped in their own countries as well as others who fled further afield as refugees.

Perhaps for the first time, the plight of IDPs became a topic for serious debate in the corridors of power.

Sudanese lawyer and diplomat Francis M. Deng was appointed to the newly-created post of Special Representative of the U.N. Secretary-General for Internally Displaced Persons, a recognition that this group of disenfranchised people needed their own champion.

After years of delicate legal maneuver and hard bargaining with governments, lawyers, academics and humanitarians, he produced a slim booklet called *Guiding Principles on Internal Displacement,* a set of 30 recommendations for the protection of this group.

A handful of governments incorporated some of the points in their national legislation and a few were willing to review the issue of sovereignty and international intervention.

Walter Kälin, a refugee law expert from Switzerland who succeeded Deng in 2004 to a slightly different post, now the Representative of the U.N. Secretary-General on the Human Rights of Internally Displaced Persons, insisted that "A few years ago it would have been impossible to talk about the human rights of IDPs with governments. Today at least, it is acknowledged by most authorities that the internally displaced do have human rights."

In the wake of Secretary-General Annan's call to arms at the end of the old century, U.N. and other specialized agencies were encouraged to take what was bureaucratically termed a "collaborative approach"—working closely together—to help internally displaced civilians. A small, specialized IDP unit was established within the Office for the Coordination of Humanitarian Affairs (OCHA) in Geneva.

Today, emergency coordinator Egeland reports biannually to the Security Council on the protection of civilians caught up in conflict. Peacekeeping operations in such countries as Liberia and Sudan have specific protection mandates for civilians and peacekeepers are obliged to intervene to help people at risk.

At a General Assembly summit meeting in September 2005, states agreed on a declaration spelling out their "Responsibility to Protect"—effectively committing governments to shield their civilians from genocide, war crimes, ethnic cleansing and crimes against humanity and empowering the international community to respond if countries did not live up to their obligations.

But this largely voluntary, softly-softly approach, still left huge gaps and it took the worsening crisis in Sudan to strip away the system's ongoing failures.

## A New Approach

Egeland ordered an urgent, independent study to "evaluate the humanitarian response system" worldwide.

An interagency internal displacement division was established in Geneva in 2004 to help usher in a new, more muscular approach to the problem.

The new initiative announced in late 2005, will reinforce and refine the existing collaborative approach towards IDPs. Major gaps and weaknesses were identified, including what Egeland called the "absence of clear operational accountability and leadership in key sectors."

Individual agencies were designated as "sector leaders" to coordinate operations in specific areas to try to plug those newly identified gaps.

UNHCR will be responsible for all aspects of protection for internally displaced people, their shelter and the establishment and running of camps, should they prove necessary.

Other agencies will take lead roles in separate areas, the children's fund UNICEF for such things as water, sanitation and nutrition, the World Food Program for logistics, the World Health Organization for health, UNICEF and OCHA for telecommunications and the U.N. Development Program for long-term rehabilitation and recovery.

Designated lead agencies will both participate directly in operations, but also coordinate with and oversee other organizations within their specific spheres, reporting the results up through a designated chain of command to Egeland at the summit.

It is hoped to establish a central emergency reserve fund of $500 million to kick-start emergency operations at short notice and individual agencies will also seek direct additional funding from donors to underwrite their new operations.

A series of pilot projects to test the effectiveness of the new approach will be launched in 2006, probably beginning in three of the largest IDP problem areas in Liberia, Uganda and the Democratic Republic of the Congo.

Dennis McNamara, the head of the interagency division in Geneva said, "The important point is that in future everyone should know who is responsible for what and that, in the final analysis, the designated lead organization must be held accountable for fulfilling the tasks assigned to it. That has not been the case in the past when there was little accountability."

According to Egeland the new initiative must be "more effective, predictable and cost effective"—all new IDP buzz words. "It must not fail as it did in Darfur in 2004," he said.

## UNHCR and IDPs

UNHCR's mandate is specific and does not cover internally displaced people. However, the agency has been involved on an ad hoc basis with them for more than three decades.

Ironically, in view of the fact that the current crisis in Sudan triggered the latest initiative, it was an earlier crisis in the same country that signaled the refugee agency's first involvement with IDPs.

In a situation remarkably reminiscent of today, peace had been declared in the south of the country in 1972 after years of intermittent war. Tens of thousands of refugees began returning from surrounding countries, but their numbers were dwarfed by civilians who also began to go back to their homes from other areas of the Sudan, people not then known by their subsequent label as IDPs. The refugee agency began helping both groups of civilians and also to rebuild a landscape devastated by conflict—the challenge UNHCR now faces again in the same region.

Since that first operation, either at the behest of the General Assembly, the Secretary-General or the Security Council, UNHCR has participated in more than 30 similar emergencies.

It currently helps 5.6 million people out of the global population of some 25 million.

There are obvious reasons for this overlap and dual role. Refugees and internally displaced people may be victims of the same war, even come from the same village, the only difference being whether they had crossed an international frontier or not. UNHCR's expertise is easily transferable to both groups in many circumstances.

But the agency has always maintained a cautious approach to a deeper involvement, worried about stretching already limited resources by taking on the burden of looking after millions of additional disenfranchised people; the so-called turf wars in an increasingly congested field of humanitarian agencies, governments and even armies; the practical difficulties faced by its staff in the field, particularly security issues; and perhaps most importantly the possibility of diluting or compromising its own "core" work with refugees.

There have been persistent concerns expressed, both from within UNHCR itself and by governments and other agencies, over the possible contradiction in trying to help the two groups at the same time. According to this logic, helping people in situ, in their own countries, could complicate another vital branch of the agency's work, helping refugees to seek asylum.

Potential receiving countries could argue, as the former Yugoslav Republic of Macedonia did in 1999, that there was no need to allow civilians fleeing Kosovo to cross into a second country where they would be eligible to seek asylum because they were already receiving aid inside their own country.

Conversely, other experts argue that states might be prepared to accept asylum seekers more readily if they are convinced that everything has been done inside a troubled country before civilians are forced, as a last resort, to seek the protection of a foreign state.

UNHCR's Executive Committee, has insisted that whatever its involvement inside states "the principles of international human rights and humanitarian law and the institution of asylum must not in any way be undermined."

The debate continues. Writing in Oxford University's Forced Migration Review journal Roberta Cohen called the lack of adequate protection for IDPs the "biggest gap" in current efforts to help the group and said the refugee agency must both expand and redefine its protection role.

"With refugees, it [UNHCR] basically defends their legal right to asylum and *non-refoulement* [the forcible return to a country where a civilian may face persecution]," she said. "With IDPs they are in their own countries and should enjoy the same rights as other citizens, but there are no international legal agreements to help," according to Cohen from the Brookings Institution in Washington. "Protection involves defending their physical safety and a broad range of human rights to which they are entitled."

In the absence of a specific IDP organization, many advocates in the last decade strongly suggested that UNHCR itself should be designated as the clear lead agency.

In the 1990s, then High Commissioner Sadako Ogata decided that the problems of trying to help additional millions of people—the need for more financial and physical resources, mandate complications and the suspicions of other agencies—were simply too enormous for one organization and backed away from that approach.

Joel Charny, vice-president for policy at the advocacy group Refugees International remains a champion of a single leadership approach. "The collaborative response remains deeply flawed," he wrote in the Forced Migration Review. The U.N. leadership should "agree to make UNHCR the centerpiece of the global response to internal displacement" such an approach bringing 'clarity' to a broken system.

High Commissioner Guterres outlined his own approach in August. The agency's traditional refugee mandate would not be compromised, he said, even as its role with IDPs expanded.

Additional funding would be vital, but he stressed the same targets as Egeland—predictability, coordination and cooperation.

"We are part of a team," he emphasized, recognizing the sensitivity of the subject. "We are willing to have a leading role in some areas, but within the framework of a team, respecting the mandates of all other agencies. We are not going to do anything alone."

## Difficult Times Ahead

The future remains uncertain. However effectively humanitarian organizations such as UNHCR respond to the legal and material needs of the world's uprooted peoples, ultimately only political solutions will solve any particular emergency.

"We have failed these people for too long," Egeland repeated recently. "Too often, we have been a big plaster covering the wound. But this will not heal without political agreements to settle the problem."

Angola is a case study, highlighting not only the worst kind of deprivation and persecution hapless civilians are subject to, but also how quickly even the most

protracted crisis can be turned around, given the political will of opposing groups.

Three years ago, the southern African state was literally a humanitarian basket case. Potentially one of the continent's richest countries with an abundance of oil, gems, minerals and agricultural land, it had been mired in civil war for more than a quarter century since independence from Portugal.

It was officially classed as the worst place in the world for a child to grow up and the legacy to its young people, even if they survived into adulthood "will be a vast plain of scorched earth," according to the U.N. at the time.

The World Food Program reported: "Civil war has been bleeding the country for so long that the cynical observer would be inclined to think it is business as usual there" where "the dead already number in the hundreds of thousands, the mutilated more than 100,000, the displaced well into the millions."

But when a peace treaty was signed between the government and rebel forces in 2002, villagers immediately began flocking back to their homes, many walking hundreds or thousands of miles without assistance to start rebuilding villages which had been razed to the ground. An estimated 900,000 went back in 2004 alone and though the country remains in a fragile state, there is at least cautious optimism for what had been one of the world's most vicious and intractable conflicts.

A power sharing agreement the following year in neighboring Democratic Congo triggered a similar mass return. There were signs of movement in the broken state of Somalia on the Horn of Africa. People on foot, in trucks, on bicycles, by air and by boat went back to Liberia, parts of Sudan and Afghanistan. Significantly, there were no major new conflicts in 2004.

However, there were as many ongoing "black spots" as there were hopeful developments. As earlier noted, for every civilian returning home, another was displaced last year.

If some governments had incorporated the Guiding Principles into domestic legislation and others at least paid lip service to the idea of honoring human rights obligations, many others ignored international pressure and insisted the concept of absolute sovereignty was paramount.

In at least 13 countries, governments responsible for the protection of their own populations were actively involved in military campaigns against those same civilians, according to the Global IDP Project run by the Norwegian Refugee Council.

Nearly 20 million civilians in 20 countries remained at "constant risk of death" because of ongoing military activity near their homes, the project reported. In 19 states there was not even any real information on the wars in those regions and the fate of millions of other people, it added.

Such precarious situations—ongoing war, scarce information, governments fighting their own populations—underlined the enormous challenges faced by the international community, particularly UNHCR and its protection portfolio—even if leading humanitarian organizations are now willing to increase their assistance.

Will recalcitrant states, especially governments such as those in Myanmar, the Central African Republic or Nepal who, according to the Global IDP Project, offer no help to embattled civilians, cooperate? How will field officials be able to offer protection in areas where conflicts continued unabated? How will protection officers protect themselves in such hostile environments?

## A Turning Point?

Dennis McNamara, the director of the internal displacement division in Geneva, believes that despite ongoing concerns about the new approach to IDPs, it nevertheless "represents a pretty dramatic development in U.N. terms." He added, "The trick now is that we must transform these commitments into action on the ground."

As well as convincing involved governments to cooperate, traditional donors must also be brought on board. Many have already expressed their concerns that victims of internal displacement have been ignored for too long, but the costs of addressing the problem will be enormous—at least $1 billion annually, according to McNamara.

The donors, needing to meet increasing global demands with smaller budgets, have, like the agencies themselves, been criticized on occasion for "picking and choosing" the crises they assist. Thus, while high profile catastrophes such as the Asian tsunami triggered an overwhelming global response and virtually unlimited funding, many far less 'glamorous' emergencies received scant attention or assistance. Some aid workers worried that as their role with IDPs increased, funds might be transferred from ongoing projects rather than new money being found.

Walter Kälin, the U.N. appointed IDP representative on human rights, believes the donors will respond ... in certain circumstances. "My feeling is that the donors are prepared to move in," he said recently after months of high level consultations. "But only if they see the agencies working effectively on the ground." He added that this could be a Catch-22 situation: "It is admittedly a vicious circle. The agencies can't work effectively without those additional resources."

The bottom line was summed up by former UNHCR Assistant High Commissioner Kamel Morjane who said: "It is neither ethical nor practical to distinguish between human beings because of a border they may or may not have crossed. Human life should have the same worth whether a person is a refugee or an IDP."

And the challenge of a newspaper editorial in the Canberra Times written after the U.N. Secretary-General's call to arms more than five years ago remains as relevant today as it did then: "On whether history will view it [Kofi Annan's initiative] as a quixotic gesture or a first and brave step towards a genuine new world order, rests the prosperity, happiness and perhaps the lives of millions of human beings."

### Questions

1. Who are internally displaced people, and what are their special needs? How does the UN hope to help these people?

2. Is it the responsibility of the world community to help people fleeing within their own country? In what ways?

*Source:* The Biggest Failure: A New Approach to Help the World's Internally Displaced People. Ray Wilkinson. *Refugees.* Vol. 4, No. 141. 2006. Reprinted by permission of United Nations High Commissioner for Refugees.

# PART V

# HEALTH

In recent decades, the world as a whole has made major gains in reducing infant and child mortality and extending human life expectancy. The gains have been very uneven, however. While some Asian countries are seeing new generations living far longer than ever before, in parts of Africa, life expectancy has dramatically decreased as young adults die from the ravages of conflicts and AIDS. While poor countries struggle to provide the basics of clean water and adequate food, wealthier nations struggle with the problem of providing and paying for increasingly expensive health care for aging populations. Rich and poor face fears of the rapid spread of diseases such as AIDS and the possibility of new epidemics such as avian flu.

One of the new words we have had to learn in the age of globalization is outsourcing: the sending of jobs to off-site locations, often overseas. Outsourcing has transformed manufacturing and is now beginning to change the world of information processing as well as software and product design. Now outsourcing has reached the world of medicine. Article 20 considers what happens to medical practice when major procedures can be done for a fraction of the cost in distant locations.

While new dangers and new procedures gain attention, the world still struggles with old killers and cripplers. Agencies such as the World Health Organization (WHO) have declared the end of active smallpox and hoped to do the same for polio. Eradicating disease involves navigating complicated social worlds and cultural practices as well as simply delivering medicine and technology. Article 21 looks at what went wrong in the final stages of eliminating polio from the planet.

As old diseases decline and disappear, all too often new diseases emerge and spread. AIDS continues to devastate parts of Africa, but it is also expanding rapidly in much of Asia and is threatening new populations in the Americas and Europe. Article 22 is an account of how European welfare states, often touted as some of the most effective in protecting the health of their populations, struggle to deal with the challenges of AIDS. Article 23 brings the health discussion full circle from exporting procedures to importing trained personnel. The United States needs nurses. But does its efforts to bring in new nursing talent further impoverish poor countries who lose their trained medical personnel? The article echoes the theme seen in each of these looks at the world of health: the interconnection of humans across the globe, sharing the same biology even as we live in very different social worlds.

20. Outsourcing Your Heart.
    Unmesh Kher. *Time Magazine*. May 21, 2006.

21. Rumor, Fear and Fatigue Hinder Final Push to End Polio.
    Celia W. Dugger and Donald G. McNeil, Jr. *The New York Times*. March 20, 2006.

22. AIDS and Health-Policy Responses in European Welfare States.
    Monika Steffen. *Journal of European Social Policy*. Vol. 14. 2004.

23. US Plan to Lure Nurses May Hurt Poor Nations.
    Celia W. Dugger. *The New York Times*. May 24, 2006.

# CHAPTER 20

## Outsourcing Your Heart

Unmesh Kher

> The high cost of medical care is leading to what has become known as medical tourism, with people traveling to distant, lower cost locations for surgery and other health care. Medical tourism brings new opportunities and also new risks.

Whiplash was just the first agony that Kevin Miller, 45, suffered in a car accident last July. The second was sticker shock. The self-employed and uninsured chiropractor from Eunice, L.A., learned that it would cost $90,000 to get the herniated disk in his neck repaired. So over the objections of his doctors, he turned to the Internet and made an appointment with Bumrungrad Hospital in Bangkok, the marble-floored mecca of the medical trade that—with its liveried bellhops, fountains and restaurants—resembles a grand hotel more than a clinic. There a U.S.-trained surgeon fixed Miller's injured disk for less than $10,000. "I wouldn't hesitate to come back for another procedure," says Miller, who was recovering last week at the Westin Grande in Bangkok.

With this surgical sojourn, his first trip outside the U.S., Miller joined the swelling ranks of medical tourists. As word has spread about the high-quality care and cut-rate surgery available in such countries as India, Thailand, Singapore and Malaysia, a growing stream of uninsured and underinsured Americans are boarding planes not for the typical face-lift or tummy tuck but for discount hip replacements and sophisticated heart surgeries. Bumrungrad alone, according to CEO Curtis Schroeder, saw its stream of American patients climb to 55,000 last year, a 30% rise. Three-quarters of them flew in from the U.S.; 83% came for noncosmetic treatments. Meanwhile, India's trade in international patients is increasing at the same rate.

That's still a trickle compared with the millions of surgeries performed each year in the $2 trillion U.S. health-care system. But a significant shift is under way. It's one that could put greater competitive pressure on U.S. hospitals as some of their most lucrative patients are siphoned off. Elective surgeries are key moneymakers for hospitals, and even a small drop-off can cut deep into their profits.

What may accelerate the trend is that some pioneering U.S. corporations, swamped by rising health-care costs, are taking a serious look at medical outsourcing. Blue Ridge Paper Products of Canton, N.C., a manufacturing company, may soon offer employees outsourcing as a health-care option. The carrot? The patient would get to pocket some of the firm's substantial savings.

The calculus behind this interest isn't complicated. Many major U.S. employers are self-insured, which means they pick up the tab for much of their employees' medical care. That's why three major corporations that collectively cover 240,000 lives asked Dr. Arnold Milstein, national health-care "thought leader" at the consultancy Mercer Health & Benefits, to assess the best places to outsource elective surgeries. Procedures in Thailand and Malaysia, he found, cost only 20% to 25% as much as comparable ones in the U.S.; top-notch Indian hospitals sell such services at an even steeper discount.

The bottom line: If more private payers sent patients abroad for uncomplicated elective surgeries, the savings could be enormous. "This has the potential of doing to the U.S. health-care system what the Japanese auto industry did to American carmakers," says Princeton University health-care economist Uwe Reinhardt.

U.S. hospitals could certainly do with a little global competition. For years, their share of the national health-care bill has grown at a rate far faster than inflation, and today they gobble up a third of all medical expenditures. At current rates, the U.S. will be spending $1 of every $5 of its GDP on health care by 2015, yet more than one in four workers will be uninsured. The ingrained inefficiency of most hospitals doesn't help. "A lot of them still don't know how to schedule their operating rooms efficiently," says Reinhardt. "They've never had to. They always get paid, no matter how sloppy they are."

That sloppiness, among other things, widens the price gap with foreign hospitals that entrepreneurs are exploiting. United Group Programs (UGP) of Boca Raton, F.L., a third-party administrator that sells a low-premium, bare-bones form of coverage called a mini-medical plan, this month began promoting Bumrungrad Hospital as a preferred provider to its customers. Employees of self-insured businesses who use the more conventional plans designed by UGP will also have access to the Thai hospital. This means that UGP offers the option of partly or fully covered medical tourism to some 100,000 people, including those who could use it most.

Mini-med plans are increasingly popular with contract and hourly workers, who are more likely than most other workers to be uninsured. But these plans are controversial because the buyers often think they cover more than they actually do. UGP's plans at best cap reimbursement for surgery at $3,000 and hospital stays at $1,000 a day. That would barely cover an afternoon in a U.S. hospital. But in Thailand, says Jonathan Edelheit, UGP's vice president of sales and marketing, a heart bypass that would cost its U.S. customers $56,000 could be had for $8,000.

Companies with traditional plans are also taking the initiative. Blue Ridge Paper, which makes the DairyPak brand of packaging, was carved out of the forest-products firm Champion International when its employees bought a few factories that were scheduled to close. But health-care costs are hurting the company. So a Blue Ridge team plans to visit hospitals in India to assess their quality of care. If it gives the green light, Blue Ridge will begin promoting the option to its 2,000 workers.

Employees who opt for India would get to take along a family member, says Darrell Douglas, vice president of human resources, and the whole experience, including a recuperative stay at a hotel, would be covered. IndUShealth, a medical tourism start-up in Raleigh,

N.C., will make all arrangements and coordinate care between U.S. and Indian providers. The sweetener: the company will share with these intrepid employees up to 25% of savings garnered from the outsourcing.

Get a new hip—and a rebate. Sounds like a bargain, but would people actually travel 10,000 miles for medical care just to make a few bucks? You bet. Polls commissioned by Milstein suggest that few consumers would opt for surgery abroad for incentives below $1,000. But raise the ante above $1,000, and the equation changes. Among people who have sick family members, about 45% of the underinsured or uninsured declare they would get on the plane; even 19% of those who have insurance say they're game. Above $5,000, the percentage of takers climbs to 61% and 40%, respectively.

State governments, which tend to offer generous health-care benefits, may find those numbers appealing. A bill in the West Virginia legislature sponsored by delegate Ray Canterbury outlines incentives for the public employee health-insurance program that are similar to Blue Ridge's. Hospital administrators attending the legislative session when the bill came up for a hearing in February nearly gagged, says Canterbury: "They were not happy. But I didn't expect them to be. The point is to make them face competition."

Is the quality of care in foreign hospitals high enough? To cater to an international clientele, many private hospitals abroad are applying for accreditation (many of them successfully) from the Joint Commission International, the global arm of the institution that accredits most U.S. hospitals. Many of the tourist hospitals teem with surgeons who have trained in the U.S. or Britain, which is a great comfort to American patients (the irony is that 25% of physicians in the U.S. got their M.D.s abroad). Escorts Heart Institute and Research Center in Delhi, for instance, was founded by an authority on robotic cardiac surgery, Dr. Naresh Trehan, formerly of New York University. Wayne Steinard, 59, a general contractor from Winter Haven, Fla., is one of these U.S. patients "who fall through the cracks" of the health-care system, as he says. Steinard landed in New Delhi last week with his daughter Beth Keigans to get a clogged artery cleared and a stent installed. Steinard, too rich for Medicaid and too poor for insurance, certainly didn't have the $60,000 he would have had to pay back home. So he contacted PlanetHospital, a Malibu, CA, medical-tourism agency, and learned he could get it done for about a tenth as much at Max Healthcare's Devki Devi Heart & Vascular Institute.

Things have not gone as Steinard expected. When surgeon Pradeep Chandra scanned Steinard's angiogram last week, he found the artery 90% blocked. "A stent is out of the question," he told Keigans. "Your father is going to need a double bypass, and he needs it immediately." The blood drained from Keigans' face. While she loved their plush hospital suite and the staff had been superb, this was all happening too far from home. Steinard, though, was blunt about his choices. It's either this, he said, or a fatal heart attack back home. The surgery last week was successful; the hospital's bill: $6,650.

"I'm not sure I'd ever want to come back to Delhi," says Keigans, "but I'll be telling everyone I know to come here if they need surgery. It's not just the price. They've made everything so easy for us."

Yet India is a developing country, and this can shake the confidence of even the most cavalier patient. First-class hotels are in short supply. Beyond that, the country's crumbling infrastructure and shocking income disparities—children pick through the garbage outside Steinard's hospital—make medical tourism seem a tad too adventurous for many. And for the litigious minded, good luck. The country's malpractice laws limit damage awards, one of many reasons that health care is cheaper.

But people don't have to be in Steinard's—or Miller's—straits before they cross borders for care. Retirees, especially the snowbirds who winter in South Texas and Arizona, have turned Mexican towns like Nuevo Progreso (pop. 9,125; dentists, 70), in the Lower Rio Grande Valley, and Los Algodones (pop. 15,000; doctors and dentists, 250), near Yuma, A.Z., into dusty dental centers. Los Algodones might rake in as much as $150 million during the winter season. People from Minnesota and California arrive in chartered planes to get their teeth fixed in these dental oases. Two California insurers, Health Net and Blue Shield, for the past few years have marketed popular health-insurance plans, aimed at Latinos, that charge lower premiums and cover treatment on both sides of the border.

Mexico's medical industry is just beginning to bubble; India's, like its other outsourcing segments, is booming. Apollo Hospitals, one of the largest private chains in the world with 46 hospitals in three countries, and Wockhardt Hospitals Group, which has eight hospitals in India, are working through agencies like IndUShealth, PlanetHospital and the Medical Tourist Co. in Britain to build business across West.

Trehan plans to launch next year, in partnership with GE, the first installment of a vast, $250 million specialty Escorts hospital complex near New Delhi that will feature luxury suites, a hotel and swank restaurants for patients and their families. "We will be the Mayo Clinic of the East," he says. Max Healthcare is also planning a specialty complex in New Delhi (fields: neurologic, orthopedic, ob-gyn and pediatric).

A corresponding boom is taking place among Western agencies that funnel patients to Asia. Eight have popped up in Canada, where national health care can mean a yearlong wait for elective surgery. In the U.S., several firms are aiming at the roughly 61 million people who are uninsured or underinsured. PlanetHospital's founder, "Rudy" Rupak Acharya, says his agency, which in the past seven months has sent some 200 patients abroad, got 11,000 inquiries in March alone. He has just retained Mercer to help him develop an insurance plan for the uninsured that will combine primary and emergency care in the U.S. with surgery abroad.

Patrick Marsek, managing director of the agency MedRetreat, says his company sent 200 people abroad last year and is already processing 320 this year. He is demanding a deposit of $195 from customers because people posing as patients have been looking for information to start up their own agencies.

Will U.S. insurers join the party? Mohit Ghose of the trade group America's Health Insurance Plans says many have taken note of medical outsourcing but are scared off by the regulatory and legal uncertainties. Aaditya Mattoo, a World Bank economist who has published a study on the potential of medical outsourcing, suspects that pure institutional inertia has something to do with the lack of interest.

Yet as the medical-cost crisis deepens, the corporations who pay insurers are likely to find the lure of outsourcing as irresistible in health care as it is in software.

## Questions

1. What factors along with cost would someone want to weigh in considering whether to have medical procedures done in another country?

2. Is medical tourism a good way for more people to get the care they need, or do you think it points to problems in our health-care system?

*Source:* Outsourcing Your Heart. Unmesh Kher. *Time Magazine.* May 21, 2006. Reprinted by permission.

# CHAPTER 21

## Rumor, Fear and Fatigue Hinder Final Push to End Polio

Celia W. Dugger and Donald G. McNeil, Jr.

International agencies are struggling to put an end to some of the diseases that have killed and crippled people for centuries. For a while, it looked like polio would be added to the list of diseases such as smallpox that have been completely eradicated or removed from human populations. Then the plans went astray.

Nearly 18 years ago, in what they described as a "gift from the 20th century to the 21st," public health officials and volunteers around the world committed themselves to eliminating polio from the planet by the year 2000.

Since then, some two billion children have been vaccinated, cutting incidence of the disease more than 99 percent and saving some five million from paralysis or death, the World Health Organization estimates.

But six years past the deadline, even optimists warn that total eradication is far from assured. The drive against polio threatens to become a costly display of all that can conspire against even the most ambitious efforts to eliminate a disease: cultural suspicions, logistical nightmares, competition for resources from many other afflictions, and simple exhaustion. So monumental is the challenge, in fact, that only one disease has ever been eradicated—smallpox. As the polio campaign has shown, even the miracle of discovering a vaccine is not enough.

Not least among the obstacles is that many poor countries that eliminated polio have let their vaccination efforts slide, making the immunity covering much of the world extremely fragile, polio experts warn. They compare it to a vast, tinder-dry forest: if even one tree is still burning, a single cinder can drift downwind and start a fire virtually anywhere.

Here in northern India the embers are still glowing. And northern Nigeria, another densely populated, desperately poor region, is aflame.

In a calamitous setback in mid-2003, Nigeria's northern states halted the vaccination campaign for a year after rumors swept the region that the vaccine contained the AIDS virus or was part of a Western plot to sterilize Muslim girls. Within a couple of years, 18 once polio-free countries have had outbreaks traceable to Nigeria. Though most have since been tamed, Indonesia and Nigeria itself remain major worries. In 2001, there were fewer than 500 confirmed cases of polio paralysis in the world. Last year, the number jumped to more than 1,900—and each paralyzed child means another 200 "silent carriers" spreading the disease.

This year in addition to India and Nigeria, cases have been reported in Somalia, Niger, Afghanistan, Bangladesh and Indonesia.

Yet no eradication effort against any disease has been as well financed or as comprehensive as the polio drive, which has cost $4 billion so far. In the balance is not just whether polio will be extinguished, many public health officials say, but whether a world that could not quite conquer polio will have the stomach to try to wipe out other diseases, like measles. The closer a disease is to eradication, they say, the harder won the gains. Interest lags as the number of cases falls. Fatigue sets in among volunteers, donors and average people. Yet even one unvaccinated child can allow a new pocket of the disease to bloom.

Here and elsewhere, eradicating polio means finding ways to get polio drops into the mouths of every child under 5—over and over. Because it can take many doses to effectively immunize a child in parts of the world where the disease circulates intensely, eradication requires repeated sweeps. Campaigns are planned to the smallest detail. Each lane is mapped. Supervisors shadow vaccination teams. Follow-up specialists pursue resistant families. . . .

## Nigeria's Agony

. . . The collapse of Nigeria's drive has become a lesson in the ways eradication campaigns can go terribly awry. "Nigeria is clearly far and away the greatest risk to the eradication effort," said Dr. Stephen L. Cochi, a senior adviser in the federal Centers for Disease Control and Prevention's immunization program. The quality of its campaigns is the worst in Africa, he said. "They're just missing lots and lots of kids."

Nigeria's president, Olusegun Obasanjo, who is from the Christian, Yoruba-speaking south, has apologized for his country's role in reigniting the disease, but officials in the Muslim north are defensive. Asked last year whether he had been right to stop the vaccinations, Kano's governor, Ibrahim Shekarau, cut off an interview. "We're not saying it didn't spread, and we're not saying people didn't suffer," he said. "But I had a moral responsibility to our population to stop it until it was clear there was no harm." . . .

As is often the case with rumors, they appeared based on distortions of fact amplified by an alarmist media and by politicians and clerics absorbed in a religiously divisive presidential election campaign. . . .

With such rumors circulating during the hotly contested 2003 elections, in which a Muslim candidate lost to Mr. Obasanjo, "The situation got hijacked," said Dr. Barbara G. Reynolds, deputy chief of the Nigerian office of Unicef. "People who had multiple agendas ran with it."

Most vocal was a wealthy Kano doctor who was both head of a campaign to impose Islamic law in northern Nigeria and a candidate for a top job in the national health department. After being denied the post, he turned against the polio drive, calling the vaccine "tainted by evildoers from America." Governor Shekarau's spokesman publicly speculated that the vaccine was "America's revenge for September 11."

With residents turning vaccinators away and the threat of riots growing, Mr. Shekarau—a well-educated rival to southern politicians—decided to halt vaccinations until doctors could test the vaccine. That took 10 months. Hearings were held, and teams visited vaccine factories in Indonesia, India and South Africa. Medical and religious experts from Saudi Arabia flew in to meet local clerics. Finally, the case was made that the vaccine was safe.

In October 2004, at a kickoff of a new round of vaccinations of 80 million children, Mr. Shekarau allowed Mr. Obasanjo personally to give his 1-year-old daughter, Zainab, the drops—a picture that became famous in Nigeria. The emir of Kano, who rarely lets himself be seen in public, allowed himself to be photographed vaccinating children. But by then, the virus was on the loose.

## New Drive, Old Obstacles

Now that official opposition to Nigeria's eradication drive has melted, it is facing its obstacles, like those in India: Scotch-tape logistics and pockets of resistance.

At 7 a.m. on the first day of a vaccination drive last year, the dirt courtyard of the public clinic in Kano looked like the deck of the world's most bedraggled aircraft carrier. Smashed-up minibus taxis, many with their front ends crumpled and doors held closed by rope, were waiting to take off. Like F-18's, each had a name painted on: Titanic, Dollars, Thank You Daddy.

By 8 a.m., after some near misses with the wobbly benches in the courtyard, most of the minibuses had left, bearing vaccinators on their rounds. But problems were quick to arise. The chief of a nearby district was unhappy that each of his teams got $23 to hire transportation for the day. Last time, he said, the money had gone directly to him, and he had made the arrangements. That was changed, a World Health Organization official said privately, because half the money was pocketed.

The vaccine must be kept chilled from the time it leaves the factory until it reaches a child's mouth, and the clinic's freezers looked as battered as the taxis. The day was already hot, and World Health Organization officials worried that the ice packs keeping the vaccines cold were not fully frozen. A big problem, one confided, was clinic officials "who take the money we give them to buy big freezers, and then buy refrigerators to keep their cold drinks in."

Finding enough women for the teams proved particularly tough. Only women can enter a Nigerian Muslim household if the husband is away, and women with children are better at persuading other mothers to vaccinate. But many men refused to let their wives leave home, and either wanted the jobs, which pay about $3 a day, for themselves, or sent their young daughters. . . .

Some families tricked the teams, erasing the chalk marks on their doorways showing that they had not cooperated, or blackening their children's thumbs with the same ink that the vaccinators had used and falsely claiming that they had been immunized.

Still, the government seemed determined to succeed. At the campaign's command center in the capital, Abuja, the officer in charge of the vaccine "cold chain"—keeping it chilled from the time it arrives in Nigeria—knew exactly which district leader in a remote part of Kano was considered a "joker" by his peers and arranged for his removal and the shipping of two new freezers.

Sometimes the new determination was a bit excessive. The chief prosecutor of Katsina, another northern Nigerian state, announced he would jail for a year any parents who refused drops for their children.

## India's Uphill Campaign

While Nigeria struggles to restart its campaign, India, whose need is such that it uses more than half the world's two billion polio vaccine doses each year, has long made an extraordinary commitment to wipe out polio. Teams . . . have made repeated sweeps in the state of Uttar Pradesh, home to 180 million people, which Dr. Cochi of the Centers for Disease Control describes as "historically the center of the universe for the polio virus."

Nowhere are the prospects for conquering polio more intimidating. Living conditions are so dense, public health services so awful, summer heat so sweltering, and open sewers and monsoon floods so common that a more perfect breeding ground could hardly be conjured.

The state, populous enough to make it the world's sixth-largest nation, has endured more than two dozen campaigns in recent years. In 2004, teams went door to door eight times. They came eight more times last year. Each round requires almost every health worker to join in for at least a week or two, local managers say, and each time vaccinators must try to get the polio drops into the mouths of 50 million children.

International leaders of the global drive were hopeful last year that the country would finish off the disease—but it still registered 66 cases. That was the lowest tally ever, but not zero. And so this year, India must repeat its consuming effort yet again, with special focus on Uttar Pradesh and other regions still trying to extinguish

the last cases. Resistance has persisted where services are weakest and distrust of public officials deepest. . . .

Polio spreads through oral-fecal contact: children can get it by drinking well water tainted by sewage, or simply by picking up a ball that rolled through a gutter choking with human waste. In warm or tropical climates, many similar viruses can attach to the same receptors in the intestine as the polio virus does, making it even harder to immunize a child. It can take up to 10 vaccine doses, spaced months apart.

With great anticipation, India and other countries began trying a new eradication strategy last year, using a "monovalent" vaccine that focuses only on the most common strain of polio, but gives immunity in fewer doses. The old vaccine attacked three strains of the virus, two of them less common. "The great hope was that monovalent vaccine would be the magic bullet and melt all polio cases away, but that hasn't happened," Dr. Cochi said.

While the new vaccine has brought India closer than ever to eradication, resistance to the vaccine has persisted in some areas. . . .

## Big Money, but Also Skepticism

The world has donated billions of dollars for polio eradication. Japan and Great Britain have given more than $250 million, and Canada, the Netherlands, the European Commission and the World Bank each have given more than $100 million. Far and away the biggest donors have been the United States and Rotary International, which initiated the "gift to the 21st century" idea. Each has given more than $500 million.

But as the polio campaign has dragged on, the voices of skeptics have grown louder. Dr. Donald A. Henderson, renowned for leading the successful war on smallpox, and currently a professor of medicine and public health at the University of Pittsburgh, said he believed the polio campaign was all but doomed. He suspects that the official caseload figures on www.polioeradication.org are incomplete and that the World Health Organization may not actually know every pocket of virus in the world.

But even if it does, and even if all the world's polio cases can be wiped out, he argued, problems that are now being nearly ignored in the all-out effort to corral the last few cases will suddenly loom large. For example, as a precaution, vaccination must be continued for many years after the last case is found, polio experts agree. (Nearly every American child is still immunized—albeit with a killed vaccine given by injection—even though polio was virtually wiped out in the United States in the 1960s.)

But in about one in three million doses, the live oral vaccine used in poor countries can mutate back into a wild-type virus that can infect and paralyze victims. They are used, however, because they give better immunity than the killed vaccine and are easier to administer.

A tiny number of healthy people with a rare immune-system defect can keep excreting polio virus for decades—creating a reservoir that could, theoretically, cause a new outbreak many years in the future. (That is what happened in an unusual case last year in an Amish community in Minnesota where some had refused vaccinations.)

Dr. David L. Heymann, of the World Health Organization, acknowledged the concerns, but said the problems were not insurmountable. For example, the use of oral vaccine could be discontinued after eradication to avoid its mutation into a wild form, he said

Through the years—as experts have sparred over strategy—thousands of Rotary volunteers have never lost faith in the prize of eradication. And they have spread their fervor into the American heartland. Dave Groner, a funeral home director from Dowagiac, Mich., and his wife, Barbara, a retired schoolteacher, have led seven teams of volunteers to India and Nigeria to help out in vaccination campaigns. On a recent trip to India, a hog farmer, a psychologist, married real estate brokers and a retired obstetrician were among those who went along.

Ann Lee Hussey, an animal medical technician from Maine who had polio as a child, got down on the floor with one little girl, and compared their deformed feet.

"The girl ran her hand on Ann's foot and scars and all the other kids scooted up," Mr. Groner recalled. "No one snapped photos. Everyone swallowed their Adam's apple."

Thousands of such volunteers have offered testimonials at club meetings back home and constitute an extraordinary grass-roots network of fund-raisers. When $93,000 was needed for balloons, whistles and other materials for an immunization campaign in the north Indian state of Bihar, Mr. Groner sent an urgent e-mail plea. In 72 hours, he had pledges for $115,000.

## "A Load on My Heart"

Success is tantalizingly close in India, but still too late for those like Amitkumar whose daily torments are a testament to polio's cruelty. A brainy, square-jawed 15-year-old, he has been paralyzed from the waist down since he was a year-old baby whose plump, sturdy legs steadily wasted away.

At 11:30 one morning at the Amar Jyoti School in New Delhi, the bell rang for recess and rambunctious children—both able-bodied and disabled—went out to play. Amit, on crutches, swung his shrunken legs at high speed, using his broad chest and shoulders to propel himself. He balanced on legs of skin and bones, held stiff and straight by heavy braces.

He has since childhood suffered the taunts of "cripple," and toughened himself to play cricket with neighborhood children. He positioned himself smack in the middle of the field this day. As a ball flew by, he lifted his powerful hand, big as a catcher's mitt, to pluck it from the air.

That afternoon, his father, Jaganath, a genial railway worker with a big belly, picked him up at the bus stop on a rusty old bicycle. The son rode sidesaddle, his legs dangling over the back wheel. Mr. Jaganath confided that he was never at peace because of his eldest son's suffering. Some years back, he and his wife stood outside the hospital door while attendants straightened their boy's twisted legs using brute force. They listened to his screams of agony.

"I feel a load on my heart," Mr. Jaganath said. Amit's mother, Arti Devi, confessed, "It's a torture for me every day to watch him."

Once home from school, Amit shed his painfully tight braces, lifting his legs, lifeless as sausages, and stuffed them into a pair of pants. His four younger brothers and sisters treat him with awe and a measure of fear. He is a stern big brother who insists that his siblings study hard, as he does. He is one of the best students in the slum.

"I want to become a doctor," he said fiercely. "I want to eradicate polio so that no other child faces the problems that I do."

---

## Questions

1. How was the World Health Organization (WHO) planning to eradicate polio?

2. What went wrong with their plans, and what do they have to do now to be successful?

---

# CHAPTER 22

# AIDS and Health-Policy Responses in European Welfare States

Monika Steffen

Much of the world's attention has focused on the AIDS crisis in Africa. But AIDS has become a major public health crisis all around the world. This article looks at European countries generally known for extensive public health programs and the special challenges of confronting the AIDS epidemic.

This article analyzes the complex policy issues set into motion by the AIDS epidemic in Europe. It shows how different health systems responded to the challenge and how the management of an epidemic influenced general trends in health-care policies. AIDS emerged as an ill-structured problem calling into question the central position of the medical profession in policymaking, institutional fragmentation in the health sector and the exclusive role of economic factors in policy reform. While the mainstream health services had to adapt to new demands, public-health services had to reinvent themselves to cope with the specific issues around prevention. The analysis thus distinguishes between the well-established medical-care sector and the weakly structured public-health sector. It focuses on the reshaping of policies in this previously neglected field, including at the level of the European Union.

## Introduction

Policy studies in the health sector have generally focused on the relationships between the medical profession, financing institutions and state authorities. International comparisons of health policies arose as growing health

expenditure came up against limited economic growth and as welfare states were confronted with the need to contain costs. The issue of cost provided the main intellectual framework for comparative studies of health systems and policies. AIDS, however, called into question the traditional medical model and the exclusive role attributed to economic factors in policy reform. This article focuses on the dynamics of change at the *periphery* of the medical sector, in the field of public health and risk management. It analyzes how European health systems reacted to the unexpected challenges of the AIDS epidemic, which constituted the most important public health problem since the Second World War. . . .

## The Challenge of AIDS

The unexpected arrival of a new public-health risk caused by an unknown agent represented a difficult challenge, especially as no expert group existed that could have spoken on the subject with the required legitimacy. The issue, complex in itself and further complicated by important national variations in content and policy timing, can be simplified through the construction of a Weberian ideal type, to which the respective country cases can be compared. This model comprises four distinct phases, each characterized by particular problems and specific actor networks:

- An initial *period of recognition,* characterized by uncertainty, lasted four years, from the diagnosis of the first cases in 1981 in the United States of America and in Europe, to early 1985 when the HIV antibody test became available. The only experts familiar with the new pathology comprised a small number of clinicians caring for the first patients, militant gay men defending the interests of the infected people and from whose ranks came most of the early recognized cases, and public-health officials, mainly epidemiologists motivated by the need to identify transmission routes. This first group of experts dominated the initial stage of policymaking, which had the aim of reducing uncertainty. Two opposing attitudes marked the period: activism on the part of the experts; and lack of attention or hesitancy to get involved on the part of politicians and public authorities.

- The second phase, a *period of controversy,* centered on the use of the antibody test and the possibilities and issues raised by its use for screening. Although this controversial phase, sometimes described as chaotic, strongly marked the history of AIDS, it was in fact very short, covering only a few months in 1985–6. In fact, the phase corresponded to a normal sequence of formulation or adjustment of most public policies, characterized by enlarging networks of actors. In the particular AIDS case, experts, politicians and bureaucrats presented and argued conflicting opinions to define the role of the antibody test and draw up an agreed policy to monitor the epidemic. Choices had to be made both for immediate action and long-term perspectives. The period was marked by the media, which publicized AIDS and actively fed controversy.

- The third period, of *public information and education,* which constituted the most visible part of AIDS policy formulation and enactment, lasted some four to five years 1986–90. Engaged early in some countries, later in others, the public information and education campaigns had in common the promotion of collective attitudes and individual behavior in line with the management of the epidemic. Substantial budgets were allocated to the fight against AIDS. Controversies were reduced to the issues of financing the measures and defining the precise content of the messages to be diffused. At this stage, social scientists entered the field as experts and policy advisers on communication and behavior.

- The final phase, a *period of institutional consolidation,* provided a sustainable base for the new policies. Prevention, care and social support were henceforth considered as long-term and lasting strategies. Initiated during the 1990s, the consolidation phase is still unfolding. The process entails reinforcing or even introducing the public-health dimensions of other policies, some of them being reformed at the same time. The reorientation of policies on drug abuse towards the reduction of harm, the stringent control of hospital hygiene and the efforts to extend access to HIV antibody tests, new multi-therapy and post-exposure prophylaxis, all illustrate the continuity of a process of normalization. . . .

## National Patterns of Policy Responses

European health systems faced the new challenges with different inputs and outcomes. For many years, France reported the greatest number of cases in the European Union, probably because of an earlier and more massive start of the epidemic, with the three main transmission routes combined. Two decades after the outbreak of the epidemic, the prevalence of HIV infection is still up to five times higher in France than in Germany and the United Kingdom. Southern European countries still face a massive epidemic due to transmission among injecting drug users (IDUs). Drug abuse represents a particularly difficult issue for prevention, but AIDS received no notable public attention in these countries until the early or even mid-1990s, when the large number of deaths among drug users could no longer be ignored. As early intervention and coherent implementation were essential to the successful fighting of the epidemic, the effectiveness of institutional support and coordination mechanisms emerge as the crucial factors in explaining the striking differences between European welfare states.

The first European case of AIDS was discovered in Paris in June 1981 by a hospital doctor who set up an informal study group of doctors and researchers. Although this initial French expert group was extremely efficient and contributed directly to the isolation of HIV, in March 1983, it remained isolated. Only a modest link with the Département générale de la Santé, the weakest part of the Health Ministry, provided some institutional support. Medical authorities and the government only reacted when an American team challenged the paternity of the virus discovery. AIDS entered the French policy agenda as matter of national pride and interests in the field of science and industry (Seytre, 1993), not as a public-health risk. In Germany, health authorities of the

City of Berlin informed the federal health authorities about the first cases. The Federal Ministry of Health reacted by setting up a consultative structure bringing together public-health authorities, medical specialists and representatives of gay organizations. In the UK, a similar process channeled the information from London genito-urinary clinics that saw the first patients up to the highest levels of the National Health Service (NHS). The government and medical authorities, convinced of the emergency, urged rapid action. In Italy, gay men launched the first community prevention campaigns, on a local basis, while the central health administration initiated traditional surveillance measures, but the mismatch between the IDU profile of the Italian epidemic and the AIDS policy promoters delayed effective action.

A major difference between the countries was the attitude of the medical profession. While doctors everywhere played an important part in health policy, their central position in France appears exceptional by comparison with other countries (Immergut, 1992; Jobert and Steffen, 1994). Therefore, French medical elite's lack of interest in public health had more crucial consequences than elsewhere. It legitimized politicians and intellectuals in their strategy of minimizing the acute risk for public health and exaggerating the virtual risk of stigmatization. In Italy, on the contrary, a group of medical professors pushed for the creation of the National AIDS Commission. This body was, and still is, responsible for drawing up the Italian policy on HIV/AIDS. The first national anti-AIDS plans became law in 1990, but implementation was hampered by conflicts and therefore remained weak. Regional and municipal health agencies opposed the central alliance between the administration, the government and interested clinicians.... Moreover, most public funding did not reach its destination at the time, being diverted to other uses, especially prescription of pharmaceuticals. Such "redistribution," including clientelistic politics and overt corruption, formed part of the then still "immature welfare states of Southern Europe" (Ferrera, 1996). Implementation improved from the mid-1990s onward, after the general reforms of the health administration and the entire political system.

In the UK, public-health specialists pushed reluctant politicians into action, using the powerful argument that the epidemic would absorb the entire health budget if it were not stopped in time. In the British system, the institutional structure of the NHS and the political level of decision making are linked through the position of the Chief Medical Officer, an independent person whose role is to advise the Minister of Health. During the early AIDS years, the position was held by an epidemiologist while

practical measures were developed under the leadership of a clinical specialist in sexually transmissible diseases. The combined approach of institutional and medical management of public health resulted in an efficient model for AIDS prevention. The UK succeeded in confirming the epidemic within the initial population at risk. However, when the new multi-therapies became available in 1996, the NHS authorities had to revise their rather restrictive testing policy, in order to orient potential beneficiaries towards effective medical treatment.

In Germany, politicians made the strategic choices. The "Permanent Conference of Health Ministers," a standing working group, brings together the ministers and their close collaborators from all *Länder,* from right-wing as well as left-wing parties according to the majorities in regional parliaments. The health ministers declared AIDS to be a public-health problem of major importance that required an urgent response in the form of a national public-health policy. They reached compromises on controversial subjects and mobilized the public-health agencies under their authority. Reluctant local or regional administrations were officially encouraged to implement the new prevention policies. The regional dynamics helped to overcome medical and political opposition, especially to prevention strategies for drug addicts....

## From an Ill-Structured Problem to New Public-Health Policies

Unlike cost-control policies which brought identified parties defending particular interests into conflict, the public-health strategies relating to HIV/AIDS provoked conflicts with less precisely defined interests and environments. AIDS presented an "ill-structured problem" to established health systems and policy networks, in the sense of Simon's work (Simon, 1973). The concept refers to situations where the available knowledge from the initial conditions is insufficient to determine what the future evolution could be and to select solutions. An ill-structured problem is characterized by incomplete information, unknown constraints and uncertainty concerning the referents and rules to apply. Problem definition and solutions depend on the divergent views of interested parties.

### CONSENSUS BUILDING FOR PUBLIC HEALTH

Political conflict arose in particular over two issues, both related to the application of previously existing law. The first issue was the question of screening. Two different arguments motivated demands for systematic screening for the presence of HIV antibodies in specific populations or situations: on the one hand, medico-professional views, aimed at epidemiological surveillance and protection of health professionals and patients from the risk of infection in hospital; and on the other hand, socio-political demands aimed at applying existing laws on infectious and sexually transmissible diseases to HIV-infected people, with the hope it would help to prevent infection in everyday life by controlling virus carriers. As medical knowledge progressed, the latter perspective was rapidly ruled out as unnecessary and even undesirable, because test results could serve interests outside the health sphere when used by insurance companies, employers or landlords. The controversy led to an interesting compromise. HIV-antibody tests could only be done with the consent of the individual, and were "systematically proposed" in a growing number of situations such as pregnancy, pre-marriage medical examinations, working with IDUs, and after each exposure to a risk. This policy combined the possibility of testing a large part of the population with the protection of marginal groups from stigmatization.

. . . It was only in France, and to a lesser degree in Germany, that screening provoked major political controversies, in both cases as part of electoral politics. . . .

The second issue was the introduction of large-scale strategies aimed at the reduction of health risks in the field of drug policies, including access to methadone as a substitute treatment for injecting addicts. The AIDS risk arrived in a policy field with a high electoral sensibility and public demands for repressive action. Furthermore, during the 1970s professional paradigms had moved away from medicine towards psychotherapeutic approaches. Consequently, in several countries, the medicalization of drug policies was not easily accepted, while AIDS experts and pressure groups insisted that repressive policies that penalized drug consumption and drove addicts underground had to be abandoned if the preventive strategies were to be implemented. As consensus building and policy timing varied considerably by country, the latter obtained very different results in fighting the epidemic.

Consensus building in the drug field depended mainly on professional agreement and practice. The prescription of substitutive medications was still in marginal use in the UK and Italy, but strictly prohibited by professional rules in Germany and France. The UK could furthermore rely on a useful precedent. "Harm reduction" strategies aimed as reducing the social consequences of addiction (such as delinquency) had already emerged before AIDS was known, in local initiatives that had brought together voluntary organizations

and social services (Berridge, 1996). With AIDS, these networks reoriented their activity towards "health-risk reduction." By the mid-1980s, needle-exchange programs and comprehensive programs for primary medical care for addicts had been launched under the responsibility of the local NHS units and with national support. The remarkable effectiveness of the British "risk-reduction" strategies made them a model for all other countries.

In Germany, health-risk reduction was implemented by professionals from the drug and public-health fields, supported by the regional health ministers. Methadone treatment encountered strong opposition from the national medical commission responsible for clinical classifications of medicines. This resistance was progressively overcome as practical reform dynamics grew, originating from the regions and cities. Left-wing administrations were the first but not the only ones to launch methadone programs. The latter received financial support from the sickness funds because they estimated that methadone provision to IDUs would be less expensive than long-term care for new cases of AIDS and hepatitis infection. When opponents resorted to the courts, jurisprudence established that the restrictions on methadone did not apply to public health strategies.

In Italy, professional consensus and effective implementation suffered from a private/public split. When AIDS arrived, syringes were accessible over the counter at low cost, and methadone was still used occasionally in public treatment centers. During the 1980s, however, a growing part of the surveillance and management of addiction was left to private associations. The care institutions linked with local governments and the political Left promoted risk-reduction strategies, including needle as well as condom provision and methadone treatment, whereas those linked with Catholic organizations maintained their traditional commitment to abstinence, in both drug use and sex. This divergence resulted in contradictory messages being delivered to people at risk, politicians and public opinion. Coherent prevention strategies depended on favorable local circumstances. New impetuses for large-scale risk reduction followed in the mid-1990s, when general reforms in the health administration and political system improved conditions for implementation.

In France, risk reduction met strong political *and* professional opposition. The professionals caring for drug addicts constituted an isolated corporatist network that escaped supervision by the health ministry and cultivated a hermetic border against medical services (Bergeron, 1998). They were affiliated to a single national association committed to a particular psychoanalytical paradigm. The medical AIDS risk was ignored as being alien to their professional concern. When growing numbers of IDUs arrived in hospitals with full-blown AIDS, the health ministry had to organize joint training sessions, from 1988 onward, for medical staff and professionals from the drug sector, to foster mutual understanding. Risk-reduction strategies were first launched by a humanitarian medical association, in the early 1990s, with a single mobile street unit operating in Paris. It was only in the aftermath of the contaminated blood trial, when the Henrion Commission was set up (1995), that the political and professional consensus on abstinence was questioned and that France started to move towards European standards. . . .

## HEALTH EDUCATION ON A LARGE SCALE

The political compromise exchanged the application of public-health regulations to AIDS for the willingness of the people at risk to adopt new patterns of behavior. Prevention policies thus stressed "individual behavior" as a risk factor. The model was promoted as a theoretical support to the educational approach. The urgency to act against the epidemic provided legitimacy to the pragmatic approaches: public authorities under-took to socialize "deviant" behavior, such as homosexual practice, sexual relationships with multiple partners and injecting-drug abuse. Instead of fighting those practices, new behavioral patterns, known as "safer sex" and "safer shooting," were officially promoted in order to stop virus transmission in circles engaged in risky behaviors. The new behavior patterns were also to be transmitted to all young people, which led to sexual education systematically delivered in school, with a shift from contraception towards the prevention of sexually transmitted diseases (STDs). The tools of the educational policies were the public promotion of condoms and the provision of clean injection equipment. . . .

The educational approach for drug addicts, infected through needle sharing, could only be effective under two conditions. First, clean injection equipment had to be provided on a large scale, through sale at low prices and free distribution by medical or social services. "Needle-exchange programs," comprising the provision of disinfecting kits or the exchange of clean syringes for a used one, proved particularly relevant because they necessitated regular individual contact with the IDUs and thus provided a suitable framework for educational intervention. Second, free medical care and access to substitutive medication had to be offered because, apart from the medical benefits, relief from suffering constituted the most powerful incentive for marginalized

people to attend the services and thereby develop health awareness. Naturally, countries were unequally equipped to implement these measures. Britain could rely on the local units of the NHS, and Germany on the local public-health offices (*Gesundheitsämter*), each of them staffed by a coordinator for AIDS prevention for at least five years (1988–93). France, in contrast, had not only to overcome the lack of collaboration between medical care providers and the centers in charge of drug users, but also to remove serious policy contractions. For example, sale of syringes had been introduced in 1987, but syringe possession continued to be treated as an official "indicator of illegal consumption" in the mid-1990s, and the police still arrested IDUs near pharmacies. Italy needed to develop the effective use of condoms and clean syringes as well as the provision of medical care. This only became effective on a nationwide scale once primary health-care centers (Unità Sanitarie Locali) had been reinforced and officially charged with financial coordination. The laggards finally achieved implementation towards the end of the 1990s.

The educational policies and their implementation showed how the ill-structured AIDS problem was transformed into a public health problem to which European welfare states could respond. The process consisted in developing and modernizing STD prevention and medical attendance for IDUs. The results were measurable: condom use increased considerably and needle sharing was significantly diminished. Both these improvements appear to have been permanent. . . .

## Public-Health Dynamics and General Reform Trends

Most of the "innovative" responses to AIDS in fact already existed, at least in part. Self-support and self-help organizations had operated in various fields in Germany, the Netherlands and elsewhere. The UK had long traditions in public-private provision of health care, in particular in the long-stay sector and home care. Social and psychological support with direct user involvement had already been developed to cope with alcoholism and chronic disease. Treatment communities with live-in arrangements, such as the French *appartements thérapeutiques* and the Italian *communità terapeutiche* operated as part of psychological care and services for drug addicts. The promotion of condoms to fight STDs was also known. What was new, however, was combined application in this unique case. Under the threat of an international public-health catastrophe, all these elements were deployed simultaneously, forming a coherent dynamic that drew public health in from the margins of the medical system to the center of political attention, in at least three ways. First, public health was considerably upgraded in the scale of political priorities. Second, European partners actively engaged in cross-national health management. Third, the medical sector engaged in coordinated care and standardization of treatment.

## THE REBIRTH OF PUBLIC HEALTH

Public health was reasserted in several ways, not least by requiring the specialty to engage in major cultural changes. The AIDS epidemic, in effect, required public-health services to become more involved in policy interventions and outcomes. At the intellectual level, public-health approaches replaced ethical and ideological considerations. Public intervention in the field of sexual behavior thus became legitimate, notably in the countries with a strong Catholic tradition. In Germany "sexual pedagogy" was even elevated to a new university discipline, based on knowledge and theories largely drawn from the experience acquired with AIDS. Risk reduction undoubtedly constituted the major example of a new public-health priority in the field of addiction. A new classification of "drugs" according to their degree of danger to health was proposed in France (Roque, 1998). . . .

Second, the systems and procedures for epidemiological surveillance were reinforced or modernized to various degrees depending on the needs in different countries. Italy improved data protection and the transmission of information between the regional and national levels, recognizing the inter-regional migration of patients towards the best treatment centers of care. France reorganized its compulsory notification system for AIDS and extended it to all cases of HIV infection. . . .

Third, the massive HIV-contamination of hemophiliacs in almost all European countries, with the exception of Finland and Belgium, led to the reinforcement of tracing systems for blood, plasma and other biological materials. In Germany and France, the "blood scandals" created a further impetus for major institutional reforms, aiming in both cases at effective control of the either private (Germany) or public (France) plasma fractionating industry. . . .

## CROSS NATIONAL HEALTH MANAGEMENT IN EUROPE

The Maastricht Treaty (1993) charged the European Commission with competence over public health, which was reinforced in the Amsterdam Treaty (1998). Thus, the advent of AIDS accompanied and amplified the organization of public health at the European level. Initially, the Commission's activity was limited to the cofinancing with the World Health Organization (WHO) of the Paris-based center for the epidemiological monitoring of AIDS in Europe, and to the coordination of loose medical and scientific networks and activist initiatives (Altenstetter, 1994).

Closer integration came in the mid-1990s with the European anti-AIDS programs, which structured research and introduced the comparative evaluation of different national intervention strategies (*AIDS Care,* 2000; Moatti et al., 2000). The EU Biomedical and Health Research Program (BIOMED) financed social science, especially in the field of sexual behavior in Europe (Campenhoudt et al., 1997; Hubert et al., 1998). The EU initiatives focused on transnational AIDS prevention and problems, in fields such as migration, geographical movement of sex workers, and specific risk situations common to all countries but unexplored, such as "new sexual encounters." European policies prioritized first the harmonization of national data collection systems and building expert capabilities; and, second, the establishment of common policy goals and similar tools. This development is illustrated by the creation of the European Monitoring Centre for Drugs and Drug Addiction. Since 1995, the Lisbon-based center has delivered annual reports to the European Commission and provided governments and administrations of member states with comparative policy advice. Furthermore, the model of HIV/AIDS monitoring was extended at European level to other transmissible diseases, especially STDs, hepatitis C and tuberculosis. Cross-national surveillance systems were thus set up for diseases with similar routes of transmission and methods of prevention. Similar monitoring systems are currently being set up for central and eastern European countries as well as for the Commonwealth of Independent States, in collaboration with, and under the technical authority of, the WHO Regional Office for Europe. . . .

## COORDINATED CARE AND STANDARDIZED TREATMENT

The response to AIDS spurred general reform trends usually considered as being exclusively linked with cost containment. In the UK, stronger public-private collaboration developed around AIDS also corresponded to the reform agenda in the NHS, with the aim of reducing the public sector's role in providing services (Berridge, 1996). Besides this classic public-private example, several other directions common to all countries can be distinguished.

First, in all the countries where universal access to medical services was not completely guaranteed, access to care was facilitated for specific groups. As the archetypical public-health threat, AIDS fuelled political awareness about the necessity to extend and secure the medical coverage at the periphery of the established service provision. The French scheme of "universal medical coverage," in operation since January 2000, was originally formulated when many homeless people and migrants were found to have HIV/AIDS and infectious diseases. Italy engaged in a program of hospital renovation to help poorly equipped and insufficiently financed departments for infectious disease cope with the rapidly growing number of HIV/IDU patients. All countries, especially those in southern Europe, improved medical-care provision for drug users.

Second, medical care for people with AIDS fostered comprehensive service structures combining hospital and home care, a particularly difficult issue in many European health systems. The patients' demand for "normal life" as well as cost containment considerations created a common pressure for close coordination of services because the disease evolved with alternate phases of acute illness and remissions allowing home care and return to work. In fragmented care systems, such as the French or Italian cases, where attempts to reorganize care structures have always met with failure, networks linking specialized hospital services with local general practitioners are now operating rather successfully for people with AIDS and also for drug addicts. . . .

Third, the rapid progress in therapy, combined with the pressure from activists for speedy access to the newest treatments, led to standardized treatment protocols and the strict surveillance of the delivery of medication. For the treatment of AIDS, doctors' traditional freedom of prescription was severely limited, for reasons of technical competence and to avoid the development of resistant virus strains. This development contributed to a learning process making the rationalization of prescription practice acceptable to doctors. . . . Last but not least, the risk of HIV transmission through medical procedures, coupled with the spread of drug resistance, made hospital hygiene a new priority. In fact, the AIDS issue served as a lens making visible dysfunctional situations in the health services and so identifying areas where control and solutions need to be applied.

Future developments and perspectives, in prevention and care, at national as well as European levels, are dominated by progress in new therapeutic regimens. Since the widespread introduction of multi-therapies reduced the mortality rate, most people with AIDS have lived longer. Treatment, however, is intensive and continuous (for life), and appears to be most effective when started early. People at risk now have a direct therapeutic interest in being HIV-tested after each risk exposure. Consequently, a growing number of people are and will be under permanent medical treatment and surveillance. This underlines the lasting challenge for health and social policies in European welfare states. In addition to growing medical expenditure and growing numbers of patients, prevention strategies have to be maintained and reinforced. The case of AIDS illustrates that the responsibility of health authorities is not diminishing but will grow in the future.

## Conclusion

The perspective of health systems adapting to an ill-structured problem helps to understand why AIDS management was dependent on existing patterns and at the same time a ground-breaking challenge. AIDS acted as a dependent and an independent variable (Steffen, 2001a). It reflected existing short-comings or capacities, and initiated changes or contributed to ongoing changes. The changes adopted to fight the epidemic were not equally important throughout countries. Those whose health system was relatively well prepared to face AIDS (such as the UK and to a lesser degree Germany), or those that did not immediately respond fully to it (such as Italy and more generally the southern European countries), were obviously less affected by pioneering reforms than those which faced up to the crisis, like France. In France, for the first time in its history, a full range of new public-health agencies and surveillance systems was set up at the national level (Morelle, 1996; Murard and Zylberman, 1996). Learning processes and institutional changes were more important in the French case because the latter combined a high degree of urgency, in terms of HIV prevalence and political contest, with a particularly weak capacity in public-health management. The French reforms responded to a logic of institutional updating under the pressure of an acute crisis (Steffen, 2001b).

Fighting the epidemic required comprehensive strategies of public-health management, beyond the limited medical model, at the periphery of the welfare state. Responding to the ill-structured problem contributed to organizing the previously weak public health sector. A lasting political consensus was elaborated for public-health strategies, and new public resources were made available for the health sector. Large-scale health education constituted the main policy tool, and the reinforcement of patients' rights was an unintended result. All these changes corresponded to current reform goals in the health sector, except to cost containment. The European Union assumed competence over this particular area where previous policies were weak or subject to ideological conflict, and where national differences were striking. The European level legitimized new policy goals and tools, and thus fostered harmonization beyond the national welfare states. The successful management of AIDS has revealed the capacity of European welfare states to respond to new social risks and major health issues.

---

### Questions

1. In what ways does AIDS pose special challenges to health-care systems?

2. How does public health differ from medical-care health? What must be done to improve public health policies?

---

## References

*AIDS Care.* (2000) Special Issue "3rd European Conference on the Methods and Results of Social and Behavioural Research on AIDS" 12 (6).

Altenstetter, C. (1994) "European Union Responses to AIDS/HIV and Policy Networks in the Pre-Maastricht Era," *Journal of European Public Policy* 13 (3): 414–40.

Barbot, J. (2002) *Les Malades en mouvement: la médecine et la science à l'épreuve du Sida.* Paris: Balland.

Bergeron, H. (1998) *L'État et la toxicomanie. Histoire d'une singularité française.* Paris: Presses Universitaires de France.

Berridge, V. (1996) *AIDS in the UK. The Making of Policy, 1981–1994.* New York: Oxford University Press.

Campenhoudt, L., Cohen, M., Guizzardi, G. and Hausser, D. (1997) *Sexual Interactions and HIV Risks – New Conceptual Perspectives in European Research.* London: Taylor & Francis.

Epstein, S. (1996) *Impure Science. AIDS, Activism and the Politics of Knowledge.* Berkeley: University of California Press.

Feldman, E. and Bayer, R. (eds) (1999) *Blood Feuds. AIDS, Blood and the Politics of Medical Disaster.* Oxford: Oxford University Press.

Ferrera, M. (1996) "The Partitocracy of Health. Towards New Welfare Politics in Italy?" *RES PUBLICA Belgian Journal of Political Science* 2: 447–59.

Freeman, R. (2000) *The Politics of Health in Europe.* Manchester: Manchester University Press.

Hayward, J. and Klein, R. (1994) "Grande-Bretagne: De la gestion publique à la gestion privée du déclin économique," in B. Jobert (ed.) *Le tournant néo-libéral en Europe,* pp. 87–121. Paris: L'Harmattan.

Hubert M., Bajos, N. and Sandfort, T. (1998) *Sexual Behaviour and HIV/AIDS in Europe.* London (UK) and Bristol, PA: UCL Press.

Immergut, E. M. (1992) *Health Politics. Interests and Institutions in Western Europe.* New York: Cambridge University Press.

Jobert, B. and Steffen, M. (eds) (1994) *Les politiques de santé en France et en Allemagne.* Paris: Observatoire Européen des Politiques Sociales, Espace Social Européen.

Kirp, D. L. and Bayer, R. (eds) (1992) *AIDS in the Industrialized Democracies: Passions, Politics and Policies.* New Brunswick, NJ: Rutgers University Press.

Moatti, J. P., Souteyrand, Y., Prieur, A., Sandfort, T. and Aggleton, P. (eds) (2000) *AIDS in Europe. New Challenges for the Social Sciences.* London and New York: Routledge.

Moran, M. (1999) *Governing the Health Care State. A Comparative Study of the United Kingdom, the United States and Germany.* Manchester: Manchester University Press.

Morelle, A. (1996) *La défaite de la santé publique.* Paris: Flammarion.

Murard, L. and Zylberman, P. (1996) *L'hygiène dans la République. La santé publique en France, ou l'utopie contrariée. 1870–1918.* Paris: Fayard.

Pinell, P. (2002) *Une épidémie politique. La lutte contre le Sida en France, 1981–1996.* Paris: Presses Universitaires de France.

Regonini, G. and Giuliani, M. (1994) "Italy: Au-dela d'une démocratie consensuelle?" in B. Jobert (ed.) *Le tournant néo-liberal en Europe,* pp. 123–99. Paris: L'Harmattan.

Roque, B. P. (1998) *Rapport au Secrétaire d'État chargé de la Santé* (Report to the Secretary of State for Health). Paris: INSERM-CNRS.

Rosenbrock, R. and Wright, M. T. (eds) (2000) *Partnership and Pragmatism. Germany's Response to AIDS Prevention and Care.* London: Routledge.

Seytre, B. (1993) *Sida: les secrets d'une polémique.* Paris: Presses Universitaires de France.

Simon, H. A. (1973) "The Structure of Ill-structured Problems," *Artificial Intelligence* 4: 181–201.

Steffen, M. (1999) "Protection sociale et management de la santé publique en Europe de l'Ouest et de l'Est," *Matériaux pour l'histoire de notre temps, Revue de la Bibliothèque de documentation internationale contemporaine* 53: 53–62.

Steffen, M. (2001a) *Les États face au Sida en Europe.* Grenoble: PUG-Presses Universitaires de Grenoble.

Steffen, M. (2001b) "Crisis Governance in France: the End of Sectoral Corporatism," in M. Boven, P. 't Hart and G. Peters (eds) (2001) *Success and Failure in Public Governance: A Comparative Analysis,* pp. 470–88. Cheltenham, UK: Edward Elgar.

---

*Source:* AIDS and Health-Policy Responses in European Welfare States. Monika Steffen. *Journal of European Social Policy* Vol. 14. 2004. Reprinted by permission of Sage Publications.

# CHAPTER 23

## U.S. Plan to Lure Nurses May Hurt Poor Nations

Celia W. Dugger

The United States is facing a critical shortage of trained and experienced nurses. Increasingly, it is seeking nursing recruits from poor countries, offering higher salaries and greater opportunities. This can, however, drain nurses from the very countries that need them the most.

As the United States runs short of nurses, senators are looking abroad. A little-noticed provision in their immigration bill would throw open the gate to nurses and, some fear, drain them from the world's developing countries.

The legislation is expected to pass this week, and the Senate provision, which removes the limit on the number of nurses who can immigrate, has been largely overlooked in the emotional debate over illegal immigration.

Senator Sam Brownback, Republican of Kansas, who sponsored the proposal, said it was needed to help the United States cope with a growing nursing shortage.

He said he doubted the measure would greatly increase the small number of African nurses coming to the United States, but acknowledged that it could have an impact on the Philippines and India, which are already sending thousands of nurses to the United States a year.

The exodus of nurses from poor to rich countries has strained health systems in the developing world, which are already facing severe shortages of their own. Many African countries have begun to demand compensation for the training and loss of nurses and doctors who move away.

The Senate provision, which would remain in force until 2014, contains no such compensation, and has not stirred serious opposition in Congress. Because it is not part of the House immigration bill, a committee from both houses would have to decide whether to include the provision on nurses if the full Congress approves the legislation.

Public health experts in poor countries, told about the proposal in recent days, reacted with dismay and outrage, coupled with doubts that their nurses would resist the magnetic pull of the United States, which sits at the pinnacle of the global labor market for nurses.

Removing the immigration cap, they said, would particularly hit the Philippines, which sends more nurses to the United States than any other country, at least several thousand a year. Health care has deteriorated there in recent years as tens of thousands of nurses moved abroad. Thousands of ill-paid doctors have even abandoned their profession to become migrant-ready nurses themselves, Filipino researchers say.

"The Filipino people will suffer because the U.S. will get all our trained nurses," said George Cordero, president of the Philippine Nurse Association. "But what can we do?"

The nurse proposal has strong backing from the American Hospital Association, which reported in April that American hospitals had 118,000 vacancies for registered nurses. The federal government predicted in 2002 that the accelerating shortfall of nurses in the United States would swell to more than 800,000 by 2020.

"There is no reason to cap the number of nurses coming in when there's a nationwide shortage, because you need people immediately," said Bruce Morrison, a lobbyist for the hospital association and a former Democratic congressman.

The American Nurses Association, a professional trade association that represents 155,000 registered nurses, opposes the measure. The group said it was concerned the provision would lead to a flood of nurse immigrants and would damage both the domestic work force and the home countries of the immigrants.

It is difficult to forecast exactly how removing the limit on nurse immigration would affect the number of nurses who moved to the United States.

Based on past trends, Mr. Morrison, the lobbyist who represents the hospital association, said he thought the numbers would grow 5 to 10 percent a year over recent levels. Recruiters would focus on countries with large numbers of well-trained nurses, mainly the Philippines, India and China.

"But it's certainly true that the longer the United States puts off investing in training nurses, the more pressure there will be to find nurses abroad," he said.

Senator Brownback, who has been an advocate for programs to combat AIDS and malaria in Africa, said he did not think lifting the cap on nurse migration would have much effect on Africa because the infrastructure of companies that did recruiting for the United States market was not set up there, nor did African nurses have a big community there to plug into.

And while the Philippines could see an increase in nurse immigration, such flows could also bring benefits, he said, not just in the money they sent home, but in the nurses' voluntary efforts to improve health care in their home countries.

But Eric Buch, the top health adviser to the New Partnership for Africas Development, an Africa-wide undertaking initiated by the continent's heads of state, said he expected that recruiting agencies would set up in African countries where nurses were trained in English and that they would advertise the change in the American law.

"You'll see that emerge, that's my guess," Professor Buch, who teaches health policy at the University of Pretoria, in South Africa said in a telephone interview. "The United States could become a place where we bleed our health care workers."

The flight of nurses from the Philippines, a former American colony, has provided a huge boost to a weak economy, through remittances. Some government agencies there have encouraged the export of nurses, who send home billions of dollars each year to their families.

A nurse in the Philippines would earn a starting salary of less than $2,000 a year compared with at least $36,000 a year in the United States, said Dr. Jaime Galvez Tan, a medical professor at the University of the Philippines who led the country's National Institutes of Health.

He said the flight of nurses had had a corrosive effect on health care. Most Filipinos died without medical attention in 2003, just as they had three decades earlier.

Based on surveys, Dr. Galvez Tan estimates that 80 percent of the country's government doctors have become nurses or are enrolled in nursing programs, hoping for an American green card. "I plead for justice," he said in a telephone interview. "There has to be give and take, not just take, take, take by the United States."

## Questions

1. What factors have led to a shortage of nurses in the United States?

2. Is it wrong for the United States to recruit nursing staff from poor countries? Is there a solution to this problem?

*Source:* U.S. Plan to Lure Nurses May Hurt Poor Nations. Celia W. Dugger. *The New York Times.* May 24, 2006. Copyright © 2006 The New York Times Co. Reprinted by permission.

---\\\\\---

# PART VI

# ENERGY

The modern world is built and driven on the abundance of affordable energy stored in our planet. Exploitation of vast energy resources fuels the engines of economic growth and the economic hopes of much of the world. Yet we are facing an energy crisis in both production and consumption. Exploiting the world's energy reserves of fossil fuels, especially coveted oil and natural gas, runs tremendous risks of outstripping supplies, destroying fragile environments, and disrupting entire societies. So great are these dangers for some societies that a few have begun to speak of the "curse of oil." Oil rich states are often marked by political repression and social unrest. Article 24 examines this problem in Africa, a continent rich in resources that nonetheless has often remained poor as the wealth flows elsewhere.

The other great concern about the world's massive consumption of fossil fuels such as oil, coal, and natural gas is what effect this is having on the global climate. Article 25 shows how concern about climate change, often called "global warming," raised alarms around the world, even as some leaders continued to question whether it was truly a problem. Article 26 discusses the policy implications of stopping global warming, arguing that the problems are real, but dire consequences are not inevitable if prompt action is taken.

24. Exploitation of Energy Resources in Africa.
    Julia Maxted. *Journal of Developing Societies.* Vol. 22, No. 1. 2006.

25. While Washington Slept.
    Mark Hertsgaard. *Vanity Fair.* May 2006.

26. Some Convenient Truths.
    Gregg Easterbrook. *The Atlantic.* September 2006.

# CHAPTER 24

## Exploitation of Energy Resources in Africa

Julia Maxted

Exploiting oil reserves has brought large amounts of money to many impoverished African nations. But oil can be a curse as well as a blessing, bringing social and ethnic turmoil and bolstering repressive regimes. Often the military is used to keep a watchful eye on the operations to protect foreign companies from resentful local communities and national minorities.

## Introduction

In this article I draw upon case studies from several countries to demonstrate that the conditions under which the current scramble for Africa's oil and gas resources is taking place are increasing social tensions and intensifying the dispossession of minority groups. American, European and Asian companies are competing to extend their command over proven and potential resources. Countries along the western coast of Africa such as Angola, Gabon, Equatorial Guinea and Nigeria have become important sources of United States' oil imports as the country seeks to reduce its dependence upon Middle East oil resources.

In testimony before the US Congress in 2001, Paul Michael Wihbey of the Institute for Advanced Strategic and Political Studies described West Africa (including Angola) as "an area of vital US interest" (Silverstein, 2002). The US already buys 15 percent of its oil from the countries in this expanded category of West Africa. This is nearly equal to the amount it imports from Saudi Arabia and is expected to grow to 20 percent in 2008 and 25 percent by 2015 (Silverstein, 2002). China is now the world's second largest importer of oil and its demand is growing rapidly. Chinese, Indian and Malaysian companies are engaged in oil exploration and/or production in a number of African countries including Ethiopia, Libya

and Sudan, countries which have been ignored by western countries, or in the case of the latter two, had sanctions in force against them.

Far from encouraging improvements in human rights and enabling further deepening of democracy and decentralization, in the countries examined in this article—Western Sahara, Angola, Morocco and Ethiopia—oil development is buffering repressive regimes and their military apparatuses. Confronting the destruction of their environments and continued underdevelopment, minority groups are actively seeking to attach socioeconomic rights more self-consciously to the demand for political rights.

## Western Sahara and Morocco

Western Sahara is a 2660 sq. km piece of desert land tucked between Mauritania and Morocco and has been at the center of a sovereignty dispute since Spain relinquished its colonial grip in 1975. Despite Spain's promise to grant self-governance (and an International Court of Justice ruling in favor of Saharan independence), Spain, Morocco and Mauritania signed the Madrid Accords, which divided Western Sahara between Morocco and Mauritania. The next 16 years were marked by a low intensity war between Rabat and the Popular Front for

163

the Liberation of Saguia el Hamra and the Rio de Oro (Polisario). The signing of the Madrid Accords sparked a civil war in Western Sahara, with the Polisario Front fighting both Moroccan and Mauritanian forces. By 1979, Mauritania had withdrawn from Western Sahara. Fighting continued on the Moroccan side until 1988, when both sides agreed in principle to a UN peace plan calling for a cease-fire, an exchange of prisoners, and a referendum designed to give the inhabitants of the Western Sahara a choice between independence or integration into Morocco.

The original date for the referendum was set for 1992; however, more than a decade later, the referendum has not been held. The UN mission responsible for organizing and monitoring the referendum, MINURSO, has spent most of that time presenting voter registration lists to Morocco and the Polisario Front. However, Morocco has raised repeated objections to the voter lists.

The Western Sahara has a population of about 250,000 and another 160,000 Saharawis live in refugee camps in southern Algeria, where they have been for up to 26 years as Morocco continues to claim it has the right to administer Western Sahara. That claim is not formally recognized by any country and the UN classifies Western Sahara as a "non-self governing territory."

Western Sahara's fish and phosphate resources are already being exploited by Morocco. The country's oil reserves have become a factor in the struggle. The US and other major consumers are looking for alternative sources to the Middle East and West Africa is seen as relatively stable and there is also a straight route to refineries on the US eastern seaboard. The US Geological Survey of World Energy 2000 estimated Western Saharan offshore oil and gas resources as substantial, while Morocco's reserves were small, producing less than 1000 barrels of oil a day and spending heavily on energy imports. Fusion, an Anglo-Australian exploration group that specializes in the region, has reported to the Western Sahara's government-in-exile, the Saharawi Arab Democratic Republic (SADR), that it believes there are commercially viable oil fields off the coast (BBC News, 2005a).

In 2001, the Moroccan government granted exploration and exploitation licenses in the Western Sahara region under its administration to US, French and British companies. In February 2002, the UN undersecretary for legal affairs, Hans Correl, ruled Morocco had no right to award contracts that would allow oil to be pumped in Western Sahara, holding that the "exploitation of natural resources in a non-autonomous territory" is only allowed "if it benefits local populations, is carried out in their name or in consultation with them" (BBC News, 2005b).

In May 2005, Polisario's chief negotiator told the Reuters News Agency that it was considering resuming the armed struggle if there was no breakthrough in the UN-led peace talks within six months. The current deal on the table provides for the Western Sahara to be given self-rule for a period of four to five years. After that, its long-term residents and the refugees in Algerian camps would vote in a referendum to choose whether the territory is to be fully integrated with Morocco, continue to have autonomy within the Moroccan state, or become independent. This plan has been accepted by Polisario but rejected by Morocco.

Following disturbances in the main city of the disputed territory Laayoune in May 2005, the Polisario Front accused the Moroccan government of ferocious repression. The Moroccan authorities maintained Polisario instigated politically motivated riots, but the independence movement countered that the demonstrations were peaceful protests against Morocco's intransigence in the long-running dispute. Arrests followed, in what an official for the UN mission in Western Sahara, MINURSO (which has spent more than US$6 million trying to settle the dispute since the cease-fire) said were the most serious disturbances in six years. In July 2005, a Moroccan court jailed 12 Western Saharan separatists following the protests.

Polisario has rejected a proposal to grant the territory some autonomy, namely to run its regional affairs "within the sovereignty of the kingdom." Protesters in November 2005 again took to the streets of Laayoune calling for independence (BBC News, 2005c).

Dispossession of natural resources has also sparked protests by Morocco's Berber population. After Mohamed VI ascended the throne, Morocco changed the Hydrocarbon Code raising the interest of foreign companies. At the beginning of 2000, Shell signed five licenses for marine exploitation over an area of 9000 sq. km in the Moroccan Atlantic. During the same period, the US Company Lone Star Energy signed three exploitation licenses for the Talsint region over an area of 6000 sq. km, and another three reconnaissance licenses—two of which were opposite Larache City. A joint American-Moroccan company, Lonestar, a subsidiary of Skidmore Energy Inc., extracts oil from the large oil fields, thought to contain 20 billion barrels in crude, near the town of Talsinnt, southeastern Morocco. The oil field lies about 160 km from the Algerian border. The oil well is heavily guarded and it requires a military escort to reach the site. One quarter of total government revenue in Morocco is spent on defense. Berbers, who comprise 60 percent of the Moroccan population, say any revenue collected should benefit them. During French colonization, a decree enabled the government to appropriate communal Berber lands. Independence has not changed this and the impetus for dispossession continues.

# Ethiopia

Ethiopia's Gambella People's National Regional State (Gambella) lies on the Sudanese border in the southwest of the country. Nuer and the Anuak are the two largest groups in the region; the third largest population group consists of people the indigenous groups refer to as "highlanders," or "*habasha*," terms which group together all migrants from other parts of Ethiopia and their descendants.

The region has recently attracted government interest, largely because of its natural resources. Gambella is the best-watered region of Ethiopia and has large tracts of uncultivated land along with deposits of gold and oil. Petronas, Malaysia's state-owned oil corporation, has acquired exploration rights in Gambella, and China's Zhongyuan Petroleum Exploration Bureau (ZPEB) has begun seismic exploration activities in Gambella under a subcontract from Petronas (Human Rights Watch, 2005).

Forced resettlement by the Derg in the 1980s generated a massive influx of some 60,000 highlanders to the region. All of the resettlement villages were located on land that the Anuak claimed as their own. At the same time Nuer refugees from the Sudanese civil war began fleeing into Gambella with many Nuer refugees then claiming Ethiopian citizenship and settling permanently in Gambella. The result has been that the Anuak are now a minority and greatly outnumbered by Gambella's Nuer population. There are persistent ethnic tensions—some traditionally Anuak lands are now inhabited almost exclusively by Nuer and the most frequent outbreaks of ethnic violence in Gambella have pitted the Anuak against the Nuer. Many Anuak also bitterly resented the arrival of the highlanders and a number of ambushes attributed to armed Anuak have left scores of highlander civilians dead.

Gambella's long and porous border with Sudan is a source of perennial concern to federal authorities. The Oromo Liberation Front (OLF) managed to infiltrate fighters into Ethiopia through Gambella in 2002, reportedly with the help of the Eritrean government; forces led by a former Derg official have succeeded in destabilizing some areas along the Sudanese border; and the Anuak-led Gambella People's Liberation Front (GPLF) has launched raids into Gambella from bases in southern Sudan.

*Targeting the Anuak* released by Human Rights Watch in March 2005 alleges that the Ethiopian army has been killing, raping and torturing people in Gambella since the end of 2003. The federal government assumed de facto control over the regional government and has stationed several thousand more Ethiopian National Defence Force troops in Gambella since December 2003. Almost all of those soldiers are highlanders and identify themselves as such in the context of highlander-Anuak ethnic conflict. The primary reason for the large military presence in Gambella appears to be an effort to eliminate armed Anuak groups in the region and assure the security of areas under exploration for oil. The Ethiopian military has undertaken operations aimed at rooting out armed Anuak and Nuer groups operating in Gambella, some of which are based in southern Sudan. Gambella currently has no regional president and no Anuak representative in the House of People's Representatives, as both sought asylum abroad in early 2004.

# Nigeria

The Niger Delta is the main oil-producing region of Nigeria, which is the largest oil producer in Africa and the fifth largest oil producer within the Organization of Petroleum Exporting Countries (OPEC). However, little of this wealth is distributed within the Niger Delta, or to the Nigerian people as a whole. Economic and social rights, such as the right to health and the right to an adequate standard of living, remain unfulfilled for many Nigerians.

Many of the traditional responsibilities of the state are fulfilled in parts of the Niger Delta by transnational oil corporations operating there, such as providing basic services or building infrastructure. These activities have left local people unclear about how to seek redress for any adverse consequences or human rights abuses as the companies frequently act on a voluntary basis without any accountability mechanisms.

Oil companies have been operating in Nigeria for over six decades. In the opinion of activists and local NGOs in the Niger Delta several oil companies have historically acted arbitrarily, or failed to deliver on promises made or thought to have been made to communities. In other cases, companies have pitted one community against another, or interfered with the traditional governance structures of the communities. For the communities, oil companies then appear as external players who are taking the wealth from the region, sharing it with the federal government, and providing little in return. Worse, the companies are seen as operating on the traditional lands of the communities without consulting them, or consulting them inadequately. When communities object to specific projects, or ask for more compensation, the companies create divisions within the communities by supporting one faction, usually the chief and groups/gangs associated with the chief, who then forcibly secure the compliance of other community factions who may be opposed to the project. This has been a repeated pattern in many statements made by stakeholders to Amnesty International during 2004 and is referred to as a policy of "divide and rule" by various stakeholders in interviews conducted by Amnesty International (Amnesty International, 2005). Finally, in 40 years of operation, oil companies have left large areas of the Niger Delta unusable for farming, due to frequent oil spills, leakages, and the effect of gas flaring or other accidents.

In many instances, the grievances turned into outright antagonism leading to frequent instances of abduction of company officials, sabotage of company property, and violence targeting companies. The companies have turned to the state security forces, which in some cases have used force, often arbitrarily and disproportionately, against individuals. The easy availability of small arms in the region has made the situation more serious. Calculations by Amnesty International based on local and international media reports show that the number of people killed in the Delta, Rivers and Bayelsa States in 2004 up to and including incidents to late August, could be in the region of 670 (Amnesty International, 2005).

There is a growing perception that the Nigerian Federal Government, state governments, the Niger Delta Development Commission (NDDC), and to a certain extent the TNCs are not transparent about their allocation of resources and their payments to communities. In addition, as Transparency International notes, there is widespread corruption in Nigeria at all levels (Transparency International, 2005). The Nigerian Federal Government is the prime beneficiary of the revenue earned from selling the crude oil abroad. As the international oil price rises, the state's share of the total oil revenue increases under a formula with companies. In spite of this injection of revenue and resources, the Nigerian Federal Government has invested little of these resources in the Niger Delta, where the oil-producing communities reside. Poverty in this area is widespread. Roads are in a constant state of disrepair; power outages are frequent; the water available is of poor quality and is often contaminated; schools are almost nonexistent; and

state-run hospitals and clinics are under-equipped or short-staffed, or both.

In early 2005, thousands of Ogoni and members of other minority communities were evicted from their homes in a Port Harcourt shantytown. The Rivers State government and the Nigerian Agip Oil Company (NAOC) are accused by the communities of demolishing their waterfront homes to facilitate planned oil company expansion. The community was evicted and the homes demolished without adequate notice or compensation. Some residents have suffered a second displacement since they were living in the shantytown following earlier destruction of their village homes due to military activities in Ogoni territories. Many had been resident in the shantytown for over 10 years. Ogoni rights groups state that residents have been left to fend for themselves and have been forced to move to other shantytowns or return to villages where their future is uncertain.

Oil exploration and production in Nigeria has led to communities successfully protesting against the abuse of general human rights and the lack of environmental protection, including the right of indigenous peoples to land and Nigerian citizens' rights to information and participation in the decision-making process relating to the environment. In the context of the Niger Delta oil exploration and production, the right to seek, receive and impart information to communities and individuals is not fully respected in the context of environmental impact assessments because the manner in which the documents are disseminated does not afford communities a realistic chance to express their opinions on planned projects, which may have a detrimental effect on their environment, as required by Section 7 of the EIA Decree. The people of the Niger Delta have waited too long for the benefits from the resources in their region to reach their communities.

## Angola

Angola pumps a million barrels of oil a day and yet 70 percent of the population lives in poverty. The World Bank and International Monetary Fund have reported that over a third of oil revenues do reach the public budget.

The US imports more oil from Angola than from Kuwait, the majority pumped from rigs in Cabinda Bay. Texaco-Chevron alone pumps 60 percent of Angola's oil and continued to do so through the country's long civil war, protected from attack by an armed base. An armed government base is still located outside the Madongo compound of Texaco-Chevron employees in Cabinda, coordinating security with the company. There are few regulations to protect the environment in Cabinda. Gas flares fill the air with an acrid brownish-yellow haze. Sixty-nine oil spills were recorded in the January–October 2003 period—reported to the government but never publicly disclosed (Eviatar, 2004).

Cabinda Province is separated from the rest of Angola by the Congo River and a strip of land belonging to the Democratic Republic of Congo. A separatist movement for independence for Cabinda has been in existence since 1961, with the formation of the Front for the Liberation of Cabinda (FLEC) in 1963. Despite huge oil reserves, Cabinda itself is very poor and has little economic development. Cabindans feel exploited by the central government and foreign oil companies. Small scale guerrilla activity has been taking place since the early 1960s to which the government has responded with repression. Conflict continues between separatist fighters and the government and large numbers of government troops continue to be stationed in the province. In the past three years there have been numerous reports published documenting abuse of Cabindan civilians by the police and armed forces (Human Rights Watch).

Cabindans have been pressing for self-rule and some separatist movement have refused to end the armed struggle.

## Conclusion

In the article and book entitled *The New Imperialism*, David Harvey argues that accumulation by dispossession is assuming heightened significance in the current structure of capitalist accumulation:

> The shape and form any new imperialism will take is therefore up for grabs. The only thing that is certain is that we are in the midst of a major transition in how the global system works and that there are a variety of forces in motion which could easily tip the balance in one or other direction. The balance between accumulation by dispossession and expanded reproduction has already shifted towards the former and it is hard to see this trend doing anything other than deepening, making this the hallmark of what the new imperialism is all about (and making overt claims about the new imperialism and the necessity of empire of

great ideological significance). We also know that the economic trajectory assumed throughout Asia is key, but that military dominance still lies with the United States. (Harvey, 2003)

One way that the new imperialism is playing out geopolitically is in the militarized control of African resources. Collaboration with authoritarian and highly militarized regimes, coupled with extensive offshore oil production has removed the necessity (at present) for direct military involvement in order to secure these. "Much of Africa's oil is offshore, thereby insulated from domestic political or social turmoil" (African Oil Policy Initiative Group, quoted in Fagan, 2002). Accumulation by dispossession can occur in a variety of ways. The monetary value of accumulation by dispossession has not yet been quantified. We do know, however, that the rates of return on US direct investments in Africa are the highest of any region of the world. The average rate of return on US FDI in 1997 for all countries was 12.3 percent. The average rate of return on US FDI for Africa for the period 1990–7 was 29 percent (United Nations, 1998). Such excess profits are possible because African assets are devalued; the social and environmental costs of production are not borne by capital or the presently privileged consumers but with the complicity of their state elites, by the millions of Africans whose basic needs go unmet.

## Questions

1. What is it about exploiting oil and gas reserves that drives social turmoil and ethnic tension in Africa?

2. Are energy reserves benefiting African nations or harming them? Are there ways to ensure that all citizens of a country benefit from its resources?

## References

Amnesty International (2004) "Nigeria: Are Human Rights in the Pipeline?" 9 November, available at: [http://web.amnesty.org/library/Index/ENGAFR440202004?open&of=ENG-NGA], accessed 18 November 2005.

BBC News (2005a) [http://news.bbc.co.uk/1/hi/business/2758829.stm], accessed 20 November 2005.

BBC News (2005b) [http://news.bbc.co.uk/1/hi/business/2758829.stm], accessed 20 November 2005.

BBC News (2005c) [http://news.bbc.co.uk/go/pr/fr/-/1/hi/world/africa/4415284.stm], accessed 20 November 2005.

Eviatar, D. (2004) "Africa's Oil Tycoons," *The Nation,* 12 April.

Fagan, C. (2002) "Bush's Search for Black Gold," *International Socialist Review* November/December. Available at: [www.thirdworldtraveler.com/Africa/Bush_Black Gold_WAfrica.html], accessed 18 November 2005.

Harvey, D. (2003) *The New Imperialism.* Oxford: Oxford University Press. See also: http://titanus.roma1.infn.it/sito_pol/Global_emp/Harvey.htm].

Human Rights Watch (2005) *Targeting the Anuak: Human Rights Violations and Crimes against Humanity in Ethiopia's Gambella Region.* New York: Human Rights Watch.

Silverstein, K. (2002) "U.S. Politics in the 'Kuwait of Africa,'" *The Nation,* 22 April. Transparency International (2005) [http://www.transparency.org/cpi/2005/dnld/cpi2005.highlights_africa.pdf], accessed 18 November 2005.

United Nations (1998) *World Investment Report 1998 Trends and Developments.* New York and Geneva: United Nations.

*Source:* Exploitation of Energy Resources in Africa. Julia Maxted. *Journal of Developing Societies* Vol. 22, No. 1. 2006. Copyright © Sage Publications. Reprinted with permission of the publisher.

# CHAPTER 25

# While Washington Slept

**Mark Hertsgaard**

Vanity Fair is better known for fashion articles than for articles on global warming and the environment. But as concern over global climate change has increased, celebrities talking about the environment is very much in fashion. In this article, the author looks at how public attention to energy and global climate grew, even as the US administration was giving the topic minimal attention.

The Queen of England is afraid. International CEOs are nervous. And the scientific establishment is loud and clear. If global warming isn't halted, rising sea levels could submerge coastal cities by 2100. So how did this virtual certainty get labeled a "liberal hoax"?

Ten months before Hurricane Katrina left much of New Orleans underwater, Queen Elizabeth II had a private conversation with Prime Minister Tony Blair about George W. Bush. The Queen's tradition of meeting once a week with Britain's elected head of government to discuss matters of state—usually on Tuesday evenings in Buckingham Palace and always alone, to ensure maximum confidentiality—goes back to 1952, the year she ascended the throne. In all that time, the contents of those chats rarely if ever leaked.

So it was extraordinary when London's *Observer* reported, on October 31, 2004, that the Queen had "made a rare intervention in world politics" by telling Blair of "her grave concerns over the White House's stance on global warming." *The Observer* did not name its sources, but one of them subsequently spoke to *Vanity Fair*.

"The Queen first of all made it clear that Buckingham Palace would be happy to help raise awareness about the climate problem," says the source, a high-level environmental expert who was briefed about the conversation. "[She was] definitely concerned about the American position and hoped the prime minister could help change [it]."

Press aides for both the Queen and the prime minister declined to comment on the meeting, as is their habit. But days after the *Observer* story appeared, the Queen indeed raised awareness by presiding over the opening of a British-German conference on climate change, in Berlin. "I might just point out, that's a pretty unusual thing for her to do," says Sir David King, Britain's chief scientific adviser. "She doesn't take part in anything that would be overtly political." King, who has briefed the Queen on climate change, would not comment on the Observer report except to say, "If it were true, it wouldn't surprise me." . . .

Temperatures are rising, the Queen learned from King and other scientists, because greenhouse gases are trapping heat in the atmosphere. Carbon dioxide, the most prevalent of such gases, is released whenever fossil fuels are burned or forests catch fire. Global warming, the scientists explained, threatens to raise sea levels as much as three feet by the end of the 21st century, thanks to melting glaciers and swollen oceans. (Water expands when heated.)

This would leave much of eastern England, including areas near Sandringham, underwater. Global warming would also bring more heat waves like the one in the summer of 2003 that killed 31,000 people across Europe. It might even shut down the Gulf Stream, the flow of warm water from the Gulf of Mexico that gives Europe its mild climate. If the Gulf Stream were to halt—and it has already slowed 30 percent since 1992—Europe's temperatures would plunge, agriculture would collapse, London would no longer feel like New York but like Anchorage.

The Queen, says King, "got it" on climate change, and she wasn't alone. "Everyone in this country, from the political parties to the scientific establishment, to the Archbishop of Canterbury, to our oil companies and the larger business community, has come to a popular consensus about climate change—a sense of alarm and a conviction that action is needed now, not in the future," says Tony Juniper, executive director of the British arm of the environmental group Friends of the Earth.

At the time of his meeting with the Queen, Blair was being attacked on climate change from all ideological sides, with even the Conservatives charging that he was not doing enough. Yet Blair's statements on the issue went far beyond those of most world leaders. He had called the Kyoto Protocol, which has been ratified by 162 countries and requires industrial nations to reduce greenhouse-gas emissions 5 percent below 1990 levels, "not radical enough." The world's climate scientists, Blair pointed out, had estimated that 60 percent cuts in emissions were needed, and he committed Britain to reaching that goal by 2050.

But it wouldn't matter how much Britain cut its greenhouse-gas emissions if other nations didn't do the same. The U.S. was key, not only because it was the world's largest emitter, but because its refusal to reduce emissions led China, India, Brazil, and other large developing countries to ask why they should do so. All this Blair had also said publicly. In 2001 he criticized the Bush administration for withdrawing from the Kyoto Protocol. In 2004 he said it was essential to bring the U.S. into the global effort against climate change, despite its opposition to Kyoto. . . .

To compel Bush to engage the issue, Blair made climate change a lead agenda item at the July 2005 meeting of the Group of 8, the alliance of the world's eight richest nations. A month before the meeting, which was held at Gleneagles, in Scotland, Blair flew to Washington to see Bush face-to-face. That same day, the national academies of science of all the G-8 nations, as well as those of China, India, and Brazil, released a joint statement declaring that climate change was a grave problem that required immediate action. . . .

In the end, however, Bush held firm. Washington vetoed all references to mandatory emissions cuts or timelines, and the climate-change issue was overshadowed by African debt relief, which had been publicized by Bob Geldof's Live 8 concerts.

No one can say for sure whether global warming caused Hurricane Katrina, which slammed into the Gulf Coast on August 29, 2005. But it certainly fit the pattern. The scientific rule of thumb is that one can never blame any one weather event on any single cause. The earth's weather system is too complex for that. Most scientists agree, however, that global warming makes extra-strong hurricanes such as Katrina more likely because it encourages hot oceans, a precondition of hurricane formation. . . .

Just weeks before Katrina struck, Emanuel published a paper in the scientific journal *Nature* demonstrating that hurricanes had grown more powerful as global temperatures rose in the 20th century. Now, he says, by adding more greenhouse gases to the earth's atmosphere, humans are "loading the climatic dice in favor of more powerful hurricanes in the future."

But most Americans heard nothing about Hurricane Katrina's association with global warming. Media coverage instead reflected the views of the Bush administration—specifically, the National Oceanic and Atmospheric Administration, which declared that the hurricane was the result of natural factors. An outcry from N.O.A.A.'s scientists led the agency to backtrack from that statement in February 2006, but by then conventional wisdom was set in place. Post-Katrina New Orleans may eventually be remembered as the first major U.S. casualty of global warming, yet most Americans still don't know what hit us.

Sad to say, Katrina was the perfect preview of what global warming might look like in the 21st century. First, Katrina struck a city that was already below sea level—which is where rising waters could put many coastal dwellers in the years ahead. In 2001, the U.N.-sponsored Intergovernmental Panel on Climate Change (I.P.C.C.), a peer-reviewed, international collaboration among thousands of scientists that is the world's leading authority on climate change, predicted that sea levels could rise as much as three feet by 2100. By coincidence, three feet is about how much New Orleans sank during the 20th century. That was because levees built to keep the Mississippi River from flooding also kept the river from depositing silt that would have replenished the underlying land mass, explains Mike Tidwell, the author of *Bayou Farewell: The Rich Life and Tragic Death of Louisiana's Cajun Coast.* "You could say that in New Orleans we brought the ocean to the people," Tidwell adds, "which is pretty much what global warming will do to other cities in the future."

What's more, Katrina was a Category 5 hurricane, the strongest there is. Such extreme weather events will likely become more frequent as global warming intensifies, says the I.P.C.C. Yes, Katrina's winds had slowed to high-Category 3 levels by the time it made landfall, but it was the hurricane's storm surge that killed people—a surge that formed in the Gulf of Mexico when the storm was still Category 5. Thus, Katrina unleashed 10 to 15 feet of water on a city that was already significantly below sea level. . . .

Since roughly half the world's 6.5 billion people live near coastlines, a three-foot sea-level rise would be even more punishing overseas. Amsterdam, Venice, Cairo, Shanghai, Manila, and Calcutta are some of the cities most threatened. In many places the people and governments are too poor to erect adequate barriers—think of low-lying Bangladesh, where an estimated 18 million people are at risk—so experts fear that they will migrate to neighboring lands, raising the prospect of armed conflict. A Pentagon-commissioned study warned in 2003 that climate change could bring mega-droughts, mass starvation, and even nuclear war as countries such as China, India, and Pakistan battle over scarce food and water.

These are just some of the reasons why David King wrote in *Science* in 2004, "Climate change is the most severe problem that we are facing today, more serious even than the threat of terrorism." King's comment raised hackles in Washington and led a top press aide to Tony Blair to try to muzzle him. But the science adviser tells me he "absolutely" stands by his statement. By no means does King underestimate terrorism; advising the British government on that threat, he says, "is a very important part of my job." But the hazards presented by climate change are so severe and far-reaching that, in his view, they overshadow not only every other environmental threat but every other threat, period. . . .

The worst scenarios of global warming might still be avoided, scientists say, if humanity reduces its greenhouse-gas emissions dramatically, and very soon. The I.P.C.C. has estimated that emissions must fall to 60 percent below 1990 levels before 2050, over a period when global population is expected to increase by 37 percent and per capita energy consumption will surely rise as billions of people in Asia, Africa, and South America strive to ascend from poverty.

Yet even if such a reduction were achieved, a significant rise in sea levels may be unavoidable. "It's getting harder and harder to say we'll avoid a three-foot sea-level rise, though it won't necessarily happen in this century," says Michael Oppenheimer, a professor of geosciences and international affairs at Princeton. Oppenheimer's pessimism is rooted in the lag effects of the climate system: oceans store heat for a century or longer before releasing it; carbon dioxide remains in the atmosphere for decades or longer before dissipating.

According to King, even if humanity were to stop emitting carbon dioxide today, "temperatures will keep rising and all the impacts will keep changing for about 25 years."

The upshot is that it has become too late to prevent climate change; we can only adapt to it. This unhappy fact is not well understood by the general public; advocates downplay it, perhaps for fear of fostering a paralyzing despair. But there is no getting around it: because humanity waited so long to take decisive action, we are now stuck with a certain amount of global warming and the climate changes it will bring—rising seas, fiercer heat, deeper droughts, stronger storms. The World Health Organization estimates that climate change is already helping to kill 150,000 people a year, mainly in Africa and Asia. That number is bound to rise as global warming intensifies in the years ahead.

The inevitability of global warming does not mean we should not act, King emphasizes: "The first message to our political leaders is, action is required. Whether or not we get global agreement to reduce emissions, we all need to adapt to the impacts that are in the pipeline." That means doing all the things that were not done in New Orleans: building sound levees and seawalls, restoring coastal wetlands (which act like speed bumps to weaken hurricanes' storm surges), strengthening emergency-preparedness networks and health-care systems, and much more.

Beyond this crucial first step—which most governments worldwide have yet to consider—humanity can cushion the severity of future global warming by limiting greenhouse-gas emissions. Hansen says we must stabilize emissions—which currently are rising 2 percent a year—by 2015, and then reduce them. *Avoiding Dangerous Climate Change,* a book based on a scientific conference convened by Tony Blair before the G-8 summit, estimates that we may have until 2025 to peak and reduce.

The goal is to stop global warming before it crosses tipping points and attains unstoppable momentum from "positive feedbacks." For example, should the Greenland ice sheet melt, white ice—which reflects sunlight back into space—would be replaced by dark water, which absorbs sunlight and drives further warming. . . .

Among the reasons climate change is a bigger problem than terrorism, David King tells me, is that the problem is rooted in humanity's burning of oil, coal, and natural gas, "and people don't want to let that go." Which is understandable. These carbon-based fuels have powered civilization since the dawn of the industrial era, delivering enormous wealth, convenience, and well being even as they overheated the atmosphere. Luckily, the idea that reducing greenhouse-gas emissions will wreck our economy, as President Bush said in 2005 when defending his opposition to the Kyoto Protocol, is disproved by experience. "In Britain," King told the environmental Web site Grist, "our economy since 1990 has grown by about 40 percent, and our emissions have decreased by 14 percent." . . .

One of the first moves Angela Merkel announced as the new chancellor of Germany last fall was the extension of a Green Party initiative to upgrade energy efficiency in the nation's pre-1978 housing stock. Most of that housing is in the former East Germany, where unemployment approaches 20 percent. Replacing old furnaces and installing efficient windows and lights will produce thousands of well-paying laborers' jobs that by their nature cannot be outsourced.

Corporations, too, have discovered that energy efficiency can be profitable. Over a three-year period beginning in 1999, BP invested $20 million to reduce the emissions from its internal operations and saved $650 million—32 times the original investment.

Individuals can cash in as well. Although buying a super-efficient car or refrigerator may cost more up front, over time it saves the consumer money through lower energy bills.

Efficiency is no silver bullet, nor can it forever neutralize the effects of billions of people consuming more and more all the time. It can, however, buy humanity time to further develop and deploy alternative-energy technologies. . . .

No one pretends that phasing out carbon-based fuels will be easy. The momentum of the climate system means that "a certain amount of pain is inevitable," says Michael Oppenheimer. "But we still have a choice between pain and disaster."

Unfortunately, we are getting a late start, which is something of a puzzle. The threat of global warming has been recognized at the highest levels of government for more than 25 years. Former president Jimmy Carter highlighted it in 1980, and Al Gore championed it in Congress throughout the 1980s. Margaret Thatcher, the arch-conservative prime minister of Britain from 1979 to 1990, delivered some of the hardest-hitting speeches ever given on climate change. But progress stalled in the 1990s, even as Gore was elected vice president and the scientific case grew definitive. It turned out there were powerful pockets of resistance to tackling this problem, and they put up a hell of a fight.

Call him the $45 million man. That's how much money Dr. Frederick Seitz, a former president of the National Academy of Sciences, helped R. J. Reynolds Industries, Inc., give away to fund medical research in the 1970s and 1980s. The research avoided the central health issue facing Reynolds—"They didn't want us looking at the health effects of cigarette smoking," says Seitz, who is now 94—but it nevertheless served the tobacco industry's purposes. Throughout those years, the industry frequently ran ads in newspapers and magazines citing its multi-million-dollar research program as proof of its commitment to science—and arguing that the evidence on the health effects of smoking was mixed.

In the 1990s, Seitz began arguing that the science behind global warming was likewise inconclusive and certainly didn't warrant imposing mandatory limits on greenhouse-gas emissions. He made his case vocally, trashing the integrity of a 1995 I.P.C.C. report on the op-ed page of *The Wall Street Journal,* signing a letter to the Clinton administration accusing it of misrepresenting the science, and authoring a paper which said that global warming and ozone depletion were exaggerated threats devised by environmentalists and unscrupulous scientists pushing a political agenda. In that same paper, Seitz asserted that secondhand smoke posed no real health risks, an opinion he repeats in our interview. "I just can't believe it's that bad," he says. . . .

Seitz was the highest-ranking scientist among a band of doubters who, beginning in the early 1990s, resolutely disputed suggestions that climate change was a real and present danger. As a former president of the National Academy of Sciences (from 1962 to 1969) and a winner of the National Medal of Science, Seitz gave such objections instant credibility. Richard Lindzen, a professor of meteorology at M.I.T., was another high-profile scientist who consistently denigrated the case for global warming. But most of the public argument was carried by lesser scientists and, above all, by lobbyists and paid spokesmen of the Global Climate Coalition. Created and funded by the energy and auto industries, the Coalition spent millions of dollars spreading the message that global warming was an uncertain threat. Journalist Ross Gelbspan exposed the corporate campaign in his 1997 book, *The Heat Is On,* which quoted a 1991 strategy memo: the goal was to "reposition global warming as theory rather than fact." . . .

The deniers' arguments were frequently cited in Washington policy debates. Their most important legislative victory was the Senate's 95-to-0 vote in 1997 to oppose U.S. participation in any international agreement—i.e., the Kyoto Protocol—that imposed mandatory greenhouse-gas reductions on the U.S. . . .

Among many rebuttals to the deniers' arguments, perhaps the most authoritative collection is found on the Web site of Britain's national academy of science, the Royal Society. But such rebuttals have little impact on true believers, says Robert May, the Society's former president. "[Nobel Prize-winning physicist] Max Planck used to say that people don't change their minds [because of evidence]," he adds. "The science simply moves on and those people eventually die off."

But if the deniers appear to have lost the scientific argument, they prolonged the policy battle, delaying actions to reduce emissions when such cuts mattered most. "For 25 years, people have been warning that we had a window of opportunity to take action, and if we waited until the effects were obvious it would be too late to avoid major consequences," says Oppenheimer. "Had some individual countries, especially the United States, begun to act in the early to mid-1990s, we might have made it. But we didn't, and now the impacts are here."

"The goal of the disinformation campaign wasn't to win the debate," says Gelbspan. "The goal was simply to keep the debate going. When the public hears the media report that some scientists believe warming is real but others don't, its reaction is 'Come back and tell us when you're really sure.' So no political action is taken." . . .

The accumulation of scientific evidence eventually led British Petroleum to resign from the Global Climate Coalition in 1996. Shell, Ford, and other corporations soon left as well, and in 2002 the coalition closed down. But Gelbspan, whose Web site tracks the deniers' activities, notes that key coalition personnel have since taken up positions in the Bush administration, including Harlan Watson, the State Department's chief climate negotiator. (Watson declined to be interviewed.)

ExxonMobil—long the most recalcitrant corporation on global warming—is still spending millions of dollars a year funding an array of organizations that downplay the problem, including the George C. Marshall Institute, where Seitz is chairman emeritus. John Passacantando, executive director of Greenpeace USA, calls the denial campaign "one of the great crimes of our era." Passacantando is "quite confident" that class-action lawsuits will eventually be filed against corporations who denied global warming's dangers. Five years ago, he told executives from one company, "You're going to wish you were the tobacco companies once this stuff hits and people realize you were the ones who blocked [action]."

The public discussion about climate change in the U.S. is years behind that in Britain and the rest of Europe, and the deniers are a big reason why. "In the United States, the Chamber of Commerce and National Association of Manufacturers are deeply skeptical of climate-change science and the need to reduce greenhouse-gas emissions," says Fiona Harvey, the environment correspondent for the *Financial Times*. "In Britain, the equivalent body, the Confederation of British Industry, is absolutely behind the science and agrees on the need to cut emissions. The only differences are over how to do that."

. . . Charles Alexander, the former environmental editor at *Time*, complains that, while coverage has improved recently, media executives continue to regard climate change as just another environmental issue, rather than as the overriding challenge of the 21st century.

"Americans are hearing more about reducing greenhouse emissions from BP ads than from news stories in *Time, The New York Times*, or any other U.S. media outlet," Alexander says. "This will go down as the greatest act of mass denial in history."

In 2002, Alexander went to see Andrew Heyward, then the president of CBS News, after running into him at a Harvard reunion. "I talked to him about climate change and other global environmental threats, and made the case that they were more dangerous than terrorism and CBS should be doing much more coverage of them," Alexander recalls. "He didn't dispute any of my factual points, but he did say the reason CBS didn't do more of that coverage was that 'people don't want to hear all that gloom and doom'—in other words, the environment wasn't a ratings winner. He seemed to think CBS News's job was to tell people what they wanted to hear, not what they need to know, and I think that attitude is increasingly true for the news business in general." . . .

American television did, however, give prime-time coverage to the latest, and most famous, global-warming denier: novelist Michael Crichton. ABC's *20/20* broadcast a very friendly interview with Crichton when he published *State of Fear*, a novel arguing that anyone who bought into the phony scientific consensus on global warming was a modern equivalent of the early-20th-century eugenicists who cited scientific "proof" for the superiority of the white race.

When Crichton was invited to testify before the Environment and Public Works Committee, observers in Britain were floored. "This is fairyland," exclaims Michael Meacher, the member of Parliament who served as Tony Blair's environment minister from 1997 to 2003. "You have a science-fiction writer testifying before the United States Senate on global-warming policy? I mean, you can almost see the little boy off to the side, like in the story of the emperor's clothes, saying, 'But he's a science-fiction writer, isn't he?' It's just ludicrous."

The man who invited Crichton, committee chairman James M. Inhofe, a Republican from oil-rich Oklahoma, had already said on the floor of the Senate that global warming was "the greatest hoax ever perpetrated on the American people." In an e-mail interview, Inhofe defended Crichton's appearance, noting that the writer holds a medical degree from Harvard. (Crichton is also a post-doctoral fellow at the Salk Institute for Biological Studies.) The senator added that he stood by his hoax statement as well.

David King responded that Britain's climate-science research is headquartered within the Ministry of Defense, "and you wouldn't find a group of people less likely to perpetrate a hoax than the people in the Ministry of Defense." . . .

Paul H. O'Neill, who served nearly two years as George W. Bush's secretary of the treasury, does not buy the common notion that Bush and Vice President Dick Cheney resist taking action on global warming because they are oilmen. "I don't think either one of them is an oilman," insists O'Neill. "You have to have success to be an oilman. It's like saying you're a ballplayer, but you never got on the field."

In 1998, while running the aluminum giant Alcoa, O'Neill was among the first U.S. business leaders to recognize the enormity of climate change. He says Bush asked him, early in the first term, to put together a plan of action, but it was ignored. Like Bush, O'Neill opposed Kyoto, so he proposed other ways to move forward. But instead, he says, the administration "cherry-picked" the science on climate change to justify taking no action, "just like it cherry-picked the intelligence on weapons of mass destruction" to justify the invasion of Iraq.

"The United States is the only entity on this planet turning its back on this problem," says Massachusetts senator John Kerry. "Even as he talks about protecting the security of the nation, the president is willfully choosing not to tackle this problem. History will record it as one of the greatest derelictions of duty ever."

Bush-administration officials counter that they are doing more to fight global warming than anyone else— just with different tools than those favored by supporters of the Kyoto Protocol. James L. Connaughton, the head of the White House Council on Environmental Quality, starts by pointing out that Bush has raised federal mileage standards for SUVs and light trucks. When I point out that the increase is tiny (a mere 0.3 miles per gallon, says Dan Becker of the Sierra Club), Connaughton maintains that over time further increases will result in substantial energy savings, especially when paired with the administration's new tax credits for efficient vehicles. It's also important, he says, to "keep personal income taxes in check" to encourage people to buy these new cars. What's more, the administration recently provided $10 billion in incentives for alternative energy development and $40 billion over 10 years to encourage farmers to plant trees and preserve grassland that can soak up carbon dioxide.

The administration opposes the Kyoto Protocol, Connaughton claims, because its mandatory emissions cuts would punish the American economy, costing as many as five million jobs. It would also dry up the capital needed to fund the technological research that will ultimately solve global warming.

"It's important not to get distracted by chasing short-term reductions in greenhouse emissions. The real payoff is in long-term technological breakthroughs," says John H. Marburger III, the president's science adviser. Besides, "there is no question that mitigating the impact of climate change as it takes place will be much less [expensive] than the costs of reducing oil and coal use in the short term."

"The world is now on a trajectory to slow the growth in greenhouse-gas emissions," concludes Connaughton, who as a lawyer represented mining and chemical interests before joining the administration. "I'm highly confident we will stabilize [those emissions]." He says that's exactly what happened over the last 80 years with air pollution. He seems to take pleasure in observing that, under Bush, the U.S. has actually reduced its annual emissions, which, he says, is more than some of its harshest critics overseas have done.

It's a cheerful story, but virtually no one else believes it. Waiting 80 years to eliminate greenhouse-gas emissions would guarantee runaway global warming, says James Hansen. In January, six former chiefs of the Environmental Protection Agency, including five who served Republican presidents, said Bush needed to do much more to fight climate change. In Britain, Peter Ainsworth, the Conservative Party's shadow secretary of state for the environment, says his party is "saddened" by the Bush administration's approach. "We would have preferred the Bush administration to take a leadership position on this problem . . . instead of allowing itself to be seen as foot-dragging."

Outsiders doubt President Bush's desire to confront the issue, pointing out that his right-wing political base agrees with Inhofe that global warming is a liberal hoax. Critics also question the administration's faith in volunteerism. They argue that imposing mandatory timelines and emissions limits would put a price tag on carbon and push corporations and individuals to use less of it. "Long-term research is fine, but to offer that as a substitute for the stark necessity of near-term cuts in emissions is a kind of magical thinking—trusting that something will happen to make everything all right," says Donald Kennedy, the editor in chief of *Science*. In fact, despite Bush's call to end our "addiction" to oil, his 2007 budget actually reduced funding for alternative energy and efficiency.

Nor has the Bush administration cut short-term emissions, says a European diplomat who requested anonymity because he has to work with Bush officials. Citing data from the Energy Information Administration, the diplomat says Connaughton is correct to say that U.S. greenhouse-gas emissions declined, but only in the single year following the 2001 terrorist attacks, owing to the ensuing economic recession. U.S. emissions increased in every other year of Bush's presidency, making it "complete hokum" to claim that Bush's policies are cutting emissions, the diplomat says, adding of Connaughton, "I'm afraid Jim has drunk the Kool-Aid."

As for John Marburger's assertion that it will be cheaper to adapt to climate change than to try to head it off, Michael Oppenheimer says, "It's a sad day when the president is being told by his science adviser that climate change isn't worth avoiding. It may be possible for rich nations and people to adapt, but 90 percent of humanity doesn't have the resources to deal with climate change. It's unethical to condemn them just because the people in power don't want to act." . . .

But the rest of the world is no longer waiting for the Bush administration. At the international climate conference held in Montreal last year, European nations called the administration's bluff when it refused to commit even to the breathtakingly modest step of someday discussing what framework might follow the Kyoto Protocol, which expires in 2012. At past summits, the administration's stubbornness led other nations to back down in hopes of keeping America involved in the process. At Montreal, the world quit waiting for Godot and recognized, as Elliot Morley, Tony Blair's minister of the environment, says, "there are a lot of voices in the United States in addition to the Bush administration, and we will work with all of them to address this problem."

The same thing is happening inside the U.S. "It is very clear that Congress will put mandatory greenhouse-gas-emission reductions in place, immediately after George W. Bush leaves office," says Philip Clapp of N.E.T. "Even the Fortune 500 is positioning itself for the inevitable. There isn't one credible 2008 Republican presidential candidate who hasn't abandoned the president's do-nothing approach. They have all adopted the approach the rest of the world took at the Montreal talks—we're moving forward, you're a lame duck, and we have to deal with it."

Regardless of what happens in Washington, D.C., state and local governments across America are aggressively confronting the problem. Two hundred and eight mayors have committed their cities to meet or exceed the emissions reductions mandated by the Kyoto Protocol, and some have gone further. Governor Arnold Schwarzenegger has committed California to 30 percent cuts by 2020.

California officials have also held talks with their counterparts in Oregon and Washington about launching a so-called carbon-trading system like the one currently in force in Europe. Such a system allows efficient users to profit while wasteful users must pay for burning more fuel. A similar mechanism worked in the 1990s to dramatically reduce emissions of sulfur dioxide—the cause of acid rain—at far less cost than industrialists or environmentalists anticipated.

New York and seven other northeastern states, which together with California amount to the third-biggest economy in the world, are also considering a carbon-trading system. Their collective actions—investing in energy efficiency, installing wind turbines, sequestering carbon—could boost production runs and lower costs to the point where the green technologies needed to fight global warming become affordable for everyone.

At the same time, investors and others worried about global warming are pressuring corporations and Wall Street to take the problem seriously. The Investor Network on Climate Risk, a coalition of pension-fund managers and institutional investors representing $3 trillion in assets, has put corporations on notice that its members will reconsider investing in companies that don't pay enough attention to climate change. In 2005, investment-banking giant Goldman Sachs pledged to embrace carbon trading and invest $1 billion in renewable energy. . . .

No matter what happens, the global warming that past human activity has already unleashed will make this a different planet in the years ahead. But it could still be a livable, even hospitable, planet, if enough of us get smart in time. If we don't, three feet of water could be just the beginning.

---

## Questions

1. How were problems of energy and climate change seen differently in London and Washington? Why the differences?

2. What are some of the effects of global climate change that have so many, including Queen Elizabeth, so worried, and what would need to be done to slow or reverse these changes?

---

*Source:* While Washington Slept. Mark Hertsgaard. *Vanity Fair.* May 2006. Reprinted by permission of the author.

# CHAPTER 26

## Some Convenient Truths

Gregg Easterbrook

Al Gore's *An Inconvenient Truth* won a 2007 Academy Award and has helped focus public attention on the problem of climate change. While some still contend the problem is exaggerated, many others find it overwhelming and maybe unstoppable. In this article, the author contends that while the problem is very real, the changes required to stop it may be very practical and well within our ability, even without harming economic growth.

If there is now a scientific consensus that global warming must be taken seriously, there is also a related political consensus: that the issue is Gloom City. In *An Inconvenient Truth*, Al Gore warns of sea levels rising to engulf New York and San Francisco and implies that only wrenching lifestyle sacrifice can save us. The opposing view is just as glum. Even mild restrictions on greenhouse gases could "cripple our economy," Republican Senator Kit Bond of Missouri said in 2003. Other conservatives suggest that greenhouse-gas rules for Americans would be pointless anyway, owing to increased fossil-fuel use in China and India. When commentators hash this issue out, it's often a contest to see which side can sound more pessimistic.

Here's a different way of thinking about the greenhouse effect: that action to prevent runaway global warming may prove cheap, practical, effective, and totally consistent with economic growth. Which makes a body wonder: Why is such environmental optimism absent from American political debate?

Greenhouse gases are an air-pollution problem—and all previous air-pollution problems have been reduced faster and more cheaply than predicted, without economic harm. Some of these problems once seemed scary and intractable, just as greenhouse gases seem today. About forty years ago urban smog was increasing so fast that President Lyndon Johnson warned, "Either we stop poisoning our air or we become a nation [in] gas masks groping our way through dying cities." During Ronald Reagan's presidency, emissions of chlorofluoro-carbons, or CFCs, threatened to deplete the stratospheric ozone layer. As recently as George H. W. Bush's administration, acid rain was said to threaten a "new silent spring" of dead Appalachian forests.

But in each case, strong regulations were enacted, and what happened? Since 1970, smog-forming air pollution has declined by a third to a half. Emissions of CFCs have been nearly eliminated, and studies suggest that ozone-layer replenishment is beginning. Acid rain, meanwhile, has declined by a third since 1990, while Appalachian forest health has improved sharply.

Most progress against air pollution has been cheaper than expected. Smog controls on automobiles, for example, were predicted to cost thousands of dollars for each vehicle. Today's new cars emit less than 2 percent as much smog-forming pollution as the cars of 1970, and the cars are still as affordable today as they were then. Acid-rain control has cost about 10 percent of what was predicted in 1990, when Congress enacted new rules. At that time, opponents said the regulations would cause a "clean-air recession"; instead, the economy boomed.

Greenhouse gases, being global, are the biggest air-pollution problem ever faced. And because widespread fossil-fuel use is inevitable for some time to come, the best-case scenario for the next few decades may be a slowing of the rate of greenhouse-gas buildup, to prevent runaway climate change. Still, the basic pattern observed in all other forms of air-pollution control—rapid progress at low cost—should repeat for greenhouse-gas controls.

Yet a paralyzing negativism dominates global-warming politics. Environmentalists depict climate change as nearly unstoppable; skeptics speak of the problem as either imaginary (the "greatest hoax ever perpetrated," in the words of Senator James Inhofe, chairman of the Senate's environment committee) or ruinously expensive to address.

Even conscientious politicians may struggle for views that aren't dismal. Mandy Grunwald, a Democratic political consultant, says, "When political candidates talk about new energy sources, they use a positive, can-do vocabulary. Voters have personal experience with energy use, so they can relate to discussion of solutions. If you say a car can use a new kind of fuel, this makes intuitive sense to people. But global warming is of such scale and magnitude, people don't have any commonsense way to grasp what the solutions would be. So political candidates tend to talk about the greenhouse effect in a depressing way."

One reason the global-warming problem seems so daunting is that the success of previous antipollution efforts remains something of a secret. Polls show that Americans think the air is getting dirtier, not cleaner, perhaps because media coverage of the environment rarely if ever mentions improvements. For instance, did you know that smog and acid rain have continued to diminish throughout George W. Bush's presidency?

One might expect Democrats to trumpet the decline of air pollution, which stands as one of government's leading postwar achievements. But just as Republicans have found they can bash Democrats by falsely accusing them of being soft on defense, Democrats have found they can bash Republicans by falsely accusing them of destroying the environment. If that's your argument, you might skip over the evidence that many environmental trends are positive. One might also expect Republicans to trumpet the reduction of air pollution, since it signifies responsible behavior by industry. But to acknowledge that air

pollution has declined would require Republicans to say the words, "The regulations worked."

Does it matter that so many in politics seem so pessimistic about the prospect of addressing global warming? Absolutely. Making the problem appear unsolvable encourages a sort of listless fatalism, blunting the drive to take first steps toward a solution. Historically, first steps against air pollution have often led to pleasant surprises. When Congress, in 1970, mandated major reductions in smog caused by automobiles, even many supporters of the rule feared it would be hugely expensive. But the catalytic converter was not practical then; soon it was perfected, and suddenly, major reductions in smog became affordable. Even a small step by the United States against greenhouse gases could lead to a similar breakthrough.

And to those who worry that any greenhouse-gas reductions in the United States will be swamped by new emissions from China and India, here's a final reason to be optimistic: technology can move across borders with considerable speed. Today it's not clear that American inventors or entrepreneurs can make money by reducing greenhouse gases, so relatively few are trying. But suppose the United States regulated greenhouse gases, using its own domestic program, not the cumbersome Kyoto Protocol; then America's formidable entrepreneurial and engineering communities would fully engage the problem. Innovations pioneered here could spread throughout the world, and suddenly rapid global warming would not seem inevitable.

The two big technical advances against smog—the catalytic converter and the chemical engineering that removes pollutants from gasoline at the refinery stage—were invented in the United States. The big economic advance against acid rain—a credit-trading system that gives power-plant managers a profit incentive to reduce pollution—was pioneered here as well. These advances are now spreading globally. Smog and acid rain are still increasing in some parts of the world, but the trend lines suggest that both will decline fairly soon, even in developing nations. For instance, two decades ago urban smog was rising at a dangerous rate in Mexico; today it is diminishing there, though the country's population continues to grow. A short time ago declining smog and acid rain in developing nations seemed an impossibility; today declining greenhouse gases seem an impossibility. The history of air-pollution control says otherwise.

Americans love challenges, and preventing artificial climate change is just the sort of technological and economic challenge at which this nation excels. It only remains for the right politician to recast the challenge in practical, optimistic tones. Gore seldom has, and Bush seems to have no interest in trying. But cheap and fast improvement is not a pipe dream; it is the pattern of previous efforts against air pollution. The only reason runaway global warming seems unstoppable is that we have not yet tried to stop it.

---

## Questions

1. How is it that the author is optimistic about a problem that has generated so much pessimism?

2. What immediate actions does he suggest? Do you believe that Americans, and the rest of the world, are ready to take these steps?

---

*Source:* Some Convenient Truths: Stopping Global Warming. Gregg Easterbrook. *The Atlantic.* September 2006. Reprinted by permission of the author.

# PART VII

# ENVIRONMENT

All of the questions considered so far must be set against the resources and limitations provided by the global environment. When we consider questions of international development and global change, we are continually forced back to basic questions: Is it equitable and broad-based, with the benefits reaching everyone? Is it safe and sustainable, with benefits for future generations as well as the present? The question of equity and the environment drives Article 27. A degraded environment is not just a concern for those wealthy enough to worry about such things. All too often it is the poor who suffer the most as they are unable to escape the most dangerous, least desirable environments. Major cities everywhere in the developing world are ringed by large and growing slums of poor and displaced people. It is here that the harsh realities of economic exploitation and environmental exploitation can squeeze the life out of communities.

New concerns about the environment have also driven new forms of travel. Increasing numbers of tourists want more than a location where the beaches are hot and the drinks are cold. They seek experiences that help them learn about and appreciate both the natural environment and the people who call these places home. Variously called "ecotourism" or "geotourism," the idea remains controversial. Does it represent a more responsible way to see the world while protecting fragile environments and cultures, or is this just a way to ease the guilty consciences of wealthy tourists? Article 28 looks at the possibilities and concerns with ecotourism. Article 29 provides a compelling example of travel intended to encounter remote people in remote places: is this responsible ecotourism or a new form of exploitation? The final article reflects back on a global voyage and its impact on college students, who must now consider the role they will play in changing the global environment.

27. A Financial Framework for Reducing Slums: Lessons From Experience in Latin America.
Bruce Ferguson and Jesus Navarrete. *Environment and Urbanization, 15* (2), 2003.

28. Tropic of Answer: Charles Munn, a Pioneer of South American Ecotourism, Answers Readers' Questions.
Charles Munn. *Grist Magazine.* April 14, 2006.

29. Strangers in the Forest.
Lawrence Osborne. *New Yorker.* April 18, 2005.

30. In American Waters.
Scott Sernau. *IU International News.* Spring 2006.

# CHAPTER 27

# A Financial Framework for Reducing Slums

## *Lessons From Experience in Latin America*

Bruce Ferguson and Jesus Navarrete

This paper describes how slums have come to house such a significant proportion of the urban population in virtually all low- and middle-income nations. It then discusses a combination of large-scale land development for housing and more efficient upgrading programs (with attention to keeping down unit costs and integrating microfinance to support house improvement), and how these approaches can greatly reduce the proportion of people living in slums, thus contributing to the Millennium Development Goal of significantly improving the lives of at least 100 million slum dwellers by 2020. The paper illustrates its points with examples of effective innovations in housing vouchers, land market reforms, and land development programs from different nations in Latin America.

## I. Introduction

Eight hundred and fifty million people currently live in urban slums in low- and middle-income countries—about one in every seven people in the world. This number is projected to double to 1.5 billion by 2025.[1] These shanty towns exact enormous human and financial costs. Slums reduce the efficiency of cities and the economic growth of countries and—most fundamental—stunt the human potential of enormous numbers of people. Slum residents bear the bulk of these costs. Lack of infrastructure and services contributes to very high burdens of injury, illness and premature death among slum dwellers. Reducing slums, therefore, should be a high priority for governments, donors, NGOs and others. Indeed, the United Nations has set goals related to "cities without slums."[2]

However, some of the literature and many shanty town-related programs show little understanding of the causes of slum formation and their financial implications. Not surprisingly, nonstrategic efforts have had little effect on the overall problem. Some slums are improved, but the accelerating rate of slum formation—particularly in much of Asia, the Middle East, and some

African countries where urbanization is still cresting—offers little hope of reducing the absolute number of people living in urban slums in the foreseeable future.

An effective approach must start with an understanding of why shanty towns form, and then put in place a financial framework to avoid their formation and to upgrade existing slums. Some middle-income countries—such as Chile and Costa Rica[3]—and cities in middle-income countries–such as Juarez, Mexico—have effectively done this.

This paper first describes the causes of slum formation and their financial consequences for households and government. It then presents a financial strategy for low/moderate-income land development—the key to stopping slum formation—and for slum upgrading.

## II. Urban Slum Formation and Its Cost Implications

Why, from a financial perspective, do urban slums and, more broadly, informal settlements form on such a large scale in low- and middle-income countries?

Fundamentally, the reason is that the low/moderate-income majority—typically 50–70 percent of the population—cannot afford to purchase the least expensive commercially built housing unit.[4] A series of interrelated factors lie behind this lack of housing affordability:

- low incomes relative to the cost of land and construction;
- high real interest rates (resulting from macro-economic conditions, fiscal deficits, currency risk, international capital flows and other factors)—often 10 percent or more—that raise the debt service on home loans; and
- high standards and a cumbersome process for formal sector subdivision development, and for building permits joined with high charges on formal sector development (for property transfer, title registration, etc.).

Other factors typically exacerbate the basic cost problem. Insecure and poorly functioning property rights systems often result in insecure tenure for a large share of "homeowners." Poorly developed and highly protected financial systems result in modest supply of credit and little competition for customers. In this context, financial institutions usually limit their lending to middle- and upper-income households and to government, and have no interest in going down-market.

These factors join to cause a phenomenon common to most low- and middle-income countries and, increasingly, to poorer parts of high-income countries (such as some parts of the US along its border with Mexico). Formal sector housing production usually covers only a modest part of new household formation. Even relatively prosperous dynamic middle-income countries suffer from a huge gap between formal sector supply of housing and household formation. For example,[5] in Mexico, new household formation runs at 750,000 families per year. However, public and private sector financial institutions extend credit for the production of just 350,000 units per year. Most of the remaining families get housed informally.

As a result, most households in low- and middle-income countries build their housing progressively over a period of 5 to 15 years.[6] This progressive building process allows families to stagger the cost of home ownership over long periods and, thus, make it affordable. Before they start building, however, these families must find a lot. Some invade land. Others purchase a lot in an illegal subdivision (an unplatted subdivision developed without the approval of government). Those who lack the resources necessary to purchase an illegal lot or to invade

and undertake the progressive building process (the poorest of the poor, temporary migrants) and families that put a premium on access to the city center often settle in inner-city buildings divided up into small units—called "tenement houses" in Jamaica and *corticos* in Brazil. Such informal settlements constitute the universe from which urban slums form.

These informal settlements, which form the bulk of most cities in low- and middle-income countries, have evolved paralegal and financial systems to handle property transactions. Families sell their house usually by transferring documents short of full legal title because the formal costs of getting such freehold tenure to begin with, and then transferring it on sale, exceed the benefits[7] and the amount they can afford. Households also often finance the improvement and expansion of their homes informally through money lenders, gifts from family members—including transfers from spouses and offspring working abroad in richer countries (Persian Gulf, Western Europe, Japan and Taiwan, US, Canada, Australia)—labor exchange and self-help agreements with other households, and popular savings clubs (where all members of the group contribute each month and one person wins the pot).

Thus, housing markets in low- and middle-income countries are highly segmented. Low/moderate-income households (50–70 percent of the population) operate in informal markets[8] largely separate from those of the small middle and upper class, who buy developer-built complete units, use banks and register their title.[9]

Most informal settlements share a key characteristic from a financial perspective. Although informal settlements help solve the individual family's immediate problem of finding affordable shelter, they generate immense private and public costs. The private costs come in the form of the tremendous effort[10] necessary for slum families to build adequate shelter over a long period of time (when unassisted by formal sector institutions and government, as is usually the case) and the higher levels of environmental health risks associated with higher prevalence of diseases, increased levels of disablement and premature death among slum populations.[11] Sometimes, such environmental health risks spill over to the rest of the city.[12]

The major public costs come in the form of the investments in basic services necessary to upgrade slums—reordering the settlement to allow an appropriate street layout, relocating families in order to do this, and the basic infrastructure (paving main roads, water, sanitation). The cost of reordering slums and providing basic road-related infrastructure to conventional standards[13] usually amounts to two to three times the cost of providing such infrastructure to new formal sector development.[14]

MetroVivienda—a city agency that engages in low/moderate-income land development in Bogotá—has quantified this cost. This agency calculates that after land costs, the basic infrastructure package for upgrading informal settlements costs three times that of formal sector development.[15] Taking into account the extra infrastructure costs and reordering, Metro-Vivienda notes that government ends up paying US$ 2,500 more per unit (in addition to the normal costs of urban development) in order to upgrade informal settlements. Another significant cost for upgrading often derives from professional staff time required to sort out ownership in informal settlements—with the area to be upgraded having a complex mix of tenure status and occupancy.[16] Generally, all of this expense comes in the form of a subsidy with minimal cost recovery. Hence, allowing slum formation creates a huge unfunded public liability.

It is useful to think of housing demand and supply in hydraulic terms. In low- and middle-income countries, the system consists of a huge pipe for low/moderate-income households that use informal markets and a small one for middle/upper-income households that use formal markets. If the flow of new low/moderate-income households greatly exceeds formal sector supply—as is typically the case—the remainder will spill over somewhere. The unsatisfied demand either goes into new informal settlement on the urban fringe or into greater density of central-city tenements, or into overcrowding.

This problem afflicts not only developing countries but also, increasingly, advanced industrialized countries. The US counties along the border with Mexico suffer from a similar situation.[17] The share of low-income households—many earning the minimum wage or below—has increased to 30–40 percent of the population in large parts of the US border with Mexico. Since these families cannot afford to acquire the most basic home, some have resorted to purchasing raw lots in semi-urban areas lacking basic infrastructure. Over half a million people live in the resulting *colonias,* mainly in Texas but also in the other border states.[18] The US border states with Mexico—particularly Texas, which has the most *colonias*—currently cannot afford to upgrade the majority of these informal settlements because of the high cost of provision of basic services—particularly sanitation[19] and water.

Similarly, because of the high cost of upgrading, most governments in low- and medium-income countries can only afford to fix the urban slum problem for a relatively small part of the population. Even relatively prosperous developing country cities can bear the costs of slum upgrading only for a small share of their population. The slum upgrading programs of Rio de Janeiro—the developing country city that has most emphasized this mechanism—have covered a population of 500,000 relative to a total population of over 10 million in the Rio metropolitan area.

Once an urban slum forms, government has lost the cost battle and can only fix a small share of the result. Hence, the best way to deal with urban slums is to decrease or stop their formation, and thereby avoid fixing them retroactively at high cost. This fundamental conclusion takes on particular importance given that urban slums in low- and middle-income countries are projected to double in population over the next 25 years. Dealing with the flow is as or more important than upgrading the stock. This strategy applies at the level of cities and states as well as countries.

The key to stopping slum formation is to increase low-cost formal sector production to rates near those of new household formation. When this happens, few or no new urban slums form. Various low- and middle-income countries and many of their cities have succeeded in stopping slum formation this way. For example, Costa Rica has stimulated large-scale formal sector production partly through a direct demand housing subsidy program established in 1988.[20] Essentially, this direct demand subsidy consists of a voucher in the range of US$3,000–5,000 assigned to individual households that then join this subvention with a market rate mortgage loan and a down payment to purchase a new core unit. Since 1990, Costa Rica's direct demand subsidy program has produced new housing at a rate averaging about 15,000 units per year, compared with new household formation of 13,000 per year. Hence, new production has exceeded new household formation by satisfying new demand and working down the backlog of pent-up demand. Hence, urban slum formation has first slowed and then stopped over the last decade. Costa Rica is now working on upgrading its existing slums.

The most critical step in increasing formal sector production is low/moderate-income land development. The next section deals with this topic.

## III. Low/Moderate-Income Land Development

Before a family engages in progressive building, it needs a lot, preferably with reasonable access to jobs. Securing a lot starts the progressive housing process. The remainder of the process depends critically on success in accessing land. Since 1980, as cities have become larger and denser, developable urban land in reasonable proximity to city jobs has become far less available in emerging countries (as early as 1985, McAuslan emphasized urban land shortages).[21] High standards and slow, cumbersome development approval processes have also contributed to reducing land supply and raising land costs. Various studies have shown that government regulations and formal and informal (i.e., bribes) charges in low- and middle-income countries raise the end cost of housing substantially.[22] Unfortunately, the idea that poorly conceived government regulations will increase the cost of private sector housing, and that streamlining such rules can reduce its cost and help private development go down-market, is still a new and unfamiliar idea in many low- and middle-income countries.

El Salvador, however, is a striking exception to this rule and demonstrates the enormous positive impact of reducing land development standards and streamlining its regulation.[23] The government of El Salvador (GOS) undertook wholesale reform of the legal and institutional structure of land development, cadastres and the property registry.[24] Before these reforms, government required full basic infrastructure (electricity, individual water connections, individual sanitation, drainage, paved roads) prior to subdividing. These high standards made the resulting development unaffordable to the majority. Box 27.1 provides details.

Now, developers need only lay out the subdivision (pegging out individual lots, common facilities and roads), and provide basic water (standpipes), sanitation (a latrine) and legal title. These changes have greatly lowered up-front costs, allowed incremental upgrading of this infrastructure, and stimulated a low-income development industry that now accounts for over one-quarter of all new lots and housing solutions in the country every year. Over 200 low-income development firms have produced lots at a rate far above new household formation

---

### Box 27.1
### Low/moderate-income land development in El Salvador

Unique in Latin America, El Salvador has a thriving national industry of developers supplying legal low-cost subdivisions. Minimized regulations make land acquisition affordable through a category of progressive subdivisions for low-income residents. These developments require the provision of demarcated lots of a minimum 100 square meters, with green spaces and planned roads, and without costly and time-consuming additional up front infrastructure investment. This arrangement facilitates private sector financing and diminishes the need for land invasions.

Housing developers account for between 50 and 70 percent of the annual growth in housing for low-income households and 26 percent of all new housing in El Salvador. While 200 firms are reportedly active, 3 have been operating on a significant national scale for 20 years or more. These developers provide 8–12 year loans for lot purchase, with affordable payments of US$15–25 per month. Many of these subdividers then offer additional financing for self-constructed housing or community infrastructure.

Argoz, the country's largest developer, has financed over 630 projects throughout El Salvador, earning over US$9 million in 2000. The company is currently financing 250,000 lots and supplying 10-year rent-to-own contracts for families with monthly incomes of approximately US$170. Families do not have to provide a down payment, and pay a fixed fee of US$17 per month, which includes insurance.

The company offers additional financial services, including immediate loans up to half of the amount paid on the lot at any time in the transaction. Families can access these funds for emergencies and home improvements or expansions. In addition, all of Argoz's developments have a community-elected Board that can organize group financing for infrastructure projects, using their own property as collateral.

SOURCE: Souza, M T (2000), "Nota sectoral: lotificaciones de desarrollo progresivo en El Salvador," unpublished paper, Inter-American Development Bank, Washington DC.

since 1996, and have rapidly expanded the developed areas of El Salvador's medium and large cities. As a result, lot prices in El Salvador have gone down in real terms by 20 percent since the mid-1990s, rather than rising fast as is the case in most low- and middle-income countries. The monthly payment for the purchase of a 100 square meter lot—averaging US$15–25—is affordable to low/moderate-income families that earn US$1,500–3,500 per year. Interestingly, these El Salvador low-income land developers have also chosen to extend micro-loans to families that purchase their lots to construct a basic home.

Although residential land development on the urban fringe is critical, it often gets bogged down in a morass of problems. Frequently, land ownership is highly fragmented among many different individuals who have varying degrees of rights to property and tangled title histories. The resulting urban expansion consists of a chaotic patchwork that costs government large sums to rationalize.

The opposite problem also occurs. One or more landowners sometimes concentrate ownership of much of the developable land on the urban fringe. As low- and middle-income country cities have very low property taxes and poor enforcement, these landowners face few carrying charges and are able to hold this land without cost for long periods, encouraging speculation, creating land shortages and raising prices.

Many other problems contribute to market failure in the supply of urban parcels for development. In some countries, the complexities of the land development process are so entrenched in laws and historical custom that this activity becomes uneconomic for the private sector, except for middle-and upper-income housing. Systems of communal and traditional property rights are a case in point. Usually intended to protect the poor, or to preserve traditional uses of land, communal and customary property systems tend to handicap private sector urban land development. For example, 65 percent of developable land surrounding urban areas in Mexico consists of *ejidos*—land with communal rights originally granted to peasant farming communities. A special, complicated legal regimen governs the use of *ejidos*, restricts their sale and greatly complicates rational urban development.[25] In Indonesia, a traditional system of property rights, and a parallel Western version brought by the Dutch, makes assembling land on the urban fringe without government intervention virtually impossible.

However, simply removing these protections and allowing the private sector free reign to urbanize agricultural land often results in a huge transfer of wealth from traditional communities to developers. It also threatens to exclude the poor from access to lots, with disastrous social consequences. Mexico has tried to strike a balance by allowing the privatization of *ejidos* in corporate form—through land development partnerships between *ejido* communities and developers, in which both parties share the profits. Indonesia has yet to attempt to strike a balance, and continues to give private sector developers monopolies and immense power over land development of traditional communities on the urban fringe.[26]

---

**Box 27. 2**
**Massive residential land development on the urban fringe in Bogotá, Colombia**

In 1998, the mayor's office in Bogotá created MetroVivienda as a public enterprise. The agency's overall goals are to "prevent chaotic urban development" (i.e., the formation of informal settlements) rather than "remediate" it through massive land development. The compelling need for MetroVivienda arises because " . . . *half of the population of Bogotá does not have sufficient resources to acquire the least expensive housing unit produced through standard urban development practice . . .*" and " . . . *land is disappearing.*" Essentially, the agency operates as a "second tier" institution, and replaces direct production of housing by the municipality of Bogotá. MetroVivienda buys large tracts of land wholesale—often getting a lower price—extends infrastructure lines to these tracts, divides them up and sells the resulting parcels, also at low prices, to builders. In turn, builders commit to construct a minimum number of units of a specified quality (size, appointments, etc.), and sell these units at a ceiling price. The process works as follows.

First, MetroVivienda buys large tracts of land that is zoned as rural or semi-rural. The organization has thoroughly studied and identified the major raw land parcels left in the Bogotá metropolitan area. Once the decision is made to purchase a particular parcel, MetroVivienda contracts the

*(Continued)*

(Continued)

local real estate appraisers organization to determine a fair market price, declares the property of "public use," and initiates negotiations with the owner. As the parcel is zoned for rural uses and lacks infrastructure, the agency typically pays substantially less than if this land were urban. Payment can consist of cash, or the landowner can have an interest (joint venture) in the subsequent development. The owner has 30 days to reach an agreement once the property is designated of "public use" (thus, this power is of critical importance in land acquisition) and an offer has been made. If the landowner is intransigent, MetroVivienda uses its condemnation powers to expropriate land, and pays the owner a fair market price set by legal fiat.

In conjunction with land acquisition, MetroVivienda applies to and obtains permits from other government entities for development. The organization then puts in place trunk infrastructure, and establishes parks and other common areas in conjunction with other authorities. Infrastructure provision starts with building trunk water and sewer lines, followed by electricity, telephone and roads. Areas reserved for commercial establishments are sold. With infrastructure in place, MetroVivienda sells parcels to for-profit and nonprofit builders, who commit to construct and sell housing at a maximum price. The builders first construct sample units to market their future developments. The subsequent competition for clients among these builders, and the sale price ceilings set by MetroVivienda, join to control sale prices and ensure quality. Thus, builders pass on to home buyers a substantial share of the great cost advantages created by MetroVivienda, which result from lower land-purchase costs, larger-scale and quicker development times. MetroVivienda delivers no subsidies itself, although the organization sometimes organizes families to access direct demand subsidies funded by central government to reach lower-income households. The resulting developments have high density—averaging 240 units per hectare—and ample public and green space (40 percent of total area).

By 2000, after its first two years of operation, MetroVivienda had bought 320 hectares and had 1,800 units under construction in three projects. The build-out of these parcels will result in 31,000 units (100 per hectare) and, with a staff of 38, the organization was lean relative to most government housing agencies.

SOURCE: Alcaldia Mayor de Bogotá (2002), "Ciudadela el recreo—memoria del modelo de gestion MetroVivienda," MetroVivienda Empresa Industrial y Comercial del Distrito Capital, Bogotá, Colombia.

An inadequate supply of basic infrastructure—especially water—often limits the areas suitable for formal sector development by the private sector. Small and even medium-sized private developers lack access to construction finance to develop parcels in many countries. This lack of credit finance reinforces the concentration of the ownership of developable land, adding to the market power of large landowners, and raising prices.

These many difficulties contribute to market failure. Hence, a role exists for the public sector in urban land development in many countries. For example, the city of Bogotá in Colombia has targeted the urban fringe land development problem through the creation of MetroVivienda (Box 27.2).

MetroVivienda assembles large tracts of land through condemnation and purchase, or through joint venture with landowners. The agency then provides trunk water and sewer infrastructure, and sells the resulting parcels to developers for subdividing and building on. These developers include nonprofit makers that build starter, expandable units for moderate-income households.

These two methods of low/moderate-income land development represent alternatives on a continuum. The first method—streamlining development standards and processes in El Salvador—relies fully on the private sector. The second method—the macro-blocks of MetroVivienda—uses the public sector to perform the key function of converting agricultural to urban land, but delegates the remainder of the process to private developers.

Other approaches exist along this continuum. Many involve a greater and more inappropriate role for government. The most common is for government to assemble land and then build and sell units directly to households. This alternative leads local governments to bank land. Sometimes, governments retain considerable parcels of developable land on the urban fringe, formerly used for parastatal agricultural enterprises or other outdated government activities such as agricultural land reform.[27]

Alternatively, local governments must buy land to feed the social housing development process.[28]

Governments, however, usually fail to manage such land reserves well and lack the market acumen and, often, the financial resources for their development. As they typically transfer land to developers at far below its market value, these agencies end up de-capitalizing their land development enterprise. These agencies also tend to deliver far less than the value of the land subsidy to households. Land subsidies typically go first to the developer (a supply agent)—who largely controls their use. Without careful controls and appropriate incentives in place, developers (and other supply agents, including financial institutions and landowners) will absorb a greater share of the subsidy amount than if the subvention went in the form of a voucher (an up-front grant or "direct demand subsidy") to households that these families could use to shop among eligible housing units.

In addition, public agencies frequently have their land invaded, and face an unenviable set of options. The agency can evict squatters at great political cost, regularize the resulting settlement or relocate households voluntarily to a different settlement at great economic cost, or leave the squatting households on the land for the subsequent government to deal with.

In summary, massive low/moderate-income land development is the key to halting slum formation. In turn, avoiding the formation of new slums—a preventative and relatively low-cost enterprise—is, strategically, highly preferable to improving existing shanty towns—a curative, high-cost and reactive approach.

Market failure, however, typically pervades low/moderate-income land development in low- and middle-income countries. Hence, government can usefully play an important role in this process. However, this role must be carefully crafted. A safe way to begin is to gear subdivision standards to the financial possibilities of the low/moderate-income majority and to streamline the development process.

In most countries, however, many other barriers obstruct substantial formal sector land development for low/moderate-income groups. Government involvement may then be necessary to conduct the first step in the urban land development process—the conversion of agricultural land to urban use through the assembly of large parcels, permitting and the provision of trunk infrastructure lines, followed by sale to private sector developers. As government involvement goes further down the residential development process, however, it carries increasing risks of inefficiency, waste and corruption.

# IV. Finance of Slum Upgrading

Although avoiding slum formation is the best overall strategy, existing urban slums are not about to disappear. New slums are also certain to form in most low- and middle-income countries. Hence, virtually all low- and middle-income countries require a financial framework to make slum upgrading—which is a relatively high-cost enterprise—bearable.

"Slum upgrading" can mean many things, with radically different financial consequences…. The most essential investments that characterize slum upgrading are those for water, sanitation, drainage, roads and land regularization. In addition, a host of other interventions are possible. The most frequent add-ons are community infrastructure such as public squares, health clinics, day care and some job or income-related intervention—typically either training or micro-enterprise loans. There are, however, many other possibilities that get added to what has become known as integrated slum upgrading programs.[29]

Hence, the cost per family of slum upgrading programs can escalate dramatically to unsustainable amounts, as more elements get added to the mix. Hence, from a financial perspective, the first step in sustainable slum upgrading is to set the cost per unit (or per family).

## a. Set the cost per unit

Three methods have some currency for setting a figure for cost per unit. The first, and most theoretically correct, is cost-benefit analysis. The second—cost-efficiency analysis—and the third—spreading available resources over need–are less correct in theory but more widely used in practice.

Both the cost-efficiency and the cost-benefit methods start with an analysis of expenditures. The initial outlays for a slum upgrading project are relatively easy to determine. Engineering studies quantify the investments necessary in a particular case or program. Based on a pilot design, these studies then determine the cost of basic services, taking into account regional variations and topographic and soil conditions. These costs account for the initial capital investment. The costs of the social components and operation and maintenance must be added to the engineering studies. These are less straightforward to calculate. When outlays occur in the future, they must be discounted to calculate their present value, based on a series of assumptions (regarding discount rate, timing of costs incurred, etc.) The end result is a total figure for the cost of the project and—taking into account the number of households—the cost per unit.

With the cost per unit established, three methods are then used to quantify the benefits of slum upgrading programs for cost-benefit analysis: property appreciation, willingness to pay, and hedonic price studies. The property appreciation method[30] determines the market value of the property after intervention, subtracts that from the market value before intervention, and the difference is the benefit generated by the project....

Willingness-to-pay studies[31] estimate the amounts that beneficiaries of the project would pay for the benefits received over time and discounts them to arrive at a total benefit figure. Hedonic price studies[32] estimate the benefit that each component of the project will produce, and adds them together.

With the benefit calculated, the analyst then compares the benefit based on one or more of these methods to the cost of the project, to calculate its benefit-to-cost ratio. In general, the project is worthwhile and a good use of funds to the extent that the benefit-to-cost ratio exceeds that of other competing projects.

In practice, cost-benefit analysis can become quite technical, and the results are highly sensitive to modest changes in assumptions. As a result, two other methods are used more frequently than cost-benefit analysis to arrive at a cost per unit. The first is cost-efficiency of the most essential investments. In most cases, the stakeholders of a slum upgrading program can agree on the investments that are the minimum and most essential for slum upgrading. Typically, these minimum investments include water, sanitation and—if they involve social services—child care facilities. Cost-efficiency analysis considers various alternatives for providing these services and determines the least-cost method. Then, a maximum amount per family is set.

The second hands-on method, spreading available resources over need, takes into account the amount that government can afford to spend and the number of unserved households. Typically, national governments start by setting a goal for producing housing solutions for both new units and improved units based on some indicator of need. New household formation plus replacement minus formal sector/private sector production is a logistical choice. Then, governments figure out how much they can spend on housing, including slum upgrading. Worldwide, central governments typically spend 2–4 percent of their budget on housing. Then, the analysis spreads the available budget over the number of required housing solutions in order to get an overall

sense of the average amount of subsidy that each family can receive. Mexico has performed a sophisticated analysis of this type to develop its official housing strategy.[33]

In practice, many governments use a combination of these three methods—cost-benefit, cost-efficiency and spreading the available budget over need—to arrive at the amount they are willing to spend per unit. There is much to be said for taking into account various approaches, either for a national program or for a particular project.

Typically, the great bulk of expenditures on slum upgrading constitute a subsidy, as government recoups little or nothing from slum residents. The actual number for the cost per unit (or subsidy per unit, as the two are frequently quite similar) varies substantially between middle-income countries and low-income countries, although it falls within predictable ranges within these country income categories. In Latin America and the Caribbean, the per unit subsidy is typically in the range of US$3,500–8,000 per unit for middle-income countries such as Brazil, Mexico, Venezuela and Chile, and US$1,000–3,500 per unit for lower-income countries such as Nicaragua, Guatemala and Honduras. These are the amounts found in project documents of multilateral donors such as the World Bank and the Inter-American Development Bank in their housing and slum upgrading programs for these countries.

b. Drivers of the cost of slum upgrading at the project level

With a cost per unit set, the next step is to select among possible projects for those that meet this cost criterion or that have priority because of unusually high benefits. Here, various characteristics of the particular slum become crucial. These include the share of households necessary to relocate, the selection of the sanitation solution and—once the area has been upgraded—the cost of garbage collection.

**Share of households to relocate.** Relocation is often a thorny issue in slum upgrading projects, for both political and cost reasons. Politically, forcing a substantial share of households out of their homes to other locations will kill a project. Financially, the relocation of more than 10 percent of households will drive costs higher than can be justified, particularly if multilateral donors fund the project.[34]

**Selection of sanitation solution.** The cost of sanitation varies probably more than any other single item in slum upgrading. A pit latrine, which is essentially a hole in the ground, is inexpensive. A septic tank is intermediary in price. Finally, waterborne sewerage can be expensive and, if it involves treatment, very expensive. The choice depends on population density, soil and water table conditions, and other factors. In the past, slum upgrading, and even housing projects, often had no sanitation solution. In effect, such projects would dump water into the area (through provision of piped water to houses or standpipes), but have no means for dealing with the resulting wastewater, causing all sorts of environmental and health problems. This approach is no longer acceptable.

**Cost of garbage collection.** The ongoing cost that looms largest is garbage collection, which cost varies between sites because of access problems, levels of community participation, levels of safety and other factors.

Considering all the above factors, prioritizing areas by cost is one way to sequence a slum upgrading program. For example, Chile started with upgrading the slums requiring the lowest cost per family, and has progressively worked through to the highest cost areas.

There are a number of other key factors that bear on cost that are common to all sites.

**Use of one contractor for all construction work.** Inevitably, pressure comes from the sectoral agency to build "their" particular infrastructure within the slum upgrading project. For example, the water company will want to extend water and sewer lines. However, the physical work for slum upgrading requires close coordination. Hence, contracting one firm to build all infrastructure offers compelling advantages.

**Involve from the start the agency designated to maintain the upgraded area.** Building the infrastructure, of course, is not enough. An agency must also take over the finished work in order to operate and maintain it. This is often difficult. The basic standards necessary to keep construction costs down often result in higher expenses for operation and maintenance for the agency that takes over. Hence, agencies and governments often resist assuming responsibility for infrastructure in upgraded slums. In Rio de Janeiro, the municipal government finally had to hire independent firms to take over the maintenance of infrastructure in its upgraded areas because the municipal departments and infrastructure companies refused. Hence, the agency designated to maintain the infrastructure is best involved from the start.

c. Recovering slum upgrading costs

Various methods exist for recouping the costs of slum upgrading, including charging for land title regularization or purchase, basic services and property taxes. However, tension exists between these charges and the objectives of slum upgrading. Essentially, households operate in the informal sector in order to avoid such costs. Families connect to water and electricity lines clandestinely, and get these services at low quality but for free. They sell and buy rights to property informally so as to avoid paying the transfer taxes, registry fees and other charges associated with formal ownership, which often represent 5–15 percent of the sale price.

Hence, charging the full amount tends to drive households back into the informal sector. In other words, they disconnect their meters, and tap into water and electricity lines clandestinely. For this and social redress reasons, infrastructure service companies and others typically charge these families lower amounts. These lower charges often take the form of lifeline rates for water and electricity for consumption below a certain level. Frequently, upgraded slum areas are exempt from property taxation for a time. In any case, property is taxed effectively at such a low level in most low- and middle-income countries that such charges recoup little in most cases.

This tension is particularly critical when basic services are concessioned and operated by a private company. Typically, slum upgrading occurs in the poorest areas that are the least attractive for these companies. In such circumstances, government usually pays for the entire capital cost and negotiates the terms of transfer of services in these areas to the private companies. In some cases—especially for water provision—governments provide ongoing subsidies to the private companies to serve upgraded areas. Another tactic is to cross-subsidize the cost of providing services to low-income consumers with that of business and higher-income consumers, although this causes as many problems as it solves.

When land has been invaded and tenancy is regularized as part of slum upgrading, governments often charge households for purchase of the land. These amounts are typically well below the market cost, but still significant, and represent substantial cash inflows to the public agency involved if the land was publicly owned prior to invasion. If the land is privately owned, law often requires government to reimburse the private owner for the land.

d. Joining slum upgrading with housing microfinance

Slum upgrading projects typically improve basic services and the physical environment around the family's house, and regularize tenancy. Highly positive externalities justify subvention of basic infrastructure. Investment in sanitation, for example, improves not only the lives, health and security of the slum residents, but also that of the city at large. However, slum upgrading programs often ignore the house itself. Hence, slum upgrading programs typically leave families in an improved environment, but living in an unreconstructed hovel.

Housing microfinance (HMF) has the potential to fund in an affordable way the costs of building a home on a serviced lot that a low/moderate-income family owns.[35] The term "microfinance of housing" refers to small loans typically for self-help home improvement and expansion, but also for new construction of basic core units.[36] Best practice involves lending at unsubsidized interest rates and for short terms, relative to traditional mortgage finance. Microfinance holds great promise for housing the low/moderate-income majority in low- and middle-income countries for three central reasons. First, it fits well with the incremental building process used by the low/moderate-income majority. Second, it resolves many of the difficulties that greatly limit the scope of traditional mortgage finance. Third, it taps into an existing network of microfinance institutions, as well as home lenders. For these reasons, HMF is spreading rapidly, largely through networks of microfinance institutions rather than traditional mortgage lenders.

HMF can be joined with slum upgrading programs (and sites and services projects).[37] Essentially, the division of labor is that the slum upgrading program subsidizes basic infrastructure and land tenancy, while households must borrow if they want to improve their individual dwellings.

There are essentially two variations on the HMF theme,[38] namely, "soft" credit and "hard" credit.[39] In one version of the soft credit approach, a community association manages a rotating fund that funds small loans. Slum households borrow these credits for improvement and expansion, and make fixed payments over one to three years, geared to their ability to pay. To the extent that they repay and that loan terms approximate market rates, the rotating fund remains capitalized to lend to other members of the community. Hence, peer and community pressure for repayment is fierce. The Fundación de la Vivienda Popular has spread this soft credit method throughout urban Venezuela.

The "soft" method has the advantage of reinforcing community solidarity and covering a large share of a slum's population, as it is reserved for a targeted geographic area. As terms typically fall short of market, however, the full present value of the principal usually fails to return to the rotating fund, which gradually de-capitalizes (although some such rotating funds recover their full costs). Thus, the soft approach is a non-banking one, and

has restricted scope, although it is, of course, more sustainable than outright subvention. Most seriously, however, the soft credit approach tends to undermine the development of hard credit for HMF, as it once did in micro-enterprise finance[40] and still does in other sectors.

The other method is "hard" credit. A microfinance institution, typically, offers HMF loans to the public at large, and some of these borrowers live in slums. Restricting availability to a particular slum and, thus, reducing the geographic diversification of the portfolio would substantially raise the risks of HMF lending. The microfinance institution is professionally managed and aims at full recovery of operating costs plus capital. The PRODEL program in Nicaragua, supported by Swedish Assistance (SIDA), uses this method as part of an integrated approach to improving poor neighborhoods in Nicaragua. More broadly, housing microfinance is rapidly becoming a major product and profit center of microfinance institutions. As microfinance institutions demand financial sustainability, only hard credit can engage microfinance networks now in place throughout Latin America, Asia and Africa.

The pros and cons of the hard credit approach to joining HMF with slum upgrading are the opposite of the soft credit approach. Because of its financial sustainability (although some hard credit microfinance institutions fail to recover their full costs), the hard credit approach appeals to most donors, to the microfinance institution industry and to these authors. The minus is that the hard approach can cover only a portion of slum residents, since a substantial fraction usually fails to qualify for a loan. However, some slum dwellers neither want nor should receive home micro-loans. Regardless, the improvement of a portion of an upgraded slum's houses can generate a virtuous circle of investment that lifts the community as a whole.

## V. Conclusion

In conclusion, the best way to deal with urban slums is to decrease or to stop their formation. Numbers of countries and cities have succeeded in this goal, including Chile and Costa Rica. They accomplish this task by increasing formal sector production of low-cost housing solutions to close to the rate of new household formation. Massive low/moderate-income land development holds the key to increasing formal sector production in many countries.

As market failure typically pervades the conversion of agricultural to urban land, governments usefully play a role in low/moderate-income land development. First and foremost, governments can reduce standards and streamline the development process in order to stimulate a private low/moderate-income land development industry. In most countries, however, just reducing standards and streamlining the development process will prove insufficient and government must also assist in the first step of the land development process—conversion of agricultural land to urban land.

Once new slum formation starts declining, governments appropriately focus on upgrading existing slums. The first step here consists of setting a maximum cost per unit through a mix of cost-benefit analysis, cost-efficiency analysis and spreading available resources over need. With the cost per unit set, the keys to reducing project expenditures include:

- reducing the share of households necessary to relocate,
- selecting the least-cost sanitation solution,
- accessibility of the area (physical and safety) for garbage pick-up,
- use of one contractor for all upgrading work, and
- involving the relevant infrastructure agencies from the start in order to assume maintenance and operation of their type of infrastructure.

While government usually subsidizes the great bulk of slum upgrading costs, some opportunities for cost-recovery arise, mainly from charging for land title or through the sale of land.

Housing microfinance can join with slum upgrading to fund the improvement, expansion and construction of a basic unit. Despite some advantages of soft credit, the hard credit approach to HMF promises financial sustainability and, thus, can leverage the institutional capacity of the microfinance industry.

This strategic approach to slum upgrading differs from that of many governments. Rather than deal with the cause—the mismatch between low-cost entry-level housing solutions and new household formation—governments of some countries, states, and cities focus mainly on the symptom—by focusing on upgrading existing slums. This reactive approach condemns government and local people to endure the tremendous costs of new urban slum formation far into the future. Instead, governments best promote low/moderate-income land development in the poorest countries and low-cost entry-level housing solutions in moderate-income countries (the flow) more than slum upgrading (the stock). This strategy holds particular importance for South Asia and Africa, where the wave of urbanization is still cresting and the costs of preventing new slum formation are the greatest.

## Questions

1. What is driving the rapid growth of urban and peri–urban (city edge) slums around the world?

2. What have been the most successful ways to reduce slums and improve housing in Latin America? How will these efforts help to meet the UN Millennium Development Goals?

## Notes

1. UNCHS (1996), *An Urbanizing World—Global Report on Human Settlements,* Oxford University Press, Oxford.

2. Specifically, the UN Cities without Slums Millennium Development Target 11 is: "By 2020, to have achieved a significant improvement in the lives of at least 100 million slum dwellers."

3. For descriptions of the Chilean and Costa Rican cases, see Ferguson, Bruce (1996), "The design of direct demand subsidy programmes for housing in Latin America," in *Review of Urban and Regional Development Studies,* United Nations Centre for Urban and Regional Development, Tokyo.

4. Ferguson, Bruce (1999), "Microfinance of housing: a key to housing the low- or moderate-income majority," *Environment and Urbanization.* Vol 11, No. 1, pages 185–201.

5. Secretaria de Desarrollo Social (2001), *Programa Sectorial de Vivienda 2001–2006; Casa y Hogar para Cada Quien: Una Tarea Contigo,* México City.

6. See reference 1; also, for a depiction of the gradual construction process, see Navarrete, J. (1990), "The progressive development of houses in a sites and services project," unpublished Masters thesis, McGill University, Montreal.

7. While De Soto documents the benefits of full legal title for the middle class, he does not take into account that, for low/moderate-income households, costs often exceed benefits—De Soto, Hernando (2000), *The Mystery of Capital,* Basic Books, New York.

8. Burns, L. and L. Grebler (1977), *The Housing of Nations: Analysis and Policies in a Comparative Framework,* Macmillan, London.

9. Called "second-best solutions" by Burns and Grebler (1977), see reference 8.

10. Ward, P. (editor) (1982), *Self-help Housing—A Critique,* Mansell Publishing Ltd, London.

11. Hardoy, J. E. and D. Satterthwaite (1989), *Squatter Citizen: Life in the Urban Third World,* Earthscan Publications, London.

12. This spill-over motivated New York City and other industrial cities in the US and Western Europe to engage in large-scale building of tenement apartments to shelter the poor of the late nineteenth and early twentieth centuries. Housing and city planning as fields of government intervention in currently developed countries date back to this era.

13. "Conventional standards" here means those specified by municipal and other governments for the lowest-cost residential

development. It is possible to make significant and worthwhile improvements to slums (putting in pit latrines, paving the main road, etc.) at much lower cost. However, the resulting settlements will be of much lower quality. The lower quality environments means that formal-sector organizations (e.g., infrastructure and urban service agencies, home finance institutions) are much less likely to serve these areas, and that the area's residents continue to bear many of the costs noted above.

14. Slum upgrading does not always cost far more than new development. Factors that reduce the cost of slum upgrading in some circumstances include: the settlement being organized in such a way as to allow a rational street layout, well-defined and appropriately sized property boundaries, and common spaces; a location that is reasonably close to existing infrastructure lines, and land with suitable topography and soil conditions; and an active and cooperative neighborhood association that participates in the slum upgrading process and continues to assist in subsequent activities, such as organizing garbage collection and helping to maintain infrastructure. In such cases, slum upgrading costs can be comparable to those of similar improvements (basic infrastructure and tenure) to new development. However, such cases are a small minority.

15. Alcaldia Mayor de Bogota (2002), "Ciudadela el recreo—memoria del modelo de gestion MetroVivienda," MetroVivienda Empresa Industrial y Comercial del Distrito Capital, Bogotá; also, see Rocha, R., L Garcia and N. Rueda (2003), "Estimacion del efecto de MetroVivienda sobre el bienestar de la poblacion de Bogotá," PowerPoint presentation, Universidad Los Andes, Bogotá; also, the cost of paving informal settlements is 1.3 times that in formal settlements, sewers 3.2 times the cost, and storm sewers 2.8 times the cost. In addition to these added infrastructure costs, government must reorder settlements by straightening roads, leaving space for communal facilities and—as a result—relocating a portion of households.

16. Payne, G. K. (editor) (1984), *Low-income Housing in the Developing World: The Role of Sites and Services and Settlement Upgrading,* Wiley, New York.

17. For a comprehensive analysis of US *colonias* and a comparison with those of Mexico, see Ward, P. (1999), *Colonias and Public Policy in Texas and Mexico; Urbanization by Stealth,* University of Texas Press, Austin, Texas. For an examination of the lessons of *colonia* development for housing programs, see Ferguson, Bruce and Michael Marez (2003), "Expand entry-level housing; a key lesson from developing countries for the US," in Daphnis, Franck and Bruce Ferguson (editors) (forthcoming 2003), *Housing Microfinance; A Guide to Practice,* Kumarian Press, Connecticut.

18. A family with 1.5 employed members earning the minimum wage can afford to buy a house for US$40,000. However, housing that costs less than US$65,000 is generally unavailable. As a result, informal subdivisions—called *colonias*—have sprung up in semirural areas (typically outside city limits in county areas) along the US border states with Mexico. Using a "contract for deed" that allows quick repossession in case of nonpayment, developers—often the original farmers of these tracts of land—subdivide them and sell lots without water, paved streets or sanitation to buyers hungry to own their own homes. The purchasers then put a trailer or some makeshift unit on the lot, and start improving and expanding it. *Colonias* now house over half a million people along the US border with Mexico, and are increasing steadily in number and population. As in low- and middle-income countries, the extension of basic infrastructure to *colonias* costs much more than for new formal sector development. See reference 17, Ward (1999) for a rich description; also see reference 17, Ferguson and Marez (2003) for a cost analysis.

19. The cost of providing adequate sanitation alone to unserved Texas *colonias* has been calculated at over US$600 million. See reference 17, Ferguson and Marez (2003).

20. Ferguson, Bruce (1996), "The environmental impacts and public costs of unguided informal settlement; the case of Montego Bay," *Environment and Urbanization* Vol. 8, No. 2, pages 171–193.

21. McAuslan, P. (1985), *Urban Land and Shelter for the Poor,* Earthscan, London.

22. Ferguson and Hoffman quantify the impact of land development regulation on social housing production costs in Indonesia, concluding that they account for one-third of the sales price. See also Ferguson, Bruce and Michael L. Hoffman (1993), "Land markets and the effect of regulation on formal sector residential development in urban Indonesia," in *Review of Urban and Regional Development Studies,* Tokyo, January.

23. For examples of public–private partnerships in land in other countries, see Payne, G. (editor) (1999), *Making Common Ground: Public–Private Partnerships in Land for Housing,* IT Publications, London.

24. Souza, M. T. (2000), "Nota sectoral: lotificaciones de desarrollo progresivo en El Salvador," unpublished paper, Inter-American Development Bank, Washington, DC.

25. Jones, G. A. (1998), "Privatizing the commons: reforming the ejido and urban development in Mexico," *International Journal of Urban and Regional Research* No. 22, pages 76–93, March.

26. In Indonesia, these monopolies come in the form of "location permits," which government grants to developers for parcels in traditional use owned by peasants on the urban fringe. Essentially, these location permits give the recipient builder the exclusive right to develop this parcel for a period of time. As a result, the builder is the only viable purchaser of land owned by peasants, greatly reducing the price (and provoking great social unrest). See reference 22, Ferguson and Hoffman (1993) for details.

27. For example, abandoned sugar cane plantations now owned by the central government sugar agency surround the capitals of the Dominican Republic and Guyana, while the national agrarian reform agency owns large amounts of developable land around medium-sized Venezuelan cities, see Ferguson, B. (1996), *Housing Sector Diagnostic—Venezuela,* prepared for the Inter-American Development Bank, Abt Associates, Bethesda, MD, USA.

28. Most Mexican states, for example, acquire land reserves (either from other government agencies or through purchase) and transfer these parcels at low prices to developers, who then use the programs of central government housing finance agencies (INFONAVIT, SHF, FOVISSSTE) to finance their build-out and sell the resulting units to moderate-income households, see reference 5.

29. Brakarz, Jose with Margarita Greene and Eduardo Rojas (2002), "Ciudades para todos; la experiencia reciente en programas de mejoramiento de barrios," Inter-American Development Bank, Washington, DC.

30. The property appreciation method is fairly straightforward, and is thus often used by multilateral banks such as the IDB and the World Bank. If similar upgrading efforts have occurred nearby, the analyst uses the figures for these to estimate the benefit for the project that is proposed. In addition to calculating the appreciation of the property that has received the investment, it is necessary also to calculate the appreciation of property in the immediate surrounding area—say 100–200 meters. This is often substantial, and as much as the increase in value to the property that receives the intervention. Adding both together gives the total benefit generated per unit.

31. Typically, these estimates of willingness to pay are done through household surveys of potential beneficiaries.

32. To get the necessary data, the analyst compares similar properties with this particular attribute to those without it.

33. As contained in Secretaria de Desarrollo Social (2001), see reference 5. This strategy started with an indicator of need announced by President Fox, while still a presidential candidate—the production of 750,000 units per year by both the public and private sectors. This figure roughly approximates the annual rate of new household formation plus replacement of deteriorated housing.

34. Multilaterals have stringent rules for relocation of households. Generally, these regulations require replacing the household's current solution with one that is better (if in the same neighborhood) or a new house (if in a different neighborhood).

35. See reference 17, Daphnis and Ferguson (forthcoming 2003); also Serageldin, Mona and John Driscoll et al. (2000), "Housing microfinance initiatives, regional summary: Asia, Latin American and sub-Saharan Africa with selected case studies," Centre for Urban Development Studies, Harvard University Graduate School of Design, draft paper for USAID Best Practices; and Ferguson, Bruce (2000), "Mainstreaming microfinance of housing," in *Housing Finance International,* Journal of the Union of International Housing Finance, September.

36. Housing microfinance lies at the intersection of micro-enterprise finance and mortgage finance. It shares characteristics with both, but also demonstrates some important differences. For example, the amount (US$300–5,000) and the length (2–8 years) of housing microfinance loans are typically much less than for mortgage finance, but greater than for micro-enterprise credits. As micro-enterprise finance, many housing microfinance programs work with paralegal title and income from self-employment—the typical security that low/moderate-income households can offer. In contrast, mortgage finance typically requires a mortgage lien and formal sector employment.

37. The World Bank is studying this approach in Vietnam and India. The Inter-American Development Bank is studying it in the Dominican Republic.

38. Mitlin, Diana (1997), "Reaching low-income groups with housing finance," IIED Working Paper, London.

39. A review of case studies of housing microfinance, such as those noted in Mitlin (1997) (see reference 38) and those profiled in Serageldin, Driscoll et al (2000) (see reference 35), shows the dichotomy between hard credit and soft credit approaches to housing microfinance. There are currently many of both.

40. Robinson, Marguerite (2001), *The Microfinance Revolution,* the World Bank and the Open Society Institute, Washington, DC.

*Source:* A Financial Framework for Reducing Slums: Lessons From Experience in Latin America. Bruce Ferguson and Jesus Navarrete.

# CHAPTER 28

## Tropic of Answer

*Charles Munn, a Pioneer of South American Ecotourism, Answers Readers' Questions*

Charles Munn

"Ecotourism" has become a common term for leisure travel and tourism that is sensitive to learning about and preserving the natural environment. Some see ecotourism as a sham that hides the negative environmental effects of world tourism; others see it as a way to make one of the world's largest industries more sensitive to environmental needs. In the following interview, one of the pioneers of ecotourism in the Americas tries to answer some of the difficult remaining questions.

*Ecotourism is promoted as a sustainable alternative to industrial development; however, ecotourism does not generate the same immediate financial returns as industrial development. How can activists formulate their argument when aiming to save pristine areas from mining through promoting ecotourism?—Jacqueline Obando, Pretoria, South Africa*

Well, yes, a gold mine, diamond mine, or oil well is going to be hard to compete within terms of gross revenues. But most places in the world don't have large gold deposits or oil fields, so it normally is not a problem we have to face. In general, we avoid areas where there is large potential for industrial development or mining, as we know we cannot compete there in terms of job creation and political power. If some amazing, unique biological feature lies in an area of major gold mining or oil production, we would still consider ecotourism-investment there. In such a situation, however, we would go into it knowing that at best we might be able to create just enough jobs and economic activity to prevent the mining or oil production from destroying the biological wonders.

*How do you facilitate so that all in a community benefit from an ecotourism venture? Often men, the most vocal, and those taking leadership roles in a*

*community benefit the most.—Jacqueline Obando, Pretoria, South Africa*

We ensure that each family in the community is an equal shareholder in the lodge and that all qualified community members who complete job training then participate equally in work rotations at their own lodge. Some of the community members show more ability than others at harder, higher-paying jobs in their lodge, such as chef or forest guide, and they do receive a higher salary for this harder, more skilled work. But, in general, between the even shares owned by each family member and the meritocracy and universal right to work, the benefits are quite widely distributed.

*I have grave moral reservations about traveling to "Third World" countries; that sort of tourism seems to encourage, if not racism explicitly, at least a certain sense that some races or nations do well to be servants of other races or nations. How do you defend ecotourism against such charges?—Mark Stephen Caponigro, New York, NY*

If you were to ask local Amerindians such as the Quichua of Napo Wildlife Center about their views of showing foreigners around their rainforest lands, they

197

would tell you that they are proud to show off their homelands and make a living doing it. And they would also say that the alternatives (cutting the forest to sell the trees or to grow subsistence crops, or working wage labor for the polluting oil companies) are far less appealing and offer them much less chance to protect their culture. While we agree that the risk does exist of having racism creep into ecotourism, we are sure that it is a much more manageable risk than those faced by indigenous people who feel forced into either cutting the forest or working for callous oil companies.

*Do you ever see a "budget" ecolodge in the future— a place where the average family of four can afford to make a trip every year?—Jon Current, Hillsboro, OR*

A family of four would find the airfare to be one of the most expensive items—if you could go to Peru in its low-travel months (November, February, March, and April) or to Costa Rica in its low-travel months (September, October, and November), you could probably get much better prices on airfare and have enough money left over to visit a good ecolodge. Within the Tropical Nature system, for instance, Sandoval Lake Lodge, in Peru, would be affordable for you if you could find a good deal on off-peak air travel. And we offer discounts and deals for families, which also helps make our lodges affordable.

*How can a newcomer get involved in ecotourism?— James Jedibudiah, Madison, WI*

Read all about it, and if possible, volunteer at some sites where you feel comfortable learning the language. If you lack the financial ability to volunteer, try studying for and applying to guiding or ranger positions in the U.S. to build up some savings so you can then consider making the leap to other countries. If you want to be guiding in the field, you can study the fauna and flora of distant lands before you ever even reach them. In your case, not only could you benefit from studying guide books and nature handbooks in good science libraries (like the University of Wisconsin-Madison), but you also could benefit from studying the immense (off-display) biological collections and scientific libraries at leading natural-history museums (notably the Field Museum in Chicago, which is not too far from you).

*I'm working in a town with no love for a well-educated environmentalist, and I'm looking for job opportunities elsewhere. Can I be of assistance?— Claude Chandler, Chesterton, IN*

Perhaps, but the first question always is, Do you speak Spanish or Portuguese, and if not, what are your skills and job experience?

*What is your opinion of certification systems for ecotourism? Are your lodges certified by any of the existing standards like Green Globe 21?—Michelle Knab, Santa Barbara, CA*

I think that the certification idea is a good one, but I am not familiar enough with the different options. We will look into Green Globe 21 and see how it works. Some of the certification efforts we have examined in the past did not appear to verify at the ground level which lodges were truly green versus brown covered with green marketing facade.

*Can eco-travel be accessible to the mildly disabled? I think of people like myself—arthritic, ambulatory, but often slow and a bit clumsy. I'm a walker but have no interest in carrying all my own food and camping equipment in a backpack.—Rebecca Phillips, Marietta, OH*

At Sandoval Lake Lodge in Peru and at Santa Tereza Lodge in the Pantanal of Brazil, we have made it easy for people with physical limitations to enjoy nature to the fullest. Neither requires much more than a five-minute walk (or even a 30-second walk or wheelchair ride in the case of Santa Tereza), and the outings at both lodges are by boat or car, so almost no self-propelled locomotion is required.

*I operate a large nonprofit recycling organization in Colorado. When I travel, I see the world flooded with trash, especially plastics, even at "eco" locations. Is anyone working to help the ecotourism industry gets its act together so that there will never be another "ecolodge" without recycling?—Eric Lombardi, Boulder, CO*

The question of recycling at ecolodges is an interesting and knotty one. Help us analyze this, please. Environmental Defense told us years ago that if we were going to have to consume significant amounts of fossil fuels to transport plastics or from our remote lodges to urban recycling sites or dumps, that it might be more justified to simply bury these items properly on site so as to prevent adding insult to injury. We do separate and recycle when feasible, but I don't think that makes sense all the time for lodges that are too distant from the closest recycling location.

*I noticed you said your favorite meal is ceviche. If you were able to institute an environmental reform where everyone was to become a vegan, would you include yourself and be able to give up ceviche?—Gill Brociner, New York, NY*

I agree that ceviche is a problem, and I realize that it contradicts my call to eat vegan. But, yes, if good vegan fare were easily available, I could give up ceviche.

*What suggestions do you have for promoting a vegan or vegetarian diet?—Marylou Noble, Portland, OR*

The main problem for me has always been lack of interesting spicing and preparation options. A chef from Lima who worked for our system amazed me with very tasty dishes made from texturized soy protein—dishes that were quite delicious and interesting. It would seem to me that with proper spicing and preparation, vegan fare can rise to the level of the best carnivorous fare.

*What are your thoughts on keeping macaws as pets?—Mark Stephen Caponigro, New York, NY*

I would not do it, but I know many people who do. I used to think keeping macaws was uniformly, universally bad. But now that I have seen how well many people treat their pet macaws, I have come to accept the practice on a case-by-case basis. The key is quality of life—many, but not all, people take excellent care of their macaws. Nevertheless, I do not recommend that people get macaws as pets (too loud, too neurotic, too complicated). I will never own one myself.

*If you are worried about your carbon lifestyle of jetting to South America and back, why not offset your carbon-producing flights with companies like Carbonfund.org, the Solar Electric Light Fund, NativeEnergy, TerraPass, or Sustainable Travel International?—Kim Fortin, Minneapolis, MN*

Thanks for these useful suggestions, which I had not heard of before.

*My husband and I recently returned from a trip to Peru and Ecuador. I was shocked to see the massive prevalence of Australian eucalyptus. What is your opinion of the situation in Peru?—Katherine Austin, Sebastopol, CA*

Although not an expert on the issue of carbon sinks and eucalyptus, I feel that it is quite unfortunate that the amazingly diverse high-elevation forests of Peru and Ecuador have given way to this biologically sterile Australian monoculture. Our projects in the cloud forests of Manu (Cock-of-the-Rock Lodge) are protecting original cloud forest from conversion to eucalyptus.

*I will be visiting Peru for two weeks this July. Hotel plans are already arranged, but I'd love to visit some of the lodges featured on your Web site. Are there any day trips available? Can you suggest any other great trips and sights to see in Peru?—Morgan Poncelet, Fremont, CA*

You may have arranged hotels through our conservation system already and not even know it! Our conservation system has Web portals and Web pages that offer hotels in Peru. Anyway, yes, there are a number of good options for day trips, please email us and we can talk to you about options, some just outside of Lima and others outside of Cusco.

*I work in southwestern China's Yunnan province. One challenge faced by ecotourism in this area is effectively accommodating local culture and preferences; for example, many of the "best" destinations are sacred to local people. Has Tropical Nature faced issues of local cultural demands or protection of sacred lands in South America?—E. Pay, Kunming, China*

We would not take tourists to any location that could not be visited while respecting the beliefs and customs of local cultures. So far this has not been an issue, but if the issue were to arise, we would try to design trips or outings in conjunction with leaders from the local cultures such that their culture is respected.

*How do you really, truly, keep whole the soul of a place and a people who are connecting with tourists daily? No matter best intentions, people get burned out answering questions about their heritage or lifestyle, or they become envious of the outsiders' stuff—their binoculars, their Ray-Bans, whatever. How has Tropical Nature dealt with the negative aspects of exploitation, even though that exploitation is welcomed by the people and needed for conservation efforts? This haunts me, as a sustainable-tourism expert.—Anne Markward, Durango, CO*

An excellent question that also haunts us. It is hard to strike the balance, but we feel that indigenous people who have significant, reliable income from protecting and showcasing tropical biodiversity are in a much better position to design systems to prevent burnout and loss of their culture than are those who are desperately scratching out an existence by deforesting poor tropical soils and frantically hunting all the game animals to sell the meat illegally to restaurants and meat markets in tropical towns.

Over 20 years of working with traditional peoples in the Peruvian Amazon, we have found that the increased pride in being forest peoples and knowing a lot about the biodiversity and making good money from protecting that biodiversity leads Indians to push back against the loss of their language and culture. Rotation of workers and continual training in total quality and in new aspects of biodiversity service industries can keep people excited about their work rather than burned out. The great thing about the tropical rainforest is that it is so diverse that there always are new biodiversity frontiers to be explored, protected, and showcased.

We are heartened by the fact that some of the jungle executives in our system are traditional Amerindians who now have the wherewithal to promote their own culture much more than they did when they were poorly

paid laborers for illegal mahogany loggers. They know we respect and value their culture and traditional knowledge, and rather than burn out, they are learning more Western techniques while teaching us more of their traditional jungle secrets. Typically, their jungle knowledge is more interesting and more useful commercially for ecotourism development than are our Western techniques, which already are both well-known and much easier to duplicate.

## Questions

1. What distinguishes ecotourism from other forms of travel?

2. Can ecotourism provide a good experience for travelers and still maintain a quality environment? What are the challenges?

*Source:* Tropic of Answer: Charles Munn, a Pioneer of South American Ecotourism, Answers Readers' Questions. Charles Munn. *Grist Magazine.* April 14, 2006. Reprinted by permission of Grist.

# CHAPTER 29

## Strangers in the Forest

Lawrence Osborne

Along with ecotourism there is growing interest in cultural tourism, or "ethno-tourism," that seeks to encounter people of other cultures, preferably as non-Westernized or as nonmodern as possible. This is also accompanied by "adventure tourism" that treks to remote and difficult locations. Here, an expedition seeks to make contact with an isolated people in New Guinea—for tourist purposes.

The jungle canopy below us was suddenly ruptured by a rectangular clearing not much longer than a suburban lawn. This was the airstrip for Wanggemalo, a tiny village in the Indonesian province of Papua, which is the western half of New Guinea. The six-seat plane carrying our tour group, which had been chartered from Seventh-Day Adventist missionaries, began a rapid descent. At the end of the airstrip, a few dozen members of the Kombai tribe waited patiently for this rare arrival. They were half-dressed, in hand-me-down clothes, and their arms were filled with arrows carved from sugarcane and bundles of limp yellow flowers. Their hair was fluffed with chicken feathers, and their thin black legs were spattered with toffee-colored mud. The wheels touched down on the crudely cut grass, and the plane came to a stop. Georg Decristoforo and Theresia Ellinger, a couple in their fifties from the Austrian Tyrol, climbed out first. They were followed by a young blond Finn named Juha. All were scientists. Georg and Theresia were chemical engineers with Sandoz, the pharmaceutical company; Juha worked for a small company outside Helsinki that designed software for the European Space Agency. They greeted the Kombai with awkward waves and smiles.

I emerged from the plane along with Kelly Woolford, our American tour guide. It was early morning; a low mist hovered over ancient ferns and tufts of flowering ginger. Starting at dawn the next day, Woolford was to lead us on a two-week trek deep into the surrounding rain forest.

Woolford, who lives in Bali, runs Papua Adventures, a small company that specializes in treks through the wildest zones of Papua. Although he has a degree in criminology from Drury University in Springfield, Missouri, he resembles an American backwoodsman of centuries past, with shoulder-length blond hair, a greyhound physique, and a rural Missouri accent. Woolford takes three or four small groups into the jungle each year. The trip, which costs several thousand dollars per person, is not for the timid: the forest terrain is punishing and remote, and there are few comforts or safeguards.

The goal of our expedition was to meet forest-dwelling Kombai who had never seen this airstrip—people who knew little or nothing of modern civilization. Many Kombai, Woolford had told us, do not live in villages. Single families build tree houses high in the forest canopy, with the aim of protecting themselves from potential enemies. There are dozens of such tree houses in the jungle; some of them had been visited by Westerners, Woolford said, and others had not. "We're going to find Kombai who may never have even heard of white people, let alone seen any," he told us. "You'll see that look in their eyes."

The fantasy of a "first contact" encounter has lured a steady trickle of Westerners to Papua, whose interior rain forests are nearly devoid of towns, roads, and other signs of modernity. Every year, a few dozen tourists visit this jungle region, either with Woolford or with a rival company such as Primitive Destinations International. The region has a reputation for looking perpetually distant and bemused.

We eventually fell to discussing our reasons for coming to New Guinea, and found ourselves rambling about "curiosity," "dissatisfaction," "boredom," a desire to see "something different."

"I maybe thought that the Kombai would teach me something," Juha said. "I'm not sure what. But life is made of romantic ideas." He nodded toward the Kombai standing there in the dark. "Or maybe not so romantic," he murmured.

The romanticization of primitive life is one of the persistent tropes in the history of Western thought. In 1755, Jean Jacques Rousseau wrote, "Nothing is more gentle than man in his primitive state." After Captain Cook visited the South Sea Islands, in the mid-eighteenth century, Enlightenment thinkers argued that the truth of human nature could now finally be revealed by an empirical study of primitive societies. Denis Diderot argued that primitive cultures like that of Tahiti were joyful because they were sexually free, unburdened by the artifice of civilization. Primitives, Diderot argued, were spiritually healthy and robust, and, as such, they were a devastating mirror held up to us.

. . . As recently as 1998, Reuters reported that two new tribes, the Aukedate and the Vahudate, had been discovered by missionaries in Papua. But Hoesterey cautioned, "I wouldn't call such tribes 'uncontacted.' These peoples are indeed caught up in modernity, even if they haven't actually seen a white tourist before." Perhaps they had engaged in trade, or seen tire tracks in the mud.

In the darkness, two shadowy figures were heading swiftly toward us. "And who is that?" Theresia asked Woolford.

A raffish-looking adolescent with wild eyes walked onto the veranda; he was closely followed by an older man in a shaggy green jacket. We asked Yanbu, the translator, to explain. The teenager, it turned out, had been accused by fellow villagers of being a demon in human form. The Kombai call such a spirit a kakua. As a test, the youth would be forced to eat a live frog, pig shit, and human excrement. If he vomited, he would be declared innocent. If not, a grim fate awaited him. A kakua is typically killed and cut into four parts; each section is then buried in a separate spot in the forest. The victim's viscera are sometimes cooked on hot stones and eaten.

"Is he really a witch?" Juha asked urbanely.

Woolford chuckled. It was dark now. He warned us that the Kombai in the jungle might not always know we were entirely human; with our strange pale skin, we certainly didn't look human. On our trek, it would be wise to wash as little as possible, avoiding shampoo and shaving products, for the forest people might consider chemical smells to be the sign of a kakua. "We don't want them freaking out, do we?" Woolford said, winking.

At dawn, the porters formed a column a quarter-mile long. They carried weapons, tent bags, cooking supplies, and food. They sang and twanged bamboo Jew's harps. Penus, our improbably named cook, laughed so loud that birds flew away.

It was soon raining hard. Wanggemalo is surrounded by dense swamps, acres of thick slime which can be traversed only by walking across fallen logs. Soaked, and covered in a toxic mixture of sweat, insect repellent, and black mud smelling of fermenting beer— a result of rotting sago-palm trees—we jumped from one log to another, teetering like high-wire artists without poles. I was the slowest, the most buffoonish, and Yanbu stopped frequently to let me catch up, a look of pity on his face. A little over five feet and probably not past forty, Yanbu wore a pair of surfer shorts, a dapper dog-tooth necklace, and rubber galoshes. A large wok was balanced on his head. He had become savvy about Western manners: when I looked at my photographs later, I noticed that Yanbu was the only Kombai who smiled at the camera.

Yanbu had relatives dispersed throughout the jungle, which facilitated his role as ambassador. There was a precise protocol for visiting Kombai tree houses, Woolford explained. A few porters would be sent to the tree house the day before we arrived, acting as emissaries and offering gifts of tobacco. (Many Kombai love smoking, though they usually puff on raw leaves.) If the men in the tree houses liked the tobacco and permission was granted for us to enter the premises, we would approach the place, with Yanbu in the lead. There would probably be an initial display of force, a tense standoff as the Kombai assessed the strangers.

By midday, we had left the swamps and entered the forest. . . .

The forest grew increasingly monotonous: dark-green carallia trees, tunnels of rattan. Very rarely, a cream-white orchid sprouted out of a tree. The other tourists and I stumbled through muddy ravines as slippery as glass. The Kombai, by contrast, navigated the forest effortlessly, like fish darting through coral. Frustration began to well up in me, for in nature the "civilized" man quickly becomes a helpless child, dependent upon people we have been conditioned to think of as helpless children.

At the end of the afternoon, we heard Yanbu, far ahead of us, yodeling into the forest. We were close to the first tree house. After a moment, we heard similar cries in response. We all fell silent.

Woolford told our group that he had taken an English investment banker along this same trail the year before. This tree house, therefore, would not be a pure first contact. It didn't matter: the scene was surreal enough. We were at the edge of a sun-flooded clearing piled with the debris of hundreds of shattered trees. It looked like the site of a meteor strike, without the crater. At its center rose a gabled thatch house on sixty-foot-high stilts. Its walls of bamboo were covered with shields painted white and ochre. The roof was festooned with mouse skulls. It swayed in the wind, smoke puffing out of its door. Below it stood a naked man, his bow drawn.

The man began creeping toward us, a look of anxiety on his face. His sugarcane arrow was three feet long, finely carved, and painted with white bands. In one hand, he held a kind of sandwich, made of sago stuffed with fat white beetle grubs, which burrow inside sago trees. A "sago burger," Juha called it later.

Yanbu pulled out a plastic bag of Indonesian tobacco. Georg suddenly volunteered to carry it over. Fanbu looked at Woolford, who nodded.

Even from a distance, we could see that the naked man was trembling and scared. Georg reached out to touch his hand. The Kombai man extended his, shaking violently, then quickly withdrew it and shook his head. They tried again. The fourth time, their hands brushed, and the tension subsided. The Kombai man straightened up, loosened his bow, and poked into the bag of tobacco. Quite unexpectedly, he smiled, showing a line of rotten teeth. "Nari," he said.

We stepped forward, half-whispering "Nari, nari, nari" and passing our hands over his. Our antagonist turned charmingly gracious. He pointed at our genitals and said, "Ringi buungkus?" This caused a moment's confusion until Yanbu offered Woolford a translation: "Shall we wrap your penises?"

It was, we gathered, a friendly overture, though we politely declined.

Two families lived here, we learned. Behind the tree house was a dark, tea-colored river. The porters pitched our tents along its banks. In minutes, they had also assembled a crude table and benches out of branches and bamboo twine—a miracle of forest engineering that they repeated every night. Nearby, on the ground, there was another small house, where the women slept. (Only men sleep in Kombai tree houses.)

Georg, Juha, and I swam naked in the cold little river. I asked Georg how he had felt handing over the tobacco. "Well, I could see the whole thing was ceremonial in some way," he said. "But the look in his eye—it was incredible. I've never seen a look like that. I don't even know what emotion it was. At first, I thought terror. But it was more complex than that."

"Paralysis?"

"I don't know what to think."

"But he's seen a white man before," Juha said. Nevertheless, the man's astonishment had been genuinely volatile.

"Did you see his knees shake?" I said.

. . . He expressed concern that the Kombai might one day be inundated by tourism. "The sad thing is, nothing remains unknown forever," he said.

At dusk, we set up candles on the table. We were soon assaulted by mosquitoes, which bear a potent strain of malaria. Wild-animal yells echoed through the forest. Without warning, two men emerged from the trees. They had daintily chiseled bodies; cassowary feathers were woven into their hair, and mouse tails were tied around their heads. Saying nothing, they glided past us, lighting their way with a sheaf of burning grass. When they noticed the hard, lucid flames of the candles, however, they stopped and lingered. Eventually, they shook our hands, and I saw that white ringworm coated their shoulders. Disconcertingly, they kept sniffing us. . . .

The following day, Georg and Theresia, taking out reference books and binoculars, scanned the forest canopy with scrupulous academic vigor. They were admirable jungle companions: tough, stoic, and perceptive. At one point, Theresia, a keen bird-watcher, pointed out the world's most imposing pigeon, which is endemic to New Guinea. And after hours of harsh bushwhacking, Theresia finally spotted a rare lizard, an emerald tree monitor, which scuttled so high up a tree that the naked eye couldn't detect it. "Schön!" she exclaimed, as the porters began scampering up after it on liana straps. "A beauty!"

Theresia followed the porters' progress through the binoculars as they climbed into the canopy. Suddenly, the lizard hit the forest floor with a thud. "Oh dear," she moaned, turning pale.

The youths jumped on the dazed reptile and gaily beat out its brain with sticks. Holding it up by its tail, they showed it off—a huge, three-foot specimen with jewel-like markings—while blood dripped from its tongue. This would be their dinner, it appeared. Theresia picked up her walking stick and moved on. I imagined her indignation and even rage. The island's beautiful parrots proved a still more anguishing problem. The porters liked them roasted on spits. What to the educated Westerner is a marvel of nature to be catalogued in a digital camera is to the Kombai a wood-smoked snack.

The forest remained sullen and densely meshed. At our feet, pink pitcher plants yawned upward, like open mouths. Yanbu sliced through barbed vines and ancient ferns with a machete. We slithered along fallen trees, stopping in the rivers to drench ourselves and refill our water bottles, shaking them up with iodine tablets. In a clearing near a stream, the porters suddenly dispersed and loaded their arrows: one of them had spotted a deadly taipan snake.

After seven hours, we reached the next tree house. It was lofty, with grand views over the forest, but it felt suffocatingly isolated. That night, over a meal of musky brash-turkey eggs, we asked two elder Kombai men living there about their myths. The men were reticent, but they did recount a Kombai creation myth.

Human beings were once as tiny as grubs, they said, and they lived inside a large woven bag, high up in a tree house. They were fed sago until one day; having grown big, they spilled out of the bag, eventually coming down from the primordial tree house to the earth.

I asked the men if they knew where we came from.

"We don't know," one of the men said.

"We don't come from the forest," Woolford said, through Yanbu. "We come from outside the forest."

At this, the men shook their heads.

I asked them about their neighbors, the Korowai.

"We don't know them," they said flatly.

During all this, they stared obsessively at a candle on the table. A candle's brilliant light is totally different from a campfire's dull orange, and it dazzled them. "It burns, but it doesn't go out," one man observed meekly to Yanbu. The men clicked a finger behind their front teeth, a gesture that translates as "Wow!" . . .

The following morning, however, Yanbu was tense. He told Woolford that the next tree house was going to be more difficult to approach. Several families, he had learned, would be gathering at the house that evening for a pig feast. (Some porters who had been sent ahead had returned with this news.) The feast was, in some ways, a political gesture: recently, a young man living in the area, suspected of being a kakua, had been murdered. The clan needed to heal the rift among its members, and the feast would be a sign of unity. But the intrusion of strangers had not been anticipated, and it was not clear that we would be welcome.

We set off once more. There was a bend in the trail as it rose toward a high crest denuded of trees. As we neared the top, cries of greeting shot back and forth. This time, it was my turn to offer the tobacco. We could tell that these Kombai were excited, perhaps agitated, by our presence; their cries seemed a little hysterical.

I nervously walked forward into the clearing, carrying Indonesian shag tobacco. There were two magnificent tree houses, far taller than the others that we had seen. In front of me were twenty men, their bows sullenly drawn. I kept advancing, pacing myself like a man on a tightrope. My feet crunched on burned twigs in the grass; the sound seemed as loud as firecrackers. At the same time, the shouts of the men, who were now closing in on me, felt oddly muted. I suddenly wondered if all this was an elaborate mise-en-scène that Woolford and Yanbu had quietly arranged. (On the coast, I knew, tourists were often treated to staged primitivist spectacles; locals would dance naked for a few hours each night before hitting the neighborhood bar.) I am not an anthropologist and was not equipped to judge the authenticity of this encounter. I knew nothing about these people. Yet the experience felt real.

Suddenly, as I was moving slowly forward, an arrow flew over my head with a crisp whoosh. Then another. An older man in a hornbill penis gourd stepped toward me, with a look of frowning amazement on his face. He swayed from side to side, glassy-eyed. Suddenly, he pushed the arrow loaded in his bow forward and indicated through gestures that I should hook the bag of tobacco on it. Apparently, he didn't want to risk touching me.

I did so, and he slipped the bag off his arrow; he felt the alien plastic and licked it. He opened the package and sniffed its contents. This meeting was dramatic and bizarre for both of us, but far more so for him, it seemed. After all, I had seen many photographs of Papuan natives in National Geographic, and I had read essays about the cultural rituals of the island. He, however, could not be prepared for my hair, my skin, my height, my eyes, the texture of my industrial clothes, my watch, my shoelaces, my copious sweat. It was not surprising that he could not bring himself to graze my hand. He looked utterly perplexed. . . .

Yanbu arrived at my side and spoke to the man in Kombai, urging him to shake hands with me. The man's name, Yanbu told me, was Mamandeo. "Nari, nari," I tried. We began saying "Nari" to each other, over and over. An hour later, all twenty Kombai had calmed down and we were smoking tobacco together, using pipes as large as didgeridoos. "When we saw you, we thought, 'What is that?'" Mamandeo admitted. "Then we were mad. Then we were scared."

The pig feast started in the late afternoon and lasted until dark. The animal was cooked in stones wrapped in leaves; its hair had been scraped off with bamboo knives.

As the men ate, they scooped up the bloody meat in large oyster shells. We watched, but did not eat. Later, I asked Mamandeo how his family had acquired the shells. Had he been to the sea? He responded with a bored shrug: he had traded with neighbors for them, he said.

During the feast, the women had sequestered themselves. Traveling among the Kombai, I had noticed the apparent severity of the division between men and women: they did not sleep together and did not eat together, and their days were often spent apart; there was little sign of what we would call intimacy. . . .

We sat down at our rustic dinner table and lit our candles. Men and boys gathered around to stare at the bright displays on our digital cameras. The older men looked fearfully at the tiny pictures on the LCD screens, but the children were quick to grasp the idea that the cameras displayed small-size images of themselves.

Woolford asked if they had seen a white man before, and, with no hesitation, they shook their heads. A man named Mauraga said, "We thought you might be people. But white skin? We were shocked."

There is no logging or mining anywhere near the Kombai forests; the charter flight to Wanggemalo is expensive. When you add the ferocity of the environment and the menace of malaria, the Kombai's isolation becomes far less difficult to understand. Equally important, perhaps, is the desire for solitude of the Kombai themselves. Rupert Stasch, an anthropologist at Reed College, and a leading expert on the region, told me that he thought the Kombai choose to be alone. "It's not a condition they sit in passively; until some great explorer comes along and relieves them of it," he said. This desire to remain in the forest should not to be confused with hostility toward others, he added. "The Kombai and Korowai people love moral relations that are demonstrated through conversation, gift-giving, and acts of care."

In fact, the forest Kombai were more than willing to sit, smoke, and talk once we had exchanged gifts and proved that we had no aggressive intentions. That night, three of them stared at the assorted campers' junk on the table. They were particularly fascinated by the synthetic ice-blue tint of our plastic water bottles. And, once again, the candles were a sensation.

"We live in darkness," a man named Andono said. "Could you bring us a candle if you come again?" Since Kombai doesn't have a word for candle, he said lilin, the Bahasa word for candle, which Yanbu had used while translating.

I then offered them malted biscuits. With extreme caution, they held them up to the candle, turned them over, inspected them gravely, then stuck out their tongues to touch the surface. They were nonplussed and suspicious. Then, egged on by Yanbu, they bit off morsels.

The Kombai have a discreet way of spitting. They form a blob of saliva on their lips, lean over and then let it fall silently.

"It makes me want to vomit," Mamandeo said.

Next, a spoonful of white sugar. They nibbled at it and then, with disgust, went through the same spitting motion.

"It makes us want to vomit," Mauraga said. We tried a simple cup of water next. But the plastic of the cup upset them, the feel of it against their lips. They spat out the water.

"It makes me want to vomit," Andono said.

Afterward, we walked with the men back up to the crest, smoking. Far across the forest, we could see people swinging handfuls of burning grass as they wound their way back to other tree houses. We listened for a long time to the Kombai men singing and playing their bamboo harps. The jungle felt dreamily serene at last. For a moment, I felt closer to these people, and to their single song, which never seemed to change; it was strange to think that a touristic enterprise had created a genuine moment of connection.

At the same time, it was hard not to wonder why the Kombai had not hit upon certain fundamental innovations. "Why haven't they improved their gardens or come up with some kind of lamp or candle?" Juha asked, as if confessing a dirty secret. "The Egyptians had oil lamps, didn't they? I thought curiosity was a universal human instinct."

As Juha and I talked, we became boorishly impatient with the Kombai. "I mean, thirty thousand years, and no lamp?" Juha said. "We shouldn't be judging them, but we do." Their isolation was equally difficult to absorb. "We can't accept their immobility, their stasis," Juha continued. "We can't help it. It's stupid of us, but there you are." He paused and laughed. "But why should they travel far and wide?" he said. "They think we're mad for doing that. They must look at all our gear, our things, and think we're insane."

We are insane, I thought.

It was also true that, in talking about their "stasis," we were speaking of them as mythical primitives—as if they were somehow living outside of history. Yet hadn't Brimob, who lived only a few days' walk from here, killed an Indonesian officer with an arrow? History was much closer than it appeared.

"Could you live here?" I asked Juha.

"It's the most beautiful place I've ever seen. But no, I couldn't live here. I would go mad."

"So would I," I said. "I would go mad, but I don't really know why."

"Because you couldn't travel?"

"Maybe. Or because I couldn't eat sago grubs."

"And yet the Kombai seem so happy, don't they?" Juha said, musingly.

Who could say? To my eyes, our Kombai porters had a sly jollity about them; they seemed to love horsing around during our long daily walks. Then again, we were providing them with food and, to an extent, were amusing them with our clownish oddities. It would have been foolish to draw any sweeping conclusions. The youngest porter, a six-year-old boy named Nehemiah, followed me to the river every day and showed me how to throw stones; in return, I taught him how to boogie-woogie, which made him collapse with laughter. But sometimes I noticed him watching me with grave earnestness. Then, when I caught his eye again, the big grin returned, and he would wiggle his hips and shout, "Boogie-woogie!" It was impossible to know what he was really thinking....

After another day's walk, we arrived at another tree house. A young man named Gagerigo came out to meet us, scowling as he chewed on a twig, and it took some time to persuade him and his old uncle, Mangnalo, that we were benign. Gagerigo wore a leaf and nothing else, and his gaze was somberly averted. Finally convinced, they took us up into the house. A stormy wind was blowing and the house swayed. Its floors were made of bamboo strips lashed together. The sago ceilings were covered with mouse and fish skulls, along with hundreds of cockroaches. Exhausted by the walk, we sat down, and Gagerigo told us that he was more afraid of us than he was of cassowaries. He said that he had never seen a white person before; none of the people had.

That evening, Mangualo told us, with Yanbu's help, that he didn't want to go to Wanggemalo because he was "scared clothes." He then added that he would much prefer it if we were naked: "We would be less afraid if you were naked, you smelled like us!" The Kombai rarely wash in rivers, whereas we plunged in at every opportunity. "It would be even better if you wore a koteka"—a penis gourd—like us." He had a point: we were now five hobos in filthy, tattered clothes.

It was starry, hot, and humid. Cicadas shrieked in the rattan. Georg, Theresia, Juha, and I talked with Woolford about how we had all adapted to the jungle, though we were also beginning to fray, mentally as well as physically. Once, our group had been surprised by a huge black spider with pencil-thin fangs; the porters had speared it to death. (Yanbu, upon being told the story,

observed that the spider's bite could kill you.) Woolford told us that our experience in Papua was perhaps more than a temporary adaptation. We could be in the midst of a more profound interior change. The trek was a short immersion, he said, but its intensity was destabilizing. And wasn't that why we had come—not to study an alien culture but to be changed ourselves? Wasn't that what travel used to be all about? . . .

The next day, a teen-age boy appeared on the trail, carrying a speared bird in his hand. His hair was threaded with pieces of wild orchid. He, it turned out, was headed to the same tree house that we were. It was a lucky break, for he had been at the pig feast and remembered us. We wouldn't have to have the usual psychodrama upon our arrival.

The chief of the tree house was Mambi, a handsomely bearded man with a sultry charisma. He shook our hands warmly: "Nari, nari, nari." We sat and smoked with him, as flying foxes shrilled in the trees. I couldn't resist asking him a question that had been nagging at me. You have seen an airplane going overhead, I said to him, through Yanbu. What do you think it is? You've seen it several times, haven't you? Do you never wonder how or why it flies?

"I never thought about it," he said, shaking his head slowly. "I just run away and hide when it passes overhead."

I explained that white people like us had made the planes. It was our machine, our way of getting about.

"How does it fly?" Mambi asked.

I was halfway through my explanation of the dynamics of winged flight when I realized that I wasn't sure exactly how airplanes fly. He looked at me intently; curious to witness a man who could not explain how his own culture's inventions actually worked. I suddenly dreaded him asking me how my flashlight worked or how my Gore-Tex boots were made waterproof. About these marvelous inventions of my culture I was essentially as ignorant as he.

Mambi then surprised me by saying, "We hope that you'll come back one day to see us." It was the first time that a Kombai person had expressed a desire to see us again.

The next morning, we went down to a part of a nearby river that was claustrophobically closed in by giant sago palms. This time, men and women were gathered together. The men were going to cut down a sago tree with their hulking stone axes. The felling took an hour. The trunk was then split open, and the women moved in with stone clubs to smash the interior to pulp.

The pulp was drained through a frond and rolled into balls. The men sat down to smoke, and a soporific mood descended upon us. I looked up and saw Juha surrounded by a large group of the younger boys. The boys shouted and stamped their feet around the tall Viking, chanting, "Juha! Juha!" For these Kombai boys, Juha was a fascinating creature: weird, exotic, entertaining. We were the tigers in the cage, not them. Juha turned to me and winked. It was a refreshing, even relieving, experience—to be the object, not the voyeur. . . .

"After we leave, what will they say about us?" I asked my companions. "What do they think about us? That's one thing we will never know, and it's the thing I'd most like to know."

In Graham Greene's novel "A Burnt-Out Case," mystified Africans sing about their European visitors: "Here is a white man who is neither a father nor a doctor. He has no beard. He comes from a long way away—we do not know from where—and he tells no-one to what place he is going nor why. He is a rich man, for he drinks whisky every evening and he smokes all the time. Yet he offers no man a cigarette."

. . . It was possible, I suggested, that the Kombai had unsettled us far more than we had unsettled them. "It isn't so much the Kombai I worry about with jungle tourism—it's the tourists themselves," Rupert Stasch, the anthropologist, had told me. "The Kombai often like tourism. It can be good for them. It's tourists themselves who are the real moral problem. Because often it's the urban Westerners who are 'uncontacted,' in the sense that they're stuck inside their own projected fantasies."

A week later, we made the last hike, back to Wanggemalo, and as we dragged ourselves through the sago swamps, slowed by heat exhaustion and diarrhea, I heard a sound that brought tears to my eyes: a cock crowing!

On our final day in Wanggemalo, I gave my Therm-a-Rest compressible mattress to Stephanus, who had hauled my pack through fifty miles of jungle. There were sad leave-takings. Nearly the whole population of Wanggemalo—a hundred or so people—came to the airstrip to see us off. (To my relief, the boy who had been accused of being a kakua was there, waving with the others: he must have survived the test.) We told the porters that we would come back. They waved at us, knowing, surely, that none of us, except Woolford, ever would. They seemed melancholy, but I wasn't certain.

Several weeks after I returned to New York, I called Georg and asked him how his re-insertion into civilization was going. How did Papua seem now that he was back in the Tyrol?

"Like a dream," he said. "A complete dream."

What did he remember most from our trip?

"Without question, giving the tobacco to the man in the first tree house," he said. "And that beautiful river by Mambi's place." He paused. "In truth, Theresia and I are having quite a hard time adjusting. We suddenly realize how weird and noisy our culture is. We miss the closeness with nature. I know it sounds hackneyed, but there it is. Perhaps we'll go again in 2007, just to keep our promise to the Kombai. Perhaps you'll join us?" I could imagine him rubbing his beard uneasily as he paused. "The Kombai will probably be the same. But maybe not."

## Questions

1. What characteristics of the tribe made them interesting and unusual to the trekkers?

2. Who had the most to learn in this encounter? Was it positive for both the tribe and the tourists?

*Source:* Strangers in the Forest. Lawrence Osborne. *New Yorker.* April 18, 2005. Reprinted by permission.

# CHAPTER 30

## In American Waters

Scott R. Sernau

The author circled the globe with 700 students aboard the MV Explorer as part of the Semester at Sea program. This article notes a few highlights of that experience and the students' mixed reactions upon returning to American waters with new impressions of globalization and the global environment.

The MV Explorer steams toward Hawaii, the final port before the Semester at Sea journey ends in San Diego, and Scott Sernau thinks about their trip around the world.

1 Dec. Honolulu

We have been crossing the Pacific for over a week. It is hard to keep track of days. It doesn't help that Tuesday, November 29 was followed by a second Tuesday, November 29 as we crossed the international dateline. We have been losing an hour of sleep each night crossing time zones. This is worse than jet lag for us Hoosiers who are not used to setting clocks ahead.

We have been crossing some of the clearest, bluest water I have ever seen. But there are also the sudden interruptions of large swirling slicks of trash floating out from who knows where. Like lost sailors of old, we were cheered to see rugged lush islands come into view. These are part of Hawaii but not the tourist belt; they are small wildlife sanctuaries assessable only by permit. The first inhabited island we pass is Ni'ihao, wholly privately owned and restricted to a small Native Hawaiian community. Gradually the numbers of soaring seabirds increase, and the great volcanoes of the big island of Hawaii emerge from the clouds. I've read that Polynesian seafarers found these specks of land in the vastness of the Pacific by following the birds and the clouds. Closer in, the dark swirls and occasional spouts of the first humpback whales returning to the islands can be seen

off the back of the ship. The shadowy whales usher us toward Diamond Head rising on the horizon, followed soon by the great hotels of Waikiki. This is not an easy day to keep students' minds focused on class.

The long Pacific crossing has provided some time for reflection, along with attempts to put some conclusions to the last 100 days. It is a magnificent world. Maybe that is easier to remember as we edge past palm-fringed beaches to dock at the historic Aloha clock tower. But we have also found that magnificence in less familiar places, from the lush Orinoco delta of Venezuela to the temple-studded plains of Bagan, Burma. It is also a precarious world. Our "near misses" have become a topic of speculation. We just narrowly escaped the fury of Hurricane Katrina as we started south. We rerouted our voyage away from East Africa and later heard of an attempted pirate attack on a small cruise ship off of Somalia. The day we left India, the Asian news was filled with reports of flooding in Chennai, with a derailed train in Hyderabad and terrorist bombings in Delhi. A day or two earlier, we had students in each of those locations. We left Burma to hear the next day that the junta is moving the capital out of Yangon into the interior and adding new travel restrictions. They claimed to have worries about invasions. Maybe our "invasion" was too much for them, although they should take some comfort in knowing that these invaders could only get in during the month's highest tides. We made it through China before the typhoon, and to Japan after the offshore earthquake, then across the Pacific beneath large winter storms. Still, while I pity parents tracking our voyage and watching the news, the world is really a much safer place than one would glean from CNN. And the scattered "hot spots" are becoming most unpredictable. Outside of the French colonial post office in Ho Chi Minh City, next to Notre Dame Cathedral, we read in the English language papers of the riots all across France. How fortunate that we were enjoying our glimpse of French architecture in a calm, peaceful country like Vietnam.

Classes for the last several days have focused on that elusive term, globalization. Certainly as we have traveled through our ports, and especially our Asian ports, we have seen the tremendous impact of economic, political, and cultural globalization. Having a conversation in English in a distant port over a Starbuck's latte, with citizens of three different countries who are all concerned about the impact of US foreign policy, is now commonplace. At the same time, globalization remains a catch-all for some very different, and sometimes contradictory, forces. The world is integrating at the same time that [it] is fragmenting. Economic globalization brings new market integration while it divides social classes further from one another and leaves many utterly cut off from productive livelihoods. Global politics keeps nations continually intertwined with one another at the same time that there are new movements for independence and autonomy and more isolated pariah states. Cultural globalization brings us not only all the same media and the same billboards around the world, but also new attempts to revive and understand old traditions. The latter is not so much a clash of civilizations as it is a potpourri of cultural identities all mixed together and trying to claim their own space. In great multicultural cities like Honolulu or Hong Kong, or Ho Chi Minh City for that matter, the heritage of many civilizations and traditions may mingle on a single block.

Our final student panel debates the pros and cons of globalization. The truth is, however, that we have found few alternatives to the forces that are both uniting and fragmenting the world. Even the ostensibly communist countries we have visited are pursuing global capitalism with a vengeance (in some cases "vengeance" may be literal). The challenge for us, then, is how to master and harness the forces that seem to be running away with the planet. Can we globalize in ways that are more humane and more respectful of the biosphere that we share? I have become convinced that such a search must be our prime motivation for overseas study and for international travel.

The idea of "ecotourism" has caught on in many of the ports we visited. Guides offer travel that focuses on learning about the natural world, and they are doing so in ways that don't damage what we have come to enjoy. Sometimes these eco-trips do just that, but at other times ecotourism seems to be nothing more than a Disney-like "jungle cruise" but with real insects. We have also had a course on the ship on cultural tourism, travel in search of greater cultural awareness and understanding. In this port, that means getting past the tiki torches and hula skirts to understand a bit of what a cultural blender the Hawaiian Islands have been for the past couple hundred years. I am intrigued by this idea of encountering both the natural world and the human cultural world, but still balk at the world of "tourism" itself. One of our daily memos began with this quote from Daniel Boorstin on tourism versus travel: "The traveler was active; he went strenuously in search of people, of adventure, of experience. The tourist is passive; he expects interesting things to happen to him. He goes *sight-seeing.*"

Our goal from the beginning has been to be travelers rather than tourists, to complete a voyage, not to take a cruise. Time will tell if we have succeeded. Students around me take study breaks on the computers by cataloging great volumes of amazing digital pictures. Nice collections all, but will they move beyond "snap shots" to form a vision for the big picture? They have been "excited for" many things on our common venture, with that great 20-year-old enthusiasm. Now we'll see if they maintain that enthusiasm as they go on to tend the amazing natural and cultural heritage we have viewed and to share it more equitably with our global neighbors.

For the moment the excitement is about coming home. A student has won the opportunity to raise our port flag over the ship. For the first time, the flag is the Stars and Stripes as we enter US waters. He waves it dramatically over his head in the strong Hawaiian breeze. We get a brief 24 hours here as the ship refuels. Exams are in two days, but for the moment the surf is up at Waikiki. I share their excitement, but also know a secret. We never left home. We need to see the whole planet as our home. And we need to straighten up our room. It is a beautiful place. Aloha.

## Questions

1. Do you believe a voyage such as the one described can provide a true global learning experience for students?

2. What does it mean to see the entire world as our home? How might this change our actions?

*Source:* In American Waters. Scott Sernau. *IU International News.* Spring 2006. Reprinted by permission of Scott Sernau.

# INTERNET RESOURCES

## A Changing World

### United Nations

The United Nations site (www.un.org) is "information central" for a host of international issues and statistics.

See also www.undp.org, the United Nations Development Program. This agency of the UN collects a wide range of data on global well-being and economic development and publishes the annual Human Development Report.

### Fair Trade

Alternate traders (sometimes called "fair traders") attempt to provide an alternative to exploitive international trade relations. Alternate traders include Ten Thousand Villages (www.tenthousandvillages.com), SERRV (www.serrv.org), Equal Exchange (www.equalexchange.com), and Marketplace: Handiwork of India (www.marketplaceindia.org). Others can be found at The Fair Trade Resource Network (www.fairtraderesource.org).

## Inequality and Poverty

### ILO

Go to www.ilo.org for information on the UN affiliated International Labour Organization. Their site has information and articles on globalization, child labor, women's work, AIDS and work, global wages, and dozens of other topics.

### Students Against Sweatshops

See www.studentsagainstsweatshops.org for the site of United Students Against Sweatshops (USAS). A quick browser search will also take you to the sites of independent students against sweatshops organizations for Canada, California, Iowa, Harvard, and so forth. On the USAS site, note "get involved" and "take action" sections. Affiliates are also listed.

National Organization for Women (NOW) at www.now.org. Under issues, note "global feminism" for articles and gatherings from around the world.

### Grameen Bank

This Nobel Peace Prize winning organization (www.grameen-info.org) helped launch the idea of micro-credit, small-scale lending to the poor for innovative business development. Based in Bangladesh, and particularly known for working with poor women who have no other access to credit at reasonable rates, it has become a global model for promoting entrepreneurship.

# Education

## United Nations

United Nations Educational, Scientific and Cultural Organization (www.unesco.org) has very good information on education, media, and literacy. True literacy is hard to measure, and governments often over-report their literacy rates, but this site provides good comparisons.

The United Nations Children's Fund, www.unicef.org, site offers good information on the status of children, reports on the Year of the Child and other material.

## Free the Children

See www.freethechildren.org. This organization was created by a 12-year-old concerned about forced child labor. It now focuses heavily on education, with information on school building projects and school kits.

# Conflict

## Interpol

The international network of police organizations, Interpol, has a site at www.interpol.int. The site has huge amounts of information on international crime including drugs and drug trafficking, money laundering, trafficking in children, as well as international crime statistics.

## United for Peace and Justice

See their site at www.unitedforpeace.org. This rapidly growing group serves as a clearinghouse for hundreds of peace groups around the country. Their issues of concern include Iraq, Israel, and Palestine, nuclear disarmament, global justice, and immigrant rights.

## Amnesty International

Amnesty campaigns (www.amnesty.org) around the world seek to end torture and human rights abuses, while championing the causes of political prisoners and other "prisoners of conscience." See their site to find out the current causes, letter writing campaigns, and other activities. There may also be a chapter on your campus or in the community.

## Human Rights Watch

At http://hrw.org/ you will find large amounts of information on human rights, including prisons, women's rights, rights and HIV, refugees, children's rights, and so forth, as well as region by region coverage of key human rights crises. See information on "campaigns" that address the trafficking of women and children, detainees, and other issues.

## UN Office of the High Commissioner on Human Rights

See their site at http://www.unhchr.ch/ for information on many aspects of international human rights, including for women, children, and indigenous peoples. They also offer information on international agreements and on human rights training and education. A daily update on human rights issues can be found at http://www.un.org/rights/.

## Overcoming Violence

The World Council of Churches, an international affiliation of Christian groups, is sponsoring a decade to overcome violence (2001–2010). Themes include the logic of violence, justice, power, identity, and pluralism. See http://www.overcomingviolence.org/ for current activities and ideas on how churches and individuals can become involved. The multilingual site also includes stories of nonviolent action from the around the world.

# Health

## Doctors Without Borders

This organization (www.doctorswithoutborders.org) won the Nobel Peace Prize for their courageous work in some of the world's most troubled places, providing critical health care to anyone in need regardless of political, ethnic, or religious affiliation. Their site contains information on health campaigns and trouble spots around the world.

## Population Connection

Formerly Zero Population Growth (ZPG), this group has changed its name to reflect a broader concern for population issues, including family planning, health care, and education, though limiting growth is still a major concern. Their site at www.populationconnection.org contains a wide array of information, legislative action alerts, and other ways to get involved. Under their "take action" section, note information on e-mail contacts, local chapters, and their campus program as well as their work for "kid friendly" and healthy cities.

## World Health Organization

This United Nations organization has been at the forefront of the campaign to eradicate disease, vaccinate children, and to improve health care and health education around the world. Their site at http://www.who.int/en/ contains information on global health concerns and their major campaigns. Special attention is given to HIV/AIDS and to global epidemics. Information can be found by country or by topic.

## AIDS Services

For information on AIDS, HIV, tuberculosis, and efforts to combat related infectious disease around the world, see the AIDS Education Global Information System at www.aegis.com.

# Energy

## Climate Change

A huge clearinghouse of climate change information now familiar to everyone who has seen An Inconvenient Truth, this site (www.climatechange.net) draws on the resources of Stanford University and a wide range of links to explain and explore issues around energy use and climate change.

## Union of Concerned Scientists

This organization (www.ucsusa.org) first came to prominence for its scientific critique of world nuclear policies. They now focus heavily on energy and climate change. The site is not only full of data, but also interesting alternatives that promise safer, cleaner, and renewable energy sources.

## Sprawl

You can learn more about sprawl, transportation, and sustainability at www.newurbanism.org. Note their designs for alternative systems including urban and intercity train systems.

## Energy Efficiency and Renewable Energy

The US Department of Energy maintains a site with information on energy efficiency and renewable energy at www.eere.energy.gov/. Note their discussion of these topics and information they provide groups and individual consumers to increase their energy efficiency and to learn more about alternative energy source.

# Environment

## Nature Conservancy

The Nature Conservancy operates worldwide, buying environmentally sensitive property and helping landowners preserve portions of their land. Increasingly, its efforts include ventures into biological "hot spots" and the "last great places" around the world. See their colorful site at www.nature.org for information on their activities, articles from their magazine, and contacts for upcoming conferences and local chapters.

## Sierra Club

One of the world's oldest conservation organizations, the Sierra Club has hundreds of local chapters and worldwide activities. These are highlighted at www.sierraclub.org along with information on current environmental issues, letter-writing campaigns, upcoming legislation, and other activities including nature trips.

## World Watch

The World Watch Institute, founded by Lester Brown in 1974, now has global partners in over 40 countries. Their site at www.worldwatch.org has an enormous amount of information on global issues related to population, energy, and the environment. Note also links to dozens of related organizations around the world.

# INDEX

A. T. Kearney, Inc., 72–73
Abdelkader, Galy Kadir, 38
Abdourahmane, Soli, 39
Abolition, of torture, 107–108
Abu Ghraib prison, Iraq:
    story of abuse at, 114 (n9)
    torture at, 109, 111
Accumulation by dispossession, 167
Acharya, "Rudy" Rupak, 145
Acid rain, 177
Acquired Immune-Deficiency Syndrome (AIDS):
    AIDS Education Global Information System, 213
    European epidemic, response to, 151–153
    European policy shifts and, 153–155
    spread of, 141
Acteal, Chiapas, 62–63
*Actualité Juive* (newspaper), 102
Adams, J. Michael, 83
Africa:
    disease in, 56
    internally displaced persons in, 135, 138
    oil exploitation of, 163–167
    poverty in, 35–36
    slavery in, 37–42
*The Age of Terrorism* (Laqeuer), 115 (n23)
Agriculture, 4, 23–25
Aid, 36, 77
AIDS. *See* Acquired Immune-Deficiency Syndrome
"AIDS and Health-Policy Responses in European Welfare States" (Steffen), 151–158
Ainsworth, Peter, 174
Alexander, Charles, 173
Algerian war of independence, 100
Allende, Salvador, 108
Altenstetter, C, 156
Alternate traders, 211
"Always With Us" (Cassidy), 33–36
Amadou, Hama, 39
American Council on International Intercultural Education, 84
American Hospital Association, 159
American Nurses Association, 159–160
American Right, 97
Amitkumar (polio victim), 150
Amnesty International:
    anti-torture campaign of, 108
    on resources exploitation of Nigeria, 166
    Web site of, 212
Amsterdam Treaty, 156
Anderson, A., 77
Anderson, Donald A., 149
Andrew, Mick, 88, 89
Angola:
    internally displaced persons in, 138
    oil exploitation of, 163, 166–167
Annan, Kofi:
    High-level Panel on Threats, Challenges and Change, 124

    on internally displaced persons, 135
    termination of MICAH, 122
    on US bombing in Sudan, 129
Anti-Slavery International, 38
Anti-torture norm, 107–108, 111–112
Anuak (Ethiopian ethnic group), 165
Argoz, 186
Aristide, Jean-Bertrand:
    election of, 120
    political force of, 124
    reelection of, 122
    removal of, 119, 123
    UN in Haiti and, 121, 125
Asia:
    cities threatened by rising sea level, 171
    poverty in, 31
    torture, human rights in, 110–111
    *See also* specific countries
Asibit (Nigerian slave), 37, 41
Astiz, M. F., 72
AT&T Foundation, 83, 85
Aussaresses, Paul, 115 (n17)
Austin, Katherine, 199
Authoritarianism, 9
*Avoiding Dangerous Climate Change* (Blair), 171
"Awakening Giants, Feets of Clay" (Bardhan), 3–11
Ayittey, George B. N., 36
Azarori, Niger, 39–40

Bain & Co., 17
Baker, D. P., 72
Bangladesh:
    GrameenPhone in, 65–68
    poverty in, 43–53
Banister, J., 6
Bardhan, Pranab, 3–11
Barriers, 83–86
Bartra, Armando, 62
"Bayou Farewell: The Rich Life and Tragic Death of Louisiana's Cajun Coast" (Tidwell), 170
BBC News, 164
Beach, R. H., 72
Beccaria, Cesare, 107, 115 (n26)
Begum, Anju Monwara, 65, 67
Begum, Laily, 67
Begum, Sharifa, 43–53
Benefit, of slum upgrading, 190
Bentham, Jeremy, 71
Berbers, 164–165
Bergeron, H., 154
Bernard, Philippe, 95, 100
Berridge, V., 154, 156
Berryhill, Melissa, 17
Besson, Luc, 98
Bhagwati, J., 72
Bharucha, Nilufer, 86

Bicycles, 18
"The Biggest Failure: A New Approach to Help the World's Internally
        Displaced People" (Wilkinson), 133–139
Biotech products, 5
Blacks, in France, 93–103
Blair, Tony, 170, 171
Blood supplies, 156
Blue Ridge Paper Products, 143, 144
Bogotá, Colombia, land development in, 187–188
Bolivia, counter-inflation measures of, 33
Boltvinik, Julio, 60
Bond, Kit, 177
Bono:
    on Jeffrey Sachs, 34
    philanthropy of, 31, 55–57
Boorstin, Daniel, 210
"Born Into Bondage" (Raffaele), 37–42
Boufoy-Bastic, B., 74
*Bound: Living in the Globalized World* (Sernau), 84
Bourdieu, Pierre, 62
Braslavsky, C., 75
Bravo, Douglas, 20
Brazil, ecotourism in, 198
"Breaking Down Notions of Us and Them" (Carfagna), 83–86
Brociner, Gill, 199
Brostuen, Kendall, 84–85
Brown, Gordon, 73
Brown, Lester, 214
Brownback, Sam, 159, 160
Bruckner, Pascal, 97
Buch, Eric, 160
Bumrungrad Hospital, Bangkok, 143–144
Bureaucracies, regulatory, 7
Bureaucratic innovation, 129–130
Burkina Faso, 73
"A Burnt-Out Case" (Greene), 207
Bush, George W.:
    global warming, position on, 169
    global warming, response to, 174–175
    John McCain and, 117 (n65)
    torture and, 106, 109–110
Bush administration:
    anti-torture norm and, 112–113
    Padilla case, 117 (n59)
    redefinition of torture, 105
    torture and power/reputation, 109–110
    U.S. torture adjustment, 110–111
Business:
    China *vs.* India, 7–8
    "A Coffee Connoisseur on a Mission", 23–25
    *vs.* government, in fighting poverty, 68
    "The Great Turning", 27–30
    The "Radical" Thesis on Globalization and the Case of Venezuela's Hugo
        Chávez", 19–21
    "The Wal-Mart You Don't Know", 15–18
Buzan, Barry, 128
Bybee memorandum, 106, 111, 114 (n15)

Cabinda Province, Angola, 166–167
Cacchioli, Romana, 41
Caldera, Rafael, 19
Campanella, Peter, 17
Campenhoudt, L., 156
Canada, medical tourism to, 145
Canales, Daniel, 24
Canales, Norman, 24
Canterbury, Ray, 144
Capitalism, 167

Caponigro, Mark Stephen, 197, 199
Carbon-trading system, 175
Cárdenas, Guadalupe, 63
Cardozo, Elsa, 20
Carey, Gib, 17
Carfagna, Angelo, 83–86
Carnegie Endowment for International Peace, 72–73
Carnoy, M., 79
Carr, E. H., 105
Carrère d'Encausse, Hélène, 97
Cartagena, Colombia, 76
Carter, Jimmy, 172
Carter Center, 113
Case, R., 74
Cassidy, John, 33–36
Catalytic converters, 178–179
Cavanagh, J., 77
CEDAW (Convention on the Elimination of All Forms of Discrimination
        against Women), 60
Cédras, Raoul, 120
Cellular phones, in Bangladesh, 65–68
Center for Global Development and Foreign Policy Journal, 77
Central Intelligence Agency (CIA), 109
Certification, of ecotourism, 198
CFCs (chlorofluorocarbons), 177
CFR Task Force, 130
Cha, Victor D., 127–131
Chad, 133, 134
Chandler, Claude, 198
Chandra, Pradeep, 145
Charity:
    of Americans, 56
    of Bill and Melinda Gates, Bono, 55–57
    polio eradication campaign, 149–150
Charny, Joel, 138
Chattel slavery, 38
Chaudhuri, S., 8
Chávez, Hugo, 19–21
Chen, S., 4
Cheney, Richard, 111, 115 (n19)
Chiapas, Mexico, 63
Child mortality, 39
Chile:
    slum upgrading in, 191
    torture in, 108, 115 (n28)
China:
    anti-terrorism in, 110
    economic overview of, 11
    ecotourism in, 199
    India, economic growth comparison with, 3
    infrastructure of, 6–8
    institutional/political issues, 8–11
    MIPONUH and, 122
    oil interests in Ethiopia, 165
    poverty/underemployment in, 4–6
    on sovereignty, 135
    on U.S. human rights violations, 116 (n52)
    Wal-Mart and, 16
Chirac, Jacques:
    on ethnic minorities, 94
    far Right and, 96
    response to uprisings, 102
    speech by, 97, 103
Chlorofluorocarbons (CFCs), 177
Chowdhury, Abdul-Muyeed, 67–68
Christianity, 102
Chuaqui, Tomas, 86
CIA (Central Intelligence Agency), 109

Circumstances, right to education and, 76
Citizenship, global, 83–84
Ciucur, Viorela, 86
Clapp, Philip, 175
Clark, Ian, 116 (n33)
Clément, Pascal, 103
Climate change. *See* Global warming
Clinton administration:
    bureaucratic innovation, 129–130
    UN in Haiti and, 120, 122
Cochi, Stephen L., 148, 149
Coffee, 23–25
"A Coffee Connoisseur on a Mission" (Weissman), 23–25
Cohen, Roberta, 137–138
Cohen, Stanley, 114 (n6)
Cold War, 130
Cole, David, 117 (n59)
Collier, Paul, 35
Collins, Susan, 112
Colombia:
    internally displaced persons in, 135
    residential land development in, 187–188
Colonialism, 73, 100
*Colonias*, 185, 194 (n17), 194 (n18)
*Columbia Encyclopedia*, 71
Common World Educational Culture, 74
Communication, 29, 66
Conditions, right to education and, 76
Confession, 107, 111, 115 (n20)
Conflict:
    ethnic minority in France, 93–103
    Haiti, UN peacebuilding in, 119–125
    internally displaced persons, 133–139
    international security, 127–131
    Internet resources, 212–213
    overview of chapters on, 91–92
    torture, 105–113
Conflict resolution, 9–10
Congo, 136, 138
Connaughton, James L., 174, 175
Constitution, U.S., 111
Content, of education, 74–75
Convention on the Elimination of All Forms of Discrimination against
    Women (CEDAW), 60
Convention on the Rights of the Child (United Nations), 71
Cordero, George, 159
Corporations:
    education and, 78
    French businesses, 95–96
    global warming and, 172
    Wal-Mart, 15–18
CorpWatch, 77
Corradi, Quirós, 20
Correl, Hans, 164
Corruption, 166
Cost per unit, 189–190
Costa Rica, demand subsidy program in, 185
Cost-benefit analysis, for slum upgrading, 190
Costs:
    of addressing IDP problem, 139
    of housing, slum formation and, 184
    of provision of education, 76–77
    of slum upgrading, 189–192, 193, 194 (n14)
    of slums, 184–185
Counter Culture Coffee, 24
Counter-Terrorism Committee (CTC), 112, 117 (n67)
Coyle, D., 72
Credit, 65, 67, 192

Crichton, Michael, 173
Cross-fertilization, 130
Cuba, schools in, 76
Cultural tourism, 201–207
Cummins, Walter, 85, 86
Current, John, 198
Curriculum, 74–75
Czinkota, M. R., 74

Dale, R., 73–74, 75, 76
Darfur, Sudan, 133–134
Davies, B., 77
De Villepin, Dominique, 99, 103
Debbouze, Jamel, 98
Decristoforo, Georg, 201–207
Demand subsidy program, 185
Democracy, 119–120, 122
Deng, Francis M., 136
Dentistry, 145
Dershowitz, Alan, 106, 114 (n14)
Desch, Michael, 131
Deshpande, L.K., 5
Desmond, C., 77
Detainees:
    at Guantanamo Bay, Cuba, 109, 110, 111–112
    torture after September 11, 2001, 106–107
    in Uzbekistan, 116 (n44)
    "water-boarding" of, 114 (n8)
"Developing Global Competencies in Higher Education" (conference), 83–85
Devidal, P., 72, 78
Devki Devi Heart & Vascular Institute, 144–145
Dhaka, Bangladesh, 43–53
Dial Corp., 17
Diamond, Andrew, 99–100
Diderot, Denis, 202
Diet, vegan, 199
"Digest for Jurisprudence of the UN and Regional Organizations on the
    Protection of Human Rights while Countering Terrorism" (UN High
    Commissioner's Office), 112
Dijbouti, 73
Disabled people, ecotourism and, 198
Disenfranchisement, 95–96
Dobbins, Steve, 16
Doctors Without Borders, 213
*Doing Business in 2006* (World Bank), 7
Donnelly, Jack, 109
Drezner, D., 78
Drug cartels, 63
Drug policy, European, 154–155
Dugger, Celia W.:
    "Rumor, Fear and Fatigue Hinder Final Push to End Polio", 147–150
    "U.S. Plan to Lure Nurses May Hurt Poor Nations", 159–160
Dutta, Roy S., 5
Duvalier dynasty, 120

Earth Community, 27–30
Earth Institute, 33
Easterbrook, Gregg, 177–179
Economic environments, 75
Economics:
    economic policy of Hugo Chávez, 21
    globalization and, 128
    politics in India/China and, 9
Economy:
    global warming and, 174, 177
    socialist to market transformation, 34–35
    Venezuelan, effects of globalization on, 19–21
    *See also* Gross domestic product

Ecotourism, 210
Ecuador, schools in, 76
Edelheit, Jonathan, 144
Education:
    articles on, 69
    of Dhaka rickshaw pullers, 44, 45
    in France, racism and, 101
    global learning, 83–86
    HIV/AIDS in Europe, 155
    in India, 4
    Internet resources, 212
    James Mokoena's dream, 87–89
    "The Right to Education in a Globalized World", 71–79
Education, right to:
    conclusion about, 79
    conditions/circumstances for, 76
    education as universal right, 71–72
    globalization and, 72–73
    how students should be taught, 75
    what should be taught, 74–75
    who gets taught, 73
    who should provide education, 76–79
Education for All, 74
Efficiency, energy, 172
Egeland, Jan:
    on failure to help IDPs, 134, 138
    on IDP initiative, 137
    protection of IDPs, 136
Eichengreen, B., 8
Einsiedel, Sebastian von, 119–125
Eisler, Riane, 28
*Ejidos* (land with communal rights), 187
El Salvador, land development in, 186–187
Elections, in Haiti, 119–120, 121, 122
Elizabeth II, Queen of Great Britain, 169
Ellinger, Theresia, 201–207
Ellner, Steve, 19–21
Elshtain, Jean Bethke, 114 (n14)
Embargo, 120
Emigration, 78
Empire, 27–30
Employment:
    in China/India, 4–6
    education and, 78
    of women in Mexico, 61
    *See also* Work
*The End of Poverty: Economic Possibilities for Our Time* (Sachs), 33
Energy:
    energy resources in Africa, exploitation of, 163–167
    global warming and, 169–175
    global warming, changes required, 177–179
    Internet resources, 213–214
    overview of, 161
Environment:
    Angola, oil industry effect on, 167
    cultural tourism in New Guinea, 201–207
    ecotourism in South America, 197–200
    Internet resources, 214
    overview of chapters on, 181
    Semester at Sea program, 209–210
    slums, financial framework for reducing, 183–193
Epidemics. *See* Acquired Immune-Deficiency Syndrome (AIDS)
Escorts Heart Institute and Research Center, 144
Ethiopia:
    aid to, 36
    oil exploitation of, 163, 165
Ethnic minorities:
    failure of the Left in France, 99–100

    far Right, philosophers and, 96–98
    in France, housing for, 94–95
    in France, poverty/disenfranchisement, 95–96
    in France, work by, 93–94
    *modèle d'intégration*, 99
    policing in France and, 96
    racism in France, 93
    Republican values in France, 98–99
    secularism/Islamophobia in France, 100–102
    uprisings, response to, 102–103
Europe:
    AIDS in, 151–158
    cities threatened by rising sea level, 171
    *See also* specific countries
European Monitoring Centre for Drugs and Drug Addiction, 156
European Union (EU), 78
Eviatar, D., 167
"Exploitation of Energy Resources in Africa" (Maxted), 163–167
ExxonMobil, 173

Fagan, C., 167
Failed State Index, 123
Fair trade, 211
Fairleigh Dickinson University (FDU), 83–86
Fanon, Frantz, 97
Farmer, Paul, 56
Farrell, R. V., 76
FDI (foreign direct investment), 34
FDU (Fairleigh Dickinson University), 83–86
Fekete, Liz, 101
Femicide, 60
Ferguson, Bruce, 183–193
Ferrerra, M., 153
Finance, 7, 189–193
"A Financial Framework for Reducing Slums" (Ferguson & Navarrete), 183–193
Finkielkraut, Alain, 97, 98, 102
Fiscal federalism, 10
Fisher, William, 117 (n63)
Fisk, Robert, 100
Fiss, Owen, 111, 117 (n59)
Foot, Rosemary, 105–118
Force, use of, 123
Foreign direct investment (FDI), 34
Foreign policy agencies, 130
Forrester Research, Inc., 78
Fortin, Kim, 199
Foucault, Michael, 107
Fouriesburg Intermediate School, Masjaing, South Africa, 87, 88
Fox, Edward, 15
Fox, Vicente, 61, 63
France:
    AIDS epidemic response in, 152–155
    colonial legacy of, 100
    far Right, philosophers in, 96–98
    housing for ethnic minority, 94–95
    Left, failure of, 99–100
    *modèle d'intégration*, 99
    Niger slavery and, 38
    policing in, 96
    poverty/disenfranchisement in, 95–96
    public health reform in, 155–157
    Republican values, 98–99
    secularism/Islamophobia in, 100–102
    struggle to include Muslim minority, 91
    uprisings, response to, 102–103
"France: The Riots and the Republic" (Murray), 93–103
Free the Children Web site, 212

Freedman, Lawrence, 129
Friedman, T. L., 3, 72, 74
Front National, 96
Funds, 139
Furio, Victoria J., 59

Gagerigo (Kombai tribesman), 206
Galeano, Eduardo, 59
Gambella People's National Regional State, 165
Gangs, 63
García, Alan, 19
Garraud, Jean-Paul, 103
Gates, Bill & Melinda, 31, 55–57
Gatrell, V. A. C., 115 (n18), 115 (n25)
GDP. *See* Gross domestic product
Gelbspan, Ross, 172, 173
Gender violence, in Mexico, 59–64
General Agreement on Trade in Services (GATS), 78
Geneva Conventions, 109–110, 114 (n14)
Geneva Refugee Convention, 134
Geography, 35
George C. Marshall Institute, 173
Germany:
    AIDS epidemic response in, 153–155
    public health reform in, 155–157
Ghana, 36
Ghose, Mohit, 145
Ghosh, Nandita, 85, 86
GIA (Governor's Island Agreement), 120
Gibbs, Nancy, 55–57
Girls, 72, 101
Giuliano, Peter, 23–24
Global awakening, 28–29
Global Campaign for Education:
    on children not enrolled in school, 72
    on provision of education, 77
    on schooling in Nepal, 76
Global capitalism, 18
Global citizenship, 83–84
Global competencies, 85
Global IDP Project, 138–139
Global Virtual Faculty, 85, 86
Global warming:
    Hurricane Katrina and, 170
    negative politics surrounding, 177–178
    public attention on, 169–175
    U.S. denial of, 169
    U.S. solutions for, 178–179
    Web site on, 213
Globalization:
    China/India, rise of, 3–11
    global learning, 83–86
    international security and, 127–131
    Internet resources, 211–214
    overview of, 1
    racism and, 95
    right to education and, 71–79
    Semester at Sea program classes on, 210
"Globalization and the Study of International Security" (Cha), 127–131
Globalization Index, 72–73
Globally Structured Agenda for Education, 74
Glucksmann, André, 97
Gonzales, Alberto R., 106, 109
González, Roberto, 61
"The Good Samaritans" (Gibbs), 55–57
Gore, Al, 172, 177
Gott, Richard, 20
Governments:

business in China *vs.* India, 8
education, provision of, 76–77, 78
land development by, 185–189
poverty and, 68
security in globalized world, 127–131
slum upgrading, 189–193
Governor's Island Agreement (GIA), 120
Grameen Bank:
    micro loans from, 65, 67
    Web site of, 211
GrameenPhone, 65–68
Grand Challenges, 55
Grants, 35
Great Britain. *See* United Kingdom
"The Great Turning" (Korten), 27–30
Greece, 108
Green, Madeleine, 84
Green Revolution, 4
Greene, Graham, 207
Green-house gas emissions, 171
Grice, Irina, 87, 88
Groner, David and Barbara, 150
Gross, Mordehai, 102
Gross domestic product (GDP):
    of Haiti, 121, 123
    spending on education, 76–77
Group of 8 (G-8), 170
Grunwald, Mandy, 178
Guantanamo Bay, Cuba:
    photographs of prisoners at, 109
    torture of detainees at, 110, 111–112
Guehenno, Jean-Marie, 127, 130
*Guiding Principles on Internal Displacement* (Deng), 136
Guilt, 107
Gulf Stream, 169–170
Guterres, António, 134, 138

*Haaretz* (newspaper), 97, 98
Haiti:
    exit strategy, 122
    first UN intervention, 119–121
    peacebuilding template, 124–125
    rebuilding failed state, 123–124
    UN peacebuilding, lessons learned, 122–123
    UN peacekeeping/peacebuilding in, 121–122, 125
Halilou (Tuareg tribesman), 41
Hallak, J.:
    curriculum for global education, 74–75
    education as universal right, 72, 73
Hanging, public, 115 (n25)
Hansen, James, 174
Hanvey, R. G., 74
Hard credit, 192
Hargreaves, D., 75
Harvey, David, 167
Harvey, Fiona, 173
Hasina, Sheikh, 67
Hasnas, J., 71
Hatcher, R., 78
Haute Autorité de Lutte Contre les Discriminations et pour l'Egalité, 96
Hawaii, 209, 210
Health:
    AIDS, health-policy responses in Europe, 151–158
    China *vs.* India, 6–7
    of Dhaka rickshaw pullers, 50–52
    globalization and, 141
    Internet resources, 213
    medical tourism, 143–145

nurses, U.S. plan to lure foreign, 159–160
polio eradication campaign, 147–148
services in Mexico, 62
*The Heat Is On* (Gelbspan), 172
Hentschke, G. C., 77
Hertsgaard, Mark, 169–175
Heymann, David L., 150
Heyward, Andrew, 173
Highlanders, 165
High-level Panel on Threats, Challenges and Change (United Nations), 124–125
Hill, D., 78
HIV/AIDS. *See* Acquired Immune-Deficiency Syndrome
HMF (housing microfinance), 192, 195 (n36)
Hobbes, T., 71
Hoff-Wilson, J., 79
Homicide, 59
Hospitals, 144
Household income, 47–50
Housing:
    of Dhaka rickshaw pullers, 44–45
    for ethnic minority in France, 94–95
    low/moderate-income land development, 185–189
    slum upgrading, financial framework for, 189–192
    slums, formation of, 183–185
Housing microfinance (HMF), 192, 195 (n36)
"How One Company Brought Hope to the Poor" (Visscher), 65–68
Hubert, M., 157
Huffy Bicycle Company, 18
Human capital, 74, 124
Human rights:
    abuses against women in Mexico, 59–64
    anti-torture norm, power of, 111–112
    of IDPs, 136
    right to education, 71–79
    torture, abolition of, 107–108
    torture, resurrection of, 109
    U.S. torture adjustment, consequences of, 110–111
Human Rights First, 113
Human Rights Watch:
    on abuses in Angola, 167
    on Ethiopian oil exploitation, 165
    on Malaysian detainees, 110
    on torture, 115 (n17)
    Web site of, 212
Human trafficking, 37–38
Hunn, Pat, 15, 16–17
Hurrell, Andrew, 116 (n37)
Hurricane Katrina:
    global warming and, 170–171
    Melinda Gates on, 56
    Semester at Sea program and, 209
Hussein, Prince Zeid Ráad Al Zeid, 85
Hussey, Ann Lee, 150

Identity check, 96
IDPs. *See* Internally displaced persons
IDUs (Intravenous Drug Users), 155
Ignatieff, Michael, 109
Illiteracy:
    China *vs.* India, 6
    in India, 4
    statistics on, 73
Immergut, E. M., 153
Immigration, 78
"In American Waters" (Sernau), 209–210
Income:

in China/India, 4
of Dhaka rickshaw pullers, 46–51
low-medium-income countries, 183–185
*See also* Poverty
*An Inconvenient Truth* (film), 177
India:
    China, economic growth comparison with, 3
    economic overview of, 11
    infrastructure of, 6–8
    institutional/political issues, 8–11
    medical tourism to, 143
    nurses emigrating from, 159–160
    polio eradication campaign, 147, 149
    poverty/underemployment in, 4–6
    spending on education, 76
Indonesia, property rights in, 187, 194 (n26)
IndUShealth, 144
Industrial Disputes Act (India), 5
INEGI (Instituto Nacional de Estadística, Geografía e Informática), 61, 62
Inequality:
    gender violence in Mexico, 59–64
    in globalized economy, 31
    Internet resources, 211
    philanthropy and, 55–57
    slavery in Niger, 37–42
    *See also* Ethnic minorities
Information power, 128
Information technology, 4
Infrastructure:
    of China/India, 6–8
    land development and, 186, 188
    maintenance of, 191
    upgrading slums and, 184–185, 189
Ingledew, Francis, 85
Inhofe, James M., 173
Institutional issues, of China/India, 8–11
Instituto Nacional de Estadística, Geografía e Informática (INEGI), 61, 62
Insurance companies, 145
Intellectuals, French, 97–98
Intelligence, 108, 112
Intelligentsia Coffee, 23–24
Intergovernmental Panel on Climate Change (I.P.C.C.), 170, 171
Intermestic security, 129
Internally displaced persons (IDPs):
    approach for protection of, 136–137
    background to problem of, 134–135
    donors for aid for, 139
    population of, 135–136
    in Sudan, 133–134
    UNHCR and, 137–138
International Civilian Mission in Haiti (MICIVIH), 120, 122
International Commission on Education for the 21st Century:
    on curriculum, 74, 75
    education as universal right, 72
*International Covenant on Economic, Social, and Cultural Rights* (United Nations), 71–72
*International Covenant on the Rights of the Child* (United Nations), 72
International Forum on Globalization, 73
International Labour Organization, 211
International security, 127–131
Internationalization Collaborative of the American Council on Education, 83, 85, 86
Internet resources, 211–214
Interpol Web site, 212
Intervention, 128
Intravenous Drug Users (IDUs), 155
The Investor Network on Climate Risk, 175

I.P.C.C. (Intergovernmental Panel on Climate Change), 170, 171
"Is Torture Ever Justified?" (*The Economist*), 106
Islam, 100–102
Italy, 153, 155–157
Iturralde, Carlos, 33

Jacobs, Heidi Hayes, 74
Jagland, Thorbjørn, 67
Jamaica, 76
*Janjaweed* (devils on horseback), 133
Jedibudiah, James, 198
Jehl, Douglas, 117 (n59)
Jenkins, R. S., 5
Jenner, W. J. F., 10
Jews, 102
Jobert, B., 153
Jobs, 16, 78
    *See also* Employment; Work
Johnson, Lyndon, 177
Juha (cultural tourist), 201–207
Jun, Z., 8
Juniper, Tony, 170
Justice system, Mexican, 63

Kakua (spirit), 202, 204
Kälin, Walter, 136, 139
Kamal, Ahmad, 83–84
Katzenstein, Peter, 129
Kelly, Paul, 17
Kennedy, Donald, 174
Kenya, poverty in, 35–36
Kerry, John, 174
Khan, A.R., 9
Kher, Unmesh, 143–145
King, David:
    on Britain's climate science research, 174
    on Britain's emissions controls, 171
    on global warming, 169
Klare, Michael, 128
Knab, Michelle, 198
Kombai tribe (New Guinea), 201–207
Korey, William, 115 (n28)
Korten, David, 27–30
Kotabe, M., 74
Krugman, Paul, 16
Kuron, Jacek, 34
Kyoto Protocol:
    Bush administration opposition to, 174
    Tony Blair on, 170
    U.S. response to, 175

Laayoune, Western Sahara, 164
Labor laws, 5
Lagarde, Marcela, 59, 63
Lagos, Richard, 115 (n28)
Land development:
    low/moderate-income, 185–189
    strategies for, 192–193
Land holdings, 44
Land subsidies, 189, 190
Laos, Hernández, 60
Lapayese, Y. V., 74
Laqeuer, Walter, 115 (n23)
Las Brumas coffee cooperative, 24
Latin America:
    neoliberal policies and, 19
    OAS on, 61

slums, reduction of, 183–193
Latortue, Gérard, 124
Law enforcement, domestic, 130
"Law of 23 February 2005" (France), 98
*Le Fabuleux Destin d'Amélie Poulain* (film), 98
*Le Monde* (newspaper), 95
*Le Nouvel Observateur* (newspaper), 97, 98
Le Pen, Jean-Marie, 96
Leahy, Patrick, 112
Learning, 83–86
    *See also* Education
Left, 99–100
Legal issues, torture, 107–108
Legal rights, 71–72
Lelyveld, Joseph, 111, 117 (n61)
Lennard, John, 86
*Les Echos* (newspaper), 94
Levin, Daniel, 106
Levin, H. M., 79
Levinson, Sanford, 106, 114 (n14)
"Liberalism, Torture, and the Ticking Bomb" (Luban), 115 (n16)
*Libération* (newspaper), 97
Lichtblau, Eric, 117 (n59)
Lifelong education, 73
Lightman, M., 79
Lindahl, Ronald:
    on conditions of schools, 76
    on curriculum in globalized world, 75
    education as universal right, 72
    on human capital, 74
    "The Right to Education in a Globalized World", 71–79
Lindzen, Richard, 172
Lipton, David, 34
Literacy, 6, 73
Loans:
    grants *vs.*, 35
    housing microfinance, 192
    micro-credit from Grameen Bank, 65, 67, 211
Locke, J., 71
Lombardi, Eric, 198
*London Observer* (newspaper), 169
Luban, David, 108, 109, 115 (n16)
Lumpe, Lora, 128

Maastricht Treaty, 156
Macaws, 199
Mach, Daniel, 103
Mackinlay, John, 109
Maddison, A., 3
Madrid Accords, 163
Magidoff, Jonathan, 99–100
Mailman, Josh, 67
"Make Poverty History" (ONE campaign), 57
Malaysia:
    oil interests in Ethiopia, 165
    torture in, 110
Mali, education in, 73
Malone, David M., 119–125
Mambi (Kombai tribesman), 206
Mangan, K. S., 78
Mangualo (Kombai tribesman), 206
Manufacturing, 5, 6
Mara Salvatrucha, 63
Marafa, Oumarou, 40–41
Marburger, John H. III, 174, 175
Mariotti, John, 18
Markward, Anne, 199

Marsek, Patrick, 145
Maschino, Maurice T., 98–99
Masjaing, South Africa, 87–89
Mathews, Jessica, 129, 130
Matsuura, K., 72
Matthew, Richard, 128
Maxted, Julia, 163–167
May, Robert, 172
Mays, R. O., 74, 76
McAuslan, P., 186
McCain, John:
    anti-torture stance of, 113, 117 (n65)
    on Army Field Manual, 118 (n71)
    standards for treatment of prisoners, 112
McKinsey & Co., 16
McNamara, Dennis, 137, 139
McNeil, Donald G., Jr., 147–150
Meacher, Michael, 173
Mead, Walter Russell, 109, 116 (n37)
Media, global warming and, 173
Medical tourism, 143–145
Medovoi, L., 77
Megret, Bruno, 96
Meier, Roberto, 135
Meir, Golda, 99
Melos, 113
Men, 62
Mercer Health & Benefits, 143
Merkel, Angela, 172
Methadone treatment, 154
MetroVivienda, 185, 187–188
Mexico:
    *ejidos* (land with communal rights), 187
    housing in, 184
    land reserves in, 194 (n28)
    medical tourism to, 145
    violence against women in, 59–64
MICIVIH (International Civilian Mission in Haiti), 120, 122
Micro-credit:
    Grameen Bank, 65, 67, 211
    housing microfinance, 192
Migration, urban, 45
*Migrations Société* (journal), 98
Militarized regimes, 167
Military, torture and, 109
Military alliances, 116 (n32)
Millennium Development Goal, 183
Millennium Project, 33
Miller, Kevin, 143
Miller, Steven E., 109, 116 (n36)
Milstein, Arnold, 143
Mini-med plans, 144
Mining, 197
Minorities. *See* Ethnic minorities
MIPONUH (UN Civilian Police Mission in Haiti), 121–122
Moatti, J. P., 156
Mobile phones, in Bangladesh, 65–68
Mokoena, James, 87–89
Mokoena, Petrus, 88
Moon Chung-in, 129
Morality:
    anti-torture norm and, 113
    torture, legal/moral abolition of, 107–108
    torture and, 105–106
Morawetz, David, 35
Morbidity, 51
Morelle, A., 157

Morjane, Kamel, 139
Morocco:
    oil exploitation of, 163–165
    Western Sahara and, 163–164
Morris, Bill, 94
Morrison, Bruce, 159, 160
Mortgage finance, 192
Muhammad, Ibrahim, 68
Multiculturalism, 99
Multilateralism, 129, 130
Multipolar world, 20
Munn, Charles, 197–200
Murard, L., 157
Murders, 59
Murray, Graham, 93–103
Muslims, in France, 93–103
MV Explorer, 209–210

National identity, 127, 131
National Oceanic and Atmospheric Administration (N.O.A.A.), 170
National Organization for Women (NOW), 211
Natural rights, 71
Naturalization, 98–99
Nature Conservancy, 214
Navarrete, Jesus, 183–193
Nayoussa, Abdou, 40
Needle-exchange programs, 155
Negative rights, 71
Nehemiah (Kombai tribesman), 206
Neoliberalism, 19–21, 60–62
*néoréac*, 97–98
Nepal, 76
New Guinea, cultural tourism in, 201–207
"The New Imperialism" (Harvey), 167
*Newsweek* (magazine), 106
Newurbanism.org, 214
NGOs (nongovernmental organizations), 112–113
*NGOs and the Universal Declaration of Human Rights* (Korey), 115 (n28)
Nicaragua:
    coffee of, 23–24
    microfinance in, 192
Niger, slavery in, 37–42
Niger Delta, 166
Nigeria:
    oil exploitation of, 165–166
    polio in, 147, 148
Nigerian Agip Oil Company (NOAC), 166
N.O.A.A. (National Oceanic and Atmospheric Administration), 170
Noble, Marylou, 199
Nongovernmental organizations (NGOs), 112–113
Non-physical security, 128–129
North Africans, in France, 93–103
NOW (National Organization for Women), 211
Nowak, Manfred, 105–106
Nuer (Ethiopian ethnic group), 165
Nurses, U.S. recruitment of foreign, 159–160
Nye, Joseph, 128
Nyerere, Julius, 36

OAS. *See* Organization of American States
OAS (Organisation de l'Armée Secrète), 100
Obaki, S., 75
Obando, Jacqueline, 197
Obasanjo, Olusegun, 148
O'Connor, Sandra Day, 111, 117 (n57)
Odremán, Hernán Gruber, 21
Office for the Coordination of Humanitarian Affairs (OCHA), 136

Ogata, Sadako, 138
Ogoni (Nigerian ethnic group), 166
Oil, in Africa, 163–167
O'Keefe, K. C., 24
Olivera, Mercedes, 59–64
O'Neill, Paul H., 173
OPEC (Organization of Petroleum Exporting Countries), 20, 165
Oppenheimer, Michael, 172, 173, 175
Organisation de l'Armée Secrète (OAS), 100
Organization of American States (OAS):
    assistance to Haiti, 122, 124–125
    on poverty in Latin America, 61
    sanctions against Haiti, 123
Organization of Petroleum Exporting Countries (OPEC), 20, 165
Osborne, Lawrence, 201–207
Oumani, Kadi, 40–41
Oumani, Moustapha Kadi, 39–41
Oumar, Foungoutan, 41
Outsourcing:
    education and, 78
    of French business, 95–96
    of jobs, 16
    medical, 143–145
    Wal-Mart and, 16
"Outsourcing Your Heart" (Kher), 143–145
Overland, M. A., 78

Padilla, Jose, 111, 117 (n59)
Papagiannios, G., 76
Paraguay, spending on education, 76
Passacantando, John, 173
Passion, 57
Pay, E., 199
"Peace and Democracy for Haiti: A UN Mission Impossible?"
        (Einsiedel & Malone), 119–125
Peacebuilding, in Haiti, 119–125
Peacebuilding Commission, 125
Pérez, Carlos Andrés, 19
Perkins-Gough, D., 74
Perspective consciousness, 74
Peru, ecotourism in, 198, 199, 200
Peters, M., 74, 75
Petkoff, Teodoro, 20
Petrella, R., 72
Peyrot, Jacques, 101
Pharmaceutical products, 5
Philanthropy:
    "The Good Samaritans" (Gibbs), 55–57
    polio eradication campaign, 149–150
Philippines:
    emigrants from, 78
    nurses emigrating from to U.S., 159–160
Phillips, Rebecca, 198
Philosophers, French, 97–98, 102
Philosophy and Public Affairs (Sussman), 114 (n8)
Physical infrastructure, 6
Pigozzi, M. J., 74, 75
Pity, 57
Planck, Max, 172
Poland, economic reform in, 33–34
Police:
    in France, 96
    in Haiti, 121–122, 124
Policy, economic, 5
Policy, for globalized security, 131
Polio, 147–150
Polisario Front, 164

Politics:
    China vs. India, 8–11
    in France, 96–100
    UN mission in Haiti, 119–125
Poncelet, Morgan, 199
Poncet, S., 8
Population Connection, 213
Positive rights, 71, 72
Poverty:
    in Bangladesh, 43–53
    Bill and Melinda Gates, Bono and, 55–57
    in China/India, 4–6
    of ethnic minorities in France, 95–96
    gender violence in Mexico and, 59–64
    in globalized economy, 31
    GrameenPhone's solutions for in Bangladesh, 65–68
    in Haiti, 123
    Internet resources, 211
    in Niger, 37–42
    in Niger Delta, 166
    plan to eradicate, 33–36
    right to education and, 76
Powell, Colin, 133
Power, 107, 108–110
Power, electrical, 6
Prejudice. See Racism
Prendergast, John, 133
Prestowitz, C., 3
Préval, René, 121, 124
Prever, Robin, 17
Prévert, Jacques, 95
Primitive cultures, 202
    See also Cultural tourism
Prisoners. See Detainees
Privatization:
    of education, 76–77, 78
    in Mexico, 62
Programma de Certificacíon Agraria (PROCEDE), 62
Property appreciation method, 190, 194 (n30)
Property rights, 187–188
Pro-poor growth, 53
Protectionism, economic, 8
Public hanging, 115 (n25)
Public-health policies:
    in Europe, reform trends, 155–157
    HIV/AIDS response in Europe, 153–155
"Pulling Rickshaws in the City of Dhaka" (Begum & Sen), 43–53

Qian, Y., 8
Quadir, Iqbal, 66–68
Quality, of education, 76
Quantity, of education, 73
Quichua of Napo Wildlife Center, 197–198

Racism:
    colonial legacy of France, 100
    ecotourism and, 197–198
    far Right, philosophers in France, 96–98
    in France, 93–94
    France's modèle d'intégration, 99
    policing in France and, 96
    poverty/disenfranchisement in France, 95–96
    Republican values in France, 98–99
    secularism/Islamophobia in France, 100–102
    uprisings in France, response to, 102–103
"The "Radical" Thesis on Globalization and the Case of Venezuela's Hugo
        Chávez" (Ellner), 19–21

Raffaele, Paul, 37–42
Ravallion, M., 4
Recycling, 198
Refugees:
    IDPs, approach for protection of, 136–137
    IDPs, population of, 135–136
    internally displaced persons in Sudan, 134
    UNHCR and IDPs, 137–138
Refugees magazine, 135
Reinhardt, Uwe, 143–144
Reinicke, Wolfgang, 127, 129
Religion, 100–102
Reno, William, 120
Republic of Korea, 76
Republican values, 98–99, 102
Reputation, 108–110
Resolution 841 (UN Security Council), 120
Resolution 940 (UN Security Council), 120–121
Resource wars, 35
Resources, Internet, 211–214
Retail, 15–17
Reynolds, Barbara G., 148
Rice, Condoleezza, 38, 109
Rickshaw pullers, of Dhaka:
    characteristics of, 46–47
    crisis events among, 50
    data on, 43–44
    financial well-being of, 47–50
    health status of, 50–52
    overview of, 43, 52–53
    profiles of, 44–46
Right, political, 96–97
"The Right to Education in a Globalized World" (Lindahl), 71–79
Rights. See Education, right to; Human rights
Rikowski, G., 78
Rio de Janeiro, slum upgrading in, 185, 191
Riots, in France:
    events of, 93
    French Left and, 100
    housing and, 94–95
    intellectuals on, 97
    policing and, 96
    poverty/disenfranchisement and, 95
    religion and, 102
    response to, 102–103
Risk reduction, HIV/AIDS in Europe, 154–155
Roberts, J., 76
Robertson, Pat, 57
Robinson, Mary, 117 (n67)
Rodley, Nigel, 106, 110
Roland, G., 8
Romero, Anibal, 20
Roosevelt, Eleanor, 79
Roosevelt, Franklin D., 72
Roque, B. P., 156
Rosenau, James, 127
Rotary International, 149, 150
Rousseau, Jean Jacques, 202
Rousseau, J.-J., 76
Royal, Ségolène, 99
"Rumor, Fear and Fatigue Hinder Final Push to End Polio"
    (Dugger & McNeil), 147–150
Rumsfeld, Donald, 110
Rural industrialization, 8
Rural poverty, 43, 44–45
Russia:
    economic reform in, 34
    MIPONUH and, 122

torture in, 107
Ryan, T., 74

Sachs, Jeffrey, 31, 33–36
Sanctions, 119, 120, 123
Sandoval Lake Lodge, Peru, 198
Sanitation solution, 190–191
Santa Tereza Lodge, Brazil, 198
Sarandon, Susan, 57
Sarkozy, Nicolas, 96–97, 103
Sartre, Jean-Paul, 97
Sauri region, Kenya, 35
Scarry, Elaine, 114 (n14)
Schools, 76, 101
    See also Education
Schwarzenegger, Arnold, 175
Schweitzer, Louis, 94
Science (King), 171
Scorza, Jason, 84, 85
Screening, HIV, 153–154
Sea level, 170
Secularism, 100, 101–102
Security, international, 127–131
Seitz, Frederick, 172
Semester at Sea program, 209–210
Sen, Binayak, 43–53
Senate Judiciary Committee, 111–112
September 11, 2001 terrorist attacks:
    global consequences of U.S. torture adjustment, 110–111
    torture after, 106–107
    torture and power/reputation, 109–110
Sernau, Scott, 84, 209–210
Sese Seko, Mobutu, 36
Seytre, B., 152
Shambaugh, George, 128
Shantytowns. See Slums
Shekarau, Ibrahim, 148
Shue, Henry, 105, 107, 110
Sierra Club, 214
Silvermine Consulting Group, 17
Silverstein, K., 163
Simon, Denis Fred, 128
Simon, H. A., 153
Singh, P., 72
SIPAZ, 63
Sitruk, Joseph, 101
Sivanandan, 99, 101, 102
Sixty Minutes II (television program), 114 (n9)
Skills, for global citizenship, 84
Slavery, in Niger, 37–42
Slum upgrading:
    costs of, 194 (n14)
    finance of, 189–192
    overview of, 192–193
Slums:
    conclusion about, 192–193
    finance of slum upgrading, 189–192
    formation of/cost implications, 183–185
    low/moderate-income land development, 185–189
    population in, 183
Smog, 178
Social environments, 75
Social infrastructure, 6–7
Social Venture Network, 67
Society:
    evolution of, 28
    gender violence and, 60–62

Soft credit, 192
"Some Convenient Truths" (Easterbrook), 177–179
SOS Racisme, 94, 102–103
South Africa, 87–89
South America, ecotourism in, 197–200
South Korea, emigrants from, 78
Sovereignty:
    globalization and, 21
    IDPs and, 135, 138
Specialization, 130
Spending, on education, 76–77
Sperling, Michael, 86
Sprawl, Web site on, 214
Spring, J., 72, 75
Standard and Poor's, 8
Stasch, Rupert, 205, 207
State of Fear (Crichton), 173
States of Denial: Knowing about Atrocities and Suffering (Cohen), 114 (n6)
Steffen, Monika, 151–158
Steinard, Wayne, 144–145
Stiglitz, J. E., 72
Still at Risk: Diplomatic Assurances No Safeguard against Torture (Human Rights Watch), 115 (n17)
Stonesifer, Patty, 55
    57, 57
Story, 29–30
"Strangers in the Forest" (Osborne), 201–207
Students Against Sweatshops, 211
Study abroad, 84–85
Subdivision, 186–189
Sudan:
    attacks in, 133–134
    population of IDPs in, 135, 136
    UNHCR and IDPs, 137
Sunstein, C. R., 72
Sussman, David, 114 (n8)

Tafan (Tuareg tribesman), 37, 41
Taiwan, 10–11
Takany (Nigerian slave), 40
Talbott, Strobe, 129
Tan, Jaime Galvez, 160
Tanzania, 35
"Targeting the Anuak" (Human Rights Watch), 165
Teachers, 76
Teaching/learning methods, 75
Technology:
    Earth Community and, 28–29
    security in globalized world, 128–129
Telenor, 67
Telephones, as income generators in Bangladesh, 65–68
Terrorism:
    global consequences of U.S. torture adjustment, 110–111
    resurrection of torture and, 108
    torture after September 11, 2001, 106–107
    torture and power/reputation, 108–110
    treatment of prisoners, 91
Texas, 185
Textiles industry, 5
Thailand, 76, 143–144
Thatcher, Margaret, 172
Third World, 19
Threats, 128, 129
Thurow, L. C.:
    on education, 77
    on human capital, 74
    on split of nations, 77
Tidwell, Mike, 170

Time (magazine), 56
"Time to Think About Torture" (Newsweek), 106
Timidria Association, 38, 41
Todo, Patria Para, 21
Topalova, P., 4
Torture:
    after September 11, 2001, 105–106
    anti-torture norm, power of, 111–112
    conclusion about, 112–113
    global consequences of U.S. adjustment, 110–111
    legal/moral abolition of, 107–108
    morality and, 105–106
    power, reputation and, 108–110
    "water-boarding", 114 (n8)
Torture: A Collection (Levinson), 114 (n14)
"Torture: The Struggle Over a Peremptory Norm in a Counter-Terrorist Era" (Foot), 105–113
Tourism:
    cultural tourism, 201–207
    ecotourism, 197–200
    traveler vs. tourist, 210
Trade, world, 4
Trafficking, human, 37–38
Transparency International, 166
Treatment, AIDS, 156–157
Trehan, Naresh, 144, 145
"Tropic of Answer" (Munn), 197–200
Trustees of Education, 73, 75
Tsunami relief, 56
Tuareg tribes, 38
TVEs (village and township enterprises), 8

UGP (United Group Programs), 144
UN Civilian Police Mission in Haiti (MIPONUH), 121–122
UN Commission on Human Rights, 108, 112
UN Convention Against Torture and Other Cruel, Inhuman or Degrading Treatment or Punishment (CAT), 108, 111, 114 (n4)
UN Educational, Scientific, and Cultural Organization (UNESCO), 72, 73, 212
UN Mission in Haiti (UNMIH), 120–121
UN Security Council (UNSC), 117 (n68), 119–125
UN Statistics Division, 73
UN Support Mission in Haiti (UNSMIH), 121
UN Transition Mission (UNTMIH), 121
Underemployment, 4–6
UNHCR. See United Nations High Commissioner for Refugees
UNICEF (United Nations Children's Fund), 136, 212
Union of Concerned Scientists, 213
United for Peace and Justice, 212
United Group Programs (UGP), 144
United Kingdom:
    AIDS epidemic response in, 153–155
    global warming and, 173
    green-house gas emissions in, 171
    public health reform in, 155–157
    torture and, 114 (n14), 115 (n17)
United Nations:
    anti-torture norm and, 112
    Earth Community and, 28
    on education as basic human right, 71–72
    on exploitation of Angola, 167
    on femicide in Mexico, 60
    on human development in Mexico, 61
    internally displaced persons and, 134, 135, 136
    peacebuilding in Haiti, 119–125
    slums and, 183
    torture, abolition of, 108
    Web site of, 212
United Nations Children's Fund (UNICEF), 136, 212

United Nations High Commissioner for Refugees (UNHCR):
    IDP challenges for, 139
    IDPs, population of, 135
    IDPs of Sudan and, 134
    protection of IDPs, 136–138
    torture and, 112
*United Nations Millennium Declaration* (United Nations), 72
United States:
    African oil, reliance on, 163–167
    anti-torture norm and, 111–113
    donations for education, 77
    Earth Community and, 28–29
    exploitation of Angola, 166–167
    global warming, denial of, 169–175
    health care system of, 143
    nurses, recruitment of foreign, 159–160
    polio eradication campaign funding of, 149
    security and globalization, 129–130
    slums in, 185
    spending on education, 76
    torture, consequences of U.S. adjustment, 110–111
    torture after September 11, 2001, 106–107
    torture and power/reputation, 109–110
    treatment of prisoners in war on terrorism, 91
    UN in Haiti and, 120–121, 122
    UN poverty plan and, 36
    Venezuela and, 20–21
    world poverty and, 34
*Universal Declaration of Human Rights* (United Nations), 71, 107
University of Wales at Aberystwyth, 105
UNSC (UN Security Council), 117 (n68), 119–125
Upgrading. *See* Slum upgrading
Uranium, 39
Urban slums. *See* Slums
Urías, Tania, 59
"US Army Field Manual on Intelligence Interrogations",
        112, 117 (n64), 118 (n71)
U.S. Constitution, 111
U.S. Department of Energy, 214
U.S. Department of Labor, 78
"U.S. Plan to Lure Nurses May Hurt Poor Nations"
        (Dugger), 159–160
Uttar Pradesh, India, 149
Uzbekistan, 110, 116 (n44), 117 (n53)

Valdés, Juan Gabriel, 125
Van Boven, Theo, 116 (n44)
Van Natta, Don, Jr., 116 (n44)
*Vanity Fair* (periodical), 169
Vargas, Rosa, 61
Väyrynen, Raimo, 128
Vegan diet, 199
Venezuela, 19–21
Verzola, R., 77
Vieira, Sergio, 117 (n67)
Village and township enterprises (TVEs), 8
Village Phone, 67
Violence, against women in Mexico, 59–64
"Violencia Femicida" (Olivera), 59–64
Visscher, Marco, 65–68
Vlassic pickles, 15–18

Waever, Ole, 128
Waks, L. J., 77
Waldman, A., 76
*Wall Street Journal*, 114 (n9)
Wal-Mart, 15–18
"The Wal-Mart You Don't Know" (Fishman), 15–18
Wang, Y., 8
Warner, John, 112
*Washington Post* (newspaper), 106, 114 (n9), 116 (n39)
"Water-boarding", 114 (n8)
Watson, Harlan, 173
Watts, Geoff, 23–24
Weather. *See* Global warming
Weila, Ilguilas, 41–42
Weissman, Michaele, 23–25
West Africa, oil exploitation in, 163
West Virginia, 144
Western Sahara, oil exploitation in, 163–165
"While Washington Slept" (Hertsgaard), 169–175
Whites, 93–94
Whitman, Andrew, 18
WHO (World Health Organization), 7, 213
Wihbey, Michael, 163
Wilkinson, Ray, 133–139
Wines, Michael, 87–89
Wiseman, A. W., 72
Wockhardt Hospitals Group, 145
Wolfowitz, Paul, 36
Women:
    in Bangladesh, economic independence of, 67
    in France, 101
    violence against in Mexico, 59–64
Woolford, Kelly, 201–207
Woolman, D. C., 74, 75
Work:
    in ecotourism, 197, 198
    by ethnic minority in France, 93–94
    outsourcing of jobs, 16, 78
    *See also* Employment
World Bank, 7, 76, 77
World Council of Churches, 213
World Economic Forum, 34
World Education Forum, 72
World Food Program, 136, 138
World Health Organization (WHO), 7, 213
World Trade Organization, 78
World Watch Institute, 214
*The Wretched of the Earth* (Fanon), 97
Wu, Y., 8

Yanbu (Kombai tribesman), 202–203, 204
Yao, Y., 8
Yin, C. C., 76
Young, Steve, 16
Yunus, Muhammad, 67

Zangaou, Moussa, 39
Zell, Doug, 23
Zhang, S., 75
Zurn, Michael, 128
Zylberman, P., 157